Winner of the 2018 International Book Award for Biography sponsored by American Bookfest.

A compelling read — the extraordinary life story of Fay Stender, whom I vividly recall as a brilliant, charismatic woman lawyer at the forefront of radical politics in the Seventies. Once again, Lise Pearlman has done a masterful job capturing this tumultuous and instructive time.
— BARRY SCHECK
CO-DIRECTOR OF THE INNOCENCE PROJECT

Call me Phaedra *is a fascinating and unflinching biography of the pioneering lawyer, prison reform activist and feminist Fay Stender. Here is a compelling account of her inspiring and tragic life, her turbulent times, and her far reaching impact, a well-told story brimming with intimate detail and political insight.*
—SETH ROSENFELD, INVESTIGATIVE JOURNALIST
AND AUTHOR OF SUBVERSIVES: THE FBI'S WAR ON STUDENT RADICALS, AND REAGAN'S RISE TO POWER.

Diligently researched and carefully written . . . Pearlman's biography accords Fay the recognition she deserves as a seminal criminal defense lawyer at a pivotal moment in the history of the California prison system.
— JONAH RASKIN
"WARRIORS NOT VICTIMS: GEORGE JACKSON AND FAY STENDER,"
COUNTERPUNCH, MAY 16, 2018

Moving, well written, at times almost poetic, Lise Pearlman's new, often thrilling book tells the story of Fay Stender, a revolutionary pioneering woman lawyer dedicated to fighting to achieve justice for some of America's most notorious prisoners. Fay was my friend from the time of our college days through the years she rose to international acclaim and notoriety until her untimely death stemming from the gun of a man who had tried to murder her. Lise's book grippingly sheds light on this remarkable woman's courageous life and the turbulent time in which she made a significant impact on the arc of justice.
— ROBERT RICHTER
AWARD-WINNING DOCUMENTARY FILMMAKER

Lise Pearlman's book generates great emotional traction recounting the heroic, tragic life and death of one of America's most zealous, brilliant lawyers. It is written with clarity and precision and is a necessary remembrance of an amazing woman.

— PENNY COOPER
MEMBER OF THE CALIFORNIA STATE BAR
TRIAL LAWYER HALL OF FAME

Call Me Phaedra *makes two major contributions to American studies. It documents the life and times of a remarkable activist woman lawyer in the men's world of the mid-20th century; Stender was a committed lawyer, exhausting and inspiring to work with. It also chronicles the experience of a strong circle of Progressives emerging from the 'Red Scare' in that Cold War era who struggled to make society more just at a time when bucking conformity was not the norm.*

— PETER FRANCK
FORMER PARTNER OF STENDER AND
2017 SAN FRANCISCO LAWYERS GUILD "CHAMPION OF JUSTICE"

I was a History Major with a Women's Study Minor in college, and this book would have been a perfect addition to my reading list. Fay Stender was a fascinating and complicated woman who lived during, and was involved in, some very significant times in our nation's history. Pearlman brings Fay, and those events, to life through the lens of Fay's legal work. This is an engaging read that will give you new insight on the McCarthy Era, Civil Rights Movement, the Free Speech Movement, Vietnam War protests, the rise of Black Power and the rise of feminism in the Women's Movement of the 1970s.

— SARAH MECKLER
GOLDEN STATE MEDIA CONCEPTS
PODCAST BOOK REVIEWER

Expertly documented . . . new biography [of] Fay Stender's fascinating life and career.

— LISA D. SMITH
PUBLISHER AND RADIO HOST
BIG BLEND RADIO

You can listen to the Big Blend Radio conversation with Lise Pearlman at Big Blend Radio & TV Magazine Summer 2018, Author Connections, p.15.

LISE PEARLMAN IS ALSO THE ACCLAIMED AUTHOR OF

THE SKY'S THE LIMIT:
People v. Newton, the REAL Trial of the 20th Century?
(2012)

AMERICAN JUSTICE ON TRIAL
People v. Newton
(2016)

WITH JUSTICE FOR SOME:
*Politically Charged Criminal Trials in the Early
20th Century That Helped Shape Today's America*
(2017)

www.lisepearlman.com

Call Me Phaedra

The Life and Times of Movement Lawyer Fay Stender

by **Lise Pearlman**

REGENT PRESS
Berkeley, California

Copyright © 2018 by Lise Pearlman

PAPERBACK:
ISBN 13: 978-1-58790-435-6
ISBN 10: 1-58790-435-7

E-BOOK
ISBN 13: 978-1-58790-436-3
ISBN 10: 1-58790-436-5

Library of Congress Control Number: 2018933614

All rights reserved under International and Pan-American Copyright Conventions. No part of this book may be used or reproduced in any manner whatsoever without the written permission of the Publisher, except in the case of brief quotations embodied in critical articles and reviews.

Cover photo of Huey Newton at a press conference on August 5, 1970, after his release, with lawyer Fay Stender standing behind him. (© Ilka Hartmann 2018.)

Cover photo of tragic mask of Dionysus, Greek God of the theater: Musée du Louvre, https://commons.wikimedia.org/wiki/File:Dionysos_mask_Louvre_Myr347.jpg. The Theatre of Dionysus Eleuthereus, on the south side of the Acropolis in Athens, Greece, is known as the birthplace of Greek tragedy.

Every effort has been made to credit sources and obtain permission where appropriate. If we have inadvertently used or credited material or images inaccurately or without applicable consent and they do not qualify as Fair Use under the U.S. Copyright Act, or are not in the public domain, please contact the publisher so appropriate steps can be taken.

Printed in the U.S.A.
REGENT PRESS
Berkeley, California
www.regentpress.net
regentpress@mindspring.com

*I dedicate this book to all the women working
for social justice throughout history
about whom it could be said,
"Nevertheless, she persisted."*

Contents

AUTHOR'S NOTE ▪ xi

PROLOGUE ▪ 1

ACT ONE
1. The Battle of Wills ▪ 9
2. Predestination or Free Will ▪ 25
3. Intellectual Boot Camp ▪ 49
4. Smitten ▪ 55
5. Renewed Ardor ▪ 63
6. Starting Out ▪ 73
7. Turbulence ▪ 79
8. Joining the Movement ▪ 95
9. Unfulfilled ▪ 107

ACT TWO
1. Second Chair at the Latest Trial of the Century ▪ 117
2. The Baton Passes to Fay ▪ 133
3. Freeing Huey! ▪ 143
4. Entering Gladiator School ▪ 159
5. "My Small but Mighty Mouthpiece" ▪ 173
6. The Shaping of a Revolutionary Hero ▪ 181
7. On a Roll ▪ 193
8. Collision Course ▪ 199
9. Blood in His Eyes ▪ 221
10. The Dragon Lady Reigns ▪ 239

ACT THREE

1. Bitter Fruit ■ 263
2. Spent ■ 273
3. Cuba ■ 287
4. *The Barb* ■ 295
5. Reflections in the Mirror ■ 315
6. *Temps Perdu* ■ 327
7. Death Comes Knocking ■ 347
8. Star Witness ■ 377
9. Nowhere to Run ■ 407

EPILOGUE ■ 437

ENDNOTES ■ 449

SOURCES ■ 467

BIBLIOGRAPHY ■ 469

INDEX ■ 475

ACKNOWLEDGEMENTS ■ 483

Author's Note

The idea for a biography of Fay Stender struck me near the turn of this century. I was attending a federal lawyer-judge conference in Napa County, California. One panel drew a capacity crowd to hear what makes a great trial lawyer. Historically, trial lawyers have seen themselves as courtroom gladiators. Federal prosecutors were taught that trial lawyers were "the fighter pilots and emergency room surgeons of the law." To craft persuasive storylines to win over juries time and again, top trial lawyers have to not only master the facts and law of each case, but possess charismatic personalities. In the traditionally macho world of the courtroom, top practitioners have often been compared to champion boxers. Like Muhammad Ali, many hone the ability to "float like a butterfly and sting like a bee." Great trial lawyers have drawn overflow galleries of spectators to admire how they established rapport with prospective jurors, landed punches in opening argument, then took punches and punched back in direct and cross-examinations and in closing arguments. As the panel discussion concluded, the moderator put up on the screen a list of about twenty famous American lawyers he thought best fit the criteria they had agreed upon. All but two of those listed were male. The two women seemed hastily named as an afterthought.

Justice Sandra Day O'Connor (one of the women named) graduated in 1952 near the top of her class at Stanford Law School. (Chief Justice William Rehnquist was first in the same class; my senior law partner John Wells was second.) Nevertheless, despite scores of applications, she could not find a job in any private law firm. (Justice Ruth Bader Ginsburg had the same disheartening experience after graduating first in her class at Columbia Law School in 1959.) At the start of her career, O'Connor juggled raising her two sons with part-time work as a government attorney. She became known for her negotiating skills — not for mastering the grueling combat of jury trials, where women litigators were still shunned. O'Connor's career path took her to working for Goldwater's 1964 campaign for the presidency, then to state political office in 1965, and a decade as an Arizona trial and appellate judge before President Reagan elevated her from relative obscurity to become the first woman justice on the highest court in the land.

The other woman lawyer listed at the panel discussion was Sarah Weddington, known for trying one landmark case before a panel of three federal judges in Dallas, Texas, in 1970 — *Roe v. Wade*. Weddington had graduated from the University of Texas Law School just three years earlier, only to face the same repeated rejection by private law firms in 1967 as Sandra Day O'Connor and Ruth Bader Ginsburg had experienced in the 1950s. Weddington instead joined activists researching ways to challenge the constitutionality of anti-abortion laws. In 1971, the twenty-six-year old advocate gained instant fame when she won her maiden argument before the United States Supreme Court. Weddington was then elected to the Texas legislature, served in the Carter administration and made her career as a professor and speaker.

Sitting in the audience as a former litigator and judge, I felt that the gray-haired male jurist who chose Weddington and O'Connor as great trial lawyers on a list headed by Clarence Darrow displayed an appalling double standard. So few women lawyers apparently came to mind that the moderator just picked two with instant name recognition for pioneering achievements in the law, regardless of their lack of jury trial experience. When the program ended, I asked Chief Judge Marilyn Hall Patel if she could think of a woman trial lawyer who should have made that list. She instantly named her deceased former colleague Fay Stender, who had served with her in the mid-1970s on the San Francisco board of the American Civil Liberties Union.

I was already aware of Stender's reputation for relentless pursuit

AUTHOR'S NOTE

of justice for unpopular causes. Nearly two decades earlier, California Women Lawyers, on whose board I served, began giving out an annual award in her name to outstanding women lawyers exhibiting similar passion for serving the disadvantaged and effecting societal change. Yet I knew almost nothing about Stender's legal career other than the realization that she must have overcome extraordinary challenges. Women litigators were still rare when I graduated from law school in 1974, a generation after Stender graduated.

I decided to follow up. I talked to Drucilla Ramey, one of the founding mothers of California Women Lawyers, who had since become the Executive Director of the San Francisco Bar Association. Through Dru I met her husband Marvin Stender, who had previously been married to Fay. Marvin Stender was himself a veteran trial lawyer still practicing in San Francisco. When I told him I wanted to write about Fay's career, he said, "It's about time," and handed me a box of her legal files he had just fetched from his attic.

I soon read a controversial tribute to Fay Stender penned by former *Ramparts* magazine reporters Peter Collier and David Horowitz. "Requiem for a Radical" was first published by *New West* magazine in March 1981, two months shy of the first anniversary of her suicide. Though cathartic for the authors, this insider criticism of the Movement by fellow Leftists caused an immediate uproar among the circle of Bay Area activists to which Collier and Horowitz were still thought to belong. Most provocative of all was their quotation of a colleague at her funeral, who called her death the "end of an era." Some branded the authors traitors to the cause. "Requiem for a Radical" did in fact presage the pair's total public rejection of Movement politics. In 1989, the two former radicals emerged as Neocons embraced by the right for their bombshell best-seller, *Destructive Generation: A Second Look at the Sixties.*

Destructive Generation led off with "Requiem for a Radical" as chapter one. The authors' portrait of Fay` — her background, career and relationships — raised more questions in my mind than answers. I then spent over a decade researching her cases, reviewing newspaper coverage of her achievements and reading her hefty FBI file, her published articles and publications by others covering Movement activities in which she participated, plus her correspondence and related papers preserved in private collections and in university libraries. I wound up interviewing several dozen people, including her husband Marvin, her sister Lisie, and friends from childhood, college and law school through her final days, "frenemies," lovers, clients, neighbors, former colleagues, opposing counsel, judges familiar with her work, and journalists who covered her unorthodox career as a Movement lawyer. The interviews took me from the greater Bay Area to Monterey, to Reed College in Portland, Oregon, to New York, New Haven, Boston and an island off the coast of Maine.

Along the way, I became fascinated by the 1968 death penalty case that rocketed Fay Stender to Lefty celebrity status and put her high on the FBI watch list. The murder trial of black militant Huey Newton for the death of a policeman first garnered international attention for audaciously seeking to put America's justice system itself on trial for a history of racism. Against all odds, the defense team was determined to seat a ground-breakingly diverse "jury of one's peers" to decide the fate of the co-founder of the Black Panther Party.

Stender was then an associate in an Old Left San Francisco law firm that often represented politically unpopular clients, including those facing the death penalty. In the Newton case, she put in grueling hours assisting renowned "streetfighter in the courtroom" Charles Garry. Though Garry garnered all the attention for his extraordinary courtroom skills, it was Stender who oversaw the equally important research and motion work and coordinated the pioneering team of experts on racism. The mostly female jury panel then chose as their foreman the only African-American among them — the first known black man ever to serve as foreman of a major murder trial in the United States. That jury spent four days poring over the evidence before deciding Newton was guilty only of voluntary manslaughter, a stunning victory for the defense. The next year, the innovative handiwork of the Newton defense team was captured in a guidebook by National Lawyers Guild historian Ann Fagan Ginger: *Minimizing Racism in Jury Trials*, which quickly became a "Bible" for criminal defense lawyers nationwide.

In August 1970, Fay Stender's brilliant brief on appeal resulted in the unexpected reversal of Newton's conviction and his release from prison. Despite its lasting impact on jury selection across the country, *People v. Newton* soon fell off the radar screen of most legal scholars. That motivated me to write a book in 2012 about that extraordinary trial, *The Sky's the Limit: People v. Newton, The REAL Trial of the 20th Century? The Sky's the Limit* has led to a documentary project, "American Justice on Trial: People v. Newton" (www.americanjusticeontrial.com) and a companion book of the same name. There was no time to waste before filming interviews with surviving participants and observers of that pivotal trial if we were to preserve their viewpoints for posterity.

Fay Stender's pioneering role in the Newton trial made more people curious about her life story. As I started readying this biography for publication, along came the 2016 election, with relentless attacks on the value of diversity amid calls to turn the clock back to an earlier time of presumed American greatness. I detoured to write another book seeking to put the yearning for a bygone era of white male monopoly power in the context of pivotal cases from a century ago that helped galvanize support for minority and women's rights. Fay Stender would have undoubtedly endorsed my 2017 book, *With Justice for Some: Politically Charged Criminal Trials of the Early 20th Century That Helped Shape Today's America*. Months before her death, she outlined a history course she wanted to teach on "socially significant cases" for college or law school students. She never got that chance. Now, here at last, is my take on Fay's own unique story, including the trailblazing cases in which she and her circle of Movement lawyers played such pivotal roles from the 1950s through the 1970s.

Lise Pearlman
Oakland, California
February 2018

Prologue

The gunman waited in the shadows near Fay Stender's front door as his companion rang the buzzer. It was after one a.m. on a quiet, tree-lined section of Grant Street in the flatlands of West Berkeley within walking distance of the police station. A young, half-dressed man, turned on the porch light and pushed aside the frayed front door curtain. He saw a light-skinned black woman standing on the doorstep and he immediately thought she must be in distress to arrive at his family home at that hour. As he opened the door, she quickly turned and ran while a black man wearing a leather jacket and a blue knit cap suddenly forced Neal Stender back inside the house at gunpoint. He then made Neal lead him to Neal's mother as she lay sleeping upstairs. The gunman followed Neal into the master bedroom and was surprised to find two women in the bed and a dog lying on top of the covers near their feet. Once Fay identified herself, the gunman told her to put something on. Her nakedness made him uncomfortable. When she had donned a nightgown in her closet, the gunman then asked her if she had ever betrayed anybody. He mentioned George Jackson, the revolutionary Soledad inmate who had fired Fay as his lawyer in early 1971 and months later died in an escape attempt from San Quentin. Fay denied that she had betrayed Jackson or anyone else.

The gunman then forced Fay to sit at her desk to write, "I, Fay Stender, admit I betrayed George Jackson and the Prison Movement when they needed me most."

Fay chided the gunman. "I will write this because you have a gun," Fay said. "But it is not true."[1] When she finished her "confession," the gunman put it in his pocket. Then he asked his three hostages for money and left Neal and Fay's lover Katherine Morse (a pseudonym) tied up. Fay offered to lead him downstairs, where she offered him a twenty-dollar-bill fetched from her kitchen drawer. Instead of taking it, he shot her five times at close range and fled out the front door, disappearing down the quiet street as she cried out for help.

The shooting early that Memorial Day of 1979 dominated local radio and television reports. Banner headlines in Berkeley and Oakland papers proclaimed, "Attorney shot, near death"[2] and "Political Murder Try?"[3] Then national wire services picked it up. For the next nine months, Bay Area media covered every development: the arrest of the suspect, his attempted escape, the contentious preliminary hearings, and the dramatic trial. Newspapers speculated that the attacker belonged to a notorious prison gang that traced its founding back to death row "Soledad Brother" George Jackson, who was killed in the prison yard at San Quentin in August 1971, days before he was to face trial for the murder of a guard at Soledad the year before. After the home invasion that nearly killed his wife, Fay's husband Marvin considered his family to continue to be at extremely seriously risk. He acquired a gun permit, armed himself and hid their two children thousands of miles away, while Fay remained, incapacitated, at another secret location in the Bay Area.

At first, no one knew if the forty-seven-year-old lawyer would survive. If she did, would she be willing to become the star witness for the prosecutor? Few reporters failed to mention the irony of the District Attorney determinedly seeking justice for a victim most members of his office despised as an enemy — a woman state prison officials nicknamed "The Dragon Lady."

PROLOGUE

Fay had once considered this slur a badge of honor. In the late 1960s and early 1970s, she had nothing but contempt for the state correctional hierarchy. She took great pride in her zealous legal representation and political organizing on behalf of Black Panther co-founder Huey Newton and death row inmate George Jackson, both accused of killing lawmen. In championing the causes of the two revolutionaries, she remained undaunted by whispered rumors that Oakland police officers used her image for target practice.

The scathing labels were, in fact, recognition of her extraordinary effectiveness. The soft-spoken attorney considered herself an impassioned insider working within the legal system to transform society's attitude toward ghettoized blacks and prisoners' rights. Fay Stender's successes made her far more threatening to the established social order than two other radical American women pilloried by the establishment at the same time — glamorous actress and anti-war demonstrator Jane Fonda and Communist lecturer and accused kidnap-and-murder conspirator Angela Davis.

But who was "The Dragon Lady" really? Almost forty years later, Fay Stender's admirers consider her a martyr to her pioneering work in California prison reform. At the height of her career, Fay was one of the most sought after "people's lawyers" in the nation. A client with a cause could not find a more energetic advocate. But in spite of her successes, many colleagues believed that Fay's untempered empathy for her clients compromised her professional judgment.

Friends could easily picture Fay as the heroine of a grand opera. A highly talented musician, she had been a child prodigy who gave up training for a career as a concert pianist during her rebellious teenage years. The five-foot-eight, dark-haired advocate often appeared striking and glamorous, whether she was passionately defending the merits of her favorite novelist, Marcel Proust, or decrying unfair penalties faced by black prostitutes, but not their "johns". Though fiercely devoted to her children, she believed the Movement came first, a commitment to political activism shared by her husband Marvin through a quarter of a century of an intermittent and unpredictable marriage.

At gatherings, Fay often dominated the conversation, while waving her expressive hands for emphasis. Upon meeting her, many people found her charismatic; she exuded an aura of sexuality not unlike that of presidents John F. Kennedy and Bill Clinton. Yet cameras seldom did Fay justice. When she was animated, her face glowed. At other times, her mood swung from contagious passion to deep melancholy. Then she might come across as eccentric and oblivious, wearing mismatched, dowdy outfits or letting her slip show. Afraid of guns herself, she acted as a cheerleader for clients bent on armed confrontation with police. Yet she never identified with the anarchism of her revolutionary clients or the militancy of some of her young Leftist colleagues.

As much as Fay worked to bring like-minded radicals together, she was also at the center of the most enduring rifts among Leftists in the tight-knit East Bay community. Muckraker Jessica Mitford — who collaborated with Fay on prison law reform — put Fay firmly in the category of "frenemy." Some colleagues found Fay's inflexibility repellent and questioned the course she charted; others felt used and dismissed when Fay's focus shifted and she no longer needed them. Yet Fay always found new collaborators as she forged ahead to her next cause célèbre.

The May 1979 home invasion left Fay both wheel-chair bound and devastated. While under twenty-four hour a day police protection, she repeatedly announced that her only motivation to live was to help convict her assailant. She told the few friends admitted to her San Francisco hideaway to "call me Phaedra [pronounced 'Fay-dra']," a tragic heroine from Greek mythology. In college, Fay had been fascinated by French playwright Jean Racine's masterpiece, *Phèdre*, the retelling of the story of the ancient queen Phaedra, daughter of King Minos of Crete. Phaedra came under the spell of the goddess Aphrodite and fell hopelessly in love with her stepson, Hippolytus, whose mother was the queen of the Amazons. Hippolytus rejected his obsessed stepmother, who sought to make him king. On the return of Phaedra's husband, King Theseus, Phaedra accused Hippolytus of attempting to usurp the throne. Outraged, Theseus had Hippolytus killed. The guilt-ridden Phaedra then killed herself.

Racine followed the classical formula that hubris leads to downfall. Fay saw parallels between Phèdre's ill-fated sexual obsession with her inter-racial stepson and Fay's own flouting of traditional taboos in becoming obsessed with her black clients Huey Newton and George Jackson. Ten years her junior, both young militants brought out Fay's strong maternal instincts as well as her passion. At the outset, Newton and Jackson greatly appreciated Fay's legal help. But the two radicals later emphatically rejected her as too controlling — a Liberal white Jewish woman who affronted their macho Black Power image with her determination to shape the world's perception of them as sympathetic victims of a racist justice system. Though Fay seemingly bounced back from her rejection by both revolutionary clients to champion other causes, she, in fact, never fully recovered.

Renewed Russian pogroms in 1905 caused Harry Aviron to flee the Polish city of Brest-Litovsk for New York to find a new home for his family. He left behind his pregnant wife Eva and two-year-old son Sam. Immigration officials anglicized the spelling of his last name to Abrahams. After months of fruitless search for carpentry work, Harry read the headlines in April 1906 about the Great San Francisco Earthquake and fire that left half the city's population homeless. He immediately headed west to be part of the rebuilding effort. After joining San Francisco's well-established Jewish community, Harry sent for his wife Eva, young son Sam, and new baby Dorie, six siblings, his Orthodox Jewish parents and his grandmother. This formal photo was taken in San Francisco around 1908. Sam is seated with his younger son Hank, born in America, on his lap. His wife Eva is standing to his left behind their daughter Dorie. Fay's father, Sam Abrahams, is the young boy standing in the right hand corner with his grandmother's arm resting on his shoulder.

ACT ONE

Photo courtesy of Fay's niece, Linda Stone

This photo taken early in World War II shows Fay and Lisie Abrahams dressed in matching outfits as children. Fay looks about 9 or 10; Lisie would have been 6 or 7. The family moved from San Mateo County to a rental home in North Berkeley in 1941 when their father was offered a prestigious new job overseeing construction and management of a plant that manufactured insulation for the war effort. By age ten Fay had long since become the focus of her proud parents and extended family as a child prodigy at the piano. In the 1970s when she and Lisie each had teenagers, Fay expressed some empathy toward her younger sister for having to grow up in her shadow.

■ 1 ■

The Battle of Wills

"At times I felt I was literally gasping for life itself."[1]
— Fay Stender describing childhood clashes with her parents

Fay likely inherited her strong will, talent and ambition from her mother. Ruby Fay Lefkowitz was a native San Franciscan, born a few months before the 1906 earthquake to an immigrant rag and bottle peddler. Louis Lefkowitz had arrived in America as a sixteen-year-old stowaway from Hungary. Ruby's mother, Lena, had been born in San Francisco of German immigrants, and boasted a rare eighth grade education. Lena, in turn, encouraged Ruby to become an accomplished piano player and star pupil at Girls' High School. Ruby then won a $100 scholarship that covered four semesters' tuition at the University of California in Berkeley. She later liked to remind Fay how she had to rise daily at five a.m. to get to the campus by street car, bus and ferry each day for the privilege of attending college.

Commuting to Cal was how Ruby met Sam Abrahams, who was taking the same time-consuming route across the bay in pursuit of a chemical engineering degree. Sam and Ruby finally saved up enough to marry in the winter of 1928 only to lose half their savings in the stock market crash of 1929. When the Great Depression followed, Ruby lost her teaching position at an elementary school to a man with a family to support. By then, Sam was earning a modest salary as a chemistry researcher. When Ruby became pregnant in 1931, the Abrahams splurged on a beautiful standing bassinette on wheels, a handsome white, wicker basket that would be reused by countless cousins and returned to Fay for her own babies.

During Ruby's last trimester, Sam suffered from a near fatal kidney infection that kept him hospitalized for three months. As his life still hung in the balance, on March 29, 1932, Ruby delivered Fay Ethel Abrahams. Ignoring Jewish custom, Ruby gave her daughter her own middle name as a first name. When Ruby and her newborn went home, Ruby was unable to breastfeed, likely due to ongoing stress. Ruby split her attention between her infant and ailing husband as Sam slowly and miraculously recovered without losing a kidney, despite the doctor's dire prediction. Yet Fay suffered all her life from mixed emotions about her mother, likely rooted in an early sense of abandonment.

Growing up, Fay was closer to her father. The Biblical injunction to help the needy was coded into the Abrahams' genes. All of the family on her father's side were brought over by her grandfather Harry Aviron from the Polish city of Brest-Litovsk, since medieval times a trading center with a longstanding Jewish population. When Harry Aviron was a youth, Brest-Litovsk had been under Russian control for over a century. Renewed pogroms caused many Jews to flee for their lives. Harry set off for New York, leaving behind his pregnant wife Eva and two-year-old son Sam. Immigration officials anglicized the spelling of his last name to Abrahams. The family would always pronounce it "Abrams."

After months of fruitless search for carpentry work, Harry read the headlines about the Great San Francisco Earthquake and fire that left half the city's population homeless. He headed west in April 1906 to be part of the rebuilding effort. He soon joined San Francisco's well-established Jewish community and sent for his wife, young son and new baby, six siblings, his Orthodox Jewish parents and diminutive grandmother. After ensuring his own family's safety, Harry Abrahams quickly joined the fledgling Hebrew Free Loan Association at his local synagogue. The group provided interest-free loans to help newer Jewish immigrants launch small businesses by buying a sewing machine or a vegetable cart to push through the streets. Harry took great pride in his own family's quick rise to the middle class and his personal role in San Francisco's recovery. He later drove family members around San Francisco, pointing out the houses he, as a carpenter, had built.

In April of 1935, Ruby gave birth to Elise "Lisie" Abrahams, just after Fay turned three. The young family was now complete. In 1936, the Abrahams' one-year-old contracted pneumonia. Lisie wound up hospitalized for several weeks as she dwindled to an alarming thirteen pounds, losing more than a third of her body weight. For another three months, Lisie seemed to wake only long enough to eat. Decades later, Lisie would speculate that her mother's prolonged distraction and grief instilled in Fay an enduring sense of abandonment and anger. Yet it was Lisie who was raised to take a back seat to her extraordinarily talented older sister in whom both parents evinced great pride.

A gifted musician with perfect pitch, Fay was eager to learn the piano at age three, but her mother made her wait until she was four to begin lessons. With Ruby as her first tutor, Fay happily practiced daily. Fay soon became the center of the entire extended family's attention. She could play a song after hearing it once. Her parents began providing her with private lessons. The first to be hired was Pauline Newman, a lovelorn spinster, who recognized in Fay signs of depression. Newman shared her concerns with Ruby and Sam. The worried Abrahams ultimately took Fay to see a psychiatrist. The subject was so unmentionable that the couple tried never to discuss it in front of Lisie. Bouts of prolonged unhappiness would trouble Fay throughout adulthood as she exhibited other classic symptoms of bipolar mood disorder.

During the 1930s, Sam developed a specialty in asbestos, perfecting a number of patents. Sam designed non-combustible covers for ships' boilers and pipes. In 1941, he was offered a prestigious job in Berkeley overseeing the construction and management of a plant that manufactured insulation for the war effort. Sam was not tall, but the successful chemist cut a dapper appearance with his well-trimmed mustache and stylish attire.

Sam and Ruby always lived in all-white neighborhoods. When they moved to the East Bay in the early 1940s, they found a modest rental home in North Berkeley and entered both of their girls in a local elementary school. School came easily to Fay, who soon skipped a grade, but Lisie always had to work harder. To assist with household tasks, Ruby hired a string of mother's helpers from the Midwest, as did many of Ruby's friends. Fay and Elise shared one bedroom; the mother's helper stayed in the third bedroom. Each boarder received "pin" money for helping Ruby prepare meals for the family and for babysitting when Sam and Ruby occasionally went out in the evening. The mother's helpers were not allowed to eat with the Abrahams. Instead, Ruby trained them to serve the vegetables at dinner in a side dish at each place setting and to answer to a bell that Ruby rang for additional assistance. Fay disliked her mother's pretentious household arrangement and objected to treating the live-in household help as servants of a lower class, unwelcome at the family table. When Fay reached high school age, she insisted on having her own room apart from her sister. That ended the era of live-in mother's helpers in favor of a once-a-week cleaning woman.

Though Sam had grown up in an Orthodox Jewish household, Fay and Lisie were raised Reform. They observed the Sabbath on Friday night, celebrated the holidays and studied for confirmation with the rabbi at a local synagogue. After dinner, the family played cards or a board game for an hour or so before each turned to other interests. Sam taught the girls the rudiments of chess, but had no patience for coaching them on the finer points of the game at which he excelled. Though Sam was authoritarian, Ruby's controlling nature weighed much more heavily on Fay. Her mother tended toward hypochondria and took Fay to the doctor frequently. Fay particularly found oppressive Ruby's preoccupation with making sure Fay's feet and smile would be beautiful when she grew up. Fay wore glasses and orthopedic shoes with arch supports Fay considered hideous and unnecessary. Her teeth were straightened with braces she also abhorred.

At a young age, Fay began nervously chewing her fingernails until they were gone, which the doctor suggested could be cured by applying a bitter coating. Ruby gave up on the suggestion after a few tries. As an adult, despite her great pride in her beautiful hands, Fay could not altogether shake the habit of nibbling her nails to the quick. A more worrisome concern to her parents was a chronic breathing problem that, in retrospect, Fay assumed was probably psychosomatic. Lisie later believed Fay may have suffered from allergies as their father did. At the time, Fay's constant snuffling perplexed them all.

Fay had many battles with her parents over breathing through her mouth instead of her nose. In the midst of a game of Parcheesi, she might excuse herself to go to the bathroom just to breathe without criticism. She told an interviewer thirty years later, "At times I felt I was literally gasping for life itself."[2] Ultimately, Fay's mother took her to an ear-nose-and-throat specialist who attributed Fay's problem to enlarged adenoids and recommended their removal along with her tonsils. The thirteen-year-old insisted that her younger sister be examined too. Much to her dismay, Lisie, who had just been along for the ride, wound up scheduled for surgery at the same time.

Encouraged by Fay's rapid progress as a piano student, the Abrahams devoted much of the family's disposable income to more expensive lessons. Fay met with a highly acclaimed tutor twice weekly, while Lisie was offered lessons by his assistant. Though proficient, Lisie soon quit, finding the contrast in their abilities too painful. When Fay periodically shirked practice, her parents threatened to discontinue the lessons, but Fay always opted to reapply herself with renewed vigor. She gave her first recital before she turned ten.

Soon afterward, Fay was accepted as a student of the renowned concert pianist and professor, Bernhard Abramowitsch. When *San Francisco Chronicle* music critic Alfred Frankenstein heard eleven-year-old Fay play, he confirmed her parents' opinion that she possessed exceptional talent. Any chance for her to become a virtuoso, however, necessitated long, regular hours of practice. Her parents decided to send Fay to the prestigious Anna Head private school — the only school around where classes terminated at one p.m., which allowed Fay all afternoon to practice.

The Anna Head boarding and day school then stood at its original 1887 location, on Channing Way in Berkeley. (It has since moved to the Oakland Hills and changed its name to Head-Royce.) Its Berkeley campus included a well-tended rose garden. In springtime, the quadrangle

When Fay turned 11, renowned concert pianist Bernhard Abramowitsch accepted her as a student. Her parents then began sending Fay to the prestigious Anna Head private school which let out at one p.m., so she could spend her afternoons practicing at the piano. The school was still in its original location on Channing Way in Berkeley when Fay Abrahams attended it. Later, it relocated to Oakland where it is now known as Head-Royce.

War reporter Marguerite Higgins in 1942, whom LIFE magazine featured as a "Girl War Correspondent," was one of Anna Head's most famous graduates. When Fay later attended Reed College, she had a month-long affair with Higgins' then estranged husband, Prof. Stanley Moore.

was surrounded by blooming wisteria. To Ruby, it seemed nearly ideal. The school had an excellent academic reputation with a top-notch faculty hired from Smith College. One of Anna Head's alumnae was celebrated war correspondent Marguerite Higgins, who had just made headlines reporting from the front lines for the *New York Herald Tribune*. Marguerite's mother was a French teacher at Anna Head. When Fay started seventh grade, the acting head mistress was Lea Hyde, a Smith Classics major who had been widowed at a young age. Smith taught English with sensitivity and compassion. It became Fay's favorite subject.

World War II imbued the Anna Head faculty and student body with a strong sense of purpose. The new school newspaper, *Quips and Cranks,* urged students to save metal, paper, cork and rubber goods for the war effort. Students knitted socks and sweaters and took first aid courses. The school social service club "adopted" two British children, mailed packages to soldiers overseas and organized a clothing drive for residents of a war-torn French town. Yet Fay hated her new regimen, particularly the drab gray skirts with white blouses and matching gray sweaters that all the girls were required to wear. Anna Head had recently established the then-novel concept of student government. The elected representatives, awed by their responsibility, dutifully issued pink slips to students caught talking in study hall or not wearing their uniforms.

What oppressed Fay most was that attending Anna Head kept her isolated from her peers in junior high school who gathered after school to socialize. Instead, Fay headed home each day for three hours of piano practice under Ruby's watchful eye. At least, unlike Lisie, Fay enjoyed exemption from household chores. Even at family picnics, Fay was not allowed to participate in volleyball for fear it would injure her hands. Ruby and Sam had grown alarmed after a game of tag ended with Lisie slamming the front door on her sister's right hand. Lessons continued with left-handed arrangements as the family waited anxiously for Fay's bandaged finger to heal. For Lisie, her parents' temporary ostracism was mortifying. For Fay, it was sweet revenge. Growing up, Fay found her younger sister irritatingly prettier than she was and disliked Lisie's normal role as the good child, far more traditional than Fay, shier and more compliant by nature.

The highlight of Fay's young musical career was a recital at the San Francisco Symphony at age fourteen. She performed the "Emperor Concerto," Beethoven's last piano concerto and an extraordinary challenge for a teenager. The thirty-five-minute piece ends with a dramatic flourish, often performed to showcase a pianist's virtuosity. The symphony gave a formal luncheon in Fay's honor to celebrate her performance. Though Fay said nothing to Lisie at the time, Fay actually felt badly that her younger sister had to suffer in her shadow in front of so many family members and friends, including their grandmother Lena, who sat in the front row with their parents. While basking in all that attention, Fay could not resist some mischief. After they reached home, a symphony staff member telephoned Ruby: Fay had been observed taking a spoon from her lunch table. Deeply humiliated, her parents made Fay return the souvenir. Sam and Ruby did not know, as Lisie did, that whenever the family dined out, Fay pocketed a teaspoon. Fay had stashed more than a dozen such flatware keepsakes in their shared bedroom.

After her debut, Fay complained to friends about feeling chained to the piano by her mother for seemingly endless hours of practice. Fay's yearning for a normal teenage existence prompted frequent feuds with both of her equally headstrong parents. At nearly five-foot-eight, Fay was tall and big-boned, with long legs and an awkward gait. Intense and forceful by nature, Fay matured into an adolescent with thick, dark eyebrows emphasizing her expressive, intelligent eyes. Her features bore some similarity to the sensuous Mexican-Jewish artist Frida Kahlo.

Soon after the San Francisco Symphony recital, Fay rebelled in earnest. Anna Head had become even more intolerable when Lea Hyde's second husband, Theophilus Hyde, returned from service in the Navy and resumed his stern leadership of the school. In shouting matches with her parents that sent Lisie scurrying out of the room, Fay declared she would no longer commit to concert piano training or go to Anna Head with its ugly uniforms. After finishing ninth grade, Fay wanted to attend Berkeley High School like her friend Hilde Stern, who had been the valedictorian of Fay's confirmation class. The Abrahams held Dr. Stern and his family in high regard. Berkeley High provided a first-rate education; it ranked among the top public schools in America. So Fay won her battle, but agreed to continue with a lighter schedule of piano lessons, giving her parents hope Fay might still make a career out of her exceptional talent.

By 1946, when Fay started high school, war-time rent control had allowed the Abrahams to save enough to purchase a small, two-story, three-bedroom home with its own garage off Arch Street in North Berkeley for $6,000. For Sam and Ruby, the dormered house on Corona Court held appeal because it was located on a quiet cul-de-sac in one of two middle class sections of the city. The upper-middle class and wealthy lived in the hills, while the poor, including many newly arrived black families, occupied the flatlands of West Berkeley. All children were channeled through local elementary schools and junior highs, segregating them by the class-based neighborhoods in which they lived.

At Berkeley High, Hilde introduced Fay to a small group of bright and motivated girl friends with whom Hilde had gone to junior high school. As a Jew whose family had fled the Nazis, Hilde noticed little overt anti-Semitism at Berkeley High. Hilde's older brother often dated daughters of well-to-do WASP families, but Hilde was drawn instinctively to those on the social fringe. More reserved than Fay by nature, the German immigrant enjoyed Fay's vibrancy. Fay seemed particularly drawn to crossing class lines when making friends and tried harder than others to understand people from different social strata.

Hilde's small group of self-described "shreds" included the daughter of a Christian Scientist family impoverished by the Depression, the daughter of a Baptist missionary back from China, the daughter of a carpenter with seven children, and the daughter of a divorced Catholic head nurse at a local hospital. Fay was the only other Jewish girl and the only girl with a grandparent born in the Bay Area.

Hilde's friends accepted Fay into their circle only as a favor to Hilde. They realized Fay was a likely fellow reject of the cashmere-and-pearl in-crowd, but left to their own devices, Hilde's friends would have been too put off by Fay's arrogant streak. All smart and college-bound, the "shreds" engaged in mostly parallel activities to the Hill girls. They rarely gathered at Fay's house where Ruby, now President of the Berkeley League of Women Voters, made them feel unwelcome.

Source of photos from 1949 *Olla Podrida*: Berkeley Public Library, https://archive.org/details/ollapodridaunse_40

Fay Stender

OLLA PODRIDA
Berkeley High School Yearbook

Source: https://www.google.com/

```
ol·la po·dri·da  ˌälə pəˈdrēdə, ˌô(l)yə/ noun
1. a highly spiced Spanish stew
2. any miscellaneous assortment or collection -
"an olla podrida of romance, comedy, and tragedy"
```

As a teen, Fay decided to expand her vocabulary by reading the dictionary from start to finish. She got as far as the letter "L." Yet she and her classmates all knew the meaning of "olla podrida." That was what the Berkeley High yearbook had always been called.

Fay joined the Pro Musica Club and, at 15, won an award as the best young musician in the Bay Area. She and her friend Hilde Stern were both members of the Honor Society, but Fay had another goal. She practiced long hours to make the cheerleading squad, to no avail.

LEADERS' CLASS

FRONT ROW, left to right: Susan Kahn, Jeannette Humfeld, Martha Shiveley, Pat Norgrove, Ida Mae Wicke, Sally Jensen, Pat Wong, Trinette Dolan, Diane Dousseau.
SECOND ROW: Sandra Waller, Dorothy Bunnel, Jackie Foster, Joyce Ussery, Laura Lehmer, Ann Wooky, Joanne Legault, Carol Webster, Judy Mayeda.
THIRD ROW: Dolores Silveria, Nate Lellep, Dolores Canuso, Jean Tharp, Joanne Crane, Georgia Gernreich, Alison Barr, Arloa Austin, Nancy Wellman.

Fay herself still pined for acceptance into the central extracurricular life of the high school. She wanted to join a sorority, but the only feasible one was composed largely of girls rejected by more prestigious sororities. Fay attempted to coax Hilde and her friends into pledging with her, but they displayed no interest. Fay also tried out for a position as a cheerleader, practicing endlessly, but failed to make the squad. Soon, Fay spent less time with "the shreds" as she initiated a series of one-on-one intense friendships that she dominated. It would be many years before Fay recognized her strong feelings for some close female friends as signs of bisexuality.

The most enduring of Fay's new best friends was Wendy Milmore, who was a year behind Fay in school. The attractive brunette was soft-spoken and a good listener as Fay confided her insecurities and unhappiness. (Wendy would later embark on a career as a psychiatrist.) Unlike the shreds, Wendy marveled at Fay's quick mind and fluency of expression. On more than one occasion, she had witnessed Fay busily writing lengthy diary entries. Stream of consciousness became Fay's writing style. As a lawyer, she rarely edited anything she wrote.

Fay and Wendy liked to go on Saturday afternoon adventures by bus. On one such excursion at the De Young Museum in San Francisco, the curious teens strolled past the public areas down restricted corridors and opened doors marked "Private" to see what was behind them. Fay would delight all her life in opening closed doors at public institutions to observe their secret inner workings. In one pivotal pretrial hearing when she represented George Jackson in the Soledad Brothers murder case in the spring of 1970, a surprised Salinas judge would grant Fay's impromptu request to enter his chambers to prove the courtroom had more than one fire exit. The stunt drew applause from the crowd of Leftists Fay had bussed down to the Conservative community. Fay had just proved the courtroom had sufficient fire exits to allow all of them to watch the trial. The chagrined judge then made county history — to avoid a media circus like that in the 1968 Huey Newton case in Oakland and the recently ended Chicago Seven trial, he transferred the politically charged death penalty case to San Francisco.

While at Berkeley High, Fay's stormy relationship with her mother

Fay Abrahams and her close friend Wendy Milmore circa 1951

As teenagers, Fay and Wendy liked to go on Saturday afternoon adventures by bus. On one trip to the De Young Museum in San Francisco, the curious girls strolled down restricted corridors and opened doors marked "Private." Fay would delight all her life in opening closed doors at public institutions to observe their secret inner workings.

continued. Freed from the dreaded Anna Head uniform, she surreptitiously snatched her mother's charge card plate to buy colorful plaid sweaters and skirts at Hink's Department Store on Shattuck Avenue in Berkeley. Of course, the new clothes did not go unnoticed and Ruby forced Fay to take them back. Fay also showed her rebellious streak by playing hymns on Sundays at a nearby Congregational Church. To the dismay of church elders and titilation of her peers, she sometimes improvised a few bars of popular music. This trend — the glee in seizing opportunities to test the tolerance of those in charge — continued throughout adulthood.

Fay joined Berkeley High's Pro Musica Club and in tenth grade, at age 15, won an award as the best young musician in the Bay Area for her performance of Chopin's "Scherzo in B Flat Minor." Her prize was an opportunity to perform as a guest artist with the Oakland Symphony and a $50 gift certificate, which Fay spent on a faddish, long-fibered coat.

For the most part, neither Fay nor her close friends paired off with a serious boyfriend in high school. Once during her junior year, unbeknownst to her parents, Fay went out driving in the Berkeley Hills with a male friend and two other couples in his family's car. Her date missed a turn on the hairpin curves of Tilden Park, throwing them both from the car, which then rolled over and was totaled. Miraculously, none of the passengers was seriously injured. The Abrahams were so relieved when they collected Fay at Herrick Hospital that they forgave her deception. The nearly calamitous accident made Fay nervous about car travel for years. She would cower in the back seat whenever Sam sped down the windy coastal road to Carmel for family vacations. Yet in her thirties and forties, Fay would herself speed recklessly behind the wheel, frightening passengers with her cavalier attitude toward their safety.

In high school, both Fay and her friend Hilde easily made the National Honor Society. Fay particularly excelled in English. She took great notes in her tiny, neat handwriting and was a voracious bookworm. Studying for the SATs, Fay embarked on a project of reading the dictionary and got through the L's before she quit. She considered herself above frivolous pastimes. She read news magazines voraciously, even managing to hide *Time* magazine issues in her music book when practicing the piano. Fay likely appreciated Berkeley High principal Elwin LeTendre's message to the graduating class of 1949. Noting it marked the centennial of the Gold Rush, the principal admonished seniors that "some philosophers think that gold is a curse.... I hope that you will find great values in other than material things."[3]

Yet Fay's awareness of the fight against racial injustice in America — what would become the cornerstone of her career — came slowly. Relatively few blacks lived in Berkeley, Oakland and San Francisco until 1940. By 1946, when Fay entered high school, several hundred thousand blacks had migrated to the Bay Area. Many only found housing in the most undesirable locations. In Berkeley, that meant the flatlands below Telegraph Avenue. In Oakland, they poured into similarly neglected neighborhoods — the streets in both cities where Fay's future Black Panther clients grew up.

When Fay started her junior year of high school, *Time* magazine printed a cover story on Jackie Robinson smashing the color barrier in baseball as National League Rookie of the Year. Prior to high school, Fay had not seen many blacks, except for a few cleaning women in her neighborhood catching the bus back to their own homes. No blacks attended Anna Head, and Fay's group of friends at Berkeley High was strictly white. But Fay and Wendy noticed with curiosity when shacks arose on the outskirts of Berkeley and filled with poor black families from the Deep South. At Berkeley High, black students were almost exclusively placed in a different educational track from those bound for elite colleges and public universities. "Shred" member Joan DeLasaux was unusual in making friends with an African-American girl in her homeroom, to the strong disapproval of many white classmates.

Probably the best student in Fay's high school class had been a Japanese-American, Margaret Ohara. Margaret's family had been removed from the Berkeley community during the war as forced internees while Margaret was in junior high school. After the war, when the Ohara family returned, no one at school discussed that wrenching experience with Margaret. It was a taboo subject, as were the Depression-era troubles of Joan DeLasaux's father. In the '40s, one simply didn't ask and didn't tell.

Source of photos from 1949 *Olla Podrida*: Berkeley Public Library, https://archive.org/details/ollapodridaunse_40

Hilde Stern

Joan DeLasaux

Margaret Ohara

In junior high school, Fay's friend Hilde from Hebrew School formed a group of self-described "shreds" outside the popular crowd and invited Fay to join them. Cross-cultural friendships like that of "shred" member Joan DeLasaux and an African-American girl in her homeroom were rare. Japanese-American Margaret Ohara was a top student whose family got sent to an internment camp when she was in junior high school. When she returended after the war, no one at school discussed that wrenching experience with Margaret. Nor did Joan DeLasaux share with school friends the Depression-era troubles of her father. In the '40s, one simply didn't ask and didn't tell.

■ 2 ■

Predestination or Free Will

"The freedom totally dominated me."[1]
— Fay Stender looking back in 1972 at her college days

When the day finally came for Fay to depart for college, Sam, Ruby and Lisie accompanied her to the train station. Fay looked elegant, wearing a new mauve suit with matching stockings and pumps — a seventeen-year-old with a ticket to an exciting new world. Lisie also felt the importance of the occasion. She looked forward to being an only child and to the peace that would settle on the household when Fay left. Ruby and Sam had strong misgivings. Cal provided an inexpensive, first-rate education right there in Berkeley. Ruby particularly wanted to have her melancholy older daughter close at hand. She had not given up hope of guiding Fay to a career as a pianist.

Cal was also the first choice of the in-crowd at Berkeley High. Fay told her close friends that it took screaming and crying to get her parents to accede to her wish to go to Reed College in Portland, Oregon — the same prestigious private school that her friend Hilde had chosen. Tuition was several hundred dollars per year, about ten times the cost of Cal. Surprisingly, Fay had not confided her ambition to Hilde. Possibly, Fay feared losing the battle with her parents, who made Fay first attend a summer session at Berkeley, before acquiescing in her choice.

By 1949, when Fay applied, Reed had a national reputation as a left-leaning haven for intellectuals, individualists and iconoclastic fine arts majors not wanting to pursue the beaten path. Reed was the West Coast answer to Swarthmore College in the East. Most locals did not hold the college in high regard; they considered it too liberal. About half of the 500 or so students at the college were women. There were virtually no minorities and no poor people.

Fay loved the college's focus on intellectualism. Her first assignment in introductory humanities focused on the ancient Greeks. The teenager eagerly absorbed her instructor's weighty pronouncement that the study of classical Athenians' politics, philosophy, literature, law, science, history and art would reveal the holiest, most glorious and sacred secrets of Western civilization. She especially found fascinating the topics of predestination and free will.

It did not occur to Fay, at seventeen, to incorporate her knowledge of ancient Jewish history from confirmation classes with what she learned in college. She had never experienced any external validation of Hebrew school teachings — that the legacy of kings David and Solomon predated the golden age of Pericles by half a millennium. Only when Fay reached her late forties did she reflect that her Reed professors never mentioned any influence on Western civilization from the earlier advanced Jewish kingdoms; nor did they acknowledge that the Greeks appropriated many of their successful ideas from other advanced Near Eastern cultures.

What mattered most at seventeen was the freedom from parental control. Fay later said that upon her arrival at the Reed campus, "The freedom totally dominated me."[2] As a first test of her independence, she introduced herself to new friends by the shortened surname of Abrams, which sounded the same as it had always been pronounced. Reed had rules by which it sought to operate in loco parentis. The girls' dorms only allowed male visitors from one to three p.m. on Saturdays and Sundays, provided the room door remained open six inches and three feet were on the floor at all times. The dorms were locked at ten p.m. on weekdays and twelve p.m. on weekends, with a procedure for signing in and out. Boys easily evaded those rules by climbing in and

"The freedom totally dominated me."

Reed College Campus

Source of headshots from 1949 *Olla Podrida*: Berkeley Public Library, https://archive.org/details/ollapodridaunse_40

Rob Scott

Rob Scott, Fay's first boyfriend at Reed, graduated from Berkeley High in the fall of 1948, six months before Fay. At Reed, Rob's roommate nicknamed her "Twinkletoes" when she gave Rob dancing lessons. Fay often played classical music on the piano in a dormitory living room. She joked to Rob that she might end up playing tunes in a bar somewhere. Her prediction almost came true.

out of dorm windows, and girls signed out to stay off campus unsupervised for entire weekends.

Fay's first boyfriend at Reed, Rob Scott, also graduated from Berkeley High. The two had first met on the eve of attending college. Fay and Rob spent many afternoons the fall of their freshmen year in the living room at Anna Mann, a dormitory furnished with a piano. Fay tried to teach Rob the Charleston, earning her the nickname "Twinkletoes" from his roommate George. More often, Fay played classical music from memory while Rob sat nearby, reading from a set of the collected works of Jules Verne. Rob asked her once how many compositions a concert pianist needed to know by heart. Fay replied with an impressive list he found hard to believe. Yet it did not even include the many popular tunes she had memorized from the radio. She joked that she might instead end up playing the big band song "Deep Purple" in a bar somewhere — a prediction that almost came true.

* * *

Fay's time at Reed coincided with a new, frightening era, the unleashing of the atom bomb and the Cold War against Communism. She was in her second semester when the FBI arrested Julius and Ethel Rosenberg for conspiracy to commit espionage by providing the Russians with top-secret information on nuclear weapons. Wisconsin Senator Joseph McCarthy then startled the nation in February of 1950 with claims that Communists had infiltrated the State Department, fueling a mounting national atmosphere of anti-Communist hysteria. Fay and her friends began to question government policies they had never before doubted, worrying about the dangers of nuclear weapons and radioactivity. Still, there was little political activism in those days. The only major urban issue Reed students tackled in Fay's freshman year was a "Fair Rose" campaign to abolish discriminatory housing practices in the Rose District of Portland. It paralleled a "Fair Bear" campaign the same year at Cal.

During Fay's freshman year, her parents moved to Pennsylvania where Sam Abrahams had been offered a promising job in the asbestos industry. Lisie, then a high school sophomore, was desperately unhappy about the change. Fay flew East that summer to join her family. Shortly after she arrived, Communist North Korea launched an invasion across the 38th parallel. This time when the United States became embroiled in war, Sam remained uninvolved, saddled back East with three unhappy women. Lisie and Ruby pined for California as Fay yearned to return to the freedom of Reed.

When Fay went back to Portland that fall, she continued dating Rob Scott, immersed herself in comparative literature courses and enjoyed ballroom, folk and square dancing — not politics yet. She joined the college's music program and performed a solo concert. She also entertained friends on occasion. One of the gathering places for students was a student-owned and operated coffee shop on campus. In the fall of 1950, the coffee shop hired a transfer student named Bob Richter as a part-time cashier. He quickly became a celebrity in Fay's small world.

Bob was a rare conscientious objector to the peacetime draft of 1948 — prior to the Korean War. He had been convicted while attending junior college in Los Angeles; his service of the three-year prison sentence for refusing to register for the draft was delayed pending appeal. Chances of reversal were slim. Conscientious objector status was then limited to Quakers and others whose religious beliefs conflicted with military service. Bob's opposition was personal; his parents were nonobservant Jews who had raised him as an atheist. In fact, his mother was a Communist who had been a teen-aged nurse in the Russian Revolution and considered religion the opiate of the masses.

As a last resort, Richter's attorneys sought review in the United States Supreme Court while Bob went back to visit his family in New York over the 1950 winter break. On Christmas Eve, Bob stood in the long line for the midnight mass at St. Patrick's Cathedral on Fifth Avenue and spotted Fay with a companion in the same queue. They exchanged pleasantries. Soon they ran into each other again heading back to Reed on the same $99 super-discount flight.

Fay and Bob began talking as they boarded the plane to Oregon and found each other fascinating company through its many landings and takeoffs. Fay particularly enjoyed Bob's attention because she had just

Bob Richter, Fay's first fiancé, at age 21 in 1950 at Reed College where he had transferred in 1949. He met Fay in December 1950 shortly before he lost his appeal from his conviction for refusing the draft as a would-be conscientious objector. In early 1951, he was jailed in Tucson, Arizona. Fay found ways to visit him there. On one trip she talked the warden into letting her perform on a church piano in the barracks. She mesmerized the inmates, many of whom had never heard classical music before — her first experience trying to humanize prison life. Bob's conviction was later expunged. Bob went on to an extraordinary, award-winning career as a documentarian. (www.richterproductions.com.)

PREDESTINATION OR FREE WILL

been rebuffed by a new love interest. Bob confided that if the Supreme Court petition for review was unsuccessful, he likely faced prison time. Fay endeared herself to Bob even more when she fell asleep leaning against him. Then a passenger died en route to Portland and the pilot made an eleventh, unplanned, stop in Montana to unload the body. During the delay, the stewardesses herded the remaining passengers into a small wooden building that served as the Great Falls airport. Bob and Fay listened to the jukebox play the "Tennessee Waltz" over and over again, wondering whether it was broken or someone else there just really loved that song. By the time they arrived at Reed they were inseparable.

In January of 1951, Bob Richter learned two pieces of bitter news: he lost his final appeal and the military rejected his offer to volunteer only as a medical noncombatant. His friends at Reed threw a farewell party for him at the end of the month. By then, he and Fay had made impetuous plans to marry after he returned from his prison term. After the bittersweet festivities and emotional parting from Fay, Bob hitchhiked to Los Angeles and turned himself in. The prosecutor sympathized with Bob's plight but felt she had no choice: the law was the law. She cried and kissed him on the cheek as she oversaw Bob's delivery to the county sheriff's deputies.

Meanwhile, Fay continued to frequent the student coffee shop and to relay Bob's travails to his former co-workers. He spent a brief time in poorly maintained Los Angeles and Maricopa County jails before reaching his final destination, a minimum security prison in Tucson, Arizona. There he would serve out his sentence with a dozen other conscientious objectors in an open barracks filled with illegal immigrants from Mexico, income tax evaders, a white murderer and a Navajo jailed for a violent felony.

Because of Bob's college education, the warden had originally assigned him to office duties. Bob complained about such preferential treatment in a letter to Fay. He had warned Fay that all his incoming mail was opened and stamped before he saw it. He learned the hard way that the warden read his outgoing mail, too. Bob spent the next several months on a logging crew paving roads for a former German prisoner-of-war camp. The camp had been newly renovated to house up to 100,000 Communists and subversives the FBI then expected to designate as too dangerous to remain at large in society. Bob assumed his own mother was among the potential internees.

Though Fay still socialized on occasion with Rob Scott, she knew she was Bob Richter's lifeline. She wrote him long letters twice a week entertaining him with her activities. That included an excursion with friends to a popular Negro night club in Portland, for Fay a novel and exhilarating experience. During spring break, Fay traveled 25 hours by bus from Portland to see her fiancé. The American Friends Service offered a place for her to stay near the Tucson prison. Visits with Bob would be supervised as they sat on chairs too far apart to touch each other, but close enough to whisper and recover a sense of intimacy.

At 19, Fay felt she was becoming a mature woman of the world. As her sister's sixteenth birthday approached, Fay shared her insights with Lisie in a lengthy heart-to-heart message beautifully printed by hand in two colors. Fay felt she was wandering in a maze, getting lost and then finding her way again. She told Lisie: "The real meaning of life is in three things, love, beauty and pain. And these three are all really one which is God or Truth. And you will only come to know and understand this by giving, and giving too much."[3] Lisie treasured the unexpected birthday letter from Fay, hid it in her drawer and kept it with her throughout her life.

Fay had already made plans for the summer that upset her parents as much or more than learning about Fay visiting her boyfriend in prison. Bob had previously worked at the local office of the American Friends Service Committee (AFSC). It advertised at Reed a Student Peace Service Program in Mexico in the summer of 1951 to inoculate villagers against typhoid. Fay felt compelled to go — to do something useful rather than sit on the sidelines. She asked her parents to pay for that trip and secretly planned to visit Bob in Arizona on the way down to Mexico and back. The Abrahams refused. Undaunted, Fay talked an older cousin who was a lawyer into providing her with the money she needed. Another volunteer from Reed agreed to detour through Arizona so Fay could visit Bob first.

Her parents were stunned at their reckless daughter. Yet over the summer Fay corresponded with her parents and got their reluctant acceptance of her choices. Most appealing to them was her decision to leave Reed and go to Cal that fall. She had become quite depressed that spring at Reed, as well as broke. At Cal, her finances would not be so stretched. Though she worked hard to repair her relationship with her parents, Fay feared from past experience that she would precipitate another rift somehow before too long.

The experience in Mexico that July and August marked a turning point for Fay. She exulted in becoming the best among the volunteers at giving shots and enjoyed learning enough Spanish to carry on meaningful conversations. She even took her turn cooking. Being paired with another volunteer helped her avoid anticipated fiascoes due to lack of kitchen skills. The villagers' joy in simple pleasures impressed her, but their living conditions and poor health were appalling. Fay even considered quitting school to remain working in Mexico with toddlers whose lives could be easily improved. What struck her most was the villagers' tolerance of invasive insects, not even batting an eyelash when flies flew in front of their faces.

Yet, most of all, Fay gained insights into herself. Once she transferred to Cal and earned her degree, she was considering graduate school in sociology. She also wanted to resume piano lessons. While in Mexico, she had heard the Emperor Concerto on the radio and yearned to reconnect with her former piano teacher. She wanted an opportunity to play the concerto as she felt it should be played, improving on her debut at the San Francisco Symphony as a young teen. Ruby would be delighted.

More troublingly, Fay had been feeling dishonest in all her cheery messages to Bob. He was hoping to win parole after one year in jail, and they talked about marrying on her next birthday. For some time she had harbored serious doubts about their future together. Fay revealed to Bob her history of alternating between wildly conflicting urges that could doom their relationship. She gave him a recent example. When Fay started working for AFSC in Portland, she had deliberately acted like a quiet, religious girl. Fay dutifully held hands before meals in silent prayer and shared weekly news from Bob in prison to reinforce acceptance into their circle. Most of all, she wanted the Quakers' social pressure to keep herself on that virtuous path. But on arrival in Mexico, Fay veered in a different direction. She joined their mutual friend Steve from Reed every night, going out drinking until the wee hours, shocking all of their AFSC campmates and feeling no shame.

Fay came to the realization she had never made decisions, but acted on uncontrollable impulses, lurching from one course to the next. She believed in predestination, not free will. She wondered aloud to Bob: "At what freakish moment will this force contort or twist my mind into doing what? It's terrible. . . . I'm left with a feeling of being on a pattern, a track that I have to go on but I don't know where it is going. . . . I am powerless to alter it or find out where it goes."[4]

On the way back from Mexico, during the third week of August 1951, Fay and Steve took several buses that connected ultimately to Tucson, a trek that left her quite ill. After visiting Bob again, Fay could not hide her unhappiness at the disparate treatment she observed in the prison camp. It bothered her that Bob had gained weight after he was reassigned to library work. Why did he and other conscientious objectors who shirked deadly combat in Korea all have easier work assignments than the Mexican "wetbacks," as Bob and the others referred to them? Though Fay had been touched when Bob whispered at their visit, "You know I'm crazy about you," she openly voiced misgivings about their marriage plans. Fay was grateful when Bob wrote back that they needed to know each other better. She wondered whether love was the deciding factor. "What do I actually want? Is it security?"[5] That question would trouble her to her dying day.

Fay's parents still lived in Pennsylvania, but her mother flew to the Bay Area that August to visit family. Somewhat to her surprise, on reuniting with Ruby, Fay enjoyed being pampered with new clothes, a comfortable hotel room and luncheons at high class restaurants. The contrast with life among the Mexican villagers unsettled her. Fay had brought back silver earrings as souvenirs, which she distributed among friends and family as she shared stories of her summer experience with the Quakers, hoping to convince them of the program's merit. She and her mother got along remarkably well on this visit, a welcome change.

Despite her growing ambivalence toward a future with Bob, Fay arranged for another trip to Tucson from Berkeley in mid-September. She asked Bob's parents to pay her way, $35 that Fay could not herself afford. Fay even arranged for a special treat. She knew that the prison had a piano. Although the barracks were off limits to visitors, an exception had been made for officials of the local evangelical church, which conducted regular Sunday services there. Fay asked the prison staff in advance if she could play the piano for the inmates. The unusual request from an attractive college coed persuaded the warden, who agreed to let her play on an upcoming Saturday afternoon.

When Fay arrived on September 15th, the warden unlocked the barracks' door and escorted Fay in. She mesmerized the inmates with her recital. Most had never heard any classical music before. After Fay left, Bob's standing among the inmates rose considerably. Her performance remained a topic of conversation for many months. Looking back, Bob likes to think that Fay's visits to him at Tucson and her small success in humanizing that bleak environment inspired her later pioneering prison work.

Fay could not resist sharing with her family the details of her prison piano performance. She also shocked them with a new announcement. Shortly after enrolling at Cal, she changed her mind and secretly reapplied to Reed in early September. She had just been accepted back at Reed and made plans to live off campus in Portland with a girlfriend. Even earning some money giving piano lessons, she could ill afford Reed's tuition. When she told her parents they exploded in anger, but Fay was not to be dissuaded.

Fay never dared tell her parents what happened next. Back in the spring she had become intrigued by a thirty-seven-year-old Svengali on the Reed faculty, Stanley Moore, a professor who was destined to become the college's cause célèbre. A Cal graduate, Moore had previously taught at Harvard where he had earned his Ph.D. in philosophy in 1940. Moore was hired to teach at Reed in 1948 on an accelerated track toward full professorship in philosophy. His peers considered him one of their most outstanding colleagues. The self-avowed Stalinist had been a Communist Party member prior to gaining tenure based on his research and writing on the economics of Marxism.

The son of a wealthy Piedmont, California, family, Moore had married war-correspondent Marguerite Higgins in 1942, but separated from her soon afterward as each pursued their own demanding careers and rumored affairs. He now lived on a romantic houseboat on a river near campus where students flocked to visit him. Bob Richter counted himself among Moore's admirers, unaware in the fall of 1951 that he was losing his fiancée to Moore's charms. Moore had already developed a reputation at Reed as a womanizer who often dated undergraduates. With Fay's uncanny instinct, she had again involved herself with the most controversial figure around. She spent one thrilling month living with Moore on his houseboat that fall, unable to break off a relationship that she knew made no sense. She wrote a lengthy poem about her decision to withdraw emotionally from Bob while immersing herself in a loveless, new liaison. Then she kept it to herself for the time being.

Fay had mentioned Moore in her letters to Bob, but for many months left out the hurtful news of their affair. Yet, as she busied herself on assembling letters of support for Bob's upcoming parole hearing, she wrote him increasingly critical letters. Going to prison for his beliefs did not make him a saint. Fay suggested it might be better to conform to society's demands and only reveal one's true thoughts to a small circle of close friends. At first, she just told Bob she needed time to herself when he was released. By mid-November, Fay told him they were now headed in different directions. Since his mailing privileges were limited, she suggested he would be better off not wasting his time writing to her. Even then she held off revealing her recently ended affair with Moore.

Family issues now preoccupied Fay. During the fall of 1951 Ruby Abrahams had developed vascular problems that required surgery. She convinced her reluctant husband to quit his job in Pennsylvania and return to the Bay Area where they would once again be in the bosom of their families. With no likely job prospects in California, Sam put heavy pressure on Fay to transfer back to Berkeley. He refused to pay for further studies at Reed after the fall semester and insisted that Fay needed to be nearer home because of her mother's ill health. This time, he did not take "no" for an answer.

Fay felt compelled to return to her mother's side, though she resented her parents' heavy-handed tactics. Sam's pride had kept him from telling Fay that money worries played a key role in his insistence that she switch schools and join them in their new apartment in San Francisco. On reflection, Fay actually felt somewhat relieved by the summons. She thought the challenge of attending Cal was probably good for her, but she refused to live with her parents. Instead, she insisted that the Abrahams pay for a room for her at the International House near campus.

In early 1952, Fay began attending Cal again, eager to find someone with whom to share what Moore had taught her. Fay quickly latched onto Betty Lee, a Chinese immigrant in her political science course. Born in Shanghai, Betty had adopted the English name when she arrived with her parents in California during World War II as a shy and passive 15-year-old who spoke almost no English. Betty's family lived in Chinatown in San Francisco. She had attended Lowell High School and only moved to Berkeley for college.

At Cal, Fay flattered Betty by aggressively seeking out her friendship as a kindred spirit. The two met often for coffee. Fay was amazed that Betty did not know a Jew from a non-Jew. She captivated her new friend as she passionately expounded on Communism, racism and imperialism. Long afterward, Betty recalled that Fay talked nonstop, "a million miles a minute." Fay bitterly complained about her forced return to Berkeley and fascinated Betty with details of her torrid affair with Stanley Moore. Moore had convinced her to reject her cloistered upbringing and bourgeois Jewish values. Betty, in turn, felt she received a fascinating insight into American Jewish intellectuals through her friendship with Fay. It was hard to tell the Jews from the Gentiles because most of the Jews she met had long since rejected their religious upbringing and cultural heritage.

As Fay bemoaned her fate and criticized her parents' values, she did not appreciate the irony that it was she who had insisted on going to Reed — an elite, private college that the Abrahams could ill afford. It was Ruby and Sam who advocated the far more accessible public university that admitted high-achieving immigrants and minorities like

Fay enjoying a trip to the snow with friends from Cal after transferring from Reed. (Likely taken at Lake Tahoe.)

Betty. Fay only knew that Reed had opened amazing doors for her. Cal felt like a giant step backward. In 1952, traditional fraternities and sororities still dominated campus life.

Much to the dismay of both sets of parents, the two friends decided to room together in their own apartment. The Lees were conservative and supported the ongoing Korean War. They considered Fay a bad influence on Betty. Their dislike of Fay hit its peak when Fay criticized Betty's kindergarten-aged brother Gus in front of his proud father after Gus drew pictures of bombs and airplanes. Fay was not invited back. (A future lawyer himself, Gus later wrote the best-selling autobiography *China Boy*.)

Betty and Fay remained close friends, though Betty felt she had little to offer her brilliant mentor. Fay frequently interrupted a conversation in their apartment with "Wait a minute," followed by a trip to her closet where she kept alphabetized 3 x 5 index cards in shoeboxes. The cards brimmed with historical facts, famous authors and notes Fay had painstakingly accumulated over several years. "Any time I had a question she would pull out a shoebox and find the answer," Betty exclaimed. Their impassioned conversations frequently lasted until one a.m.

Despite their cramped quarters, Betty tolerated Fay's eccentricities and her disregard for housekeeping. An undisciplined student, Fay often kept the light on, working deep into the night as due dates loomed and almost always pulled A's. As an English major, she wrote papers every week or two, typing with an impressive staccato style she developed as a pianist. Fay's eating habits also astonished Betty. Fay still had few culinary skills — scrambled eggs were her mainstay — but Fay had a voracious appetite for meat that she often satisfied with trips to a pet store that sold horsemeat. Fay explained to a skeptical Betty that horsemeat was a staple of French cuisine.

Shortly after she arrived at Cal, Fay joined a chamber music group and started dating a gifted cellist named Stan Seidner. A graduate student in psychology ten years her senior, Seidner was still working on a Ph.D. he would never complete. At the public library in the early spring of 1952, shortly before her twentieth birthday, Fay met another graduate student reworking his dissertation on Shakespeare. Then 28,

Robert Gene Pippin would become a lifelong confidante. "Pip," as he was often called, was brilliant and loquacious. As romantic partners, Pip preferred petite women like his second wife, Anne, who was then finishing her Ph.D. in Classics.

Even though Fay reminded him somewhat of his mother, Pip quickly developed a serious crush on the nineteen-year-old coed. Whenever Fay and Pip met for coffee, conversations between Fay and Pip volleyed like championship ping pong. He was impressed with Fay's vast knowledge of literature and the way she leapt from one observation to another. Fay was equally taken with Pip's insights. She was particularly amazed that a Gentile could have such extensive knowledge of ancient Jewish history. As a special gift, she gave him her own leather-bound, official translation of the Old Testament. It would travel with him throughout his life.

When Pip's wife Anne accepted a teaching job back East, Pip stayed behind at Cal to complete his doctorate. Both Stan and Pip then came often to visit Fay at the small apartment she shared with Betty. As Betty watched their verbal sparring, Fay impressed her as never giving ground to a man. Looking back, Betty characterized Fay as a feminist before feminism was defined by the larger population.

Fay found Pip almost as easy to entrust her innermost thoughts to as her close friend Wendy Milmore had been. Fay told him of her impassioned month with Stanley Moore, including Moore's penchant for bondage. She said that Moore had transformed her world view. She could not imagine herself pursuing an academic life like the one Pip was headed toward. For her, writing and lecturing on literature was too tame. Fay's goal became etched in his mind: "Pip, I want the power to change things."

After nine months, Sam finally found work as a corporate consultant with a pest control company. Sam bought a house in the upscale Claremont Uplands neighborhood in South Berkeley. Sam and Ruby moved in with Lisie, enabling her to finish her senior year of high school at Berkeley High. When Fay introduced Betty, Pip and Stan to her family, Lisie knew that Pip was married, but her parents did not. Sam and Ruby noted that neither Stan nor Pip was Jewish. The Abrahams somehow blamed Betty, believing that Fay's friendship with Betty reduced her chances of marrying the right man. Fay started sneaking Betty with her on visits to the Abrahams' new home when no one else was there.

Bob Richter won parole at his first opportunity and was released from prison a year to the day from being jailed. Anxious to see Fay, he invited her to fly to Portland in February of 1952. Fay had written him in December to let him know her parents had moved back to San Francisco and she was joining them for Christmas. She no longer intended to marry him, but had torn up several drafts of letters that explained why. By early February, she felt obligated to confess her betrayal of their relationship with Stanley Moore the prior fall. Yet she sent contradictory signals when she then joined Bob in Portland for a passionate couple of days that meant far more to him than to her.

In April, Bob came down to Berkeley during spring break anticipating Fay to be waiting for him with open arms. Instead, she met him in the parlor room of International House and suggested they talk there. Only then did Bob fully appreciate that Fay had cast him aside. As he began discussing what he would do while waiting for her to finish college, Fay stunned Bob with news that she had just decided to go to law school. She told him that she did not think it made sense for him to wait for her. Miserable and befuddled, Bob headed back to Portland.

While at Cal, Fay occasionally saw her friend Hilde on trips home from college to see family. Hilde had transferred from Reed to Cornell her junior year. As a student of modern philosophy, Hilde considered herself far more progressive than Fay, whom she still regarded as relatively apolitical. On a double date weekend trip to Monterey during Fay's senior year, Fay also startled Hilde with news of her intention to go to law school. Hilde wondered what, if anything, her flamboyant friend would wind up doing with her law degree.

In fact, Fay had for some time admired her free-thinking older cousin who was a lawyer. Fay herself was now paying closer and closer attention to the swirling First Amendment controversies around her. She had signed up for an undergraduate constitutional law course and began to explore law schools. Twenty years later, reflecting on her mindset back in 1952, Fay explained, "I felt people who were lawyers . . . might be listened to."[4] Fay also credited the esteem her parents placed

These photos of Fay were likely taken on a trip to Carmel her senior year at Cal. That was when she surprised her friend Hilde with news she planned to apply to law school. She explained to her new close friend Pip, "I want the power to change things."

PREDESTINATION OR FREE WILL

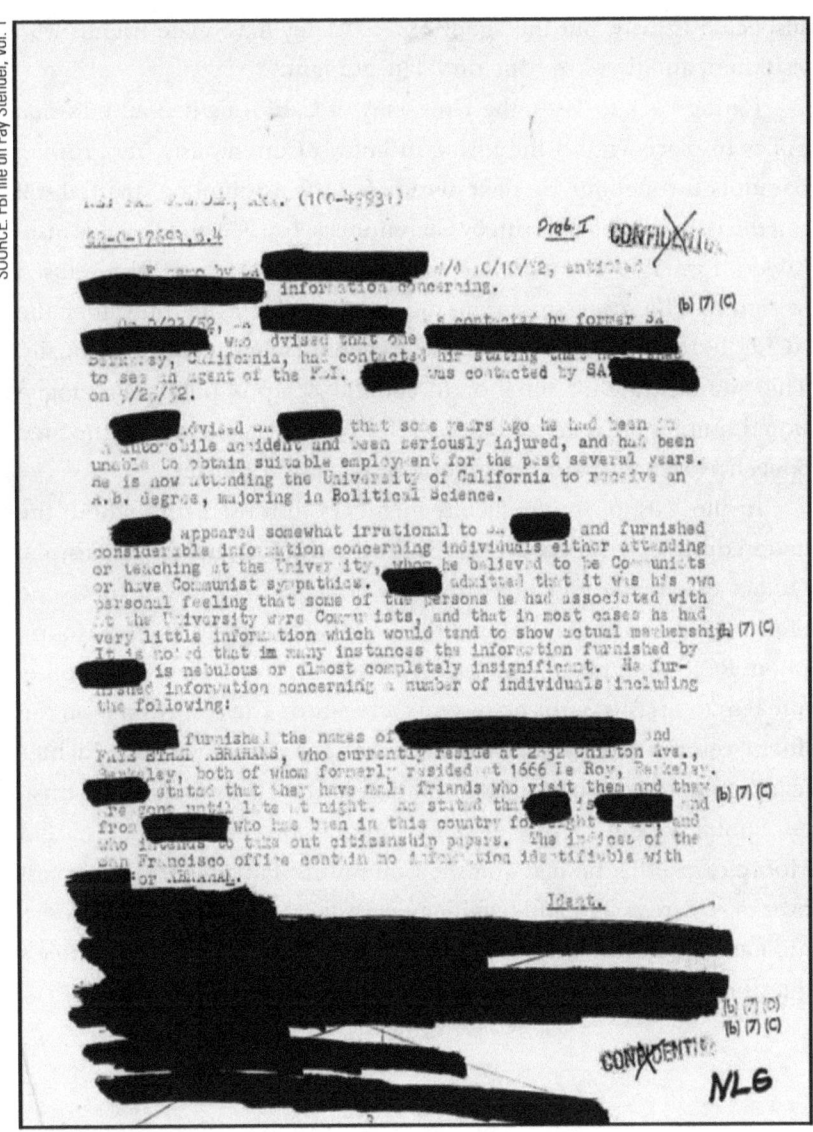

Fay first became a blip on the FBI's radar screen in September 1952 when she was a senior at Cal – just one entry. The FBI agent considered the informant "somewhat irrational" and his observations "nebulous or almost completely insignificant." Yet the agent duly recorded the address of Fay and her foreign roommate [Betty Lee] and noted, "They have male friends who visit them and they are gone until late at night."

suspected activity, but the agent noted, "They have male friends who visit them and they are gone until late at night."[9]

Dating back to 1940, the University of California had an informal policy in place against the hiring of known Communists. Yet growing paranoia throughout the next decade fed the assumption that Cal still ran the risk of being overrun by Communists. In 1949, the Regents instituted a formal loyalty oath and fired eighteen professors who refused to sign it. The professors' reinstatement in 1951 came only after the ACLU obtained a ruling that the Regents' acted unconstitutionally. The administration's attempt to muzzle campus political dialogue would simmer for years and ultimately erupt a decade later in the Free Speech Movement, with Fay among those at its forefront.

In the '50s, of the 69 faculty members dismissed throughout the nation during the McCarthy Era, 31 were at the University of California. Others were scattered among 26 other colleges. As Fay well knew, one of the academics at the center of this political storm was Stanley Moore, whom Reed would be forced to fire in 1954. Moore suffered the consequences to his career for many years afterward. The controversy on the liberal campus reverberated for more than forty years, with Bob Richter leading the charge among Reed alumni in the 1990s to have the trustees apologize and its president welcome Moore back. Only then did Moore reveal that he had quit the Communist Party in 1953 in protest over mass arrests and anti-Semitic persecutions by Stalin. When Moore was hauled before HUAC in 1954, his refusal to answer the committee's questions had been solely a matter of principle.

* * *

Fay graduated Cal in January of 1953 with honors in English. Still under Stanley Moore's lasting influence, she felt no loss in missing the June celebration with its senior ball, beach party, banquet and barbeque. But the class motto seemed appropriate: "The sky's the limit." She obtained a part-time job at the Bacteriology Department at Cal. Fay worked as a secretary, while she enrolled in graduate school courses in political science and looked into law schools.

The University of Chicago Law School had a reputation as one of the best in the country. It also generated excitement among progressives familiar with Professor Karl Llewellyn, who had just recently joined its faculty after a quarter of a century at Columbia. He was one of the leaders at the time of the "Legal Realism" school of thought developed in the first half of the twentieth century — the belief that the law was a flexible tool which balanced competing interests to accomplish particular public goals. Legal Realism would later be credited as the forerunner of a number of multi-disciplinary programs in law and economics, political science, feminist theory and racial studies.

The University of Chicago Law School had a large Jewish contingent of students and professors and, in 1953, was one of the top ten choices in the nation for women applicants. It also offered a full academic scholarship. This was key. Annual tuition was $738, several times the cost of a legal education in state law schools. Fay's parents would not support her going to graduate school in Chicago. Fay eagerly registered for the new LSAT, given in February, obtained letters of recommendation and accompanied her application with a short essay on Chaucer, the $5 application fee, and a recent head shot of herself in ponytail and bangs.

Fay also described a novel project she proposed to undertake in law school — looking for correlations between the judges' political party and their rulings in various types of cases. Maybe that was what caught the admissions' committee's attention. In the last week of June, Fay received her letter of acceptance, followed a month later with a full tuition scholarship. Fay was Chicago bound.

Fay included a recent head shot of herself in ponytail and bangs with her application to the University of Chicago Law School. She received a full tuition scholarship to attend that fall.

Fay Abrahams, U.C. Berkeley senior year, 1952

The University of Chicago Law School was known for promoting "Legal Realism" – the belief that the law was a flexible tool that balanced competing interests in pursuit of societal goals. Legal Realism was the forerunner of future multi-disciplinary programs in law and economics, law and political science, feminist theory and racial studies.

■ 3 ■

Intellectual Boot Camp

and I lust for justice . . .

. . .

*and I invent the mother of courage
I require not to quit.*[1]

— JUNE JORDAN

In September of 1953, Fay joined nine women among over 100 students in the University of Chicago's entering law school class. The progressive university had admitted women since its founding in 1902, although their attrition rate had always been high. Its first dean concluded coeducation was the wrong approach and, upon returning to Cambridge, experimented with a short-lived female-only law school.

Fay's parents could take some comfort from the fact that Chicago boasted the third largest concentration of Jews in the world. Prominent Chicago labor lawyer Arthur Goldberg had recently served as President of the American Jewish Congress. (He would later be named a Supreme Court Justice and Ambassador to the United Nations.) Sam Abrahams may have been aware of physicist Enrico Fermi's war-time nuclear experiments completed at the University of Chicago that permitted America to bomb Hiroshima and Nagasaki and usher in the atomic age. (Years later, the government revealed the location of Fermi's makeshift laboratory in an underground squash court a couple of blocks from the law school.)

The city also had a large African-American population, renowned for gospel singing and innovative jazz. Louis Armstrong, Jelly Roll Morton, and Nat King Cole had honed their styles in Chicago. The "King of Swing" bandleader Benny Goodman hailed from the Windy City. He was born to a large Jewish family in a westside slum near the railroad yards. In the 1930s, Goodman introduced audiences at the historic Congress Hotel on Michigan Avenue to the first integrated big bands.

Fay harbored only a vague awareness of Chicago's persistent racial divide, where tensions had begun mounting during World War I when the "Black Belt" south of the Loop could no longer accommodate newly arriving African-American families. Full scale riots had erupted in July of 1919, causing by far the worst racial violence Chicago ever experienced. Similar incidents of beatings, torture, lynching and arson across the country that summer of 1919 gave rise to the term "Red Summer" — the most horrific interracial strife that the country endured in the twentieth century.

In the aftermath of Red Summer, many white homeowners put restrictive covenants on their deeds to prevent blacks from moving into their neighborhoods. Fay undoubtedly had an index card in her shoebox file with notes on *Hansberry v. Lee*, the ground-breaking 1940 United States Supreme Court case challenging Chicago's restrictive housing covenants. As an avid reader, Fay was struck by Richard Wright's *Native Son*, set in the South Side of Chicago in the '30s. It narrated the powerful story of an angry black man raised in poverty and helplessness, who was then jailed for murder and rape. Fay later became fascinated by the details of her death row client George Jackson's similar childhood in Chicago's poor black neighborhoods in the 1940s and early '50s. When Fay enrolled in law school Jackson was just twelve years old, a frequent truant in nearby city streets, while Fay remained in a world apart and still largely self-absorbed.

Focused on making an impression, Fay cut a striking figure as she entered the University's Gothic village on the South Side to register for classes. She had abandoned her bangs and let her hair grow long. To new acquaintances, she projected the slender and willowy build of a dancer, though she still perceived herself as clumsy. Reed had exceeded her expectations. Fay had similar high hopes for the University of Chicago, but harsh reality soon dashed her fantasies.

The law school's distinctive stone towers rose high above dilapidated two- and three-story wood and brick tenements. In the early 1950s, speculation on its precarious future hit Chicago's newspapers. Without redevelopment of the neighborhood, there was little hope to attract needed funds and sufficient students. World War II had so decimated the law school's student body that the board of trustees had considered its permanent closure.

Former Chief Judge Mary Schroeder of the Ninth Circuit later recalled that accommodations for women students at the University of Chicago Law School were "not for the faint-hearted." Schroeder's mother cried when she saw her daughter's first apartment in an isolated tenement on 55th and Ellis Streets, which had been officially designated as graduate women's housing. "The only reason she did not haul me out of there physically was because leaving my roommate there alone was tantamount to reckless endangerment."[2]

Fortunately, Ruby Abrahams had no idea that her daughter's new university sat right in the middle of a neighborhood surrounded by slums. Two years earlier riots had broken out in nearby Cicero when a black veteran and his family tried to move into an apartment. Governor Adlai Stevenson had ordered in the National Guard, marking the first time since the deadly 1919 race riots that troops had been required to end a racial disturbance.

Over time, Fay would question the university's ownership of slum property. The city's failure to plan for the enormous increase in its black population since the turn of the century confronted Fay and her classmates whenever they left the campus. The air in Chicago crackled with racial tension, but Fay did not focus on that at first. Fay's life instead centered on the internal world of a brick building on the corner of Ellis and 58th Street. Unlike undergraduate courses, classes for the entire law school had been conducted for fifty years in that single imposing structure. A glass case in the lobby showcased Clarence Darrow's collected works. Most new students shared both Fay's excitement and fear of failure. Edward Levi, the first "home-grown" dean, was determined to elevate his alma mater to an intellectual rival of Harvard.[3]

Fay lived in the women's dormitory at Blake Hall on campus, only a block away from the law school. Women were expected to follow the typical 1950s rules of modesty and decorum. The women in the class appreciated the couch in the ladies' rest room and the attention of male students willing to help them with their studies. Most had husbands or boyfriends who were law students or lawyers. Only half of the ten women in Fay's class of 1953 ended up graduating; the others gave in to the pressure to quit and become homemakers.

Even those who earned their degrees had limited expectations. Scholarship recipient Kathleen Bouffe, who also had been a friend of Bob Richter's at Reed, was one of the few who planned a career in law. Kathleen had received strong encouragement from a successful woman lawyer her grandmother knew. For a long time, no law firms in Chicago accepted women law clerks. Only recently had the individual influence of male relatives begun to extend the old boy network to sisters or daughters.

Soon the enormity of the undertaking overwhelmed Fay. She began to entertain grave doubts about her decision to attend law school. Everything was so structured, with so much required preparation for class that last-minute cramming was not an option. Fay was unused to struggling in school. Here, she could even imagine herself failing. One promising first year woman classmate from Cornell did not even last six weeks. Another classmate, Alice Wirth, only nineteen, found herself smoking three packs of cigarettes a day to deal with the pressure. Alice's late father had been a highly regarded professor of sociology at the University of Chicago. As a family friend, Dean Levi had admitted Alice without a B.A. Some males were solicitous, others resentful. Sexism had been endemic at the law school from its earliest days.

Fay did not distinguish herself among her peers at the time as being politically outspoken or radical. The rigid structure of law school provided no opportunity for anyone to express any political opinions in class. Students simply were called upon in lectures to answer precise legal questions posed by the professors. Yet Fay did stand out as more passionate about everything — she was always more dramatic than her fellow classmates whether they were discussing the law, politics, recently read works of fiction or music.

The professors used the prevailing and intimidating Socratic method. Dean Edward Levi taught "Elements and Materials of the Law." Every year he opened the first day by announcing sternly, "This is intellectual boot camp. You will never be the same again."[4] Still, Levi was popular with students because he had a sharp wit and played no favorites. In fact, most of the faculty called on men and women equally, unlike a Harvard law professor in that era who never called on women at all except on Ladies' Day. Adding to students' anxiety, professors gave them little feedback during their first year. Only two courses gave midterms. Fay and another friend, Suzanne Brussel, persuaded second year student Bob Hamilton to conduct review sessions for them. The future law professor had already developed an extraordinary grasp of complicated issues and a knack for getting to the heart of them.

Professor Karl Llewellyn wanted to impress on all new students that the law did not operate in a vacuum. Oral argument before a judge was like asking a couple if their house was clean. The wife might look at the windows, the husband might have a different focus. Both would then make an assumption about the whole house. His point: students needed to learn how each judge made decisions.

As the fall progressed Fay felt a spiraling loss of self-confidence. With her history of undisciplined study habits and frenzied last-minute all-nighters, she struggled and despaired. Fay found a new friend in Bob Hamilton's wife, who was in her class. Dag and her husband had to pinch every penny while living in a ghetto neighborhood on $44 per month. They had qualified for prefabricated housing for married students — a two-room unit with no kitchen and only a hotplate to cook on. Fay had trouble imagining living in such a primitive setting. Yet, while offering sympathy to her new friend, Fay provided Dag only a partial glimpse into her own unhappy history and strained family situation. Fay was not about to divulge to Dag a description of her torrid affair with a married Marxist. Throughout her life, Fay followed a pattern of distinguishing among confidantes. She cultivated socially conformist friends as well as radicals and selectively held back key personal information from those she feared might be appalled by the truth.

Everything seemed to conspire to defeat Fay's high expectations of a glamorous adventure. During her first quarter at law school, Fay repeatedly wondered aloud if she had made a serious mistake and should have pursued a career as a concert pianist after all. Wherever she could find a piano on campus she entertained friends with popular and classical music. Even into the wee hours she could be heard pounding the keys in the social hall of the men's dormitory. Was she destined to follow her mother's bidding? Music was a powerful outlet for her emotions, but Fay yearned for something more soul-satisfying.

In January 1953, while still at Cal, Fay joined her extended family celebrating her parents' 25th anniversary at the Claremont Hotel in Berkeley. Fay is seated to her parents' left. Ruby is wearing a large corsage as she sits at the head of the table with her husband Sam. Closest to the camera on the same side of the table as Fay is her beloved grandmother Lena, who died later that year. At similar formal gatherings at restaurants when Fay was a teenager she often took a spoon as a keepsake.

■ 4 ■

Smitten

*Find your passion and pursue it,
with whole heart and single mind.*[1]
— Gail Sheehy

F ay had one professor she particularly admired. Malcolm Sharp taught contract law, but was a Renaissance man with a strong commitment to improving society. Fay discovered that Professor Sharp was working on the controversial criminal appeal of Martin Sobell, one of the co-defendants in the world-famous Rosenberg espionage trial. Sobell had been sentenced to thirty years in prison for his role in the conspiracy for which the Rosenbergs were executed in June of 1953. Sharp had been a latecomer to defending the treason case, but found the cozy relationship between the prosecutor and the trial judge appalling. Professor Sharp had started writing a book criticizing that trial (later published as *Was Justice Done? The Rosenberg-Sobell Case*).

Fay also learned that Professor Sharp was the incoming president of the National Lawyers Guild. Fay was then only generally aware of the Guild, founded in 1937 as the nation's first racially integrated bar association. Like the "shreds" Fay had hung out with in high school, the Guild functioned outside the mainstream. For the next two decades, Fay would embrace the Guild's civil rights agenda, siding with her future husband and other young Turks bent on expanding the Guild's focus from civil rights to other Movement causes.

Guild lawyers attacked Jim Crow laws and had met with their first major success in the 1940 landmark U.S. Supreme Court decision of *Hansberry v. Lee,* which opened the door to challenging racially restrictive housing covenants. When the Guild continued to champion Leftist causes into the late '40s, the onset of the Cold War greatly diminished its membership. By 1950, fewer than half of the original 35 chapters of the Guild still functioned. HUAC then recommended that the Guild be classified as a subversive organization, its members barred from federal employment and banned from membership in the American Bar Association (ABA). The conservative leadership of the ABA went further, urging states to disbar lawyers who advocated Marxism and to discipline those who took the Fifth Amendment in HUAC hearings. In 1952, Attorney General Herbert Brownell added the Guild to his list of subversive organizations.

Some of the excitement Fay felt as Moore's protégé surged within her once more. Membership in the Guild gave her a ready way to participate in transforming society. As Fay arrived at law school, the Guild's most pressing local issue was to address the loyalty oaths required to live in Chicago housing projects. The Guild would ultimately get the Illinois Supreme Court to strike down that requirement. The Guild's biggest national concern was then the McCarran-Walter Act, which imposed severe immigrant quotas and permitted suspected subversives to be rounded up under "loyalty clearance programs." Almost half a million Mexicans had been deported in 1953, leaving many more farm laborers at risk.

A month into law school, Fay was curious to attend the first fall meeting of the Guild's student chapter. Professors Sharp and Llewellyn stood grimly before thirty to forty students, informing them that the Illinois State Bar Character and Fitness Committee had just denied admission to George Anastaplo. The married World War II veteran pilot had graduated first in his class at the law school in 1951, but refused to answer the committee's questions about membership in the Communist Party or other organizations deemed subversive. Ignoring the advice of professors and classmates, Anastaplo had also defended

Thomas Jefferson's view of a right of forceful revolution to achieve meaningful change.

Professors Sharp and Llewellyn announced that Anastaplo had appealed, but the outlook did not look promising. The Illinois Supreme Court would in fact twice deny Anastaplo admission, and the United States Supreme Court would deny him relief.[2] Sharp and Llewellyn worried aloud whether all the students in the room faced similar risk of being denied their licenses. With Attorney General Brownell branding the National Lawyers Guild "the legal mouthpiece of the Communist Party," then third-year-student Marvin Stender vividly recalled what the two professors told the students: "You've got to disband. You would be foolish not to disaffiliate."

Stender took charge of the October meeting as the club's current president. Tall and earnest, the dark-haired, bespectacled young man was less than fifteen months' older than Fay. His self-assurance and steadfast commitment to the Guild's goals — despite the obvious political risks — impressed Fay greatly. Marvin realized that membership in the student chapter was vague anyway. It basically consisted of those who came to meetings. Heeding the professors' warning, the students voted on the spot to disaffiliate from the National Lawyers Guild and reconstitute themselves as a different organization that just happened to be dedicated to similar objectives.

Fay was physically attracted — as always — to a natural leader, someone who took personal risk in stride while he championed unpopular causes. Acting on impulse, she approached Marvin at the end of the meeting. Encouraged by his engaging smile, she began excitedly talking about her experience with the Quakers in Mexico that had convinced her to become a lawyer. He responded warmly to her enthusiasm. Each was smitten with the other and their courtship began. It proved a fitting start to a lifelong political bond that would carry their inconstant marriage far longer than many of their friends would have predicted. For the time being, Fay shelved her ongoing obsession with Stanley Moore.

Marvin came from a well-off Chicago family. In late October of 1953, soon after the two met, Fay asked to borrow the Stenders' relatively new family car to drive into the Chicago Loop on an errand. Fay was too nervous to go alone, so she invited her friend Dag to join her on her adventure. Fay arrived at a busy intersection, hesitated, and then started forward when she shouldn't have and immediately hit another car. The minor accident rendered Fay practically inconsolable, tearfully moaning about her terrible driving skills. She wailed to Dag, "How can I tell Marvin?" Fay feared that the dented car would surely ruin their relationship. Dag reassured Fay that this could have happened to anyone. In fact, the minor accident cemented Fay's relationship with Marvin. He had completely surprised and disarmed Fay by being so understanding. Fay decided that this steady, patient man, committed to the same causes as her, was in fact the perfect soul mate.

Despite looming exams, Fay and Marvin focused on wedding plans. The couple married on January 5, 1954, in a simple ceremony in Chicago just three months after they met. At the time, it did not feel like a whirlwind courtship. They were in love and, at nearly 22, Fay was not a young bride in comparison to her peers. Joan DeLasaux had been the first among Fay's high school friends to marry and become a mother during Fay's senior year of college. Hilde had soon followed suit.

Fay's parents were thrilled and much relieved to have a third-generation American Jew, and, especially, a promising young professional, as a son-in-law. The wedding took place during the winter break before only a few friends and Marvin's family. Fay and Marvin then moved into a tall apartment building with an awning and began accumulating wedding gifts. Their prize possessions included a record player and record collection, a refrigerator and a stove. The newlyweds lived in luxury compared to their classmates.

Fay enjoyed law school far more her second quarter. She now worked part-time for Professor Sharp on research for the Sobell appellate brief. With Bob Hamilton's continued tutelage, she grew more skilled at legal analysis. By the spring, Fay exhibited tremendous self-confidence. She had developed rapport with several faculty members, including the Dean and the sole woman professor, Soia Mentschikoff, and her husband, Karl Llewellyn. By her very presence teaching advanced commercial law courses and working on the Uniform Commercial Code,

Soia Mentschikoff advertised to Fay and her female classmates that the law school truly esteemed women after all.

Yet what really riveted Marvin and Fay were the McCarthy hearings, much as law students twenty years later would be fascinated by Watergate. Very few students had a radio or television of their own; they watched the hearings in the student lounge on campus or at a local bar. CBS television's hard-hitting commentator, Edward R. Murrow, host of "See It Now," impressed them all in March of 1954 when he aired a program highlighting news clips of McCarthy's most outrageous charges, including his claim that the presidencies of FDR and Truman constituted twenty years of treason.[3]

The students again gathered in the lounge later that spring, all cheering as Joe Welch, the Army's chief counsel, famously stood up to McCarthy on national television. McCarthy had just tarred a lawyer in Welch's office as a suspected Communist simply for once having been a member of the National Lawyers Guild. Welch accused McCarthy of "reckless cruelty," and ended his comments with a rhetorical flourish that made Guild members proud: "You've done enough. Have you no sense of decency, sir? At long last, have you left no sense of decency?"[4] Alice Wirth felt particularly vindicated as Senator McCarthy's power evaporated. Her father, Professor Louis Wirth, had been accused in 1951 of being a Communist and died at age 55 of a sudden heart attack shortly before his anticipated grilling by HUAC.

Fay dared not share with Marvin or any of her law school classmates her own former lover's recent devastating experience with HUAC. Stanley Moore had been named a full professor at Reed in 1953, two years after Fay's parents forced her to transfer. Divorced from Marguerite Higgins, he remarried one of his students in December 1953. The following spring, Moore was called before HUAC where he refused to answer whether he was a Communist. That prompted the local Portland papers to stir up a furor in the conservative community, using Moore as a lightning rod for growing discontent with the liberal professors and student body at the college. The Reed faculty, in a show of solidarity, circled their wagons around Professor Moore, strongly urging that the board of trustees take no action against the tenured

Philosophy Prof. Stanley Moore with his second wife, Annie Laurie Malarkey, Reed Class of 1953, at their wedding in December 1953. In the spring of 1954, Prof. Moore became the center of controversy for his Marxist teachings. He was fired from Reed for refusing to answer if he was a Communist – the only tenured professor Reed ever dismissed. In 1981, Robert Richter co-led the successful effort to have the Reed Board of Trustees formally apologize to Prof. Moore.

professor. Reed had not instituted a loyalty oath. Professor Moore had not tried to recruit anyone to become a Communist. He simply held Marxist philosophical views. Fay followed the saga from afar, with no one to share her growing anxiety.

Meanwhile, Fay still played piano to entertain friends, but now found contentment in her career choice. At Fay's instigation, she and Marvin planned to move to San Francisco after he graduated. Fay had survived her first brutal Chicago winter and had had enough of the windy city. She wanted to rejoin her close friends and finish law school at Boalt Hall. With Marvin as her anchor, Fay looked forward to finishing her legal education and proving she could make good on her pledge to become an agent for change.

Left: Portrait of Fay and Lisie as teenagers which hung in their parents' living room in Berkeley. Fay was about 16 and Lisie about 13. To Lisie's dismay, the artist emphasized Fay's hands –underscoring her training as a pianist. Lisie got in rare trouble with her parents after accidentally slamming the front door on Fay's right hand during a game of tag. Fay could only practice piano with her left hand until her right hand healed. The positioning of Fay's left hand over hers bothered Lisie enough over time that when she later owned the painting, Lisie had it split into two separate portraits.

Lisie and Don Stone being congratulated at their marriage ceremony in the Abrahams' living room Labor Day weekend 1955. The painting of Fay and Lisie is visible in the background. Fay and Marvin traveled from Chicago to join in the celebration for which Fay played the family piano. In the summer of 1954, Fay's parents had hosted in their living room a similar celebration of Fay and Marvin's January 1954 wedding.

5

Renewed Ardor

"Whereas the law is passionless, passion must ever sway the heart of man [and woman]."[1]
— ARISTOTLE

The newlyweds celebrated their marriage a second time with a large wedding reception for family and friends at the Abrahams' home in Berkeley. Fay was excited to be reunited with her old companions, oblivious that her younger sister had delayed her finals in hopes of spending more time with Fay. It must have raised eyebrows in the Abrahams' social circle when Fay and Marvin then decided to start out married life by sharing a house with Betty Lee. For a surprisingly affordable price, the trio rented a large home in the Berkeley Hills that resembled a drafty, Italian villa. Betty thought Fay had found a real gem of a husband. She was surprised and delighted that Marvin took his turn washing or drying dishes without a murmur, unlike all the other men Betty had met.

Betty remained one of Fay's few confidantes about Stanley Moore's ongoing troubles. In the summer of 1954, a group of influential Oregon businessmen pressured the trustees to ignore the faculty and fire Moore or see Reed closed. Moore kept silent on his party affiliation throughout the political storm, but challenged the trustees to consider that they might stand condemned by history for their action should they reject the faculty's ringing endorsement of his fitness to teach. The trustees yielded to the outside pressure and fired Moore, outraging faculty and students and prompting the college president to resign. In spite of her distress at this alarming turn of events, Fay likely felt enormous relief at not having been caught up in Moore's public shaming and ostracism.

* * *

Though Marvin had to hunt for a job, Fay already had hers secured. Dag Hamilton's in-laws had just rented a house in Berkeley. Walton Hamilton, then in his early seventies, had been an economist in the Roosevelt administration. The retired law professor remained still as sharp as a whip, but almost totally blind and in need of a reader and researcher. Fay and "Hammy" quickly proved even more simpatico than Dag had anticipated. Fay read him music and art books and shared his satisfaction as the Indian rights case he was working on progressed toward the United States Supreme Court.

When Professor Sharp came out to the Bay Area that summer to visit his son, he stopped by to ask Fay and Marvin for help. He was fund-raising for the Rosenbergs' two orphaned children then being reared by another family. Marvin immediately began passing out leaflets at a factory gate in Emeryville. This time Marvin's decisiveness alarmed Fay. She confided her panicked reaction to Betty. It was too dangerous. Fay pictured a steel worker punching Marvin or the FBI adding him to their list of undesirables. Yet, despite agonizing over the issue, Fay soon swallowed her fears and joined Marvin. In the years to come, Fay would take far greater risks, once she concluded that there was no safe middle ground on which she could live with herself.

After a heady summer of intellectual dialogue with Hammy, Fay came down to earth with a crash when she arrived for classes at Boalt Hall. Fay had grown up with only a dim awareness of the nearby law school as a more prestigious alternative to Hastings in San Francisco. In deciding to transfer from the University of Chicago, Fay had simply assumed that it would provide a parallel experience. She did not realize that no Malcolm Sharps could be found on its conservative faculty, whose members had all signed a loyalty oath and remained totally silent on the issue of forced relocation of Japanese-Americans during World War II. Even among Boalt students in the early '50s, being a Democrat was unusual and passed for flaming radicalism.

Within days after starting classes, Fay begged Marvin to return to Chicago. Marvin had by then obtained a temporary job as a law clerk for the office of famed torts attorney, Melvin Belli. Unlike her parents' reaction when Fay had demanded to switch schools in the past, Fay found Marvin completely supportive of her wishes. He suggested to his distraught bride that she call Dean Levi. Marvin later recalled that when Fay reached Dean Levi to ask if she could undo her horrible mistake and get her scholarship back, he laughed and said, "Sure." The earliest that the University of Chicago would accept her return was for the spring term. In the meantime, Fay told Marvin "I can't stand it here" and immediately withdrew from Boalt. She had lasted only a week.

So far Fay's iron will and headstrong, passionate nature set the path for her and Marvin. She decided to use the unexpected window of time before they moved back to Chicago to tackle a reading project her friend Pip likely encouraged — reading the English translation of the entire seven volumes of Marcel Proust's *Remembrance of Things Past* (*A La Recherche Du Temps Perdu*). The ambitious work with 2,000 literary characters had received acclaim as the greatest novel of the century, perhaps, the best ever written. As usual, Fay immersed herself completely in her latest project. She was fascinated by the author's reflections on time and memory, the role of the subconscious and of art and music in life among the French aristocracy and the emerging French middle class. Taking full advantage of Marvin's indulgence, Fay spent hours on end reading chapters and trading insights with her friend Pip over coffee at outdoor cafes. This interlude had a lasting impact. Fay would name her only daughter for Proust's heroine, the Duchesse Oriane de Guermantes, and, in her late forties, immerse herself in her own self-reflective, lengthy sojourn in Europe.

Meanwhile, Marvin left the chaotic Belli law office and worked as an editor for the legal publishing company Bancroft Whitney. When Fay tore herself from the adventures of the Duchesse Oriane de

Fay and Marvin Stender with their friend Ying "Betty" Lee when she stayed with them in Chicago in the fall of 1954.

Guermantes, she sometimes joined Marvin for lunch in San Francisco. His new work address was right across the street from Hastings School of the Law. One day in the early fall, Fay suddenly recognized a young woman on the steps of the publishing company as Alice Wirth. Fay surprised her former law school classmate by greeting her as if she were one of Fay's oldest and dearest friends. The two acquaintances had mostly spent time together in a first-year study group.

Alice was now Mrs. Gary Gray. Since leaving Chicago, she had reenrolled in the four-year law school program at Hastings as a first-year student. Fay was incredulous. She considered Hastings a dreadful school, a factory not suitable for someone who cared about the public good. Fay invited Alice to bring her husband to Fay and Marvin's home in the Berkeley Hills for dinner. The house impressed Alice as damp, dark and Gothic. Marvin caught Alice looking skeptically at the meal that Fay placed on the table — two cans of Dinty Moore beef stew, baked potatoes and sour yogurt, a product not widely in use at that time. Marvin firmly told Alice and Gary, "This is the way we eat." Alice found Marvin blunt; Fay found her husband's emphatic dismissal of bourgeois culinary skills another of his endearing qualities.

One afternoon, Fay asked Alice to walk with her to the San Francisco municipal court to see if they could observe a jury trial. Fay's flamboyant outfit included several bangle bracelets which clattered whenever she moved. Alice and Fay discovered a case in progress, opened the door and spotted available seats all the way in the front. The entire courtroom stared open-mouthed as Fay noisily made her way forward with Alice in tow. The pair stayed all afternoon to hear the details of a woman's slip and fall on a shattered jam jar at a local Safeway grocery store. It amused them both that neither attorney could correctly pronounce the names of the plaintiff's broken tibia and fibula. These bumbling litigators were undoubtedly among the men who were so dismissive of women law students.

Heeding Fay's sharp criticism and her own mounting dissatisfaction, Alice soon quit Hastings. She and her husband Gary spent many evenings socializing with Fay, Marvin and Betty. When they discussed music and literature, Fay mostly did the talking, mesmerizing Alice both with her intelligence and with her phenomenal talent on the organ installed in the Stenders' living room. Fay also dominated their frequent political discussions, though she still lived in great fear of the Cold War. The boldness that later characterized Fay's public persona took years to develop.

* * *

Dean Levi was quite tickled by Fay's return to the University of Chicago law school after just one semester's absence. He told anyone who would listen how his law school was considered by a woman student to be so much better than the law school she transferred to that she immediately sought to retransfer. Fay eagerly started attending classes while Marvin went to work for Professor Hans Zeisel on an experimental jury project that Dean Levi had launched two years earlier with a grant from the Ford Foundation. The project ultimately took fifteen years and cost the staggering sum of one million dollars to publish a definitive study of criminal trials. Some of the findings set forth in *The American Jury* later played a key role in assuring a diverse and sympathetic jury for the Huey Newton murder trial.

The outrage of Chicagoans at Mississippi's lack of justice temporarily took the focus off of Chicago's own largely unaddressed race problems, which Fay observed daily in her run-down Hyde Park neighborhood. When Betty Lee came to visit that fall of 1954, Fay delighted in giving her friend a tour of the ghetto she had originally found so appalling. Marvin's father was himself a local landlord. Betty had just emerged from an intense love affair, feeling wounded and looking for a place to recover, which Fay and Marvin gladly offered. In the close quarters of their apartment, Betty again became accustomed to Fay's late night staccato typing. She felt sorry for Fay's classmates, knowing that Fay brought her typewriter to exams and likely unnerved anyone seated nearby. By mid fall, Fay's interest had alighted on local politics. Abner Mikva, whom Marvin had met at the jury project, was making his first run for state office. Fay and Marvin joined Mikva's volunteers, while their friend Betty Lee joined his paid staff.

In the spring and summer of 1955 Fay concentrated on her studies, finding it increasingly difficult to suppress her disapproval of how the law aided the haves over the have nots. Meanwhile, with many of their old friends gone, she cultivated new friendships at the law school, including Brian Gluss, a young Ph.D. in mathematics from Cambridge University, who had been hired to assist on the jury project on a one-year worker's visa. With his heavy accent and eccentric habits, this tall, skinny Brit in army shorts stood out in sharp contrast to the rest of the jury project staff. Brian also liked to live dangerously, a wild partier who often hung out at black clubs with an inter-racial couple from the project.

Fay often played Beethoven sonatas on the grand piano in the lounge at the International House where Brian lived. She drew him out in private conversation, unearthing painful secrets he had not spoken of in fifteen years. His parents had fled devastating pogroms in the Ukraine for London in 1906, around the same time Fay's ancestors fled the border city of Brest-Litovsk. As she coaxed Brian to share his stories, she was soft-spoken, gentle, and reassuring. Years later, those nurturing traits disarmed her most aggressive black militant clients. In response to her probing questions, Brian revealed to Fay that he had been a survivor of the London blitz during World War II: the bomb that hit their home left him and his parents with only a few scratches, but killed his visiting grandmother and his twelve-year-old brother in the next room. His parents had never recovered.

* * *

After the summer quarter ended, Fay and Marvin returned to the Bay Area for Labor Day weekend. Fay played the piano for her sister Lisie's wedding to her long-time boyfriend Don Stone at a small ceremony in their parents' home in Berkeley. That same weekend, national and international headlines decried the apparent lynching in Mississippi of black Chicago teenager, Emmett "Bobo" Till. Emmett's gruesome remains were displayed in an open casket visited by thousands of mourners at an African-American church in Chicago's South Side, not far from where Fay and Marvin lived. The murder of Fay and Marvin's neighbor Emmett Till would ignite the Civil Rights Movement.

Fay now took her studies far more seriously. In her third year she took antitrust law from Dean Levi and earned a high A from him. Generally perceived as a cool, unemotional person, he spoke of Fay glowingly at alumni functions. The esteem he held her in undoubtedly dissipated over the years as he became increasingly conservative. He was later appointed President of the entire University of Chicago and ultimately named United States Attorney General for Republican President Gerald Ford. By that time, Fay had gained a national reputation for radicalism.

Yet Dean Levi had a temporary sojourn as a suspected Lefty in the eye of a national political storm himself, during the quarter that Fay took his course, and it centered on his ambitious jury project. In October, all hell broke loose. Brian Gluss feared he would lose his worker status and be deported. Marvin, as the sole support for himself and Fay, also had his job on the line. It was another lesson close to home, underscoring the dangerous third rail of the McCarthy era in politics.

The jury project on which Marvin was working had started as a small study of jury deliberations to refute critics who ridiculed jurors as mere pawns of veteran attorneys. The designers of the project anticipated tape-recording a hundred jury deliberations with the consent of the lawyers on both sides. Though the experiment was backed by the Chief Judge of the circuit, some judges and lawyers became immediately alarmed at the idea of "jury bugging." The Department of Justice strongly opposed the project, which conservative radio commentators derisively dubbed jury "snooping" and trumpeted as a national scandal.

As a liberal think tank, the University of Chicago remained under great suspicion that it might be infiltrated by Communists. In early October of 1955, Dean Levi was called to Washington, D.C., to appear in front of a House subcommittee investigating whether the law school was attempting to undermine the integrity of the entire American jury system. Warren Burger, the future Chief Justice, and then Assistant Attorney General, accused the law school of plans to eavesdrop on 500 to 1,000 juries nationwide.

This public display of shocked disapproval contrasted markedly with the Department of Justice's own secret program. In the spring of 1954, Attorney General Brownell had secretly authorized bugging by the FBI in the purported interests of national security that defied limitations recently imposed by the Supreme Court. The FBI then installed hundreds of electronic bugs in traditional criminal investigations totally unrelated to national security.

None of this was public when Congress grilled Dean Levi about the jury project or when President Eisenhower followed the hearing up with a call for a ban on bugging juries in his next State of the Union speech. Congress responded by adopting a new federal law, outlawing the secret recording of jury deliberations. The media soon moved on to other concerns.

Meanwhile, Fay turned her focus to an impetuous personal project. She talked her friend Alice Wirth Gray into asking her influential mother to help Fay and Marvin adopt an eleven-year-old homeless Wisconsin Native American girl. It would be an uphill battle given that the couple were only 23 and 24 and married for less than two years. A very dubious Mrs. Wirth then wrote letters to help facilitate the inter-racial adoption only to learn a few weeks later that Fay decided it was all a mistake and no longer wished to pursue the adoption. Fay was oblivious to what she had put Mrs. Wirth through to support the ill-conceived adoption efforts. (Over the course of Fay's career many people who did her favors felt similarly used and unappreciated.)

The next semester Fay and Marvin house sat for Professor Sharp while he was on sabbatical. Entertaining friends in his posh penthouse overlooking Lake Michigan, Fay enjoyed the life style of the upper middle class. When on an emotional high, as she was at the time, Fay had the capacity to assume that whatever choices she made were consistent with her Leftist ideology. This one was easy. After all, the apartment belonged to the President of the Lawyers Guild, who offered it to the couple for free.

By taking summer courses, Fay made up for her lost quarter following the transfer to Boalt. In June of 1956, Fay obtained her law degree with the rest of her class and finished in the top third. Fay and Marvin applied for jobs in both Los Angeles and San Francisco but received no offers. At Fay's urging, they once again headed for the Bay Area, this time with a letter of introduction from Professor Sharp to two prominent Leftist lawyers in San Francisco, Charles "Charlie" Garry and Benjamin "Barney" Dreyfus, whom Professor Sharp had come to know well through their many years together in the Guild. Fay and Marvin packed their few belongings, their diplomas and their idealism and headed west for good.

Photo courtesy of Fay's niece, Linda Stone

As a child, Fay was closer to her father than her mother, but his political outlook remained far to the right of Fay's while her mother's evolved over time. When Fay became well-known as an activist in Berkeley in the mid-1960s, Sam bristled at being introduced as "Fay Stender's father."

■ 6 ■

Starting Out

*To love what you do and feel that it matters,
how could anything be more fun?*[1]
— KATHERINE GRAHAM

That summer of 1956, Fay and Marvin found a Berkeley apartment at the top of a large house the color of gingerbread, with a turret and rounded windows. Friends thought it characteristic of Fay to live somewhere so strikingly different. Fay particularly enjoyed reuniting with Betty Lee and Gene Pippin. Pip, since divorced from his wife Anne and involved in another relationship, was again rewriting his dissertation. Fay's family found Marvin charming, though Fay herself resumed a sometimes prickly attitude toward her parents and her sister. Fay's politics would always remain far to the left of her father's.

Local headlines were then being made by a treason and sedition trial in San Francisco against a fellow Reed graduate, Sylvia Powell, and her husband John. A decade older, the Powells had been sympathetic to the Chinese Revolution and later published charges made by Chinese officials that the United States had used germ warfare against the North Koreans. Professor Sharp's friend Charles Garry took on the Powells' defense and got the treason charges dismissed in 1959. Attorney General Robert Kennedy would drop the remaining sedition charges in 1961. The Powells' lengthy ostracism and legal troubles must have reminded Fay of what had happened to Stanley Moore. After he was ousted from the Reed faculty in 1954 as a Communist, Moore could only find a part-time teaching position at Barnard College. Both the Powells' situation and Stanley Moore's ongoing academic problems underscored why Fay had good reason to fear for Marvin when Professor Sharp had asked them to distribute fund-raising leaflets for the Rosenbergs' two sons.

The first professional hurdle Fay and Marvin faced was the California Bar. Marvin took the expensive review course and brought the notes home for Fay to study. Sam Abrahams said that if only one of them passed the Bar, he hoped it would be Marvin, the breadwinner. Both passed on the first try and were sworn in together in December of 1956. Neither found work in private law firms. The handful of Leftist lawyers in the Bay Area were barely eking out a living for themselves. Marvin signed up to take court-appointed criminal cases and tried whatever personal injury cases he could obtain. Fay found a position clerking at the California Supreme Court.

Fay's new job brought her into the prestigious inner sanctum of the state's highest court to get a firsthand glimpse of how its decisions were made. From the briefs raising major civil and criminal issues that crossed Fay's desk, she quickly learned what techniques best appealed to the justices' individual proclivities (as Professor Llewellyn had suggested to his law school classes). In the process, she absorbed reams of California law. For Fay, it opened another door that members of the public and most lawyers never penetrated. Yet it had its drawbacks. Fay had been hired to work for an octogenarian Republican, Associate Justice John Wesley Shenk.

Shenk was totally unlike Fay's elderly friend Hammy, with whom she had gotten along so famously in her law school summer job. The mild-mannered, church-going Mason first made his mark as City Attorney of Los Angeles, where he had overseen the controversial acquisition of water in San Fernando and Owens Valley later made infamous in the movie *Chinatown*. Shenk soon became known statewide for his expertise in municipal water law. Though Fay found Justice Shenk affable and grandfatherly, his prejudices appalled her. Back in the

1920s, he had supported "Oriental exclusion." Fay was amazed to learn he still used the term "the yellow hordes" to describe Asian-Americans.

Meanwhile Fay, in her spare time, found an outlet for her activist energies. She volunteered to do research for a ground-breaking ACLU case challenging hiring discrimination. A white woman employed in the Alameda County Probation office was forced by an anti-nepotism policy to leave her job because she had recently married a black colleague in the same office. Mrs. Gaines then applied for a job as a probation officer in a neighboring county but was turned down.

Fay looked up legal precedents for the complaint the ACLU filed in June of 1957 on Mrs. Gaines' behalf. Marvin acted as her consultant. He considered the joint political enterprise far more interesting than his day job. The principal case the ACLU relied on was a landmark 1948 decision of the California Supreme Court that involved the refusal of the Los Angeles County clerk to grant an inter-racial couple a marriage license. State law at the time — like that in 29 other states — flatly prohibited such unions:[2] California's ban dated back to the state's admission to the Union in 1850.

California's attorney general argued that the marriage prohibition remained justified on the basis that Negroes were socially inferior and the children of mixed marriages would likely suffer rejection by both races. While this case was pending, President Truman issued his historic order banning racial discrimination in the nation's armed forces. Then still an associate justice, Roger Traynor led a bare majority of the California Supreme Court to make California the first state to hold an anti-miscegenation law unconstitutional.

When Fay read the vigorous dissent in *Perez v. Sharp*, she discovered to her dismay that it was written by her own boss, Justice Shenk. He argued with spirited stubbornness: "The Legislature certainly had as much right to . . . prohibit [marriage] between persons of different races as they had to prohibit it between . . . idiots."[3] Justice Shenk relied on a nineteenth century federal decision enforcing Georgia law. Fay boiled down her boss's perspective to its essence: "If it is good enough for Georgia, it is good enough for me."[4] At about the same time, Fay learned that a male law clerk, hired when she came aboard, received

$110 per month more than she did for doing the same work. After six months, Fay could no longer stomach Justice Shenk's racism and sexism. Fay assumed correctly that Marvin would support her decision to quit. Over and over, Fay's uncompromising nature would find a safety net in Marvin's generous support.

Armed once again with Guild President Sharp's recommendation, Fay asked Charles Garry for a job. Garry had just formed a new law partnership with his long-time fellow Guild member Barney Dreyfus. Both were becoming legendary for their vigorous defense of unpopular causes. Her quest for work at the new firm was ill-timed. The week after the partnership opened its doors on Market Street in San Francisco, three of its four principals were subpoenaed to appear before HUAC in San Francisco. The Committee was particularly bent on exposing Barney Dreyfus as a Communist: Dreyfus had played a leadership role in opposing Smith Act loyalty oaths and convincing the State Bar's most prominent attorneys to champion the rights of HUAC targets.

Both Garry and Dreyfus were identified by a witness who had attended clandestine Communist educational programs in San Francisco with them back in the '40s. Yet, much to the HUAC panel's chagrin, the Bay Area hearings attracted large crowds who sympathized with the lawyers and applauded their refusal to cooperate. Still, when Fay came calling, Garry and Dreyfus did not know if their new firm would have any future. Garry suggested that Fay instead seek a job with Claude Allen, a black solo practitioner in the East Bay.

Allen was sixteen years Fay's senior, but had just become a lawyer in 1954, two years before Fay. Born and raised in Mississippi, the World War II army lieutenant had supported his wife and four children as a bar owner while attending night law school for five years. Allen did not provide Fay with much guidance as he set her to work handling minor charges against black prostitutes. Fay convinced judges to order the same lenient sentences as white prostitutes routinely received.

While working for Allen, Fay became attracted to a young black lawyer. She confided to her friend Pip that she was tempted to cheat on Marvin with this handsome colleague. Despite this distraction, Fay soon became disillusioned with her new job. Allen had little idea how to run a practice. Shortly after Fay joined his office, he became desperate for witnesses to corroborate his client's version of a two-year-old car accident. Allen paid an agent to hire a pair of "witnesses" who turned out to be staff members of the district attorney's office. Allen pleaded guilty to perjury and was disbarred.[5] This again left Fay without a paying job. Relying on Marvin's support, Fay decided to join her good friends Pip and Stan, who were still in graduate school. She re-enrolled at Cal in political science.

Meanwhile, Fay and Marvin still worked on the ACLU's job discrimination lawsuit for Mrs. Gaines. Their aim was to destroy the credibility of the Chief Probation Officer, who had been well-coached to cite legitimate reasons for not hiring Mrs. Gaines. The conservative judge was expected to accept any potentially plausible explanation given by this trusted long-time county employee. Yet the ACLU's legal challenge coincided with an escalating national racial crisis.

At the beginning of September 1957 — two weeks before the hearing — an ugly confrontation in Little Rock, Arkansas, began to draw international attention to lack of progress in integration in the United States since the landmark decision in *Brown v. Board of Education* three years earlier. Governor Orval Faubus decided to take a stand for segregation by ordering the National Guard to block access of nine black teens trying to enroll in an all-white high school. As the situation intensified, President Eisenhower felt compelled to call in federal troops to ensure the black students were admitted. Ike then gave a televised speech explaining the necessity of that drastic action to redeem America's tarnished image in the world.

Judge Hugh Donovan took the President's speech to heart and gave the Gaines matter careful consideration before issuing his ruling on February 10, 1958. Relying on *Perez v. Sharp*, he found in Mrs. Gaines' favor. The judge wrote: "Can it be validly contended that an inter-racial marriage does not come within the constitutional prohibition against discrimination because of race, creed or color? . . . To permit such action to go uncorrected should be of grave consequence to believers in the democratic system."[6]

Fay and Marvin were elated. Spurred by the international spotlight on American racism, a conservative judge had unexpectedly rejected the testimony of his own chief probation officer. The two of them had helped the judge look with fresh eyes on the weight of the evidence and case law. Marvin remembered with fondness that they turned to each other and said: "This is so easy. Look what you can do!"

Fay and Marvin Stender with their first baby, Neal Aviron Stender, taken by Fay's friend Robert "Pip" Pippen around the fall of 1958. The new parents were living in a cottage in a wooded area of Palo Alto, California at the time. Fay made use of a family heirloom –the same white bassinette her parents had bought back in 1931 when Ruby became pregnant with Fay. Fay and Marvin's second child, Oriane, was born in January 1960.

■ 7 ■

Turbulence

> *Fay . . . surveys the tangled jungle and
> . . . offers a toast:"To chaos."*[1]
> — JUDITH NIEMI

Fay became pregnant in the early fall of 1957, finished her classes and prepared for the baby to arrive. Marvin had found work as an associate in the offices of Martin Jarvis in San Francisco, trying criminal defense and personal injury cases. Marvin's new boss was among the most stalwart of the small circle of local lawyers, including Charlie Garry and Barney Dreyfus, who had challenged political persecutions during the Cold War. As Marvin worked long hours, Fay retrieved from her cousins the bassinette her parents had bought to welcome her own birth and made it ready for her infant son, born the first week of June 1958. The delighted new mother named her baby Neal as an anagram of Lena, her favorite grandparent. Fay gave Neal the middle name Aviron for her paternal grandfather's Russian family.

Fay decided to nurse Neal. By 1958, when Neal was born, breastfeeding in the United States had dropped to close to 20 per cent and the term was not even accepted in polite company. By then, Fay and Marvin had moved to a rental cottage in a wooded area of Palo Alto. Often isolated, Fay surprised some of her old friends by taking up the cause of the newly formed La Leche League. They, too, supported breastfeeding, but found the organization too preachy.

Fay also found herself drawn to join those who challenged the modern opposition to natural childbirth. Expectant mothers, discouraged from home births as outmoded and too painful, were instead rushed to hospitals where obstetricians made nearly all the decisions. The mother was often anesthetized. The father, prohibited by law from entering the delivery room, was consigned to waiting in the hall or visitor's room for some word about his wife and newborn. The child was commonly delivered by forceps and then whisked off to a communal nursery tended by hospital personnel.

Realizing that her brother-in-law Don now had medical privileges as a new doctor, Fay convinced her pregnant sister to get Don to join her in the delivery room. Lisie had already suffered one miscarriage. Don grew alarmed when his tiny newborn daughter showed signs of serious problems, but said nothing until the crisis had passed. At Fay's urging, Lisie immediately started nursing her new baby, Linda, who quickly lost ten ounces and weighed slightly over five pounds by her tenth day. Lisie's alarmed pediatrician warned, "Well, Mother, you keep this up and she'll be in an incubator next week." Fay insisted that her sister ignore the doctor's advice and was angry when Lisie instead switched to bottled formula.

Fay herself had been nearly eight months pregnant when Lisie gave birth. In late January of 1960, Fay had her own newborn daughter, Oriane. Soon Fay's toddler Neal nicknamed Oriane "Fifi," and the name stuck throughout her childhood. Fay stayed home with her babies essentially full-time for three years. In an interview at the height of her career, Fay recalled only the joy she had experienced as a new parent. Yet, at the time, she grew increasingly depressed. She could not keep up with the demands of motherhood and had no desire to manage a household. So she threw her energy into another cause — an organization recently formed in Los Angeles, the International Childbirth Education Association.[2]

Fay embraced ICEA's promotion of freedom of choice in childbirth and family-centered maternity care. Best of all, the loosely run organization gave her lots of latitude. Fay received the lofty title of Western

Regional Director, a post she held for the next four years as she busied herself with ICEA and La Leche League projects. She authored a widely distributed pamphlet, "Husbands in the Delivery Room," and listed her home phone as a resource for new mothers under the name "Nursing Mothers Anonymous," with the slogan, "Don't reach for the bottle, reach for the phone." With help from a local lawyer, Fay brought suit to challenge a hospital policy that then barred fathers from delivery rooms. The case resulted in a settlement through which the hospital agreed to change its practice.

All the while, Fay's relationship with Marvin deteriorated. By the end of 1960, he was routinely gone for long days, leaving Fay miserable and lonely. When Fay learned that Marvin was involved with another woman, she concluded her marriage had failed. Fay made a distraught call to her sister Lisie in San Diego, where Don was fulfilling his postponed military service following completion of medical school. Lisie and her husband welcomed Fay and her two young children unhesitatingly to their tiny, two-bedroom home.

Fay returned to the East Bay a few weeks later, in early 1961, to rent a small apartment in Berkeley for herself and her two small children. Still despondent, she channeled her pain into a sixteen-line poem and sent it to her close friend Pip. Fay told him she thought haiku would have matched her feelings better, but found herself "too turbulent" inside to express herself in this simple Japanese form, as the rainy winter weather persisted. Nursing her baby gave her pleasure, but her consignment to domestic tasks left her feeling isolated from political movements. She wove into her poem literary allusions that she knew Pip would appreciate. Yet she could not help also sharing her despair at "keeping down the terror . . . ."[3]

Pip grew quite anxious about Fay's depressed mood. Likely through his connections in Cal's English Department, Fay was soon offered a job teaching an introductory speech course to undergraduates. Ruby volunteered to help with Neal and Oriane during the week. On Saturday mornings, Fay brought the children to her parents' home where Marvin would fetch them at day's end to spend Saturday night and Sunday with him and his current girlfriend. Yet, on weekdays, single parenting still overwhelmed Fay.

Fay and Marvin's acquaintances in the Guild were not surprised by their separation. Some thought Fay was single-minded and humorless, difficult to get along with. Marvin's easygoing nature often seemed to bore Fay. She continued to delight in caustic, verbal sparring with men, which was not Marvin's style. He, in turn, had developed a reputation as a ladies' man. Long before she fled to her sister's, Fay had broadcast her unhappiness to friends, frequently complaining that her husband did not offer her enough emotional support. To a few close friends, Fay confided her own continued obsession with Stanley Moore. Since 1957, Moore's career had been on the rebound following publication of *The Critique of Capitalist Democracy*, which synthesized the writings of Marx, Engels and Lenin. He had meanwhile separated from his second wife. In 1960, Stanley was at work on another ambitious book while Fay battled with postpartum depression and her own unrealized aspirations. Fay had fantasies of ending her broken marriage and reuniting with Stanley.

A more practical idea for adding meaning to her life soon came to Fay. As she nursed her newborn, and chased after her toddler, Fay followed political developments related to the most recent HUAC hearings in San Francisco focused on exposing Communist affiliations among California teachers. When police had hosed protesters down the steep steps of City Hall and conducted mass arrests, "Black Friday" May 13, 1960 had made national headlines. In April of 1961 Charlie Garry and former prosecutor Jack Berman represented Robert Meisenbach, the lone prosecuted defendant. The trial was all over the front pages and the talk of the Leftist community. By then, Fay had had enough of being a stay-at-home mom and part-time teacher. She asked Garry once again if he might hire her. Garry made Fay an offer on a part-time basis, contingent on her successfully completing a research project for his partner Barney Dreyfus. Garry knew that Dreyfus was far more exacting than he was. As she turned the work in, Dreyfus intimidated Fay by asking, "Are you good?" Fay replied, "I think so," and that was how she became the firm's first woman attorney.[4]

Barney Dreyfus concentrated on criminal defense, constitutional law and civil rights. The third partner, Frank McTernan, was an earnest, New Deal enthusiast who started practice in the '30s as a labor lawyer and expanded his practice to include civil rights law. By the time Fay started work, the firm's first black lawyer had left and another associate, James Herndon, had taken his place. Herndon, a past employee of *The San Francisco Chronicle*, was politically connected in the black community, with many contacts who referred him personal injury work. Fay was impressed — she never expected to bring in clients herself. Marvin, in his own law practice had, by now, learned the same pragmatic lesson most Guild attorneys understood: "P-I cases pay the office expenses, and most political and criminal cases don't."[5]

At the firm, Charles Garry brought in the most revenue. Fay described the dynamics of that Leftist firm: "Charles is the heart, [Barney Dreyfus] is the brain of the human enterprise in which Frank McTernan supplies humility . . . and Herndon the young blood."[6] At the time, criminal defense and personal injury practice were considered combat zones for which women were presumptively unsuited. At day's end, war stories were exchanged with free-flowing liquor. Gathering evidence in criminal cases sometimes included payoffs to cooperative police officers. That was how Charles Garry and Jack Berman had obtained copies of crucial police reports to help acquit Cal student Robert Meisenbach in the Black Friday case. This rough world, rife with illegal bribes, was not much different from Clarence Darrow's day.

For a woman lawyer in the '50s and '60s attempting to parent small children, courtroom work was especially difficult. Garry had spent years developing his trial practice skills by working day and night and often slept in his office. Though he made time for a mistress, he rarely saw his long-suffering wife and had no children. Many women who could have easily handled law school in the '50s opted instead for careers as legal secretaries because of the huge disparity in job opportunities. That included women already working at the Garry, Dreyfus firm when Fay was hired in 1961. The only one Fay met who wielded significant responsibility was the office manager. It was an open secret that she was also Barney Dreyfus's mistress. While Fay was there, the office manager continually studied for the California Bar, ultimately passed it and left the firm.

At first, Fay was overwhelmed by juggling her parental responsibilities

> Source: FBI file on Fay Stender, Vol. 1
>
> SUBJECT **Fay Abrahams Stender**
>
> FILE NO. **100-49931**
>
> VOLUME NO. **1**
>
> SERIALS **1**
>   **40**
>
> ---
>
> OPTIONAL FORM NO. 10
> UNITED STATES GOVERNMENT
> *Memorandum*
>
> TO : SAC (100-49931*)   DATE: 12/28/64
>
> FROM : ▓▓▓▓▓▓   (b) (7) (C)
>
> SUBJECT: FAY STENDER   **NLG**
> ▓▓▓▓▓▓▓▓▓▓▓▓▓▓▓▓▓▓▓▓▓▓▓▓▓▓▓▓
> She works for SF law firm of Charles G. Garry and Benjamin Dreyfus.
>
> File# 61-363-1193 p.3

The FBI began tracking Fay Stender's civil rights activities after she joined Charles Garry's law firm.

in Berkeley around her part-time job in San Francisco, despite its flexible hours. Fay dropped her one-and-a-half-year-old daughter and three-year-old-son at nursery school each morning. Each afternoon, she would rush from work to pick up Neal and Oriane, shop, make dinner and put them to bed. She told an interviewer years later, "My goal was to get through each day and not go to the looney bin."[7] Both Ann Fagan Ginger and Doris "Dobby" Brin Walker, prominent Old Leftists in the San Francisco Lawyers Guild, also raised children for a period of time as single parents. Fifty years later, with a shudder, Ann vividly recalled going it alone after her divorce from labor historian Ray Ginger. "As a single parent for five years, I know how you do it. You go crazy. Doris would say the same thing: 'Who in the Hell's got time to have friends?'" Ann quickly added, "I mean that's a terrible fact. But to be a woman lawyer in this era that we've lived through and to be a political lawyer [is a recipe for chaos]."

Attempting to meet her children's needs on top of racing back and forth to work often filled Fay with a sense of hopelessness. She started seeing a psychiatrist again, but quit when it became too costly. Her life seemed to reach bottom in the fall of 1961. Fay had sneaked a visit to Stanley Moore in New York a few years earlier and still corresponded with him. Over Christmas, Fay again saw Moore when he came to town to visit his family. She was still estranged from Marvin. Moore invited Fay to spend the next summer with him, but refused to consider another marriage and had no interest in raising children. Fay did not think she could survive another intense interlude with Stanley, only to be dropped at summer's end.

Over New Year's, Fay took a short vacation alone with Marvin to celebrate their wedding anniversary. Despite all their difficulties, she appreciated his ongoing commitment to both her and the children's financial support. Marvin offered to give Fay money to resume analysis from funds he was about to receive from a family trust. By the spring of 1962, Fay was upbeat. She had just passed the milestone of her thirtieth birthday. She cut her hair to shoulder length, kept her nails painted with bright red polish and decided to buy a car. She felt like a new person and told Stanley Moore she never wanted to see him again. Fay and Marvin took the children on a family camping trip together. They postponed any thought of formal separation papers, though they still had no plans for reuniting.

By then, Fay's work for the Garry, Dreyfus firm had evolved into a steady, half-time position. A side benefit was introduction into the inner circle of Garry's Leftist friends Bob Treuhaft and his celebrity wife Jessica "Decca" Mitford. Almost a generation older than Fay, the Treuhafts made a strikingly odd couple. Bob was a thin, dark-haired Jew with a heavy Bronx accent. He had never made friends with any Gentile until he went to Harvard. Decca was tall and blue-eyed, a broad-boned brunette with an unmistakably upper crust enunciation.

The Treuhafts had been members of the American Communist Party from the mid-forties to 1958. Decca enjoyed being known as the defiant "red sheep" daughter of an ultraconservative British peer and his wife, Lord and Lady Redesdale. Both of her parents supported the German Nazi rise to power, as did one of Decca's sisters, who joined Hitler's inner circle.

The Oakland firm of Treuhaft and Edises had represented mostly black clientele since 1948, back when Fay was still in high school. In 1951, Senator McCarthy named Treuhaft one of the most subversive lawyers in America, which Bob and Decca considered high praise. When Fay joined the Garry firm, Decca and Bob were in the midst of exposing outrageous practices of the funeral industry. *The American Way of Death* became a best-seller. The book prompted Congressional hearings into the unconscionable fees the funeral industry charged unsophisticated mourners unprepared to resist aggressive sales pitches while still mired in grief over a lost family member.

Fay would later learn that Bob Treuhaft was one of Huey Newton's childhood heroes. Treuhaft had gained instant renown in the black community for winning an improbable appeal in 1951 of a murder conviction. The defendant was a local black shoeshine boy named Jerry Newson, whom police had beaten to obtain a confession that Newson later repudiated. Even while still in elementary school, Huey Newton and his friends had appreciated the significance of that historic case.

In the early '70s, Fay and Decca would work closely together on

TURBULENCE

Jessica ("Decca") Mitford Treuhaft
(1917–1996)

Bob Treuhaft
(1912–2001)

In 1951, Senator Eugene McCarthy named Bob Treuhaft one of the most subversive lawyers in America. Bob and his wife Decca were delighted. When Fay joined Charles Garry's firm, she made the "A" list to the Treuhafts' famous Leftist parties. By the mid-1970s, Fay would stop speaking to Bob, and Decca would describe Fay as her "frenemy." (Both photos circa early '60s.)

prison reform. What impressed Fay back in 1961 was that Decca and Bob knew anyone who was anyone nationally in radical politics; the couple threw the best Leftist parties around. When she joined the Garry firm, Fay made the "A" list of invitees. Decca did not mind when Fay brought Neal and Oriane along.

Being at the Garry firm also placed Fay at the center of Leftist efforts to change the status quo. By 1961, Decca had already published her first memoir, *Daughters and Rebels*. In it, Decca famously observed that "You may not be able to change the world, but at least you can embarrass the guilty."[8] By then, Garry and Dreyfus had both achieved widespread recognition as criminal defense lawyers for getting psychiatric evidence admitted to avoid the death penalty. The partial defense of diminished capacity was afterward known in California as the *Wells-Gorshen* rule for the last names of their clients in two landmark cases. Expert testimony was now permitted to show that a homicide might have resulted from uncontrollable psychological impulses. Garry credited the *Wells-Gorshen* rule with being "an invaluable lever in the plea-bargaining process," dramatically reducing the number of executions for what would otherwise have been capital crimes.[9] "Sleepy Nick" Gorshen only served three years of his sentence before he was paroled and went back to work as a longshoreman. When Fay started work for the firm, Garry was still working periodically to secure Bob Wells' release, a long-term project finally realized in 1974.

Fay started out by assisting the partners with research and drafting briefs for personal injury and criminal matters. The Garry firm handled personal injury cases the same way as did other lawyers in the field, on a fee contingent on whether they won or settled a case. The firm made substantially less money from its personal injury practice than many other lawyers because their black clientele routinely received smaller jury awards than whites with similar injuries. Newspapermen covering Oakland reflected similar prejudice. Warren Hinckle, who became the editor of the Leftist *Ramparts* magazine in the late '60s, later recalled the guidelines followed when he had started out as a cub reporter. The newsworthiness of traffic deaths depended on the race of the victim. Working for a leading San Francisco daily, Hinckle was taught: "No niggers after 11 p.m. on weekdays, 9 p.m. on Saturdays (as the Sunday paper went to press early)."[10]

Fay handled the appeal from one particularly discriminatory verdict. She accused the defense attorney of appealing to racism for telling the jury that "Negroes have a tendency to exaggerate their complaints, to have poor memories, and to be unable to remember events." But Charles Garry had failed to ensure that the court reporter typed up the closing arguments — a lesson for Fay for the future to make sure that every significant misstep by opposing counsel was captured on the record.

The partners soon realized that no matter how routine the assignment, Fay would exhaust all possible avenues, thinking both inside and outside the box. Garry liked her unrelenting approach. Fay found a sharp contrast in working with Barney Dreyfus. Unlike Garry, Dreyfus demanded disciplined writing and never simply signed his name to an associate's draft. She later reflected that Dreyfus was "not the easiest type of person for a woman to work with in sexist America. Despite his name, his identity as Jewish is virtually non-existent. We are representatives of completely differing styles of being, personality, expression, consciousness. There was a lot of pain (for me—whether for him, I never was sure)."

Dreyfus held doors open for women and displayed great chivalry, but in meetings either ignored women altogether or behaved in a patronizing manner, often admonishing the object of his dismay with "Now, now, little girl." Yet Fay grew to admire Dreyfus. She credited him with "charm, manners, elegance, wit, elitism, anachronistic integrity, enigma; one would not mistake another for him." After years of his tutelage, Fay conceded that "He taught me more than anyone else about the practice of law. 'It is,' he said, 'the meticulous attention to detail.' Truer words few people have spoken."[11]

To Fay's relief, as the firm's business expanded, she retained a permanent part-time position. Among the appeals she handled, Fay found she particularly enjoyed wrongful termination cases even though she lost a major case about the scope of the Regents' authority to fire university staff. It would be cited again and again over the years by lawyers on the other side. Still, administrative appeals were the type of "bread and butter" cases Fay would turn back to in the '70s after she no longer represented criminal defendants.

In 1962, the partnership moved to more spacious quarters and added a new associate, Don Kerson, in the office next to Fay's. Though the two did not interact much, Don always knew when she was in her office because the walls shook whenever she typed. Don could also hear her yelling at hospital administrators over the telephone as she pursued her ICEA mission to transform delivery room policies.

It was not long before the partners decided it was time to let Don and Fay try a criminal case together to gain trial experience. The case was a "dog" — one the partners expected to lose. *People v. One 1954 Ford Station Wagon* involved a car confiscated by police after they claimed to have found a marijuana cigarette in it. Don could not dissuade Fay from challenging the routine test the police used for analyzing the presence of marijuana. Watching Fay emphatically wave her hands in court to underscore her arguments, Don could see the judge was unimpressed. Don was not surprised they lost.

* * *

Fay's niche largely remained brief-writing for Garry and Dreyfus as she shuttled her children to school and extracurricular activities, commuted across the Bay Bridge and spent much of her time at the firm scurrying between its law library and her office. Still separated in the spring of 1963, Fay told hardly anyone that she had rekindled a romance with her former fiancé, Bob Richter. After Fay rejected him following his release from prison in 1952, Bob had earned his degree at Reed and married another Reed student before moving to Iowa and obtaining an M.A.

During Fay's first semester of law school in 1953, Bob had brought his new wife to visit Fay in Chicago. Fay did not see Bob again for almost another decade, while Bob volunteered for civil service and received a pardon from President Eisenhower, erasing his conviction. By the time Fay saw him again, Bob's career had begun to take off. He had already assisted screenwriter Richard Maibaum and was now a producer and reporter for Oregon public television and radio. *The New York Times* also employed him as a part-time journalist.

Bob contacted Fay in the spring of 1963 and arranged to come down from Oregon for a weekend together. He was unhappy in his own marriage and knew that Fay remained separated from Marvin. Fay had Neal and Oriane that weekend and brought them along when she and Bob stayed at a beachside motel south of San Francisco. Unlike Stanley Moore, Bob enjoyed young children. He relished catching up with Fay as they walked along in the sunset with Neal on his shoulders and Oriane in Fay's arms. Even more, Bob would cherish the memory of putting the two preschoolers to bed in an adjacent room so he and Fay could spend a torrid night together.

From then on, Bob visited Fay whenever he had business in California — once every month or two — until she reunited with Marvin in 1965. When Fay and Marvin separated again later on in their marriage, Bob and Fay discreetly revived their long-distance affair. At one point he proposed to her, but Fay resisted. They kept up sporadic trysts over an eighteen-year period, ending in 1979 shortly before she was wounded.

While separated from Marvin in the '60s, Fay saw her old law school friend Alice Wirth Gray and her husband Gary fairly often. Fay confided to Alice that she and Marvin were planning to divorce and asked Alice to play matchmaker. Fay's fantasy was someone with whom she could play "The Trout Quintet" arranged to be performed as a duet on a piano and string instrument. The challenging Schubert composition included a famous fourth movement that evoked the image of a trout skimming the surface of a river. Alice coincidentally knew an academic psychiatrist who was single, an opera buff and amateur violinist. He had also been looking for someone to accompany him on the piano playing "The Trout" transcribed for two musicians.

Alice excitedly told Fay about her psychiatrist friend and invited both to dinner at the Grays' home to perform the piece for a few friends. After the performance ended, Fay stomped into the kitchen to speak with Alice privately. Alice assumed she was upset that the psychiatrist was not as accomplished on the violin as Fay was at the piano.

No, an irate Fay turned to Alice and exclaimed, "You didn't tell me he was a midget!"

In addition to seeing Bob Richter, Fay managed to renew her sado-masochistic relationship with Stanley Moore. He had finished his second book, *Three Tactics*, and was on the brink of accepting a professorship in philosophy at U.C. San Diego. Contradictory impulses never gave Fay much pause. As Neal and Oriane grew, Fay also felt a surge of religious identity that she had abandoned under Stanley Moore's influence. Much to Marvin's surprise, Fay determined to raise her children celebrating Jewish holidays.

Marvin had never exhibited an interest in following his family's religious traditions, but Sam Abrahams always presided over a Passover Seder with a large family gathering that Fay and Lisie usually attended. Every year, the Abrahams extended family focused on the Exodus of Jews from Egypt and celebrated their freedom from bondage. Fay felt that her children would benefit from exposure to the Torah's ideals of justice and freedom. She even sent Neal to an orthodox day school for a short time, with Marvin's acquiescence.

Fay's old friend Betty Lee (now going by her given name Ying and married name Kelley) came on a now rare visit to Fay's home with her own five-year-old and was astonished that Fay had a menorah and toy dreidl. "What are you doing?" she asked. "I want the children to know their heritage," Ying recalled Fay replying. Yet Fay shocked her parents just as much by taking Neal and Oriane and Lisie's two young daughters, Linda and baby Lora, on an Orthodox Christian Easter egg hunt.

In the early '60s, besides renewing a long-distance relationship with Bob Richter, Fay dated several local men. These included her old friend Stan Seidner, the perennial psychology graduate student and classical cellist. Stan now spent most days among the lost souls and panhandlers on Berkeley's Telegraph Avenue. At the end of November 1963, Fay's high school friend Hilde stayed a few days with Fay after Hilde's own marriage had begun to crumble. In her short stay in Fay's untidy apartment, Hilde met the unimpressive Stan and a couple of other men Fay was then seeing. They seemed to drop by Fay's apartment at will.

Finding a rare moment for some private conversation, Hilde and

Fay exchanged bitter observations of the inappropriate reactions of the men they were with as a national paralysis set in on the somber November day of President Kennedy's assassination. Hilde's husband had taken advantage of the halt in ordinary activity to sell his car. When the shocking news hit the airwaves, Fay had been shepherding a famous philosopher visiting the Bay Area. He wanted to take her to bed. "Men!" they said. But Hilde had been disconcerted by Fay's chaotic approach to life as a single mother and viewed it as a cautionary tale.

Fay herself had grown unhappy with her current situation and longed for more stability. She and Marvin remained on cordial terms as they drifted toward divorce. Yet the idea of being totally on her own with two children and no husband filled Fay with increasing anxiety. As much as she disdained her sister's safe life in the suburbs, Fay had her own traditionalist streak that counted on Marvin for security. The family still took camping trips together and socialized among the same circle of Leftist friends. In their spare time, both Fay and Marvin became increasingly active among friends supporting bold civil rights projects. Over the next two years Fay sought to entice Marvin to give their marriage another try. The excitement they both felt as they launched themselves into Movement activity was a powerful catalyst.

Source: San Francisco Public Library History Center, Stephen Vincent, "Tracy Sims and the Civil Rights Protests," 1964.

Nineteen-year-old Tracy Sims (left) was one of the leaders of the protesters arrested in the spring of 1964 for picketing discriminatory hiring practices at the Sheraton Palace and Auto Row in San Francisco. Lead defense lawyer Beverly Axelrod stands center; co-counsel Mal Burnstein stands left behind Sims; defense team member Patrick Hallinan is to Axelrod's right. The arrests resulted in the longest municipal court jury trial in the city's history and almost bankrupted Axelrod. This ordeal was fresh in both Burnstein's and Axelrod's minds in the summer of 1965 when they opted to waive a jury for the trial of 155 representative Free Speech Movement protesters arrested in December of 1964 for occupying U.C. Berkeley's Sproul Plaza — a decision the civil rights lawyers later vowed never to repeat in a political trial.

■ 8 ■

Joining The Movement

*There's a battle
Outside and it is ragin'*

. . . .

*[T]he present now
Will later be past
The order is
Rapidly fadin'*

—BOB DYLAN, "THE TIMES THEY ARE A'CHANGIN"

F ay and Marvin's circle of Leftist friends paid close attention when Dr. Martin Luther King's Southern Christian Leadership Conference (SCLC) instigated the formation of the Student Nonviolent Coordinating Committee (SNCC). Fay and Marvin joined thirty activists who formed East Bay Friends of SNCC. With mailers, radio pitches, house parties and garage sales, East Bay Friends of SNCC sponsored hundreds of events over several years' time. In the process, they accumulated a long list of contributors and achieved a reputation for being among SNCC's most productive financial supporters in the nation. In the fall of 1963, SNCC sent word out to Northern students and lawyers to help reverse seven decades of voter suppression. Dubbed the Mississippi Summer Project and later "Freedom Summer," the project's goals were threefold: registering voters, organizing the

Mississippi Freedom Democratic Party as an alternative to the white-controlled Democratic Party of Mississippi and conducting Freedom Schools. Coming out alive from some areas of the state would itself be an achievement. Training would include the Magnolia State's grim history of race violence and what to do if arrested. The planners were also concerned about how local blacks would react to Northern white volunteers, particularly white women who might be seeking their "summer Negro."[1]

Fay and Marvin joined the growing faction of lawyers lobbying the National Lawyers Guild to endorse the project. Fay had joined the fifty-member San Francisco branch of the Guild shortly after starting at the Garry, Dreyfus firm in 1961, but was rarely active in it while her children were toddlers. In 1962, the FBI duly noted her as a new Guild member. Fay enjoyed the ringside seat Guild membership gave her to the fight among Old Leftists over shifting the entire Guild's focus to civil rights abuses in the South. Though SNCC welcomed the Guild's help in launching Freedom Summer, the NAACP Legal Defense Fund threatened to cancel its own participation. Dr. King's SCLC was also unwelcoming.

Undaunted, Fay's mentor Barney Dreyfus, the long-time executive director of the San Francisco Guild chapter, had made civil rights work a priority when he assumed leadership of the national association in 1963. Dreyfus then collaborated with Detroit labor lawyer Ernest Goodman, the Guild's new president, and his partner George Crockett, the Guild's first black vice president. Crockett proposed to head a new Guild outpost to document abuses in Jackson, Mississippi — "the belly of the beast."[2] Fay and Marvin eagerly recruited young blood to support this effort.

Momentous changes were already in the air. Responding to a dire report from the federal Commission on Civil Rights on the situation in Mississippi, Congress passed the 1964 Civil Rights Act. President Johnson would soon add his signature to abolish all remaining Jim Crow laws, prohibit mandatory racial segregation in schools, housing, or hiring by the government or private sector. Mississippi officials geared up as if they were refighting the Civil War.

Two teenage black civil rights workers, Charles Moore and Henry Dee, had just gone missing in May of 1964. In early June of 1964, Fay joined the other members of her office at a luncheon at the Sheraton Hotel to hear Goodman speak about the Guild's summer plans in the Cotton Belt. Ironically, three months earlier Fay had gone to the Sheraton to observe picketing and arrests of activists protesting the hotel's own racist hiring policies.

Goodman sought volunteers to offer legal assistance in Mississippi during the coming summer: one or two weeks each; pay your own way. Fay was inspired to sign up. Marvin agreed to watch Neal and Oriane in her absence. He planned to go to Mississippi on a different week that summer, equally impressed with the historic occasion it presented. In late June, three other civil rights workers were declared missing, two whites and one black student — New Yorker Andrew Goodman and CORE workers Michael Schwerner and James Chaney. At George Crockett's request, the trio had planned to investigate the burning of a church in Philadelphia, Mississippi. The assumption among SNCC staff and volunteers was that all three were dead. The mutilated bodies of Moore and Dee, along with two unknown other bodies, would be found that summer in the Mississippi River while search teams looked for Schwerner, Goodman and Chaney.

The danger did not dissuade Fay from her plans to go to Jackson in August. Before she left, she began volunteer work in her own office library, doing research for the Guild's Mississippi Project. Under Barney Dreyfus's direction, Fay helped address the constitutional issues raised in three cases arising from prosecutions of volunteers in the City of Greenwood, including SNCC leader Stokely Carmichael, charged with willfully obstructing public streets and a creative array of other charges. To the Guild lawyers, the official's real purpose was obvious — to intimidate local blacks from registering to vote.

Less than a week before Fay's departure for Mississippi, searchers found the bodies of the three missing civil rights workers buried in a red clay dam in Neshoba County. When Fay arrived on August 10, 1964, tensions in Jackson remained high. Local newspapers reinforced the hostility that filled the air. *The Clarion-Ledger* and the *Jackson Daily News* repeatedly referred to the 1964 summer volunteers as "unkempt agitators" and "race mixing invaders."[3] Crockett and his volunteers kept risks down by sleeping on cots in the Guild's new office.

During Fay's short stay, local toughs beat a voter registration worker over the head with a baseball bat outside his office; others shot at a carload of volunteers. No one saw who set crosses on fire in front of the hotel where many visiting lawyers, doctors, ministers and news correspondents stayed. A city commissioner speculated that blacks had likely burned the crosses themselves to "agitate trouble."[4]

Five days after Fay's arrival, on the evening of August 15th, a black man was shot while sitting in a parked car in Greenwood. Segregationists targeted Silas McGee for trying to integrate "whites only" movie theaters. On August 16th, several hundred blacks gathered at a local church to protest McGee's shooting and were met by Mississippi police in full riot gear. The FBI responded slowly. Its agents preferred to document suspected subversives like Fay, noting the dates of her short visit to Jackson, Mississippi, to work at its newly opened Guild office.

Shortly after Fay returned, Marvin went to Mississippi to take depositions to support suits challenging the way state and local taxes shortchanged black neighborhoods. Nearly half of the state's black housing units lacked piped water; almost two-thirds had no flush toilets or lacked other municipal and state services routinely provided to white neighborhoods. The pervasive antagonism, the smell of fear and the risk of death in Mississippi left Fay and Marvin with the shared impression of having just been observers in a war zone.

On her return, Fay felt energized. She relished seeing the Berkeley campus develop into a hotbed of Movement fervor. One of her new acquaintances, Mario Savio, a twenty-year-old junior at Cal, had just been named SNCC's spokesperson on the Berkeley campus. An FBI agent showed up when they both spoke at a Berkeley middle school about Mississippi Freedom Summer and noted their radical affiliations.

When Mario returned to Berkeley in September of 1964 from Mississippi, he became incensed that his own university was banning all political activities, including solicitation of SNCC volunteers and funds to support civil rights efforts. In mid-September Mario helped lead a demonstration and was suspended with five other students. That led to more demonstrations and arrests. Peter Franck, a new Guild Board member recruited by Fay and Marvin, had just set up his first law practice in Berkeley. Franck began representing students in the dispute.

On December 2, 1964, thousands of students amassed at noon on the plaza outside Sproul Hall to protest the threatened suspension of Mario Savio and other student activists. Savio then gave his famous call to action:

> There is a time when the operation of the machine becomes so odious, makes you so sick at heart, that you can't take part; and you've got to put your bodies upon the gears and upon the wheels, upon the levers, upon all the apparatus and you've got to make it stop . . . to indicate to the people who run it, to the people who own it, that unless you're free, the machine will be prevented from working at all.[5]

When he finished, Savio and singer Joan Baez began singing "We Shall Overcome" as they led more than 1000 students inside the building to occupy all four floors. The students set up study areas, a first aid station, a food station and space for recreation. Some, for inspiration, watched *Operation Abolition*, a slanted HUAC documentary widely disseminated to sway public opinion against the San Francisco protesters on "Black Friday," May 13, 1960, that had also involved students from Cal. The FSM demonstrators planned a prolonged protest until the administration heeded their demands.

Over six hundred uniformed police officers showed up that night to reinforce the University and Berkeley Police Departments as they carried out orders from Governor Edmund G. Brown for the largest mass arrest in California history.[6] Savio had earlier contacted Bob Treuhaft, who arrived just in time to become the first arrestee. Inside Sproul Hall, the police then arrested everyone they saw as they worked their way down from the top floor. By the time the police arrived, Joan Baez was among those who had already left. Men and women were separated, fingerprinted and searched, then loaded into buses and paddy wagons. The men headed for the Berkeley City Jail, the Oakland City Jail or the Santa Rita Rehabilitation Center. No one knew where all the women had been taken. Bob Treuhaft went with the first batch to the Santa Rita jail, as did Mario Savio. A borrowed office in Wheeler Hall was immediately dubbed "Legal Central."

One of the earliest calls for help went out to Fay. She rushed over. The student in charge, Milton Hare, had no idea who had called this pony-tailed, Leftist attorney. She looked under thirty, dressed like a student in a pale cotton work blouse and pants. Her skin glowed. Fay appeared like a ray of sunshine — beautiful, warm and knowledgeable. Everybody at Legal Central secretly fell in love with her. Milton said, "You couldn't help it."

Milton and Fay started making phone calls and got almost forty lawyers to offer free representation to the arrestees. Fay then tracked down the whereabouts of the arrested women being held in an armory south of the Oakland airport. When they got word that Santa Rita was ready to release the arrestees on bail, Milton had been awake for at least forty hours. He and Fay gathered up the paperwork, Milton borrowed a co-worker's Volkswagen and Fay hung on white-knuckled and silent while Milton drove like a maniac. (Running another errand, later in December, Milton totaled that same car and was sidelined with injuries.)

The Santa Rita jail was surrounded by barbed wire. It had previously been an army installation and appeared quite intimidating. When they arrived at the entrance gate, Fay took charge. She opened her billfold for the guards, reached past Milton, stuck it out the driver's window and said, "We're lawyers for the Berkeley arrestees." They were waved through. This ploy worked at other checkpoints, including the main reception desk. Fay and Milton were permitted to speak for half an hour to a large crowd of unwashed, sleep-deprived students in a sparsely furnished detention room. While Bob Treuhaft remained fuming in a nearby isolation cell, Fay explained the bail bond process and assured the arrestees they would be released promptly. A week after the demonstrations, negotiators reached an agreement with the administration. The university backed down. Political speech would be permitted on campus starting January 4, 1965.

After Fay moved to a larger Berkeley apartment, she decided to hold a Seder for SNCC friends at her home. She incorporated into it references to Martin Luther King, Jr., and the Civil Rights Movement. Jewish activists had, by then, been in the forefront of the Civil Rights

Movement for decades, empathizing with blacks because of shared histories of bigotry, slavery and violent death. That spring of 1965 Fay was more upbeat than she had been in several years. Despite Marvin's involvement in a serious relationship with another woman, he and Fay maintained strong ties through their political activities and shared parenting of Neal and Oriane. By then, Fay had gotten over Stanley Moore. When Marvin began to talk more seriously about divorce, Fay campaigned hard to win Marvin's return and prevailed. One spring day, she excitedly burst into Barney Dreyfus's office to announce that she and Marvin were getting back together.

The Stenders celebrated their reunion by leasing a house on Grant Street in the Berkeley flats that had previously belonged to a friend in the Guild. It was the one Fay would still occupy when she was shot in 1979. Located in an area her parents had always looked down upon, the gray, two-story, five-bedroom house was not stylish and had no central heating. But it stood in a sociable, biracial neighborhood and came with an affordable purchase option. Fay loved the plum tree in the front yard.

The Stenders wasted no time making their new living room a gathering place for Leftist friends, galvanized by the escalating Vietnam War. Holding meetings at home was far easier on Fay. Her kids could simply go in and out. Potluck barbecues at the Stenders were the norm long before most people considered the idea. Fay rarely cooked and felt little urge to clean her cluttered house before inviting friends over.

That summer of 1965, Peter Franck and fellow civil rights activist Aryay Lenske had an idea for a new project they discussed over breakfast with Marvin and Fay and a few other young Turks from the local Guild. Franck had begun handling conscientious objector cases under the tutelage of Frances Heisler, who had been among the first lawyers to take such cases during World War II. Now in semi-retirement, the Austrian-born pacifist resided in the wealthy coastal town of Carmel. Heisler had a rich friend who offered to help bankroll Franck's proposal to set up an umbrella organization to oversee the defense of draft resisters and other anti-war demonstrators. Fay and Marvin suggested expanding legal assistance from just representing draft resistors to include the Movement's wide range of social and political causes. Over the Stenders' breakfast table, the gathered friends gave the proposal the ambitious title "Council for Justice" and considered who else to recruit.

The CFJ would be run by an executive committee. With proper coordination, they could avoid repeating past mistakes in discrimination suits against the Sheraton Palace and Auto Row in San Francisco and the Free Speech Movement (FSM) case in Berkeley. One of their members, Beverly Axelrod, had almost gone bankrupt in aggressively defending the San Francisco protest prosecutions the year before. In the FSM case, Axelrod and lead counsel Mal Burnstein had opted instead for a judge trial, greatly surprising prosecutor Lowell Jensen. Peter Franck had assisted the defense, biting his tongue as a lawyer too green to voice his serious misgivings about the decision to waive a jury. The grueling trial lasted most of the summer of 1965, drew little public attention and resulted in the judge imposing some heavy sentences. The lawyers vowed never to forego a jury again in a political case.

The original aim of the Council for Justice was to provide legal support for the Vietnam Day Committee (VDC), formed earlier that year by two anti-war activists. Co-chairs Jerry Rubin and Robert Hurwitt hoped to launch the world's largest anti-war demonstration, convinced that by dramatically increasing the visibility and numbers of those opposing the war, they might force withdrawal of all U.S. troops from Vietnam.

A thirty-six-hour VDC teach-in held in May 1965 had already put Berkeley "on the war-protest map"[7] with total attendance exceeding 35,000 people. The CFJ executive committee made a detailed plan of action assigning different roles to various lawyer volunteers. Marvin was designated as "bail central" — the source whom lawyers stationed at the jailhouses would consult to arrange for bail money. Fay would play the safer role of dispatcher, along with Guild lawyer Al Brotsky.

On the date of the march, more than ten thousand demonstrators walked without incident until they were attacked by Hell's Angels near the Oakland border. Jerry Rubin and his fellow planners wanted to mount an even larger parade in late November. Fay and Marvin helped prepare a complaint challenging Oakland's denial of a permit, which Peter Franck and Barney Dreyfus then successfully pursued in federal court. The resulting late November march from the Berkeley campus

Fay's former law partner Peter Franck. (Photo circa 1981.)

As a Cal undergraduate in 1957, Peter Franck helped found SLATE, the first Progressive campus political party to emerge in the Cold War era. SLATE brought the world's issues to campus, opposing discriminatory housing, the nuclear bomb, the death penalty, and HUAC persecutions. In 1964, as a new attorney, Franck represented leaders of the Free Speech Movement. Then the Stenders invited him to join the San Francisco Lawyers Guild board, where he led young Turks prodding the Guild to become more activist. In 1965, Franck began representing the rock band "Country Joe and the Fish," launching his long, successful career in entertainment law. That same year, he and Aryay Lenske cofounded the Council for Justice over breakfast at the Stenders.

to DeFremery Park in North Oakland drew the largest crowd yet to engage in an anti-war rally in the entire Bay Area. Flush with success, VDC planned more protests for 1966.

Meanwhile, a major new opportunity surfaced for the Council for Justice. From 1962 to 1965, labor leader Cesar Chavez had organized farm workers in Tulare County in the Central Valley of California, assembling a large union with the help from outside activists. Through Frances Heisler, Chavez soon approached Peter Franck and the Council for Justice for legal help in support of strikers. Franck sent new Guild member Alex Hoffmann 250 miles south from Berkeley to Delano. The Viennese-born Yale Law School graduate quickly gained the respect of his Latino clients. Soon, a political firestorm enveloped the union. Escalating boycotts had spread to cities across the country and catapulted the farm workers to national attention, gaining support from traditional labor, civil rights and religious groups. New York Senator Bobby Kennedy and California Senator George Murphy scheduled hearings in Sacramento for March of 1966 on the problems of migratory labor, prompting the strikers to plan a three-hundred-mile *peregrinación* (march) from Delano to the hearings. With help from everyone in the Council for Justice, the pilgrimage proved wildly successful, convincing Senator Kennedy to endorse the union's objective of a $1.25 minimum wage and a guarantee that farm workers could engage in collective bargaining.

Peter Franck also recruited Marvin to represent Chavez in defense of criminal charges arising from his union organizing. The labor leader was charged with illegally used a bullhorn from a truck on the highway to address farm workers in the fields. Fay worked behind the scenes to research and draft the brief challenging the constitutionality of the anti-bullhorn ordinance.

At the same time, in Washington D.C., the civil rights cases Fay had begun work on in Mississippi in the summer of 1964 had just reached an ominous crossroads: the United States Supreme Court granted state officials a hearing on their request to reverse a partial victory Crockett's legal team had obtained. Fay likely contributed one unusual argument before the Supreme Court. The high court still had one traditional

Jewish seat among the nine old men. It was now occupied by Abe Fortas, her late friend Hammy's ex-partner. To capture Fortas's attention, the *Peacock* brief compared African-Americans' plight in the United States to Jewish flight from bondage in ancient Egypt, using the same theme as Fay's Seder for SNCC friends the prior spring.[8]

Fay flew to Washington, D.C. to hear the historic oral argument in the *Peacock* case the weekend of April 23–24, 1966. It was the best time of year to visit Washington, when the temperature was moderate and the cherry trees were in bloom. The imposing neoclassic temple across the street from the Capitol had only been completed in 1935. It was younger than Fay. Climbing the wide steps of its main entrance, visitors could read the words "EQUAL JUSTICE UNDER LAW" carved in the façade.

The immense courtroom was on the first floor, facing a main hall filled with statuary. High on its north and south walls were two forty-foot friezes depicting great lawmakers throughout history. One could easily pick out Moses with the Ten Commandments in Hebrew. A bronze railing separated public seating from the central rows reserved for the Supreme Court Bar, which now included Fay. On Monday, April 25, the *Peacock* team had an opportunity to observe other oral arguments. In the center sat Chief Justice Earl Warren himself. Fay easily recognized the spry William "Wild Bill" Douglas with his shock of white hair, whom her friend Bob Hamilton had clerked for a decade earlier. Fifty-year-old former athlete "Whizzer" White stood out as well. Fay also recognized Hugo Black, now eighty, whom she had spilled wine on at a reception at the University of Chicago when she was a law student.

On Tuesday morning, Fay could hardly contain her excitement. For the occasion, she had bought a stylish suit accessorized with an orchid, likely bestowed by a chivalrous New Orleanian colleague to adorn the only woman on the *Peacock* legal team. Another civil rights case was heard first. Fay watched Stanford Professor Tony Amsterdam argue for the integration of Atlanta restaurants. Fay left feeling giddy from the experience. She boarded the plane home still wearing her orchid. It had been fifteen years since Fay informed her good friend Pip, "I want to change things." Her fervent desire seemed about to come true.

Sam Abrahams' asbestos consulting business took him around the world in the late 1950s. Here, Sam and Ruby are pictured in Athens in 1958 leaving the Parthenon — 20 years before Fay would get there. Sam most enjoyed working in Bilbao, Spain. In 1966, he startled Fay with news that he and Ruby planned to retire to Bilbao. But it was not to be. That fall he was diagnosed with mesothelioma and died just shy of his 62d birthday.

■ 9 ■

Unfulfilled

*Sometimes blocked in,
sometimes reaching out,
one moment your life is a stone in you,
and the next, a star.*[1]

— RAINER MARIA RILKE, "SUNSET"

Just a day after the *Peacock* oral argument, without explanation, a bare majority of the Supreme Court dismissed from its docket another pending civil rights case. The case permitted punitive damages against the NAACP. The four dissenting justices warned that the high court's action paved the way for "crushing verdicts that may stifle organized dissent."[2] Still, Fay retained faith in the judiciary to advance civil rights.

The Vietnam Day Committee had just held another major peace rally in April. This time arrested demonstrators were advised to plead guilty to most of the minor offenses, pay fines and receive no jail time. Charles Garry represented them with Fay's assistance on one key issue: challenging a city ordinance against the use of a sound truck without advance permission from the local chief of police. Fay had handy her First Amendment research for Cesar Chavez's case. Unlike in Tulare County, where Alex Hoffmann had warned Fay and Marvin that the local municipal court judge was "a son of a bitch," the Berkeley judge readily agreed that the Berkeley ordinance was invalid. At least one anti-bullhorn ordinance was now history.

There was no shortage of potential cases for the Council for Justice. They represented grape boycotters arrested for leafletting cars in a Safeway parking lot and for protest "shop-ins" where they abandoned full baskets in the grocery store's aisles. Francis Heisler handled tax work for pacifist clients like Joan Baez, who sought refunds based on conscientious objection to the Vietnam War. Assisting Heisler, Fay added to the celebrities among her growing list of contacts. Meanwhile, as legal costs mounted, the CFJ Executive Committee orchestrated a series of fund-raisers, including a brunch Fay and Marvin held at their home for Cesar Chavez.

On June 20, 1966, the Supreme Court issued several rulings from its spring session, including *Peacock*. By a five-to-four vote, the Supreme Court ordered the *Peacock* case sent back to the Mississippi state courts — ensuring years of delay before federal courts ever took a look at the claimed wholesale violations of the defendants' civil rights. The dissent penned by Justice Douglas captured the frustration of Fay and her co-counsel at this defeat: "[T]o deny relief [is] . . . to aggravate a wrong."[3] Activists had already turned to Congress to provide more relief through the hotly contested Civil Rights Act of 1965. The direction racial confrontations would take remained to be seen.

One major court battle lost, Fay soldiered on. Back in Tulare County, Cesar Chavez still faced potential conviction for the use of his bullhorn in recruiting union members. When the local judge denied relief in the summer of 1966, Marvin appealed, relying on Fay to write the brief. The following year, Marvin and Peter Franck would fly down to Fresno in Franck's Cessna to handle oral argument. The pair later received all the public credit for Chavez's ultimate victory. Still, Fay could take private satisfaction in her key role in persuading the appellate court to repudiate its own prior position: "The Tulare ordinance presents a great opportunity for discrimination, political preference and the type of censorship that is repugnant to the very concept upon which our free form of government is founded."[4]

This victory was a confidence builder for Fay. By the time the opinion issued, however, the Council for Justice had long ceased to exist.

Back in the summer of 1966, it had become clear that the group was but a small band-aid for Cesar Chavez during a time of transition to in-house lawyers with help from a new state legal assistance program. By October of 1966, the CFJ collapsed under mounting debt and closed its doors. In December, Alex Hoffmann turned over his remaining matters in Delano to new counsel and headed home. Ancient Spartan warriors went off to war directed to come back with their shields or on them. Alex Hoffmann, suffering from a slipped disc, came back flat on his back.

* * *

As the CFJ was on its last legs, Fay was preoccupied by her parents' decision to move permanently overseas. Still conservative in his politics, Sam disliked Fay's growing recognition in the Berkeley community as a proponent of Leftist causes. When meeting someone new, he bristled at being identified as "Fay Stender's father," emphatically telling his wife and close friends that was not why he had come into this world. Sam decided to retire young. He and Ruby had traveled abroad often in recent years whenever Sam was hired to design plants for manufacturing asbestos insulation materials or consulted on existing factories. The couple had grown particularly enamored of life in the Basque city of Bilbao. But the move was not to be.

Sam's own father had died at sixty-two and Sam had a premonition he would die at that age as well. In September of 1966, Sam fell ill and his doctors scheduled immediate surgery. Sam looked at his watch as he entered the operating room. He checked it again as soon as he awoke. Sam realized from the little time that had passed that the surgeon had found his abdomen filled with tiny asbestos fibers and hopelessly closed the incision again. The diagnosis of terminal mesothelioma came three months before Sam's sixty-second birthday. Many of his old colleagues from the war days were then dying of cancer as well. Sam grew despondent, lost faith in his religion and refused to see a rabbi as he lay dying.

Meanwhile, Fay's days grew increasingly hectic — crammed with part-time work, her children's music lessons, dance classes, sports, and political get-togethers. A young mover-and-shaker then lived behind the

Stenders, law student Neal Goldschmidt. Goldschmidt threw frequent parties. Fay relished adding him to her growing network. Ambitious and talented, within little more than a decade Goldschmidt would hold a cabinet position in President Carter's administration and later be elected Governor of Oregon. Still, Fay missed the electricity of the Council for Justice and Friends of SNCC.

By mid-1966, local support for SNCC had dissipated after SNCC purged its ranks of white activists. A turning point came in early June, following a voter registration "March Against Fear" to Jackson, Mississippi, by James Meredith, the first black student admitted by Ole Miss. On the second day, a sniper wounded Meredith with a shotgun blast. Dr. King and SNCC leader Stokely Carmichael decided to continue the march for Meredith. Carmichael was arrested and decided it was time to announce a new strategy. He then sent shock waves across the country from the Greenwood, Mississippi, jail by making an historic "Black Power" speech in which he repudiated Dr. King's pacifist approach to civil rights.[5]

Despite their stark differences on domestic strategies, Dr. King later joined forces with Carmichael in openly opposing the Vietnam War. The two helped lead peace marches on April 15, 1967, in New York and San Francisco that, combined, drew over 250,000 supporters, including Fay and Marvin. The FBI kept busy, noting the names of all the professionals who now openly opposed the war.

As more young men publicly burned their draft cards or otherwise resisted the draft, Fay focused her practice on representing them. She wrote a how-to article for Guild lawyers, exploring all the different angles one could pursue if time and money permitted. Yet the results ultimately demoralized Fay. While she delayed or thwarted the 1-A classification of middle class whites, young men of color often took their place on the front lines in Vietnam. "I knew for every one [case] I handled, there were many Third World People who really needed a lawyer and couldn't get one."[6]

Fay soon had a confidant at work in Al Brotsky, a transplanted New York Jew who joined the Garry firm in mid-1967, evicting Don Kerson from the office next to Fay's. Brotsky had already met Fay and Marvin through the Lawyers Guild. The jovial, happily married labor lawyer was then in his forties. With both kids now in elementary school, Fay finally began working at the firm full-time, including frequent Saturday mornings. Al occasionally asked Fay for research on a labor or personal injury case. Fay still found working with Barney Dreyfus on death penalty cases the most thrilling. It also raised her stature among Leftist lawyer friends.

Yet, stretched in two directions, Fay found her situation increasingly unrewarding. Even on weekends, the only offspring welcome at work were Al's teenagers, who covered the phones for absent staff. Al noticed Fay's growing despondence and provided a sympathetic ear. Her home life was miserable. Marvin was absent long hours, uncommunicative and having another affair. That did not surprise Al, who could see how Fay's intensity might be overwhelming.

Fay also confided to Al her growing frustrations with her role at the firm. She saw no prospects for partnership and felt mired in a rut worn between the library and her typewriter. Other women in their small Leftist community had already made substantial impact on the world, though most were a generation older than Fay. Decca Mitford and Elsa Knight Thompson, the former BBC announcer who became KPFA's Public Affairs Director, were internationally renowned. Ann Ginger had just founded the Meiklejohn Institute for civil rights research. Dobby Walker was a name partner in the Treuhaft firm. Like Ann Ginger, Walker had garnered national recognition for her Guild work.

Fay most envied the achievements of Beverly Axelrod, who was eight years her senior. Axelrod, recently divorced, had raised two sons while practicing law and achieving extraordinary accomplishments for the Movement. She had risked jail in Louisiana for the Congress of Racial Equality, coordinated the 1964 Sheraton Palace and Auto Row employment discrimination lawsuits in San Francisco, defended Free Speech Movement protesters at Cal, and championed farm workers through the Council for Justice. Axelrod also traveled to North Viet Nam in 1965, where she met with Foreign Minister Madame Binh of the provisional revolutionary government, and followed up by organizing the first American anti-war protest to include women and children.

KPFA Public Affairs Director Elsa Knight Thompson (1906–1983). (Photo circa 1964.)

Alex shared a two-bedroom apartment in Berkeley with Elsa. She, like other close friends and family, called him by his nickname, "Sasha." Alex later became a close confidant of Huey Newton. On Newton's release from prison in August 1970, Elsa and Alex's apartment was the first place he stayed.

The following year, Beverly Axelrod was once again in the spotlight after she signed up a serial rapist at Folsom as one of her new clients. Inspired by Malcolm X, Eldridge Cleaver had begun writing in prison about his fixation on white women, which Cleaver viewed in retrospect as politically motivated. Cleaver was aware that convicted Lover's Lane rapist Caryl Chessman, the infamous "Red Light Bandit," had written four best-selling books while on death row in the 1950s. Cleaver believed his own work had similar potential. He wrote to every criminal lawyer listed in a directory, offering an interest in his manuscript as compensation for helping him win his freedom. Axelrod read his powerful essays and began corresponding with Cleaver. As she worked to gain his release, Axelrod fell in love with Cleaver. This new romance was spurred in part by Cleaver's resemblance to Beverly's recent lover Reggie Majors, a prominent black journalist who had refused to leave his wife to marry Beverly.

Axelrod sent best-selling author Norman Mailer parts of Cleaver's manuscript and letters. With Mailer's strong endorsement, she got the essays published in *Ramparts* magazine. By the time Axelrod obtained Cleaver's release from Folsom in December of 1966, his essays had won him a national following and a job offer from *Ramparts*. Within months, Beverly's friends in the Lawyers Guild gathered to celebrate publication of Cleaver's essays in the book, *Soul On Ice*, dedicated to Beverly — his new love. As Fay joined friends toasting the happy couple, she hungered for more meaning in her own career. Fay had no idea her chance for similar glory lay just around the corner.

ACT TWO

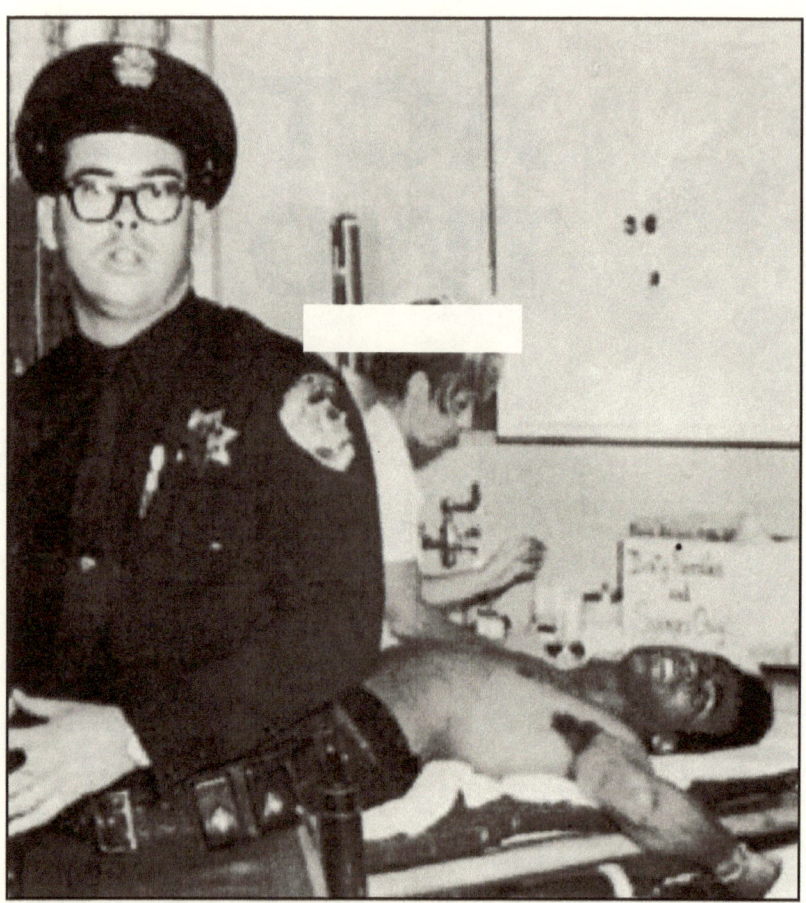

Fay first saw Huey Newton in the hospital under armed guard. This newspaper photo the day he was shot become the cover of a pamphlet the defense team quickly distributed to gain community support for his defense. The caption asked: "Can a black man get a fair trial?"

■ 1 ■
Second Chair at the Latest Trial of the Century

Every Negro ever convicted of killing a police officer has died in the gas chamber. So what chance did I have?[1]
DEATH-ROW INMATE AARON MITCHELL INTERVIEWED THE DAY OF HIS EXECUTION ON APRIL 12, 1967

I don't remember anyone thinking that Huey Newton, a person who advocated the use of guns, could shoot an Oakland police officer and expect to walk away from it. Everyone thought that surely he would be convicted of first-degree murder.[2]
PIONEERING AFRICAN-AMERICAN TV REPORTER BELVA DAVIS

By late October 1967, Fay might have thought she knew what her opportunity would be. Oakland made international headlines following a blockade of the Oakland Induction Center by thousands of demonstrators during Stop the Draft Week. The largest anti-war protest to date began on October 16 and ended several days later when demonstrators were forcibly dispersed by heavily reinforced police armed with pellet guns, stun grenades and nightsticks. Covering the confrontation for her San Francisco TV station, cub reporter Belva Davis knew she was witnessing history: "The Bay Area felt like ground zero in a generational battle for the soul of the country."³ Charles Garry signed up to be lead counsel for seven activists arrested for organizing Stop the Draft Week. But barely a week later he got a call to take on an even bigger challenge.

The lead story in *The Oakland Tribune* on October 28, 1967, blamed a local black militant named Huey Newton for an early morning shootout in West Oakland resulting in the death of one Oakland policeman and the wounding of another. At the time, Garry knew little about the Black Panther Party for Self-Defense or its co-founder, who lay hospitalized with a bullet wound in his abdomen. A few days later, when Charles Garry poked his head into Fay's cubicle on his way to see his new client in the hospital, Fay jumped at the chance to accompany him.

Garry really could not handle another high-profile case at the same time as he agreed to lead the Oakland Seven defense team. Yet Garry could not resist Beverly Axelrod's urgent plea for help. Beverly and her new lover Eldridge Cleaver had befriended Huey Newton the prior spring. The two had helped launch the Panther underground newspaper in Beverly's living room just weeks before the mainstream media first focused on the Black Panthers as a dangerous new militant group from Oakland, California who prompted the state's enactment of strict new gun control laws.

Garry developed instant empathy for Newton when Garry had rushed with Beverly to the hospital to meet the accused cop killer. Fay, too, would never forget the impact of seeing Huey Newton lying half-naked under armed guard as he recovered from life-saving surgery. At first sight, she felt a strong sexual attraction. She also reacted with indignation at his helpless condition. She would do whatever it took to save Newton's life. It would be a monumental task.

Staunch opponents of the death penalty like Fay Stender and Charles Garry knew that Governor Reagan had strongly endorsed capital punishment in his 1966 campaign. In April 1967, the popular new governor had followed through by declining to halt the execution of an African-American man on death row for killing a policeman in a botched robbery. Sending a leader of black militants like Huey Newton to the gas chamber for another officer's death would be a crowning achievement for Governor Reagan. The path to save Huey Newton's life would be to win his acquittal at trial — an unheard-of result when the victim was a policeman.

Charles Garry planned a two-pronged approach: a super-aggressive defense in court raising every possible factual and legal issue, and a major publicity campaign. For both aspects Fay's skills would be essential — particularly in researching and writing motions addressed to technical defects in the prosecution. Garry had developed no skills of his own in this critical area.

First, publicity was needed to generate sympathy for Newton as a victim of police aggression and to harness support for the Panthers. The small militant group already had gained admiration in the local black community for lobbying for stoplights at dangerous intersections and for challenging oppressive police tactics. In addition, unlike Stokely Carmichael and other black militants, the Panthers welcomed the support of radical whites. The Panthers had been impressed by white anti-war activists arrested during Stop the Draft Week and wanted to reach out to the coalition already rallying in support of the Oakland Seven.

Fay had two quick assignments addressing both the legal and political angles. A local physician contacted their office after she saw the photo of Huey Newton grimacing in pain, his arms pulled back by tight handcuffs securing him to the gurney. The doctor was appalled that Kaiser staff had allowed police to aggravate their patient's injury while he was awaiting abdominal surgery. Garry immediately asked Fay to file a lawsuit against Kaiser Hospital for malpractice. Garry then trumpeted Newton's ordeal to the press as another example of how black men were systematically mistreated. Garry also directed Fay and Alex Hoffmann to prepare papers seeking to compel the prosecutor to reveal evidence taken from the crime scene — ballistics reports, police files related to the Black Panthers, anything that might be useful to the defense.

Fay and Alex worked nonstop to get the discovery motion done for the first hearing on November 16. Their office also had its hands full preparing a leaflet for volunteers to distribute to the crowds, announcing Garry's first press conference. The flyer also informed the public about the Panthers' ten-point political platform, which included armed self-defense against police brutality. The Panther leader's legal team hoped to convince as many members of the community as possible that Huey's practice of following the police around on patrol with a law book to read arrestees their rights made him a target for harassment.

On the morning of November 13, prosecutor Lowell Jensen presented evidence to the county grand jury to support Newton's indictment. Defense lawyers had no access to that confidential proceeding. They only learned its outcome at the same time as the press that afternoon after the panel indicted Newton for murder, assault and kidnapping. A fourth charge was based on Newton's prior record as a convicted felon. The purpose of that charge was to increase the sentence for conviction of any new crimes. The murder charge by itself justified the death penalty.

The following day brought some heartening news for the defense from the California Supreme Court, which had just stayed two pending executions while the high court considered the constitutionality of the death penalty. Fay hoped for a similar reprieve if Newton were convicted. She assumed, like Charles Garry did, that the more they publicized Newton, the more carefully the courts would scrutinize the prosecutor's case against him for possible flaws, especially with Newton's life on the line.

To the defense team's delight, the Panthers' chief of staff David Hilliard made good use of a bullhorn. Hilliard drove a borrowed van through flatland neighborhoods to urge a crowd of demonstrators to gather outside the courthouse on the day of the first hearing to ensure that Huey was treated fairly. Outside, they chanted, "Free Huey, Jail the Pigs," and promised to keep picketing the courthouse daily until Huey was free. Some filed into the gallery where Huey gave them a clenched fist salute. More than anything the defense needed to buy time to prepare for trial. Garry quickly asked the judge for a delay of the proceedings so the defense could review the grand jury transcript.

Over the next couple of days, Fay and Alex Hoffmann both pored over the transcript, learning that the police had only found one gun but believed three were used. Newton's bloodied law book was found at the scene as was a half-written ticket with his name on it. The pathologist concluded that the deceased policeman, Officer John Frey, was shot five times, twice at close range from behind. The bullets recovered from Frey's body did not come from surviving officer Herbert "Cliff" Heanes' revolver, the only gun found at the scene.

Heanes had been released from the hospital still recovering from his wound and gave the grand jury dramatic firsthand testimony about the shootout. Heanes swore that he saw Frey writing a ticket for Huey Newton as Frey stood with Newton behind Frey's patrol car. Then gunfire erupted from Newton's "general vicinity" and Heanes shot back before blacking out from his own wound.

More damaging testimony came from an African-American man named Dell Ross. Ross had been parked around the corner at the time of the shooting. He testified that two men jumped into his car and kidnapped him at gunpoint. Ross told the grand jury that one of the men was wounded, but still bragged to his companion when they were riding in the car, "I'd a kept shooting if the gun hadn't jammed, I'm too mean to die." The other reassured him, "You shot two dudes. You still got two dudes."[4] The two had bolted from the car at an intersection and disappeared. Ross later identified a photo of Newton as the wounded man with a gun. This was not going to be an easy case to defend.

Fay immediately went to work with Barney Dreyfus to prepare a constitutional challenge to the composition of the grand jury that indicted Newton for murder. The Alameda County grand jury serving in 1967 had only one black member, who was not present the day Newton was indicted. The two lawyers argued that the grand jury appointments were skewed by county judges who systematically left out young people, blacks and other minorities, poor and low-income wage earners. When the argument failed, they took an appeal. When that did not succeed, they sought further review in federal court.

As Fay dived into the efforts to free Huey, she should have paid closer heed to what had just happened to Beverly Axelrod. After Beverly won Eldridge Cleaver's freedom and launched him as a journalist and acclaimed new author, Cleaver dumped his middle-aged fiancée. In the spring of 1967 Eldridge had fallen in love with a young black SNCC activist when he had taken a trip back to Vanderbilt University in Tennessee sponsored by *Ramparts* magazine. Much to Beverly's dismay, Kathleen Neal had come out to visit Eldridge that summer. When Kathleen returned to California again to help Eldridge launch Newton's defense committee, Eldridge told Beverly he was through with all white women.

To add insult to injury, Eldridge gave his new fiancée the title of Communications Director for the Panthers. Beverly had never been officially acknowledged for her far more extensive work to date on the Party's behalf. Huey still welcomed Beverly's visits at the jail and offered to dub her an honorary black woman, but Beverly was devastated. By December 1967 when Eldridge and Kathy Neal married, Beverly fled from the Bay Area, miserable at her callous treatment by the man she believed to be her long-sought soul mate.

In January, Fay started making regular visits to Huey Newton in the Alameda County Jail. Her aim was to gather personal information in the unrealistic hope she could demonstrate that Newton was a good candidate for release on bail prior to his death penalty trial. Huey, in turn, was highly motivated to win her over, just as Eldridge had been when his freedom from prison depended on Beverly Axelrod's legal talents. Fay did not know what to expect when she interviewed her militant client, but was delighted at his warm reception. She was amazed to hear that Huey had classical music training as a child, and particularly enjoyed playing Tchaikovsky's Nutcracker Suite.

Fay would work night and day for this Movement hero over the following months. Marvin welcomed her restored passion for life. Yet Fay saw little of her husband while consumed with freeing the man some Leftists now dubbed America's Che Guevara. She often gulped down dinner and returned to work after the family went to bed, sometimes attending Panther meetings into the wee hours. In her spare time, Fay heeded Newton's request that she read the writings of Malcolm X and Frantz Fanon to gain better insight into the Panthers' own philosophy. Fay felt like a highly valued comrade in a joint cause to transform society — not unlike the euphoria Beverly had felt before she bolted into exile.

Charles Garry told Fay that what he needed her help with most of all was to get the newly assigned trial judge to delay the trial from its scheduled early May 1968 start date. Without more time, the chances were slim to none that they could develop a winning strategy for Newton's defense. A major obstacle was all the bad publicity the Panthers had gotten in the mainstream press. The defense team assumed *The Oakland Tribune's* negative coverage of the shooting had already infected many people in the local jury pool. Yet no other county in California would have provided a better place to try the case than the Panthers' home town.

To generate more favorable publicity, Leftist reporters like Karen Wald, who wrote for *The Movement* newspaper, were given open access to Huey. Fay or Alex would stay by their client's side to make sure Newton said nothing that could be used against him at trial. Their office also tracked all negative stories in the media so they could bring them to the court's attention to argue that a delay of the trial was needed to help ensure an impartial jury.

Meanwhile, Fay put together a panel of sociologists from Cal to help uncover race bias in the anticipated jury panel. Her first call went to a Cal graduate student working on his Ph.D. in race relations who was on the staff of *The Movement* newspaper. Since 1964, David Wellman had also been a great fan of Fay's, stemming from when her soft-spoken words of wisdom first impressed him at a strategy session of Friends of SNCC. Wellman considered the Newton trial an opportunity he could not pass up and convinced two of his mentors on the faculty to join him at Fay's home. Together the four brainstormed ways to expose people with undesirable profiles and to identify members of the jury panel they would like to see in the jury of Newton's "peers" that would control whether Newton lived or died.

Just after their first meeting, the community grew far more polarized with shocking news on April 4 of Martin Luther King, Jr.'s assassination. King's death prompted riots across the country like the ones of the long hot summer of 1967. Two days later, Eldridge Cleaver led a caravan of armed Panthers into a confrontation with Oakland police. Several were arrested. After a siege of a house where Cleaver and 17-year-old Bobby Hutton were holed up, Cleaver surrendered stark naked. Hutton emerged wearing a coat and was shot dead on the street, unarmed. Eldridge Cleaver's probation was summarily revoked, and he was escorted in the middle of the night back to prison. The police accused the Panthers of attempted ambush and the Panthers accused the police of murdering a defenseless teenager. With the community split into two angry camps, Fay had no trouble getting Newton's trial postponed until June 10. Garry was desperate for yet more time. Fay put her long-planned overseas family vacation on hold and redoubled her efforts.

Prosecutor Lowell Jensen had been keeping Dell Ross in seclusion as well as another unnamed key witness. Fay argued that the defense could not prepare for trial properly unless Jensen revealed the name of the final witness. She also sought the location of both witnesses so the defense could send investigators out and the attorneys could have a chance to conduct interviews. At the time, Fay had no sympathy for the prosecutor's desire to protect his star witnesses from potential death threats. To her, the witnesses' fears paled in comparison to the needs of the Newton defense team.

For the last two months, they had been awaiting a key ruling from the United States Supreme Court that criminal defense attorneys expected would increase the number of women and minorities who could serve on death penalty juries. At last, *Witherspoon v. Illinois* issued in the first week of June. The high court ruled that death penalty juries could not consist solely of people predisposed to embrace the death penalty, excluding half of the adults in the country who had doubts about its wisdom. Outraged prosecutors were faced with the possibility of having to retry all the men on death row nationwide. Fay was pleased that the high court relied extensively on jury studies done by her husband Marvin's old boss at the University of Chicago, Professor Hans Zeisel. Judge Friedman granted another month's delay of the trial.

Meanwhile, Fay contacted Professor Zeisel and persuaded him to come west from Chicago to testify for free in the Newton case about the studies Zeisel had conducted. The defense had no money for experts, but they did have the hottest Movement case in the country as a lure. Professor Zeisel was happy to oblige. Then Fay turned to the volunteer experts she had already recruited from the Cal sociology department to draft hundreds of questions to ask potential jurors to smoke out evidence of racism. Fay had also been assigned other pretrial motions to make, including an unsuccessful attempt to move the trial to a larger venue. The defense wanted to accommodate the hordes of reporters, both mainstream and from the underground press, from across the country and overseas as well as local, who flocked to Oakland to cover this latest "trial of the century."

By June 1968, the Peace and Freedom Party named Eldridge Cleaver its candidate for President, Huey Newton its candidate for Congress, and Kathleen Cleaver and Bobby Seale its two candidates for the State Assembly from San Francisco and Oakland. Panther supporters busied themselves passing out campaign literature as well as "Free Huey" buttons, bumper stickers and signs to post on telephone poles. Security at the courthouse was the highest it had ever been. As recent Panther recruits with military training organized hordes of demonstrators, David Hilliard and Kathleen Cleaver led chants of "Free Huey." Followers carried signs that threatened "The Sky's the Limit" if he were not acquitted.

On the first day of trial, Fay and Charles Garry arrived late, looking exhausted. By then Fay was routinely putting in twelve-hour days and had had no weekend break. She sat down in the front row with Alex Hoffmann, just behind Charles Garry at the defense table. Given her pivotal role, Fay should have been seated next to Garry, but he had offered that chair to Ed Keating, the lawyer-publisher of *Ramparts* magazine, who had activated his law license just for the privilege of this ringside seat.

After several pretrial motions were denied, the trial started with Garry offering the evidence Fay had gathered, seeking to establish the unfairness of the jury panel. Both Charles Garry and Lowell Jensen reported death threats against them, yet Garry argued that all the security precautions would alienate the jury against the Panthers. Judge Friedman was not about to order any of the security withdrawn. Nor did Garry have any realistic hope to convince the skeptical judge that a fair trial could not be conducted. At least, they would make a record for appeal.

Fay had prepared an outline for Garry to use in handling each expert they called to testify on juror bias. Among them was a professor who had co-authored a book on the type of personality predisposed to convict defendants. Fay hoped Dr. Sanford would convince Judge Friedman to allow each potential juror to be isolated for interrogation to enhance the likelihood they would answer questions about bias honestly. That approach was rejected, yet the effort Fay had orchestrated to educate Judge Friedman had been time well spent because the expert testimony sensitized the judge to signs of deep-seated prejudice to which he would otherwise have not paid much attention. Judge Friedman was also persuaded to be very cautious about disqualifying jurors who expressed doubts about the death penalty so long as they promised that they could impose death if it was warranted under the judge's instructions.

Up until April of 1968, there had been another reason that far fewer minorities were permitted to serve on the Alameda County jury panel. Most failed an "IQ" test designed by the local bar association. The test assumed a shared cultural background. Fay's friend Penny Cooper and another deputy public defender brought a constitutional challenge to the IQ test before a sympathetic local judge. Much to Fay's delight, the judge banned use of the test because he found it unfairly discriminated against minorities. As a result, the Newton jury would be drawn from the entire county's voter list.

Fay's elation did not last long. She saw one after another member of a minority group claim that they could never render the death penalty against anyone, no matter the evidence. It was hard to tell whether that was really true or just an easy excuse to avoid serving on such an intensely polarizing case. Both Fay and Charles Garry were hoping that minorities would soft-peddle their misgivings about the death penalty, rather than leave Newton to the greater risk of capital punishment from an all-white panel who were less likely to have such qualms.

As the trial progressed, Fay took extensive notes to pass to Charles Garry or share with him at breaks. At night, she prepared witnesses, did research as needed and addressed procedural issues. Deputy Public Defender Penny Cooper observed the trial occasionally and realized Fay was the brains behind the legal issues raised by the defense who deserved equal credit with Garry for the amazing work being done on Newton's behalf. It bothered David Wellman to see Garry take Fay's role so much for granted. Garry took no notice of her. After the lunch recess on Wednesday, July 17, he did let Fay address the court briefly on a procedural matter before she resumed her note-taking.

To the disappointment of Fay and the professors with whom she collaborated, Garry never planned to read to each potential juror all or even most of the questions they prepared. He was an old-time, shoot-from-the-hip trial lawyer, with little patience for this new-fangled, scientific approach to jury selection. Garry's aim was to assess the jurors' body language more than their answers. Expert Bob Blauner, who had joined the defense team as a consultant, was particularly dismayed to see his and Fay's input ignored.

Garry assumed an impartial jury was unachievable. He stunned observers by forsaking the usual deference lawyers showed to potential jurors. Instead, Garry aggressively challenged those he believed were biased against his client and sought to intimidate others from acting on their racism. In contrast, he questioned lightly those he felt might be biased in his client's favor so the prosecutor had no excuse to toss them from the panel.

Underground papers had begun touting the prosecution as one that put America itself on trial for its history of racism. Jensen had reason to be particularly sensitive to the appearance of bias. The week before, another Alameda County judge had broken new ground by ruling that a prosecutor could not use his challenges to eliminate every person of the defendant's race. In doing his job, Jensen was both a stickler for high standards and worked hard to avoid even the appearance of bias. He wanted the entire community to feel Newton got a fair trial. Fay and trial consultant Bob Blauner were ready to accept the jury sooner than Charles Garry, who trusted his gut to keep using every challenge until there were none left. Jensen was willing to trust anyone who gave him reason to believe he or she could be fair, leaving a higher percentage of minorities and women on the panel than other prosecutors would likely have done.

Garry favored women and minorities and wound up with seven women out of the panel of twelve. One young woman juror was Latina and worked as an entry-level secretary. Another woman, whom some observers mistook for Latina, was a Portuguese-American bookkeeper married to an Hispanic construction worker. Three of the men were minorities: a Cuban-American machinist, a Japanese-American lab technician, and an African-American banker, David Harper. The defense team worried that despite Harper's reservations about the death penalty, the banker was likely an Uncle Tom, with no sympathy for the Panthers. But their strategy did not permit excluding any minorities from the jury, so they took their chances. Not trusting the jury panel's makeup, Garry argued motions Fay had prepared to challenge the entire jury and alternates on the grounds that they were not Newton's peers from the flatlands. Judge Friedman denied both motions. Harper still sat on the jury, proving no pattern of race discrimination by the prosecutor. (To their amazement, Harper would be selected foreman and do a masterful job steering the jury to consensus.)

On her way into the courthouse during July and August, Fay shared Garry's disdain for Lowell Jensen. Garry later realized he misjudged Jensen and publicly praised the prosecutor as a worthy adversary. It would be more than a decade before Fay truly appreciated Jensen's dedication as a career public servant who sought justice for all crime victims, herself included. All that Fay could focus on in the summer of 1968 was that Jensen, as representative of the People of California, was doing his best to get her hero Huey Newton executed. Fay threw herself into gathering all available legal ammunition for Garry to torpedo the prosecution. Garry also relied on Fay to work with the Panthers to help orchestrate political support from the growing coalition of anti-war activists, minorities and Movement sympathizers whom Newton claimed as the real "People" whom the revolutionary sought to empower.

When Jensen was forced to reveal the name of his second star witness, it turned out to be a middle-aged black municipal bus driver named Henry Grier. Grier had identified Newton to police as the civilian he saw grappling with a policeman as the bus pulled up to a nearby stop on the early morning of October 28, 1967. Grier said that he observed the civilian draw a gun and start shooting. If believed, Grier's testimony alone could send Newton to the gas chamber.

As Fay led the hunt for evidence to use to cross-examine Grier, Garry invited the other star witness, Dell Ross, to his office. Much to prosecutor Jensen's and the judge's surprise, Ross would show up represented by his own lawyer at the trial — a law partner of Fay's friend Peter Franck. Ross would then claim no memory of what he told the grand jury and plead the Fifth Amendment in refusing to testify at trial, drawing Jensen's frustration and anger that the kidnapping charge would have to be dropped.

Meanwhile, Fay worked with Alex Hoffmann and volunteers to dig up whatever they could to discredit bus driver Henry Grier. Alex found a passenger on the bus who disputed Grier's vantage point. Fay combed Grier's prior statement to the police and the transcript of Grier's trial testimony on direct examination for discrepancies. She found that, among other things, Grier had given conflicting descriptions of the clothes the civilian was wearing, one when first interviewed by the police and another at the trial. Only at the trial did Grier's description match the clothing Newton wore when admitted to the hospital. Garry would use Fay's work to great effect, accusing Grier of tailoring his testimony to what the prosecution wanted him to say. (Many years afterward, Newton's good friend David Hilliard revealed that, before he and his brother dropped Huey at the hospital, family members had stripped off Huey's bloody shirt and jacket to cleanse his wound, and given him another shirt and jacket to wear.)

Fay kept making herself lists week after week of potential witnesses to interview and legal research to do. Most lawyers would have found her daunting workload all-consuming. Yet Fay made a lasting impression on her young next-door neighbor, by pausing to offer her assistance. Marling Mast was recently divorced and leaving shortly for Spain to act on her dream of studying art abroad. Fay empathized with Marling's anxiety about traveling to a foreign country with two small children and limited finances. As the Stenders stowed Marling's unsold furniture in their attic, Fay took Marling aside to tell her to contact them if she fell short of funds in Europe. It touched Marling that Fay was so solicitous. To Fay, Marling's obvious need for a kind act and her gratitude were irresistible. The gesture had not taken much effort.

Fay quickly returned to trial preparation. Among the witnesses she located was a high school student, who told Fay that Officer Frey used the word "nigger" at least once in a career talk to his class. But the teenager balked at saying that in court, so Charles Garry called Fay herself to take the stand briefly. Fay then testified to the racist language the student had told her Frey used. As the trial began its second month, Bob Blauner grew disturbed at headlines from overseas that described the Russian government's brutal suppression of an uprising in Prague. Blauner commented to Fay that "The Russians are pigs, too" and was disquieted that she showed no reaction.

Actually, Fay grew to appreciate his point. The following year, among her prized acquisitions to decorate her new office was a poster by artist David Lance Goines of a man confronting a Russian tank on Prague's city streets. "QUI TACET CONSENTIT" was written in large print underneath: "He who is silent consents." In the summer of 1968 Blauner did not have the same reservations about the Black Panthers as he did about the Russians, but he later realized the danger signs he had ignored. Fay would belatedly do so, too.

The day Newton was scheduled to testify, spectators waited in line hours before dawn. The force of the crowd broke the courthouse door as they all scrambled to be close enough to get admitted. When he took the stand, Newton acted as if he were conducting a class for the jury instead of defending his life. The whole courtroom strained to listen as he gave the background of the Panthers and their focus on the history of racism in America. He explained how he and other Panthers followed police on their rounds to ensure that arrestees were read their rights.

When questioned briefly by Charles Garry about the events of October 28, 1967, Newton denied having any gun in his possession. Newton said he had been harassed forty to fifty times by Oakland police before he was stopped and frisked abusively by Officer Frey. He accused Frey of manhandling his genitals and told his spellbound audience that as he grappled with Frey, he felt a sensation like hot soup in his stomach. He thought he had been shot by Frey. Newton added that he had no memory of what happened after he was hit until he arrived at the hospital. On the last day of trial, Garry finished laying the groundwork for the jury to find that Newton lacked criminal intent to commit murder even if they found he shot the fatal bullet. Garry put on the stand his favorite forensic expert, Dr. Bernard Diamond, who testified to the amnesia experienced by soldiers who suffered similar abdominal wounds in combat.

Lowell Jensen gave a chilling, matter-of-fact account of the evidence of the shootout. In closing, Jensen asserted that Newton had motive to precipitate a gun fight with the two policemen to avoid going back to prison for possession of marijuana in the car. Charles Garry gave an impassioned plea that blamed Officer Frey for his own death and reminded the jury that just days earlier the whole country had witnessed television coverage of abusive police bashing demonstrators and reporters at the 1968 Democratic Presidential Convention. Garry compared Oakland's force to Chicago's and choked back tears as he proclaimed Newton's innocence of all charges. Despite Garry's extraordinary performance, it was hard to tell its impact on the jury or what to make of the remarkable news on the first day of deliberation that the panel had selected its lone black member as the foreman.

Reporters anxious for the first word on the verdict camped out in the courthouse with some of the attorneys and Newton's family. Bets were exchanged on the outcome. As time passed, conviction of first degree murder became the odds-on favorite. When the jury requested a copy of bus driver Grier's original statement to the police, the defense lawyers realized that they had never been given the chance to verify the transcript against the original police tape of the bus driver's interview. Only prompted by the jury's inquiry did Jensen produce the tape itself along with the transcript. Garry then got Judge Friedman's permission to allow the defense to check its accuracy. Fay quickly pressed her husband Marvin into service. He left with Ed Keating to find an expert to transcribe the tape in a hurry. The new transcription had a small, but significant wording difference from the one used at trial. On the tape, the driver had said he "didn't" get a good look at the civilian. The first transcript said he "did."

Fay and Bob Blauner were among those who passed some of the time sitting on the floor playing chess as they awaited the verdict. Working so closely with Fay all summer, Blauner sensed she was attracted to him. Though he had no romantic interest in her, Blauner did enjoy their collaboration and beating her at chess. Fay's father excelled at the game, but she had not absorbed much of his technique and usually lost.

When the jury came back to the secured courtroom on late Sunday evening, September 8th, Fay squeezed Huey's hand in anticipation of the reading of the verdicts. The jurors remained impassive as Harper handed the clerk the results of their efforts. Fay inwardly rejoiced as the judge announced Huey's acquittal of the murder of Officer Frey. Unlike most observers, Fay had considered the death penalty simply unthinkable. She had also expected Huey's acquittal of assault on Officer Heanes so that jury verdict also came as a relief, but no surprise. Fay then had to absorb the shock of Newton's conviction for manslaughter. One of Huey's sisters fainted. Movement reporter Karen Wald wept in dismay, only to be comforted by Charles Garry. Alex Hoffmann, who had spent the most time keeping Huey company in jail, also found the verdict traumatic.

Garry kept a straight face, but was ebullient. Once the proceedings were over, he decried the verdict to the press as a "chicken-shit" compromise. Beneath Garry's bluster was a realist weighing probable outcomes. At the same time as he complained to the press, he privately assured his client's family and defense team members that the result was a victory. Of course, the reporters all crowded around Garry, with no questions for Fay Stender. Looking back after her long career as a journalist, Belva Davis realized that Garry commanded all the attention, making Fay Stender one of the "most under-reported" players in the Newton trial: "It was only those who dug deeper that found out what her importance had been to the verdict that was rendered."[5]

Fay was a devotee of the cause to her core. From the first sight of her wounded client in custody, she had fixated on the goal of complete acquittal. In her view nothing short of that achievement constituted justice.

End of round one. The responsibility for round two — the appeal — would rest largely on Fay's shoulders. She would be satisfied with nothing less that Huey's freedom.

■ 2 ■

The Baton Passes to Fay

"In the early '70s, you could expect that an appeal would be successful in a criminal case one time out of 20 times, maybe one out of 25 . . . even if your issues were strong. [To do] that in a case as fraught with . . . implications as Huey's case was, and in a case in which . . . the jury had been thoughtful . . . [would be] pretty extraordinary."[1]

CRIMINAL DEFENSE LAWYER DORON WEINBERG

The finale of the grueling, two-month Newton murder trial brought Fay no respite. Yet she was energized by the realization that responsibility for liberating the Movement's revolutionary hero now depended mostly on her. Except for his appearance at the bail hearings, Charles Garry would soon be overwhelmed with other commitments. Garry was representing Eldridge Cleaver in his probation revocation proceedings and was still listed as the lead attorney in the Oakland Seven conspiracy trial headed for trial in the spring of 1969. Garry had also just been asked to represent Bobby Seale in Chicago on charges of conspiring to incite riots outside the August 1968 Democratic Convention. In both Oakland and Chicago, the defense teams intended to put the Vietnam War itself on trial, if the judges would let them.

As a consequence, Fay was happily left to oversee the slow process of Newton's appeal. Monday morning after the Sunday night verdict, she began work on a motion for new trial and a request for probation and bail pending appeal. Fay was sure she could demonstrate serious errors were made. Two mistakes loomed large. The first was that the judge allowed prosecutor Lowell Jensen to read the grand jury transcript of witness Dell Ross's testimony to the jury. The problem was that Ross claimed memory loss about the grand jury testimony and was never cross-examined about it at trial. The second claim of error was the judge's failure to alert the jury to the correction in bus driver Henry Grier's statement. Meanwhile, the "Free Huey" campaign publicized the jury's implicit acceptance of key parts of Newton's trial testimony: that Officer John Frey was a racist who had abused and degraded Newton when Frey pulled the Panther leader over on the fateful morning of October 28, 1967; that Newton was unarmed; and that Officer Heanes shot Newton first, before Newton struggled with Frey for the policeman's gun and Frey died.

An appeal would take at least a year to be briefed, argued and decided. The 4,000-page trial transcript and list of exhibits had to be reviewed and corrected first. That initial process would itself take months. Since Newton was no longer facing the death penalty, Fay thought they now had a winning argument for his release on bail. He had already been jailed for the better part of a year. If he stayed in prison pending appeal, he would serve at least two years even if he was ultimately exonerated — the same term as the minimum sentence for being found guilty.

In support of the bail petition, Fay drafted a statement for the Free Huey committee to circulate in the community for signatures. She wanted to impress the judge with the groundswell of support for Newton's release. On Thursday, September 12th, Fay and Garry returned to court. When brought from his cell, Newton now sat attentively next to his counsel, concentrating on convincing Judge Friedman he presented no risk to society.

Both of Newton's parents took the stand, noting their youngest son's consistent track record of showing up for court appearances. An association of black clergy supported Newton's release as a force for peace in the community. The Panther leader's pastor, Rev. Earl Neil, called

Huey "the personification of what our American ideals are set up to produce in all of its citizens."[2] He told Judge Friedman that just a week before the verdict was reached — when Newton had no idea whether he might face execution — Newton had made a tape recording for students at Oakland's predominantly black McClymonds High School warning them against reacting violently to whatever the jury decided. Duly impressed, Judge Friedman turned and commended Newton.

Newton then took the stand. He told the judge that he had advised his own followers in advance of the verdict to "keep cool" no matter what resulted.[3] The judge questioned Huey at length about his prior record. The veteran jurist did not need the prosecutor's reminder that Newton no longer enjoyed the presumption of innocence. A decision on bail would wait until receipt of the formal probation report on September 27th. In the meantime, Fay phoned in to the probation department her own limited observations of Huey. She had seen "a definite change in the defendant's personality" and strongly felt that he did not currently represent "even the mildest aggressive threat to others."[4] Fay had, of course, only met Huey while he was in custody and had never seen him in a situation where he might endanger others.

By the next hearing, volunteers obtained twenty thousand signatures from the community urging Newton's release. But Judge Friedman focused more on Huey's six prior arrests, two convictions and history of risk-taking and violent behavior. Jensen argued that "Newton has demonstrated nothing but contempt for the rules that govern civilized men."[5] Huey's statement in his own defense was terse: "I will stand on the record as to this case." He thought he should be free on probation "so that I can help Black People gain power to determine the destiny of our people."[6] His fiancée cited their intent to marry and Huey's interest in furthering his education. His parents contended that their son was the victim of a frame-up by the Oakland police, who had stalked him for months looking for an excuse to kill him.

African-American deputy probation officer Thomas Broome candidly acknowledged Newton's positive attributes, but added: "I could write you a book on Huey P. Newton. One of Huey's major problems . . . is his distrust of and fear of his fellow man. . . . It is fairly meaningless to talk about rehabilitation as I think he is as he is and will be. He will react in situations of stress. . . . You'll have no problems with Huey as long as he is not threatened. . . . When he is, good luck."[7]

Not surprisingly, Judge Friedman sentenced Newton to an indeterminate prison sentence of two to fifteen years without releasing him on bond pending appeal. Newton was immediately whisked from his cell at the Oakland jail for evaluation at the Vacaville medical facility. From there, he would be transferred directly to the California Men's Colony (CMC) in San Luis Obispo, 215 miles south of San Francisco, a four-hour drive from his followers.

The modern, medium-security penal facility housed 2400 mostly white, nonviolent prisoners, a large number of whom were gay. Unlike prisons where Newton had previously been held, the Men's Colony offered inmates extensive recreational and sports programs, access to a library, television and radio, and vocational training. Reporter Gilbert Moore, who had covered the trial for *Life* magazine, was among many reporters who came to interview Newton in prison. At the Men's Colony, the Panther leader had become an instant celebrity. Moore found the facility quite impressive. Moore noted with irony, "Perhaps, the only worldly pleasures denied the inmates of the California Men's Colony . . . is the freedom to leave the institution at will and the possibility of heterosexual intercourse."[8]

Fay rushed to start work on an appeal of the denial of bail. The court of appeal quickly, without opinion, denied the request, as did the California Supreme Court. That was consistent with Fay's prior experience when she clerked there. Still Fay would not take no for an answer if there was anywhere else to turn, so she immediately began preparing a petition to the federal district court, urging that it set reasonable bail to remedy the failure of the state courts to do so. She framed it as a civil rights issue. Criminal defense lawyers told her that most white prisoners facing similar sentences for manslaughter were released on bail pending appeal. Still, there was little realistic hope the federal court would intervene.

In the meantime, Fay wrote upbeat notes to Huey, worried that his new environment would depress him. Apart from his lawyers, Newton was limited to receiving letters and visits from a total of ten people. Though visitors could stay for up to five hours at a time, Newton found initial visits from his fiancée frustrating. Unlike his lawyers, she could only meet him in the large visitors' room or a nearby courtyard under the watchful gaze of the guards.

Alex Hoffmann also helped maintain Newton's spirits. Alex had become Huey's confidante after months of almost daily visits at the Alameda County jail to keep Huey company and bring him books to read. Hoffmann had also managed to visit Newton in his brief stay in Vacaville after the trial ended. Alex and Fay then made plans for a Thanksgiving trip to San Luis Obispo with her family and his housemate Elsa Knight Thompson.

At the beginning of November, Newton lost most of his privileges after he refused to work in the dining room for inmate pay of three cents per hour. When Newton insisted on the minimum wage, prison authorities thought it was a publicity ploy. As his punishment for disobeying the rules, Newton was placed in lockup in a poorly ventilated, windowless cell, four-and-a-half feet by six feet. As in the Alameda jail, he often stripped naked to tolerate the heat. When Fay complained, prison staff cut a hole in his door, which they covered with thick wire mesh. At least it improved the air flow.

Soon after moving to his isolated cell, Newton alerted Fay and Charles Garry that their assistance was urgently needed. A young, white Leftist inmate named Michael McCarthy appeared marked for death. McCarthy was a fellow Marxist and Panther supporter, who had been at CMC for over two years when Newton arrived. McCarthy was then in his fifth year of a one-year-to-life indeterminate sentence for robbery. The sentence had been his twenty-first birthday present from the state following a drunken spree at several gas stations in Southern California. McCarthy had tried to rob them by poking his hand inside his trench coat, pretending it was a gun. At the time of his imprisonment, McCarthy was dating a black woman. She came to visit him, which incensed his guards. Decades later McCarthy still recalled what a prison official told him during his second year inside: "As long as you got that nigger coming to see you, you don't get a parole."

At the Men's Colony, McCarthy quickly figured out how to meet Newton even though they were housed in different wings. McCarthy sent word through the prison grapevine suggesting they both seek medical attention at the prison hospital on the same day. They spent a half hour together in the hospital corridor before guards separated them. McCarthy pledged his support to the Black Panthers and told Newton about other revolutionaries in the prison.

McCarthy later smuggled a note into Newton's isolation cell urging him to reconsider his refusal to work, explaining that failure to adhere to prison policy would only play into the officials' hands. Newton's lack of cooperation could give the warden an excuse to transfer Newton to San Quentin or Folsom where he could be set up to be killed by white racist gangs. McCarthy also explained in the note that at the Men's Colony several prisoners had started a Marxist study group with contraband books. If Newton regained his library privileges, he could join them. Some of the members were becoming eligible for parole. Upon their release, they could then assist in organizing prisoners from the outside. McCarthy's risky note was found in Newton's cell and wound up in the warden's hands.

The interception of McCarthy's detailed message to Newton sent shock waves among prison personnel. McCarthy was immediately isolated in "the hole." His next parole board hearing involved a packed house of Department of Correction officials determined to quash prison revolutionaries once and for all. McCarthy was told the only way he would now ever get out was "in a pine box." Newton heard through the prison grapevine that following the parole board hearing in mid-November, McCarthy had been abruptly removed from CMC East to an unknown destination.

To Newton, this disappearing act meant that McCarthy would likely never surface anywhere, killed en route as stories had circulated of other "disappeared" prisoners who had battled the system. Newton sounded the alarm to Fay. Though she had never met McCarthy, she instantly started phoning every likely prison destination, frantically trying to track his whereabouts. Charles Garry made some phone calls, too. It took Fay two days, but she located McCarthy at the Deuel Vocational

THE BATON PASSES TO FAY

Institute in Tracy and was told he was headed either to Folsom or San Quentin. McCarthy wound up being transferred to San Quentin, with the prison system now well aware that Fay would instantly advertise to the outside world any harm that might befall him. Absent Fay's urgent queries at Newton's urging, McCarthy assumed he would have instead quietly disappeared forever. He owed her his life.

Newton turned his focus back to Party concerns. He found it difficult to be sitting inside prison while Eldridge Cleaver sought to control the Panther Party on the streets. Since well before the trial, Newton had spent much of his time in his isolated cell in Oakland contemplating the political situation. He had begun to reassess the Party's priorities. Newton now wanted to dispel the Panthers' image as "trigger-happy, gun-toting thugs."[9] The best way of gaining more community support for the Party was to expand its existing programs.

The Panthers' free breakfast programs in Oakland and in Los Angeles were already feeding thousands of children daily and building much-needed alliances within black communities. The programs also lured large numbers of new recruits to the Party. From his visitors, Newton learned with alarm that Cleaver had a totally different agenda in mind. Cleaver was making plans for a final bloody confrontation with Oakland police in November of 1968. After the appellate court revoked his parole, Cleaver faced certain return to prison Thanksgiving week. Cleaver preferred to go down in glory as a fiery revolutionary. Newton flatly rejected Cleaver's plan. Newton had been deeply grieved by Bobby Hutton's death, which he blamed on Cleaver's recklessness. If the Panthers followed Cleaver's lead, Newton felt the Party had no future. Through Charles Garry, Newton sent Cleaver a different agenda.

On November 24th, Cleaver disappeared without a trace, much to the chagrin of the FBI and local police. With careful planning and lots of help, Cleaver had fled secretly to Cuba through Canada. Cleaver was on a new mission — to further international support for the Panthers from the safe haven of Havana. Ironically, Beverly Axelrod would within several months' time also head to the Caribbean. She kept in touch with Alex Hoffmann and Elsa Knight Thompson and asked them to convey her love to Huey and Fay and the few other friends she missed. Axelrod had, in her own words, "fallen off the edge of the world."[10] She relocated from New Mexico to Trinidad and then Grenada in the British West Indies. There, she rented a house for $20 per month, devoid of radio or television and sheltered from news about the Panthers and her former lover Eldridge Cleaver.

The Wednesday before Thanksgiving, Garry officially reported to the court that Cleaver was not to be found. Cleaver had left his pregnant wife Kathleen in San Francisco and forfeited the $50,000 bond posted in June for his release. That same day, Alex, Elsa Knight Thompson, Fay, Marvin and their two children traveled to San Luis Obispo for the long holiday weekend. Newton was eager to learn Party news. Before he left, Cleaver had given a fiery speech further radicalizing black students at San Francisco State College, who were already incensed at the firing of Black Panther Minister of Education George Murray from the English Department faculty. It was the same college where Newton had his first paid speaking engagement in 1967 and Bobby Seale had later electrified a largely white audience by advocating that all blacks carry guns. Escalating clashes with the administration of the urban campus made front-page news, dwarfing the impact of all protests to date in Berkeley. The increasingly polarized situation would also have a tremendous ripple effect on other colleges throughout the country over the next several months.

Delighted with the impact the Panthers were having at San Francisco State, Newton was full of ideas. With Cleaver gone, it was time to reorganize the Party. Newton wanted to abolish the category of "Pantherettes" that labeled female recruits as second-class members. Women had turned out to be the major work force behind popular free breakfasts and other Panther community outreach. Treating all women as equals would encourage them to redouble their efforts to expand successful Party programs.

It became instantly clear to Fay and Alex that Newton could only maintain his leadership role with the Panthers if they made frequent trips to the Men's Colony to act as his messengers. Newton's optimism also appeared fragile and likely short-lived. Fay knew he was subject, like herself, to mood swings. She came back by herself to see Newton privately for several hours on Tuesday, December 2d and brought him Christmas and holiday messages. Newton was skin-searched both before and after all visits. But the guards left the two alone, only peering occasionally through the conference room window and taking notes. In talking with Newton, Fay tried to be very careful, realizing they might be taped. She whispered whenever she needed to convey critical information.

Fay thought what Huey needed most was more companionship. She and Alex Hoffmann agreed to return to San Luis Obispo once every three or four weeks to see Newton, putting in for reimbursement by the Garry firm of the $10 in gas and occasional motel bill as part of the cost of defense. When Alex Hoffmann's VW bug proved unequal to the long road trips, the Stenders offered him the use of Marvin's Mercedes instead.

After two trips in December, Fay made regular monthly trips to San Luis Obispo to visit Newton on weekends. As his lawyer, Fay usually still met with Newton in a conference room where they enjoyed relative privacy. On one occasion, a shocked guard reported seeing her bent down, apparently engaged in oral sex with Newton. The guard did not enter the room, but his report went all the way up the chain of command to Corrections Chief Raymond Procunier in Sacramento. In a few years' time, Fay would encourage women in her prison law collective to boost the morale of men in maximum security by engaging in whatever sexual activity the women could get away with. If she took that risk with Huey at the Men's Colony, it must have contributed to the bitter memory in her last days of the lengths she had gone to for her revolutionary client, only to be ultimately rejected.

Newton's authorized visitors still included the media. Fay suggested to other supporters that they obtain press credentials to gain access. She herself began smuggling in letters and photographs from friends to show Huey. She brought them back with her when she left to avoid having them discovered and confiscated. Between visits, Fay frequently wrote to Huey, assuming that all correspondence would be opened and read. That meant picking safe topics and saving sensitive Party business for in-person visits. Fay thought he would enjoy knowing that a photographic essay of "The Black Panthers" had opened at the De Young Museum in San Francisco. To cheer him up, she included pictures of her kids and her house, and relayed return messages from Huey to Oriane and Neal, treating Huey as extended family. It never occurred to Fay back then that there should be any barriers erected between her family and her militant clients.

■ 3 ■
Freeing Huey!

The case [against Newton] . . . was very complicated. . . . And Huey Newton went free. . . . That case was tried in a ground-breaking way, and he went free![1]
HALL OF FAME CRIMINAL DEFENSE LAWYER PENNY COOPER

On Christmas Eve 1968, three months after Huey's transfer to the Men's Colony, Fay assured her moody client that Charles Garry would be down soon to meet with him. In fact, the Oakland Seven trial was now scheduled for late January and Garry had his hands full seeking to turn that trial into a referendum on the Vietnam War. As Fay made more frequent decisions on her own, she increasingly resented working in Charles Garry's shadow.

Al Brotsky remained the most sympathetic to Fay of the partners. He was then helping her get the Lawyers Guild to support Newton's federal bail petition with a brief arguing that whites convicted of the same crime would be released pending appeal. When Fay complained to Brotsky about Garry not putting her on a path to partnership, Brotsky offered to intercede. The response from Garry was dismissive: "She can't handle cases herself. She's perfect helping us." He felt she empathized too much with her clients to be a good trial lawyer. Fay shelved her frustration for the time being, glad that Garry had given her free reign on the Newton appeal. After obtaining help from the Lawyers Guild, Fay pursued support for Huey's release from rabbis in the East Bay who were civil rights activists. Fay relished making connections between her religious heritage and her current mission. In her view, Newton's freedom should be the rabbis' cause as well.

Because of the distance to San Luis Obispo, Fay sometimes spent the night in a motel, bringing Oriane with her for the weekend. Fay and Alex Hoffmann were now sneaking tape-recorded messages from Black Panthers into the prison to deliver to Newton. They returned with his tape-recorded instructions. Given that Newton's short list of approved visitors excluded Party members, Newton had little choice but to use Fay as a go-between.

At Newton's bidding, Fay also continued to do what she could for his inmate friends. Sometimes Newton would be asked to vet names of people the Panthers did not know whether to trust. Fay thrived on her role as gatekeeper and official Huey spokesperson. She sometimes blocked people from communicating with him. Alex took no such liberties. Like Fay, Alex rationalized acting as a go-between, though officials would take an exceedingly dim view if they were caught. (A similar role of go-between for an Arab client in New York would get criminal defense lawyer Lynne Stewart disbarred and sent to prison in 2005 despite the best efforts of Fay's old friend Mike Tigar as Stewart's defense attorney.)

Soon there was grim news to report — the murder on January 17, 1969, of two Black Panther leaders on the UCLA campus in Los Angeles by two members of Organization Us, a rival militant group headed by ex-Oaklander Ron Karenga. Later, proof emerged that the FBI's Counterintelligence Program ("COINTELPRO") had instigated the killings. By 1969, COINTELPRO was focused on eradicating the Panthers. It was what Fay suspected at the time.[2]

Over the winter, Fay brought her Guild friend Peter Franck to visit Newton. On their way to the Men's Colony, Fay learned of Franck's plan to expand his Berkeley law practice. She shared with him her unhappiness in her current situation. She felt she could develop her own practice in selective service cases but would never have the opportunity if she was always assisting Garry.

Franck invited Fay to join him and his partner Doug Hill. Their law office was still on Telegraph Avenue in Berkeley, where he had previously operated the short-lived Council for Justice. The pair were adding two other young partners to form a legal collective that Franck envisioned would handle selective service cases as well as a broad range of other Movement lawsuits. Fay was flattered to be offered full partnership in a law collective.

Meantime, Fay refocused on completing her work at the Garry firm. Newton was never far from Fay's thoughts. Unlike Garry, Fay considered her role of emotional support for her client as important as her legal work. She sent him a valentine and received back a handwritten note that he thought it was very beautiful and had it hanging in his cell. He sent his own birthday greetings to "Fifi" and asked Fay to inquire whether her daughter would be his valentine. He gave his regards and love to her son Neal as well. She gathered birthday cards to bring to Newton and drove down again at the end of February.

In March, Fay and Marvin switched their focus temporarily to the new conspiracy indictments against Seale and seven other leaders of the August 1968 demonstrations in Chicago. They had received a call for assistance from their old friend Jerry Rubin, now infamous among Leftists for his role as co-leader with Abbie Hoffman of the Yippies. Fay contacted a Chicago lawyer who was assisting her in the Newton case and urged him to help Rubin: "Anything you can do will be for the cause —I really can't put it more strongly."[3]

That spring, inspired by the events at San Francisco State, student anti-war demonstrations erupted at 300 college campuses amid unprecedented attempts to interfere with national commerce by acts of arson, explosions and violence reported almost daily in the media. In the last week of March, Garry and his co-counsel completed the Oakland Seven case, winning surprising acquittals of all seven protest leaders. Following the trial, Garry took advantage of the temporary break in his schedule to visit Newton in early April. Within the next week, twenty-one members of the New York branch of the Panthers would be indicted on bombing conspiracy charges and held on $200,000 bond each. The criminal charges the Panthers faced seemed never-ending. Yet Huey's morale remained first and foremost in Fay's thoughts. As political violence escalated throughout the country, San Luis Obispo prisoner officials kept an even tighter watch on the revolutionary hero in their keep. Newton could no longer receive literature in the mail from his friends. He could only keep ten books in his cell at one time and they had to be shipped directly from the publisher.

Fay realized that, in Newton's absence, she could offer her voice in his stead. Organizers of a teach-in on May 5, 1969, at San Diego State University invited Fay to be the keynote speaker on political oppression. She spoke from her heart with compelling conviction. The FBI sent an undercover agent to attend the event. Over 1,000 people heard Newton's soft-spoken lawyer bring to life not only his persecution, but the plight of others she described as unjustly imprisoned. The FBI covert agent paid close attention. He found her surprisingly persuasive as she described the Black Panthers in glowing terms as the best thing to ever happen to African-Americans. The FBI also had to be impressed by her energy. The next day Fay was back in San Francisco attending yet another rally in support of her jailed client.

Yet most of Fay's time that spring was spent closeted in her office or at home, devoting extraordinary hours to write the brief she hoped would win Newton's freedom. She asserted every possible ground of error. The "brief" ran almost 200 pages in length. When she turned it in, it must have felt like giving birth. From the time Fay had started preparing the notice of appeal, this labor of love on Newton's behalf had taken almost nine months. She gave it deluxe treatment. Although typed briefs were the norm in the state court of appeal, she used a printing service often used by lawyers filing briefs in the United States Supreme Court. Printed and bound, her argument looked even more impressive. She ordered scores of copies to distribute to a long list of colleagues and professors.

The prosecutor would need a few months' time to respond and Fay would have the final say in reply. Oral argument was still months away. Then the appellate court would take whatever time it needed to issue its opinion. Since the federal court had just denied relief, it looked certain Newton would remain imprisoned for at least a year and a half before a decision was known.

Meanwhile, Fay anxiously observed the deteriorating political situation. Governor Reagan had just ordered police to retake People's Park in Berkeley from activists who had claimed it in April. During the melee a bystander was fatally wounded, another blinded. Scores of protesters and some of the police suffered injuries. Governor Reagan declared a state of emergency and occupied the city with 2,700 National Guardsmen. For two weeks, its streets were barricaded with rolls of barbed wire and National Guard helicopters sprayed tear gas on anyone who gathered in more than small groups.

The eerie imposition of martial law in her home town was followed by revelation of the gruesome murder of Black Panther Alex Rackley in New Haven. The two chilling events increased Fay's sense of urgency in getting Newton out of prison. The man suspected of ordering Rackley's execution was National Black Panther Field Marshall George Sams, who had just taken off for parts unknown. Was he an agent-provocateur? One of the others being investigated was Ericka Huggins, widow of Panther John Huggins, whom Organization U.S. rivals had gunned down on the UCLA campus back in January. Ericka had recently started a new Panther chapter in New Haven, her deceased husband's home town — at the same time that Panther offices were being shut down in many places. With the government prosecuting so many of Newton's followers, Fay felt the Party leader needed to be back on the streets as soon as possible to rally his remaining troops.

Fay went down to visit Newton on the weekend of May 24th just after the Rackley murder hit the newspapers. She promised to return once again the following month, just before leaving for Europe. As usual, she radiated optimism about the prospects of Newton's eventual release. Fay wrote to author James Baldwin, asking him to interview Newton and publicize his denial of privileges at the Men's Colony. Occasionally during this time, Fay ran into former Deputy Public Defender Penny Cooper, now keeping quite busy in her new private practice in Berkeley representing arrestees at People's Park. Fay admired the no-nonsense Boalt graduate for going out on her own. Fay herself could not have managed that bold move. When they talked about the Newton case, Fay oozed confidence. Losing was not possible. Cooper knew the opposite to be the norm — winning any appeal from a conviction was an uphill battle. She thought Fay highly unrealistic in her expectations. But failure was not an outcome that Fay entertained at all.

In early June Fay finalized plans for a six-week trip to Europe and Israel with her family. On her return, she planned to leave the Garry, Dreyfus firm. Fay had a soft spot in her heart for her mentor, and could not face telling him in person. She decided the best thing to do was to leave a note on his desk. Unlike her usual typed messages, it was hand-written and short, but penned with obvious enthusiasm:

I'm leaving here Sept 1
Partnership at Peter Franck[4]

* * *

During the past several months working on the Free Huey campaign, Fay had become very close to Huey's strong supporter Elsa Knight Thompson. Since 1956, Elsa had been on the staff of KPFA, first as a volunteer and then its controversial programming director. Over the years, she had become a mother figure to many young Leftist volunteers, including Mike Tigar, Mario Savio and Elsa's housemate Alex Hoffmann.

Fay ferried Elsa around when they both attended events for Newton. At sixty-three, the short, green-eyed brunette was still both beautiful and polarizing. She commanded attention by force of personality, impressing friends and foes alike as a hell-raising force to be reckoned with. Detractors nicknamed her the "Wicked Witch."[5] To Fay, she was a "SHE-ro" who had been a broadcaster for the BBC in London during the Blitz. By the end of the war, Elsa had engaged in a torrid affair with a Polish Socialist leader who then left England to help form a new government in Warsaw. At some point, Elsa realized she was bi-sexual, sharing with select women friends her view that sex was a legitimate part of any two-person relationship as an expression of mutual regard and closeness. Fay developed a similar view.

* * *

The FBI was aware of Fay's plans for an overseas vacation. Fay's summer trip had taken months of planning. The first stop would be London; then Paris. Lastly, the family would go to Israel, a long-awaited opportunity for Fay and Marvin to view firsthand the Jewish state established by bloody battle after the Holocaust. Fay looked forward to Neal and Oriane having a chance to connect with Marvin's relatives and other Israelis. The overseas travel did broaden the entire family's horizons; it also changed the course of Neal's life. In Paris, the Stenders stayed with transplanted friends from Berkeley, the Grossmans. Ten-year-old Neal enjoyed the experience so much that the childless Grossmans asked the Stenders to allow Neal to return to live with them for a year. Fay startled her family that September by putting her ten-year-old on a plane back to France, a sojourn overseas that presaged Neal spending much of his adult life as an expatriate.

Fay and Marvin had been shocked upon their arrival in Paris to see policemen carrying automatic weapons. Fay had admired the Panthers' introduction of armed patrols in East Oakland as an effective strategy to counter police brutality, but she personally abhorred violence. The Grossmans told them that heavily armed law enforcement had been commonplace in Europe since World War II. Neither Fay nor Marvin had seen similarly fortified policemen walking city streets before. The Grossmans said the French police presence had heightened as officials prepared for possible assassinations sparked by a German gang of international terrorists.

The frightening omnipresence of weapons on the streets of Paris did not dissuade Fay from arranging to meet up with European Panther supporters on July 9th. The gathering included an FBI informer. The FBI was aware that Fay's trip coincided with plans for the first Pan African conference in Algiers, where Eldridge Cleaver now lived in exile, just joined by his very pregnant wife Kathleen. The informer noted that one person Fay met asked her if he could attend the historic event as a Party representative. By then, the Black Panther Party had officially been invited to send a delegation to the conference, now less than two weeks away. Others Fay met wondered out loud about how the Panthers would handle Stokely Carmichael's recent split and denunciation of the Party. Carmichael was planning to show up in Algiers as well.

Federal agents could relax at the Stenders' last destination on their overseas trip — there was no likely Panther connection in Israel. Yet the young, industrialized country made by far the biggest impression on Fay and Marvin. When Louis Brandeis had first visited Palestine in 1919, he described it as a land of depleted soil, severely blighted by swamps. What had struck Brandeis most on that visit was the resignation of the inhabitants to the inevitability of catching malaria. The flies were so plentiful that "people did not even bother to flick them off their faces."[6] The same look of resignation on the faces of local families had been etched in Fay's memory from her college summer trip to Mexico with the Quakers.

Fay and Marvin marveled at the transformation in Israel wreaked by the collective blood, sweat and tears of so many Jews. Yet it was obvious that hostilities there had not ceased, particularly in the Gaza Strip where Palestinian guerrillas were now active. A distant cousin of Marvin's showed Marvin and Fay around the newly liberated West Bank, with his Uzi slung over his shoulder. Both Fay and Marvin had been appalled by the weapon and feared for Israel's future.

* * *

Fay returned to California with renewed energy, excited to be headed to a new firm of young Movement lawyers. Yet she could not help but feel some guilt. Charlie Garry appeared seriously ill. In July, he had experienced severe stomach pains that resulted in his hospitalization. Garry's doctor had allowed him to finish the Panther trial he was then defending, but only on the condition that Garry schedule gall bladder surgery immediately afterward. There would be little time for recuperation. The veteran litigator had just agreed to represent Bobby Seale in the upcoming Chicago conspiracy trial, by far the highest profile political prosecution in the country. Garry begged Fay to help him part-time in the fall. Fay could never turn down a role that might prove crucial to the Movement. She agreed to split her time between both firms for the time being.

Events quickly took both Charlie Garry and Fay out of the infamous Chicago trial and turned Bobby Seale into the next Movement icon. At the end of the first week of August, the police tracked down George Sams, who confessed to the May 21st killing of Alex Rackley and implicated Bobby Seale. A Connecticut grand jury then indicted Seale, Ericka Huggins and seven other New Haven Panther Party members on charges of Rackley's torture and murder. To counter the negative press, Garry immediately jabbed back with an attack on the FBI and COINTELPRO. The old street fighter was now the unquestioned lawyer of choice for all the Panthers. Writing from his San Francisco cell, Seale described Garry as "the most beautiful lawyer in the world."[7]

Though Fay remained as dedicated to the Panthers as ever, their multiplying problems sometimes appeared to defy solution. By the late summer of 1969, Fay had begun to realize the way the Panthers operated often hindered meaningful assistance. A frustrated lawyer who was trying to represent several Panthers in Los Angeles with "their asses at stake" in a criminal case, wrote to her in despair over his difficult clients. Fay wrote back:

> It isn't that the Panthers don't want to cooperate, I think—having given some serious thought to the problems; but, they really do operate in another state of mind, culture, scheme or relevancy, habit, and ultimately, of organization for relating to the details of middle class life that we are trained for in such early youth. What the outcome will be of all this is not clear, but at times it is tragic, almost always frustrating, and worse, not clear what is best to do. . . .[8]

Fay put off thinking beyond the immediate future and concentrated on proving her worth to her new partnership. One new partner, Phil Ziegler, already owed Fay an enormous debt of gratitude. Like Fay, Ziegler had started his practice representing draft resisters. Ziegler then received his own draft notice and called Fay in a panic because he could see no way out from being shipped to Vietnam. Fay offered to pull strings. She had a cousin in the California office that handled local

Selective Service appeals. With one call to her cousin, she got Ziegler's file pulled for review of the draft board's action. By the time the review was completed, Ziegler was over 26 and ineligible for the draft.

Ziegler thought it was a coup that Peter Franck had lured Fay away from the legendary Garry, Dreyfus firm. Fay had a decade's more experience than Ziegler and had established her reputation as one of Huey Newton's lawyers. But Phil had arrived in the new firm first, so he claimed the last spacious office in its new quarters. Fay would have to settle for one of the two somewhat smaller rooms in the back. The other new partner, also relegated to an office in the rear, was Ezra Hendon. Fay had only met Hendon casually at a social event. After passing the California Bar in 1968, the former D.C. Circuit law clerk had gone to work for the Treuhaft firm. Soft-spoken and introspective by nature, Hendon bonded quickly with Fay through their shared Jewish heritage and similar politics.

Peter Franck wanted to celebrate Berkeley's first radical law collective in style — the New Age counterpart to Oakland's Treuhaft & Walker and Garry, Dreyfus, McTernan & Brotsky in San Francisco. The event was catered by a top East Bay restaurateur with printed invitations designed by Free Speech veteran David Goines, who was just launching his career as a graphic artist. Goines also created a poster for their opening. He drew a bridge and under it printed a translation of the famous quote from French novelist Anatole France: "The law in its majestic equality, forbids the rich as well as the poor to sleep under bridges, to beg in the streets & to steal loaves of bread." It would later become a collectors' item. Fay soon put another of Goines' posters — QUI TACET CONSENTIT — on her office wall near her father's painting of a rabbi blowing a shofar to celebrate the Jewish New Year. Whoever is silent consents. Their law firm would speak up about all injustices they could take on.

At the opening, Fay wore a skintight black sheathe. She draped herself across a desk as friends and fellow activists arrived to toast the opening of the new law partnership. Ziegler was amazed at Fay's transformation since the first time he met with her a year-and-a-half earlier. She appeared slimmed down, far more sophisticated and alluring. Nearly forty years later, he would exclaim in amazement: "The lady was hot!"

Ziegler also noticed how sharply Fay dressed for work these days.

Fay relished the short commute to the Oakland office and did not mind operating out of the converted library in the rear. Her only request was that Peter Franck buy her a small, wheeled typing table so she could produce her own documents. Franck was happy to oblige — Fay typed faster on her manual typewriter than the secretaries could on their electric typewriters. Fay's self-sufficiency put less pressure on the small staff. It was also in keeping with the firm's effort to break down traditional barriers. Attorneys answered the phone themselves. Secretaries were encouraged to do almost everything the attorneys did short of sign court filings. Sometimes Fay's daughter Oriane, now temporarily an only child, joined her mother at the office, another major change for Fay from Garry's more traditional law firm in San Francisco. Fay enjoyed hanging Oriane's cheerful drawings on the wall by her father's painting.

The dynamism of Fay's new younger partners energized Marvin as well. Much to his delight, they started dropping by the Stenders' home on Grant Street on Sunday afternoons to join Marvin's neighborhood touch football games. Fay stayed busy inside, only emerging from the house to protect her beloved plum tree in the front yard from damage when the football crew threatened to crash into it.

Fay soon resumed her monthly prison visits to Newton. She had informed Panther headquarters she was going down to see him at the Men's Colony the Friday after her firm's opening party on September 5th, 1969. Any documents they wanted Huey to receive should be delivered to her the night before. The FBI took note.

On her visit to Newton, Fay brought bad news about Seale's upcoming conspiracy trial. The prior week, Garry had flown to Chicago to argue a motion Fay had prepared to delay the Chicago Eight trial because of Garry's impending gall bladder operation. The motion was denied. Seale would have to proceed without Garry to defend him. Though veteran Movement lawyer William Kunstler offered to represent Seale, as the trial progressed into the latter half of October, Seale angrily kept insisting on his right to represent himself. Seale called the judge names until the infuriated jurist ordered Seale bound and gagged.[9] His case was then severed from that of the other seven defendants and ultimately dismissed.

As the national media focused on what became the infamous Chicago Seven trial, Fay had other priorities closer to home. During Charlie Garry's hospitalization, Fay coordinated local defense attorneys representing Panthers in the Bay Area. Fay's desk was a wildly disorganized vortex of ever-churning papers. Documents accumulated in stacks on any available surface.

Unlike her meticulous partner Ezra Hendon, Fay was willing to ignore the constraints of rules she considered unfair, though she tried not to run unnecessary risks. A recurring issue in representing arrested teen-aged Panthers was that they could only be released from custody to family members. At first, when parents were unreachable, Fay had no qualms substituting a staff member posing as an arrested girl's uncle, but the FBI was tapping Panther headquarter phones and Fay became too nervous. She flatly informed the Panthers she was unable to obtain their release unless they could locate a parent or guardian. Meanwhile, Fay insisted the Panthers make good on a promise to pay a fee for her firm's services, money needed to cover payroll. Getting compensated enough to live on was a problem Fay did not enjoy addressing and never solved.

Whenever Fay was not interrupted with a current emergency, she returned to work on the reply brief for Newton's appeal. In early December 1969, shocking news came from Chicago. Chicago Panther leader, Fred Hampton, was killed in a predawn invasion by police. Fay assumed COINTELPRO was behind Hampton's death. Four days after Hampton's murder, in another early morning raid, the Los Angeles Special Weapons Tactics Team used a weapons search as an excuse for invading the Panthers' Los Angeles headquarters. Three Panthers were seriously wounded in the ensuing shootout.

Both Fay and Charles Garry reacted with alarm. To forestall a raid on the Oakland Panther office, Garry immediately called a press conference. He charged that, to date, twenty-eight Panthers had been murdered by the police and that the ongoing raids were "part and package of a national scheme by various agencies of the government to destroy and commit genocide upon members of the Black Panther Party."[10] Meanwhile, Fay talked San Francisco Guild board members into each spending a couple of nights with the Panthers at their Oakland headquarters. One of Fay's overnight volunteers, Marvin's best friend Gordon Gaines, admitted afterward he was more afraid of the gun-toting Panthers than he was of the police.

Civil rights leaders and mainstream press took up the cry that the Black Panthers had been targeted by the administration for political assassination. A Senate Committee in the 1970s would later document the FBI's lawless scheme. Focus on police-Panther confrontations remained on the front pages of local papers as Fay completed the reply brief on Newton's appeal on January 23, 1970. Fay had agonized about what to say in conclusion — what words were best calculated to prick the consciences of the three appellate justices as their deliberations began. She knew how common it was for appellate courts to reject alleged errors in a criminal trial as "harmless" in light of other evidence. That was what most observers expected to happen here. She challenged the justices to reject that inclination:

> Where assessment of credibility determines a case . . . and the issues on credibility are close and vigorously contested, every error affecting credibility assessment is extremely important. . . . [They] cause a miscarriage of justice and are of constitutional dimension. . . . In this case there were major errors affecting the issues of credibility . . . none of the errors . . . can possibly be deemed harmless beyond a reasonable doubt.[11]

Fay then pointed to the jury selection processes that failed to reflect Newton's peer group. She ended, "In today's America, when too often white men and black men are opposed, the administration of justice cannot constitutionally proceed on the basis of grand juries or trial juries from which the black or the poor or the young . . . have been systematically excluded."[12]

Oral argument on the Newton appeal had been reset for Wednesday, February 11, 1970. Outside the State Building that morning, several hundred supporters gathered for a three-hour "Free Huey" rally. It was the same office building Fay had worked in more than a decade earlier as a law clerk for Justice Shenk and appeared in as a lawyer many times since. Emerging from the elevator into the appellate court's reception area, Garry, Fay and their entourage encountered for the first time the encouraging sight of one black and one white bailiff at the entrance.

Garry and Fay split the argument, with Fay handling the more technical issues she had so meticulously briefed. Garry took it upon himself to assail the character of Judge Monroe Friedman. It did not bother Garry in the slightest that Friedman had made a number of key rulings favorable to the defense at the Newton trial. Before the appellate panel, Garry argued: "The court didn't care what kind of evidence went before the jury just so he got a conviction."[13] Fay then laid out all the reversible errors she claimed Judge Friedman had made.

The Panthers were duly impressed with their counsels' efforts, only to feel deflated when the state's lawyer recited at length all the incriminatory evidence that supported the manslaughter verdict. A Panther reporter wrote, "We all left the courtroom knowing full well that the pigs had no intention of allowing Huey to receive anything close to another trial."[14] Yet, from the jurists' probing questions on key issues, Garry and Fay felt that the panel was leaning toward reversal. After attending another "Free Huey" rally, Garry told Newton, "Let's keep our fingers crossed that you will be comparatively a free man in the next few days."[15] A Panther reporter told readers otherwise: "We know that the only way Huey will be set free is for the people to do it. . . . [L]eft to the pigs we will always be slaves. SEIZE THE TIME." [16]

A heavily promoted birthday benefit for Newton was scheduled the following Sunday. Money was badly needed to defray the costs of the appeal, but the event drew only a few hundred attendees. What if the Panthers were simply losing popularity? Fay worried about the impact of the passage of time on Newton's ability to galvanize the Movement if and when he was released.

Actually, the Panthers were still capable of gathering large crowds on the East Coast. National attention shifted that spring to Bobby Seale and Ericka Huggins as they faced joint trial on murder charges in New Haven. Both Fay and Charlie Garry were delighted when Yale President Kingman Brewster announced to faculty that he doubted that a black revolutionary could obtain a fair trial anywhere in America. Brewster's words would be quoted in every brief Fay and other Panther lawyers filed from then on.

Days after bloodshed was narrowly averted in New Haven, at Kent State in Ohio, National Guardsmen killed four students and wounded nine others. A week and a half after the Kent State massacre, two students were killed and a dozen more wounded at Jackson State in Mississippi. Tensions were high across country when Fay learned at the end of May that the appellate decision in the Newton case was finally about to issue. Fay heard through the grapevine that the opinion was long and had a panic attack. She thought the justices wanted to explain in detail their rejection of all her arguments. Her co-counsel Alex Hoffmann had just the opposite view — that a long opinion was needed to justify a decision in Newton's favor.

The California First District Court of Appeal issued its unanimous decision on May 29, 1970. Alex Hoffmann was right — they had won reversal of Newton's conviction and a new trial limited only to the manslaughter charges. The press tried to contact Newton by telephone for his reaction, but prison officials would not bring him out of his cell for an interview. The amazing news spread immediately. The Men's Colony prison yard erupted in glee while the rest of the country reacted with astonishment.

The panel did reject many of Fay's arguments. Yet she convinced the three jurists that a new trial was needed. The court of appeal held that Judge Friedman should not have allowed prosecutor Lowell Jensen to read the grand jury testimony of witness Dell Ross in front of the jury. The appellate panel also faulted Judge Friedman for the way he handled the key transcription error in bus driver Henry Grier's taped statement to the police.

Another key reason for the reversal was that Judge Friedman did not tell the jury that they could acquit Newton altogether. The defense expert at trial had compared Newton to soldiers in combat who could not recall their actions — including return fire — after the soldiers suffered stomach wounds. The appellate court reasoned that after Newton was wounded, he could have reflexively grabbed Officer Frey's gun and shot back in self-defense. On retrial before a new jury, the appellate court ordered that the jury be instructed to consider unconsciousness as a complete defense to the manslaughter charge. Meanwhile, Newton was to be released on bail with the very real possibility that a retrial could result in his acquittal.

The dumbfounded Attorney General's office filed for Supreme Court review, which was denied. Huey's release date was set for August 5, 1970. In his first interview, Newton credited the reversal in large part to "the pressure the people brought to bear on the case, as well as the work of my attorneys Charles Garry and Fay Stender...."[17] Both lawyers echoed Newton's comments. Yet Fay and Charles Garry both knew that they had engineered a remarkable legal feat. While Garry had taken center stage at the trial, their success owed as much to Fay's key motion work and extensive trial preparation. It was Fay who laid the groundwork for the appeal, which itself had been almost entirely Fay's labor of love. The police were livid and immediately pressed for Newton to be retried. Jensen steeled himself for another battle with Garry, vowing to convict Newton once more. This time the death penalty would no longer be an option — just jail time if the manslaughter charges stuck.

While Fay took immense pride in her achievement, she had scant time to celebrate. For the last three-and-a-half months, at Huey Newton's instigation, Fay had worked sometimes almost around the clock putting together a new defense team for another prisoner, Soledad inmate George Jackson. Fay assumed Jackson's life was at stake. It did not occur to her that her own life had just taken another fateful turn.

■ 4 ■

Entering Gladiator School

Prisoners who actually think they can get justice from the system are usually the ones who go mad.[1]
— Fay Stender

At first, Fay had only offered to see if she could help George Jackson gain his release on parole after serving nearly a decade for a $71 gas station robbery. By the date of their meeting, Jackson and two other inmates instead faced murder charges for the recent death of a popular young prison guard.

On Friday evening, January 16, 1970, twenty-five-year-old John Mills had been found near a prison stairwell with his skull fractured — the first guard killed in Soledad's long history. Local papers assumed that the sensational murder was in retaliation for the killing of three black inmates earlier that week by a prison sharp shooter. One of the dead inmates had been a good friend and mentor of George Jackson's. The defense team held out no hope for the trio's acquittal if the death penalty trial proceeded in ultraconservative Monterey County. They also faced long odds against getting the case transferred from the central coast city of Salinas. The key hearing on a motion to change venue to San Francisco was set for late June 1970.

On Fay's first trip to Soledad in the spring of 1969 the prison had looked to her like a large factory. She did not focus on the gun towers as

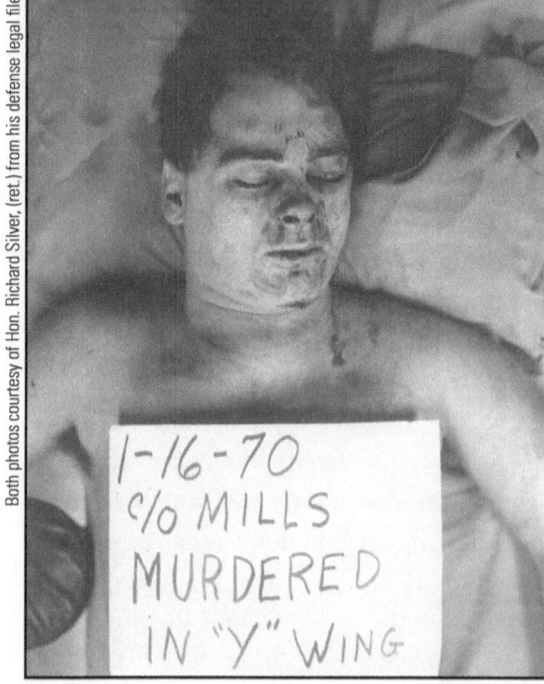

Official photos of the murder victim, John Mill, and blood on a stairwell in "Y" wing at Soledad Prison, taken on January 16, 1970.

she would on later visits. Fay parked in a visitors' lot, found her way past the barbed wire fence to the sergeant at the registration desk and asked to see Michael McCarthy. Shortly after Fay had tracked McCarthy's transfer from the Men's Colony to San Quentin in November of 1968, he had been hurriedly retransferred. The warden wanted no possibility of interaction between McCarthy and Eldridge Cleaver, who was scheduled to surrender himself for parole violation just before Thanksgiving and be imprisoned at San Quentin.

When McCarthy was moved south to Soledad, he had been accompanied by a special armed escort. Advance word to Soledad's warden described McCarthy as an extremely dangerous close associate of Huey Newton. Upon his arrival, officials at Soledad assumed a mistake had been made. McCarthy was white. Against stereotype, McCarthy joined a small group of black prisoners in a clandestine Marxist study group.

One of the militant Leftists at Soledad whom McCarthy befriended was George Jackson. The twenty-seven-year-old was just a few months' older than Huey Newton. Though housed in different wings, McCarthy and Jackson shared the main exercise yard. Among the state's African-American prison population, Jackson had already become a legendary figure for his tough, unbroken spirit and rage against the system that had kept him behind prison walls for his entire adulthood, mostly in solitary confinement.

* * *

George Lester Jackson, named for his parents Lester and Georgia Jackson, was born in September of 1941 in a poor black neighborhood by the noisy El close to the University of Chicago. Georgia had first recognized her namesake's unusual intelligence when he was two years old and could repeat from memory what he heard on the radio. Until he was kindergarten-aged, Georgia sheltered him and his older sister Delora from the neighborhood's rough crowd, isolating the two children on the roof, which was their sole playground. By the time he was five, George had little exposure to children outside his family and no experience at all interacting with any white kids. Lester Jackson argued that George would turn into a mama's boy.

Lester pushed George to play outside with other boys and punished him severely when he misbehaved. George was unimpressed with his father's long hours and low pay. George's favorite adult was his mother's father, who also lived in Chicago. His grandfather had an aggressive streak. George liked his attitude.

Despite his parents' best efforts, George started getting into trouble in his early teens. For several summers, the Jacksons sent their son to visit Georgia's relatives in the Southern Illinois countryside to get him away from Chicago's street life. Ironically, it was when visiting family in the country that George learned to use rifles, shotguns and pistols. He stole ammunition and used small wildlife for target practice.

Back in Chicago, the Jackson family moved into the projects. By then, George had two more sisters, Frances and Penelope, and a newborn brother Jonathan. George became a frequent truant. If there was a fight, he was in it. The police frequently picked him up for muggings or just on suspicion of misconduct. His father accepted a transfer to a postal job in Los Angeles where he and his wife hoped George would be free of bad influences. After the move, George was seldom at home.

When Jackson first arrived at Soledad at age eighteen, he had already incurred several major run-ins with the police. His juvenile record included a burglary in which George was wounded. That was what first got him sent to the California Youth Authority where he received vocational training and impressed his counselors by his superior intelligence and aptitude for assigned tasks. After fifteen months, the parole board considered Jackson rehabilitated and released him to obtain a job in the community.

It was only a short while later that Jackson was rearrested for the $71 gas station robbery that now kept him behind bars. Jackson had gone to the gas station with a friend. Neither was armed, but the two had with them George's little brother Jonathan's cap pistol, which George's friend brandished at the station attendant. When caught, the two teenagers had both pleaded guilty, which the public defender who represented George believed would result in leniency. Instead, Jackson was sentenced by the judge to prison for one year to life. His mother was heartbroken. Georgia stopped eating at the family dinner table when George went to jail.

By all accounts, Jackson was politically unaware when he first arrived in prison. He played poker, grabbed extra food, disobeyed orders and was described as "sullen, uncooperative and self-absorbed."[2] It did not take long, however, before Jackson started getting angry about racist prison policies. He realized that black prisoners drew longer sentences and faced far greater risks behind bars. White inmates were seldom searched for weapons, but blacks would be searched often and face additional charges for any weapon found. So black inmates were far more likely to suffer severe injury or death if attacked by a white prisoner with a concealed weapon.

Jackson and his best friend Jimmy Carr got into a race fight after another black inmate was stabbed. The two were then transferred. From San Quentin, George wrote his father about a prison official he believed wanted him dead and confided that he wanted to slit the man's throat.[3] Lester wrote to the administration in alarm, hopeful that they might offer George psychiatric help to address his self-destructive tendencies. His father's letter only resulted in George's placement in temporary lock up.

On his release from lock up, George requested work in the all-white electronics shop and instead was offered a job sweeping the yard. Jackson later told a biographer that when some of the black prisoners went on strike, a white gang calling itself Hitler's Helpers tried to lynch one of them. Jackson, with Jimmy Carr's help, organized his own gang they called the Wolf Pack. He exacted cigarettes or contraband in exchange for protection or revenge and sold drugs and alcohol to other inmates. He also grew attached to a gay inmate called Sweet Pea, who shared his stash of food and money. Jackson said nobody left without being perverted by prison in some way, whether sexually or otherwise.

It was while at San Quentin that George first formed a group of inmates focused on the revolutionary ideas of Lenin, Marx and Frantz Fanon. In his cell, George conducted imaginary conversations with famous economists and revolutionaries and wrote position papers he distributed throughout the prison. He and other members of his Marxist group fantasized about creating a trained army of inmates that could somehow escape and travel to Africa to join uprisings that were already liberating African nations from European colonialism. Jackson planned to pull bank robberies in order to finance his dream.

George decided to pursue parole. He avoided trouble for two years to convince the Adult Authority that he was rehabilitated. The parole board told George he could expect to be released the next time if he maintained his good behavior. His father promised to have a job waiting for him on his release. But the board composition changed; Jackson was denied parole twice more and transferred back to Soledad. Jackson ultimately concluded that the parole board had been playing with his mind, raising false hopes only to dash them.

At Soledad, George spent long hours perfecting his skills in the martial arts, earning him the nickname "Karate George." More rule violations were soon listed in Jackson's official file. Jackson assumed he was marked for death by prison officials. A carton of cigarettes was enough to induce an inmate to commit murder. George counted twenty attempts on his life. One white prisoner later signed an affidavit that he had been approached by Captain Moody at Soledad to kill Jackson.

By 1969, Jackson had given up hope of ever gaining freedom. Indeed, he had spent about two-thirds of his time in the last six years in isolation at San Quentin or Soledad in cells the inmates called "the hole." These fetid concrete boxes resembled zoo cages — nine or ten feet long by four feet wide with a mat in place of a bed and no toilet. All that the inmate was provided as a place to relieve himself was a raised platform in the floor with a hole in it. A heavy screen covered the door opening. Three years earlier a federal judge had declared the unsanitary state of these isolation cells illegal, but the prison had been slow to respond. While "in the hole," Jackson could expect to be let out only half an hour per day for exercise. He showered once or twice a month. The overwhelming monotony was relieved by infrequent visitors and letters to and from his family.

* * *

Fay knew nothing about George Jackson the first time she visited Soledad, but had only come at Newton's urging to help McCarthy win his release. If she could establish that prison officials simply wanted to punish McCarthy for his politics, their decision to keep him behind bars violated his First Amendment rights. Fay put McCarthy in touch with two attorneys from the local office of California Rural Legal Assistance to help him succeed at his next parole hearing.

McCarthy joined a discussion group and writing class conducted by a professor who convinced a sympathetic Catholic priest to obtain access to McCarthy's official prison files, or "jacket," and smuggle the jacket out to the CRLA attorneys. Intended for the eyes of officials only, the file had candidly referred to McCarthy's Marxist political beliefs as the reason for denial of parole. By December of 1969, McCarthy's new attorneys won his release.

Meanwhile, on one of Fay's visits to Newton at the Men's Colony in the fall of 1969 Newton asked her to help George Jackson get his release, too. McCarthy had smuggled word to Newton that Jackson wanted to join the Black Panther Party. Newton already knew about Jackson from Jimmy Carr, a weight-lifting champion at the Men's Colony whom Newton recruited as a bodyguard. Newton called him "Jackal Dog." Carr told Newton that Jackson was a close friend since the two had met as teenagers at the Duell Vocational Institution in Tracy and later served time together in San Quentin and Soledad.

Newton was impressed with what he learned about Jackson from Carr and through the grapevine from Panther Party member Earl Satcher, then also an inmate at Soledad. Newton named Jackson a field marshal of the Black Panther Party in charge of recruitment at Soledad. When Newton asked Fay to help Jackson get paroled, he knew Fay well enough to anticipate her outrage at Jackson's treatment. The average time served by prisoners with Jackson's robbery sentence was then three years; Jackson was serving his tenth.

Fay's schedule in the fall of 1969 was hectic. She had to appear in Kings County courthouse in early February of 1970 anyway to fight a speeding ticket, so she decided that trip south would provide a good excuse to return to Soledad. Fay did not know that the last time Jackson had showed up at a parole hearing at Soledad, in 1969, he learned that the best he could expect, with his past record, was transfer to Chino in a few years' time. That pronouncement was, to Jackson, a death sentence. He did not believe he would survive past thirty within prison walls. When the next opportunity for parole came up, Jackson had refused to humiliate himself by appearing before the Adult Authority.

When Fay arrived at the prison's main waiting room and showed her identification, she had to wait quite a while for the guards to fetch Jackson from solitary confinement. She did not realize Jackson was being escorted through five sets of secured, double doors from his cell to the hallway outside the visitors' rooms. Two inmates had recently implicated Jackson and two other black prisoners in "O" Wing—John Clutchette (pronounced Cloo-chay) and Fleeta Drumgo—in the January 16, 1970, killing of unarmed guard John Mills. The common assumption was that Mills died in retaliation for the felling of three black inmates in the prison yard three days earlier by sharpshooter Opie Miller. After closing that area for nearly two years because of ongoing race fights, prison officials had suddenly opened up the exercise yard on January 13 to a mixed-race group of violent felons. One of the men was boxer W. L. Nolen, who had been a plaintiff in the federal lawsuit that forced the prison to improve conditions in lock up. Witnesses later testified that as soon as fist fights started, the sharpshooter in his guard tower opened fire without warning, aiming only at black inmates.

Black prisoners smelled a set up and immediately went on a hunger strike. Then, on January 16, District Attorney Bertram Young went on the news to announce he saw no reason to prosecute Opie Miller. Only half an hour later, guard John Mills was found dead. A week and a half later, Young convened the grand jury, which indicted George Jackson, Fleeta Drumgo and John Clutchette on charges of murder and assault. As a lifer, Jackson faced death on both counts. Clutchette and Drumgo faced the death penalty only on the murder charge.

Meanwhile, the Monterey County grand jury quickly exonerated sharpshooter Opie Miller for his actions on January 13. The grand jury concluded Miller had first issued a warning and that he had acted reasonably in using a rifle instead of tear gas and in failing to follow prison rules that required him to aim at the prisoners' legs, not their chests. A later civil action for the three men's wrongful death would find otherwise.

While Soledad's black inmates seethed at the apparent whitewash of the deaths of the three black prisoners, the District Attorney turned his attention to avenging the death of guard John Mills. On February 4, 1970, Judge Elmer Machado appointed a public defender to represent George Jackson. Meanwhile, Clutchette and Drumgo's mothers frantically looked for private lawyers for their sons.

That week, as Fay sat waiting to meet Jackson, she had plenty of time to think about why she should avoid personal involvement in this new case a hundred miles from her office. When the guards returned to the visiting room, Fay was shocked that the inmate shuffling along with them had shackles on his feet and chains on his hands and under his crotch. One of the guards entered the room with the powerfully built, light-skinned prisoner and indicated his intention to stay at Fay's side for her protection while she conducted the interview. It had not dawned on Fay that this was standard Soledad policy for violent felons. Even Huey Newton had never been brought out to see his lawyers in chains or been denied private interviews with his attorneys.

Fay immediately demanded that Jackson's shackles be removed and that the guard leave. She offered to sign a waiver releasing the prison of responsibility in case anything happened to her. The guard was taken aback. He offered to wait outside the visiting room with the door open while she interviewed her potential client. The guard remained adamant, however, that the chains stay on Jackson. Fay would not take "no" for an answer and stormed down the hall to find the officer in charge. Burst in upon by this unexpected visitor, Captain Moody likewise refused to remove Jackson's chains.

Undaunted, Fay marched in to see the superintendent of the entire prison, Cletis Fitzharris, who insisted that the chains must stay in place because Jackson was extremely dangerous. Fay replied, "He's done nothing. All he has is a charge, and he is presumed innocent. So take off the chains." Fitzharris still refused. Fay realized there was nothing more she could do for the moment. Undeterred, she told Fitzharris that she would take the matter to federal court because he gave her no choice.[4]

At this point, of course, Fay had not even interviewed Jackson or decided to take the case. But the prison's policies enraged her. How dare this institution treat anyone like a beast? Fay felt that it smacked of the Nazi concentration camp at Dachau. In this frame of mind, she returned to meet George Jackson, determined to show him the basic human kindness the prison lacked. With the door open and the guard just outside, Fay conducted the interview in whispers. She did not know at the time that she was the first woman outside his family Jackson had had any conversation with since his arrest. He called her "Mrs. Stender" and told her he could not see that well without his glasses. Her heart melted. Jackson, in turn, basked in the unaccustomed warmth emanating from a white, middle-class professional woman — part of the establishment he had long since given up on.

Jackson later told Fay that when he had been fetched by the guard to finally meet Huey Newton's lawyer, his heart felt "as cold as Antarctica."[5] Jackson had earlier written to his mother asking her to recall her most depressing moment and she would know how he felt every day in prison.

As Jackson stood humbly before Fay in chains, he quoted Che Guevara. He also curried favor with Fay by telling her how much he admired Huey Newton as America's Chairman Mao. Jackson actually had reservations about Newton's bona fides as a true revolutionary. Fay was immediately drawn to the charismatic inmate but could make no commitment, except to investigate the case further. Jackson urged her to give him plenty of notice before she came again to visit. He wanted to be clean and presentable when he saw her next.

After she left, Fay researched the violent history of Soledad and became even more incensed at the deep-seated racism of the "Gladiator School." Meanwhile, *The Monterey Peninsula Herald* ran eulogies of John Mills. Potential jurors could read how in his past assignment in "C" wing, prisoners, both black and white, had taken a liking to the affable guard who planned to become a prison counselor. Correctional officers had already established a memorial fund for his grieving young widow and the future education of his four-month-old baby son. Readers were told the trust fund received an immediate donation from white inmates in "C" wing.

Fay realized there was no time to lose. The arraignment was set to take place on February 17. Back in her office, she received a message from State Senator Mervyn Dymally, still one of only a handful of high profile African-American politicians in the state. Senator Dymally had received letters from the inmates' families urging him to beg Fay to take the case. She consulted Newton, who encouraged her to put together a new team of lawyers for Jackson. Fay knew she would have to associate someone with far more criminal trial experience. She excelled at the organizational aspects of a trial, not performance in front of a jury. Even so, such a huge undertaking would undoubtedly stretch her new firm's finances to the limit as the Newton trial had strained Garry's firm.

Fay was concerned about her new partners' willingness to take the case on. She called an emergency meeting of the law collective to consider the issue. Fay's excitement was contagious. This was a major opportunity for a political trial. She told her partners that she intended to clear her calendar of other cases and ask John Thorne of San Jose to become lead counsel. Thorne was an aggressive criminal defense lawyer well known in the Lawyers Guild. There was no money in the case, but the families were prepared to help Fay with extensive community fund-raising. Her partners all voted yes without hesitation.

Fay then brought John Thorne on board. A bear of a man in his mid-forties, the Guild lawyer was in the prime of his career. He was also a committed Marxist. To improve their chances before Monterey county judges, Fay wanted local counsel for both Drumgo and Clutchette. She brought in a young lawyer associated with Carmel attorney Francis Heisler to represent Fleeta Drumgo.

Silver was an Oaklander who had moved to the Monterey peninsula in 1968 after a tour of duty in Vietnam. He had been a member of the same Boalt class of 1966 as Mike Tigar and Fay's partner Phil Ziegler. Silver recommended a law school friend, Floyd Silliman, to represent John Clutchette. Silliman came from a wealthy Republican family in Salinas but was himself a liberal Democrat with a burgeoning reputation as a criminal lawyer. Silver's recent service as an army captain gave them additional credibility with the conservative local bench.

Thorne made an appointment to meet Jackson while Fay took charge of the public relations and legal briefs. As Garry had taught her, Fay considered a successful media campaign a key strategy. Fay

The Soledad Brothers

John Clutchette, Fleeta Drumgo, and George Jackson

John Thorne, Fay Stender's co-counsel for George Jackson, is on the left facing Floyd Silliman (who represented John Clutchette) in the middle and Richard Silver (who represented Fleeta Drumgo) on the right.

immediately circulated a court picture from the first February hearing. It depicted Jackson chained like an animal to his two co-defendants. He looked handsome and his seldom-worn prescription glasses added poignancy to the photo. It incensed Fay that her second and third meetings at the prison with Jackson, like her first, had taken place with an open door and the guard just outside. The only way to preserve confidentiality was by whispers and written questions, answers and sketches, impeded by Jackson's shackles and handcuffs. She lobbied successfully to gain free access to her client.

Fay soon attracted many volunteer law students and paralegals to the high profile pretrial proceedings — with herself at the center of all the frenzied activity. Jackson later described her waving her long arms like an orchestra conductor. Silver saw it the same way from his vantage point as her co-counsel. He added, "Fay played half the band instruments as well." Most of the legal papers were drafted at her desk in Berkeley. In his adjacent office, Phil Ziegler noticed how thin Fay became as she cocooned herself in her office, oblivious to those around her. She seemed to spend night and day on the new murder case, typing or on the phone, barely eating and sleeping.

As soon as she could fit it in, Fay made a plane trip to Los Angeles where she met with Jackson's family to enlist their help in obtaining community support for the newly named "Soledad Brothers." At the airport waiting for a commuter plane back to Oakland, Fay ran into a fellow Berkeley activist, legal secretary Jerrie Meadows. Meadows was helping coordinate the New Mobilization Committee to End the War in Vietnam. She had just attended a planning meeting in Los Angeles and was also on her way home.

Meadows' organizational skills were highly prized in Fay's circle, as well as Meadows' possession of a set of nearly a thousand index cards with names and addresses of generous donors to Leftist causes. Grabbing a seat next to Jerrie, Fay exuberantly explained that she had just taken on the Soledad Brothers' representation and was setting up a fund-raising committee for the defense. She asked Jerrie to head it. Meadows firmly rejected the idea, telling Fay, "I can't, I'm up to my ears in the peace movement."

On the hour-long trip home to the Bay Area, Fay tried hard to convince Meadows otherwise. It amused Meadows how Fay insisted that her new cause was the most important thing in the whole world. Not so for Meadows — ending the war emphatically came first. But Meadows also noted with alarm that Fay had a transfixed look on her face when she described George Jackson, the same look that Jerrie's friend Beverly Axelrod had when she first met Eldridge Cleaver. Meadows wondered how this would end; Beverly Axelrod's life was shattered.

■ 5 ■

"My Small but Mighty Mouthpiece"

You're like no one I've ever met from across the tracks.[1]
— GEORGE JACKSON TO FAY STENDER

F ay galvanized Leftists to George Jackson's cause with the same grim visions that haunted her: "Three young black inmates of Soledad prison, may soon be murdered by the State of California. . . . They are innocent. Their right to a fair trial is being systematically and intentionally destroyed by the prison administration. . . . They will be railroaded to the gas chamber unless we move to stop this injustice and show the state that the lives of black men and prison inmates are not expendable."[2]

The number of local volunteers quickly outgrew Fay's law office. The Soledad Brothers Defense Committee then opened its own headquarters at 1708 Grove Street in Berkeley. To cover the escalating expenses of the defense, they raised money as they had done for other causes — with wine and cheese parties, cocktail parties, dinners, flea markets and art auctions. Jackson's supporters spoke on campuses and churches, asked rock groups to perform concerts, issued press releases and wrote letters.

Branch committees opened in San Jose (where John Thorne's office was located), Santa Cruz, Los Angeles and Marin County. The

Los Angeles Soledad Committee included Jackson's mother Georgia, his sisters and younger brother. Michael McCarthy also joined that group. He had introduced himself to Los Angeles Friends of the Panthers shortly after his December, 1969, release from prison. Fay got playwright Jean Genet, anti-war activist Dr. Benjamin Spock and Congressman Ron Dellums to lend their names to the effort. She persuaded black clergymen in Oakland to write a "friend of the court" brief to the presiding judge objecting to shackles as vestiges of slavery.

Fay even wrote to the Cleavers in exile in Algiers through a confidential local contact. Fay pleaded for Cleaver to add his voice in protest: "We need your help to save them — it's 10 times harder than Huey's case." Fay promised to send copies of Jackson's letters — "they're beautiful and you'll weep."[3]

Still, there was little hope of shifting public sentiment in Monterey County. On the Friday before the postponed arraignment, the guard's widow was invited to Soledad where white inmates presented her with a scroll of sympathy signed by hundreds of prisoners and a check for additional pledges to the Mills Memorial Fund. *The Monterey Peninsula Herald* ran a large picture of three white inmates presenting the scroll to Mills' pretty, young widow.

To counter the sympathy for Mills' widow, Fay's flyers proclaimed that Jackson, Drumgo and Clutchette were staring at the death penalty as scapegoats: "The Soledad Brothers will find justice in the courts of Salinas only if, by our actions, we make it impossible for the state to execute them. We urge you to help us prevent the deaths of these three young men as a first step in exposing and transforming a brutally destructive legal system."[4]

Radicals from the Bay Area swarmed the Salinas courthouse on February 24th for the Soledad Brothers' arraignment before Presiding Judge Gordon Campbell. A reporter for the *Salinas Californian* noted that "the talk around the courthouse is that Monterey County may have another Huey P. Newton trial on its hands — a gigantic legal spectacle with a heavy emphasis on race."[5]

At the hearing, Fay had several motions ready. Silver was in awe, watching Fay prepare. He had never seen anyone else like her. She analyzed every issue with extraordinary agility, then grabbed a typewriter and rattled out papers at lightning speed. One motion asked the judge to lift his recent gag order preventing both sides from talking publicly about the case. Fay also challenged the judge's decision to keep the three inmates dressed in prison garb and shackled when they came to court. Huey Newton had been jailed all during his trial but was still allowed to dress up for court and appear without restraints of any kind. It was clear that made a huge difference in how the jury reacted to him. Fay felt the Soledad Brothers were doomed if the Salinas jury feared the trio on sight.

Jackson left that hearing without making eye contact with either of his attorneys, upset at the court's rulings and with his passive role. Sitting silently in court while he raged inside exacerbated his feeling of impotence. George bristled at a publicity campaign portraying him as haplessly suffering cruel indignities and chafed at playing the role of victim. He had always rankled under attempts to view him through rose-colored glasses. In a letter to Fay shortly after the hearing, he explained that his mother liked to tell people he was a good boy, but it wasn't true, "I've been a brigand all my life."[6]

After the hearing, Fay rushed back to Berkeley for more help. She called David Wellman, the graduate student in sociology at Cal who still showed up for demonstrations on Newton's behalf. Wellman would do whatever she wanted. Fay asked him to interview white prisoners at Soledad and help analyze census data for their attack on the constitutionality of the jury composition. Wellman accompanied Fay as she drove at full throttle back down to Salinas. It made him quite nervous how she often kept only one hand on the wheel as she gestured to him in animated conversation or reached to hand him papers, jot down a note or take a drink.

When David Wellman was introduced to Thorne, Thorne's ego and chauvinism reminded him of Charles Garry. David grew incensed watching Thorne dismiss Fay's input and flirt with their paralegal. David's anger remained etched in his memory decades later. After the meeting, when Fay invited him out for a drink, David asked her, "Why do you let them treat you like that?" She shook her head, "That's the

The cover of a pamphlet the Soledad Brothers Defense Committee distributed seeking support — showing the defendants chained hand and foot. Left to right behind the guards: John Clutchette, George Jackson and Fleeta Drumgo.

way they are." It struck Wellman as a bitter pill for Fay to let such blatant sexists as Thorne and Garry take credit for her hard work in feeding them lines.

Both Richard Silver and Fay had a different take. There was nothing personally offensive to Fay in Thorne's behavior. Fay considered Thorne gregarious, smart and good on his feet in the courtroom. All four of the Soledad Brothers lawyers were simpatico collaborators. When they had a rare chance to relax after a long day, Silliman entertained them with his guitar and singing. If a piano was available, Fay played as well. Yet mainly they worked.

The defense team's principal focus at that time was finding evidence to refute the three inmates who had testified to the grand jury that they witnessed the attack on John Mills on the third tier of the stairwell. A black British-born inmate named Yorke had given particularly damaging testimony. Yorke's companion Eskew corroborated that account with some variation in the details. A third inmate, William Worzella, testified he saw Jackson and Clutchette standing over a body on the tier above. The defense needed to interview these purported eye witnesses as soon as possible. The prosecutor had an extraordinary advantage — unfettered access to the crime scene and the prison's interviews of all of its inmates in that wing on the evening of the killing.

The defense team learned that, when interviewed by officials on the evening of the crime, Worzella had originally reported seeing and knowing nothing. Yorke and Eskew's files also yielded useful information. All three had since been transferred. On March 16, 1970, Fay and Silver flew to Southern California to interview the three. Yorke refused to discuss anything about the case without an attorney present. The two white inmates were hostile but answered questions for several hours. Fay and Silver flew back from the interviews buoyed with their view that none of the three men would make good witnesses.[7]

The next morning, a hundred spectators squeezed into the Salinas courtroom. Others were turned away for lack of seats. Most had come by the busload from the Bay Area at Fay's request. She had seen how judges seemed more careful when they were in the spotlight. The bailiff warned the spectators at the outset that Judge Campbell would tolerate no unruly behavior. The three prisoners arrived again in their prison clothes, shackled together, shuffling forward to keep from falling.

All three now wore red buttons with black letters that proclaimed them the "Soledad Brothers." Many spectators also wore the distinctive buttons. A few had pinned on "Free Huey" buttons. One reporter noted some hippies in the audience, but most who attended dressed more conventionally. Judge Campbell looked askance at his audience and admonished them that they needed to remain silent. The Soledad Brothers' attorneys began the hearing by objecting once more to their clients' chains. The inmates were not even seated next to their counsel and could not communicate with them during the hearing. The diminutive judge cut them off in mid-sentence, swiftly denying their renewed motion to have the shackles removed. Judge Campbell and everyone else who read the local papers knew that two days earlier another racial brawl had broken out between black and white inmates of Soledad, resulting in a lockdown of all six hundred inmates in the North facility.

The defense counsel asked for additional time before their clients were required to enter pleas so they could interview all 130 remaining inmates in "Y" wing and get access to the physical site where the guard's body was found. Fay presented the constitutional attack on Monterey County's grand jury, pointing to the lack of Blacks, Mexicans, young people and the poor. No one with a Spanish surname had served on it in the past thirty years. Even the county's majority of Democrats were underrepresented. Two-thirds of the panel were Republicans. Judge Campbell insisted the grand jurors were chosen for "fairness of mind." Thorne responded, "We need understanding of soul as well as fairness of mind."[8]

Judge Campbell asked the defendants whether they pleaded guilty or not guilty to the charges. A verbal free-for-all ensued. Judge Campbell struggled for control while the defense lawyers refused to be cut off. They declared that the judge had made it impossible to advise their clients how to plead and the defendants would instead "stand mute." Judge Campbell decided to enter three "not guilty" pleas. He ordered the grand jury transcript released to the public and scheduled trial to take place on June 22. He then took up pretrial motions, quickly granting some and denying others. As the hearing drew to a close, defense counsel became convinced Judge Campbell was on a steady march to send their clients to the gas chamber.

Outside, the defense team complained to reporters that the proceedings had become a "sham and farce."[9] The defense had only fifteen days to attack all of Judge Campbell's rulings. Fay worked past midnight almost every night to meet that deadline. The defense team had also begun work on a motion to get the trial out of Monterey County. Its prospects were dim. Yet they felt that their only hope for their clients' lives was to move the case to either Los Angeles or San Francisco.

They had to assume Judge Campbell would reject the idea of a transfer out of hand. In the hundred-year history of the Monterey County bench, no change of venue had, to anyone's knowledge, ever before been granted on the basis of excessive pretrial publicity. Could they somehow get a different, more sympathetic, local trial judge?

Back in court on March 27th, Judge Campbell was temporarily replaced by his colleague Judge Larson. Fay was glad to see that Decca Mitford had accepted her invitation to that hearing. The best-selling author of *The American Way of Death* had recently published another book, *The Trial of Dr. Spock*. Mitford sat through his criminal trial for conspiring to interfere with the Vietnam War draft. Mitford's presence in the Salinas courthouse caused speculation in the local press that the muckraker might be working on a book about the trial of the Soledad Brothers.

The defense team realized with great relief that Judge Larson came to the hearing with an open mind. Judge Larson gave the district attorney until April 10 to furnish the witnesses' statements. He assessed each issue on its merits, ruling sometimes for the prosecutor and sometimes for the defense. Fay and her co-counsel reveled in their progress.

The one person seated at the defense table that day who harbored serious misgivings was George Jackson. He had vetoed a request for a change of venue to Los Angeles, where his family lived because the courthouse in L.A. would likely be on the fifteenth floor and heavily secured. His focus was on his avenues of escape. Jackson did not believe his lawyers could convince any jury in the state to keep him from the gas chamber.

George felt the same way about sitting mute before a jury as he did about presenting himself humbly one more time before the parole board. He wrote Fay that every man who got parole "crawled into that room . . . [and] surrendered . . . some part of his face (read mind, or pride, or principle). . . ." If an inmate had any record of past violence, the parole board scrutinized him for telltale signs of total submission. "[Y]ou can't fake it — resignation, defeat. . . ."[10] Watching his lawyers gear up for trial, Jackson remained filled with fury and committed solely to revolution.

■ 6 ■

The Shaping of a Revolutionary Hero

If he had been outside, he would never have belonged to us in the same way, but locked away, he was ours.[1]
—JACKSON'S BOOK EDITOR, GREGORY ARMSTRONG

Fay had to work hard to keep up Jackson's morale. After their first meeting, she corresponded with him frequently. Jackson wrote often, using the stubby pencil that was the only writing implement officials permitted in his cell. Most letters to family and friends went through several levels of censorship, read by the mail clerk and his superiors and on occasion referred to the warden before being photographed and placed in his jacket. Letters to attorneys were exempt. In his first letter in February of 1970, Jackson still addressed her as "Mrs. Stender." He asked if she would urge the judge to order that he not be chained whenever he left his cell. He told her how much he appreciated her efforts to cheer him up. "Hope and I are old friends." She told him he could drop the formalities. His next letter began with "Dear Fay," and responded to her inquiry about his need for clothing.[2]

Jackson confided that he considered "the cruelest aspect in the loss of one's freedom of movement . . . the necessity to repress the sex urge." But he said that over a decade in prison he had controlled that by doing a thousand fingertip push-ups each day. He guessed he held the world's record.[3]

Thorne made numerous road trips to Soledad to visit his new client. When not in court, the burly lead counsel wore blue jeans, a Chairman Mao cap with a red star and a denim jacket, with a gold, clenched-fist pin in its lapel. On her own trips to see Jackson in the spring of 1970, Fay usually dressed in a leather mini-skirt with her hair tied back in a ponytail. Though Fay was thirty-eight at the time, to freelance reporter Susan Berman, Fay looked more like a graduate student than a dedicated career woman. Some thought Fay was consciously imitating infamous Weathermen leader Bernadette Dohrn. On one of Fay's earliest visits, Fay smuggled in a taped message to Jackson from Huey Newton. Jackson wrote her that the tape left him feeling better than he had felt for at least ten years.

Thorne, like Fay, exuded love and admiration for the charismatic revolutionary. Both attorneys wanted to buoy his spirits and often brought their chain-smoking client cigarettes and candy from the vending machines in the main waiting room. Fay had instantly responded with a fierce protective instinct, succumbing, as she had with Newton, to the physical attraction of the handsome political icon. Fay's law partner Ezra Hendon exclaimed, "She visited him and she was nailed."

George Jackson held out little or no hope for success at trial and hardly recognized himself as the innocent victim at the heart of all his defense team's rhetoric. But, by March 5, Jackson was apologizing for his aloof behavior in court that day. He praised Fay's intelligence and sensitivity but voiced his dilemma in responding to the victim's image she painted, "wedged between me and who knows what fate." He found it both a cause for elation and fury, asking her why should he be relegated to "such a position of weakness?" George figured she could help him understand this as they worked together over the next several years. This time he signed it simply "George."[4] Soon he was calling Fay his "favorite person."[5]

Fay cherished these letters. It did not bother her that Jackson had a growing female fan club, to each of whom he professed equal love. Yet he fantasized about meeting a true revolutionary woman who would escape with him into the underground and live off the land. Jackson described his ideal companion to Fay as a woman who would carry only a flight bag, be willing to sleep in freight cars, always on the run and ever on the watch. "She would own nothing, not solely because she loved me, but because she loved the principle, the revolution, the people."[6]

Jackson left out of his verbal sketch to Fay other requirements he had formulated: that his soul mate not be overprotective like his mother and older sister and that "she has got to rob with me, steal with me, cut throats with me."[7] Fay was elated to be Jackson's trusted confidante. She considered their closeness a partnership against oppression, just as she still viewed her relationship with Newton. Fay could no longer think of Newton and Jackson as her clients, but as revolutionary comrades, for whom practically no sacrifice was too great. Her long hours week in and out without payment strained the partnership's finances. But Fay was oblivious. She welcomed any new recruit she could instill with equal zeal for the two revolutionary prisoners' freedom.

At the Co-op in Berkeley in early March, Fay ran into Karen Wald, just returned from Cuba. Wald had spent months as part of the defense team's inner circle when she covered the 1968 Newton trial. Fay tried to convince Wald to join the Soledad Brothers Defense team, but the Newton trial had taken a major toll on her. Even if the defense team were successful, Jackson also would remain in prison. For Wald, it was too heart-rending. Fay invited her to come for dinner the next week. In Fay's kitchen, Fay pulled out one of Jackson's letters and read it to Wald. That was enough. She was hooked, just like Fay.

* * *

When Jackson saw Fay at their March 17 hearing, he aggressively embraced her and she backed off, saying she did not know him that well. Jackson then asked her to reconsider: "I encircle the people that I dig." Flattering her as a committed comrade, he added that he sensed from their first meeting that the two were "kindred spirits." But he warned her it was impossible for her to really know him.[8]

Jackson tried to bridge the gulf between them, explaining to Fay that he had always reacted to crises by provoking a more desperate situation. He told her he likely would not have survived so far if he did not habitually overreact: "I seize the bull by the horns . . . ride him till his neck breaks or until he pins me to the wall."[9] He told her "if they would reach me now, across my many barricades it must be with a bullet and must be final."[10]

Since she started in February, Fay had spent seventy hours per week, generally ten hours per day, including weekends representing Jackson. Soon, Jackson began calling Fay his "small but mighty mouthpiece." He indicated that prison officials were making it hard for him to get what he required and said they could discuss it when she visited. In future visits to the prison, the two repeatedly managed to embrace, despite his shackles, the prison rules against touching inmates, and a guard posted at the door, who peered in from time to time. Fay found herself even more drawn to Jackson than she was to Newton. She told friends that both militants occupied a place in her heart nearly equal to that of her family. Fay remained undeterred even after an embarrassing incident when a guard at Soledad came in and pulled Fay and her client apart.

Fay made no attempt to hide her emotional attachment to Jackson when co-counsel were present. She let Jackson hug her tightly in front of them. Fay must have felt Jackson suffered such degradation in the skin searches he underwent to see visitors that letting go of decorum was the least she could do. Silver admired Fay greatly but worried about the outcome of this intense infatuation: Jackson faced capital punishment if they lost, and continued imprisonment, probably for the rest of his life, even if they won.

Meanwhile, Fay organized satellite Soledad Brother support groups. Among other speaking engagements, she had arranged for a public forum on the case at Victoria Hall in Los Angeles in March with Jackson's family and the mothers of the other two accused inmates. A hundred or so adults assembled, young and old, mostly black. In the audience was a young instructor from UCLA named Angela Davis. Davis had reacted with anger in February when she saw on the front page of *The Los Angeles Times* the now famous picture of the three Soledad Brothers draped in chains and shackled together. The prisoners looked like slaves still in bondage. For the next few days she had been haunted by memories of their faces.

Fay, as the principal speaker, was seated at a table in the front of the room. She must have understood that her credibility with the largely black audience depended on the presence on the panel of members of the Soledad Brothers' families. Fay was joined by Jackson's mother, Georgia, and his sisters Penny and Frances, as well as the mothers of Fleeta Drumgo and John Clutchette. Georgia was as spirited, quick-witted and stubborn as her first-born son. She fervently hoped that Huey Newton's lawyer could get her son exonerated. Losing was unthinkable. Fay was in her element. She addressed the crowd with a vivid description of the structure of Soledad and its history of encouraging the formation of gangs. She described the history of often bloody confrontations between Chicano and black gangs and the Aryan Brotherhood at Soledad. The Aryan Brotherhood had a "blood in, blood out" policy requiring the killing of another inmate to gain entry. Those who wanted to quit were threatened with death. Then she focused on the suspicious circumstances surrounding the opening of the yard at "O" Wing on January 13th, the day a sharp-shooting guard killed three black prisoners.

It reminded Davis of incidents of police officers in Los Angeles shooting defenseless blacks. Fay described the grand jury's whitewash of prison guard Opie Miller for the killings, the black prisoners' angry protest, and the death of the new guard who "stumbled into the brothers' fierce, but chaotic rebellion." Sitting there listening, Davis heard Fay say "no one knew who pushed the guard over the railing," but that the three defendants stood accused because they were black militants the officials wanted to see executed.[11]

Though instantly drawn to the cause of the Soledad Brothers, Davis felt distanced when Fay launched into a legal analysis of their situation. Davis could not relate to this white, middle-class woman playing such a central role in the life or death of black brothers. Many other African-Americans in the hall likely felt the same way. What moved that gathering in Victoria Hall most was Georgia Jackson's heartfelt speech. Years later, Davis vividly recalled Georgia Jackson's "unashamed maternal pain. . . . Black, woman, mother; her infinite strength undergird[ing] her plaintive words."[12]

The crowd had gone silent when Jackson's mother struggled to maintain her composure, describing how George had been taken away from his family for one year to life at the age of eighteen. Georgia believed her son was sitting innocently in the car when his friend held up the service station. The system had been stacked against him, the public defender had failed him and George was stuck possibly for life behind bars. Similar emotional pleas were made by Inez Drumgo and John Clutchette's mother. The crowd was electrified. Davis was among those who committed to do whatever possible to save the trio from "legal lynching."[13]

At the end of that meeting, Davis volunteered to coordinate campus appearances for the defense committee while she was conducting a statewide campaign to keep her job. Davis faced being fired as a philosophy instructor at UCLA for her membership in the Communist Party. Davis donated all of her speaking fees to the defense fund and played a key role in launching their cause as a popular, grassroots political campaign. Jackson read a newspaper account of Davis's activities and urged his mother to let Davis know he would like to meet her.

Jackson now relished being the center of a flurry of attention. The enthusiasm of the newly formed Soledad Brothers Defense Committee was contagious. It sometimes gave him faint hope of deliverance from the gas chamber — if he could make himself follow his lawyers' advice. Yet, when Jackson met with Fay and Thorne, he still spoke frequently of escape.

Fay thought George's chances of acquittal would increase if his writings were disseminated widely. With Jackson's permission, she gathered his prison correspondence from family and friends. Based on Beverly Axelrod's success in marketing Eldridge Cleaver's essays, Fay saw enormous potential. By the spring of 1970, the classic *Soul On Ice* had already gone through several printings. It had quickly joined *The Autobiography of Malcolm X* and Claude Brown's *Manchild in the Promised Land* as essential reading for students of Black Power. Cleaver had been a confessed rapist, which even many of his supporters found difficult to consider a revolutionary crime. Jackson had the potential to be viewed far more sympathetically as an innocent victim of a racist prison system.

Fay selected the most eloquent portions of Jackson's letters to attract a publisher's interest. With Jackson now facing execution, she had an extraordinary story to market. Meanwhile, Fay constantly needed to reassure Jackson that he should follow her advice. To keep him motivated, she sent him Ann Ginger's new handbook on the Newton trial, *Minimizing Racism in Jury Trials*. She also sent Jackson a copy of her brief to the court of appeal on Newton's behalf. Jackson was impressed by the amazing results the legal team had achieved, but warned Fay that success in his case was most unlikely. He described himself among "dull, heavy-handed" desperados who predictably violate the law. In contrast he considered Fay an exemplar of "the gracious, sensitive, brainy types" who make "the legal pigs" adhere strictly to the Constitution. "The cynic in me . . . sees another situation building down the road. . . ."[14]

Jackson explained to Fay what he meant: "They won't defeat my revenge, never, never. . . . I'm going to charge them reparations in blood . . . like a maddened, wounded rogue male elephant, ears flared, trunk raised, trumpet blaring. . . . War without terms."[15]

Fay had won Jackson's complete trust in just two months. The first week of April, he gave Fay authorization in writing to hire a literary agent and to negotiate with book publishers on his behalf. At the time, he had no idea that Fay had removed his threats of retaliatory violence from the manuscript in order to portray him as a sensitive victim. Beverly Axelrod had never sought to bowdlerize Eldridge Cleaver's raw voice in such fashion. Fay's extensive editing unwittingly sowed the seeds of a major rift with the death row inmate.

Meanwhile, Fay sought to convince her skeptical client that taking his chances at trial was a better option. Even if he were successful in breaking out, his plan would place him perpetually on the run as a fugitive. Jackson did not disagree. That was the only future he could envision for himself. Jackson tried to persuade Fay that revolution was the only path, an altar upon which he was willing to sacrifice his beloved younger brother Jonathan as well as himself — "extreme measures to solve extreme problems."[16]

* * *

Michael McCarthy shared Jackson's pessimism and wanted to help plot Jackson's escape. But when McCarthy approached the Los Angeles Panthers, they were suspicious of the white ex-felon. Their paranoia was understandable. Undercover agents had been infiltrating many chapters of the Party and enticing members to join in plans for which they wound up imprisoned or killed.

McCarthy referred the Los Angeles Panthers to Fay to verify that he was a bona fide revolutionary friend of Huey Newton and George Jackson. Fay had still not met McCarthy, they had only corresponded and spoken by phone. Fay surprisingly refused to discuss McCarthy with the Panthers over the telephone. McCarthy was furious. Fay had just put his life at greater risk. He asked her to help him contact Jackson in prison to vouch for him. Fay refused; she thought it was dangerous and not in Jackson's interest. Friends like McCarthy only encouraged Jackson's delusions of escape, undermining his cooperation with the legal defense team. Fay told McCarthy to lay low. McCarthy instead came to the Bay Area behind her back to speak with others on the Soledad Brothers Defense Committee. He enlisted John Thorne and Jackson's sisters as go-betweens to George. Jackson responded with a tape-recorded message that McCarthy was trustworthy. Jackson also sent word back that he had talked to Fay and "straightened her out" about McCarthy.

In April, McCarthy published a long article in the *Los Angeles Free Press* under the pseudonym Micha Maguire. He asserted that Jackson, Drumgo and Clutchette were headed for lynching by the state — one more genocidal act linked to the execution of Chicago Black Panther leader Fred Hampton and the upcoming murder trial of Bobby Seale. McCarthy soon became close to Jonathan Jackson. At Georgia Jackson's request, McCarthy sought to act as her younger son's mentor. Jonathan's goal to break George out had McCarthy's wholehearted support, but McCarthy worried that Jonathan was associating with untrustworthy collaborators.

*   *   *

While George Jackson mapped his own road to freedom, the defense team began interviewing prisoners at Soledad. It was a daunting task since they had no idea which inmates, if any, might be called as prosecution witnesses. To the lawyers' dismay, the warden had told the inmates they had the choice to have a guard present. Only one out of ten sought a private interview. The lawyers felt many were intimidated into silence. Still, they found inmates prepared to swear that Jackson was in the television room when Mills died in the stairwell.

Jackson continued to be impressed with Fay's efforts. She convinced three prominent black politicians to call for a blue-ribbon panel to investigate claims of racism at Soledad. When Fay joined an inspection tour, Jackson assumed she was the first woman ever permitted entry into Soledad's maximum-security wing.

Time was ticking. The defense lawyers were desperate to knock Judge Campbell off the case. On May 2, Fay and Thorne and two other members of the team met with Professor Anthony Amsterdam at Stanford University, to strategize on possible federal intervention. Amsterdam advised the defense to exhaust all state court remedies first. Amsterdam agreed that Jackson's status as a lifer for assisting as a teenager in a friend's $71 robbery smacked of racism. Amsterdam also endorsed the idea of a federal suit challenging Judge Campbell's gag order as a violation of the defendants' free speech rights. Fay left the meeting on a mission: to file every conceivable motion in the trial court before the next hearing.

For a change, George Jackson looked forward to his next court appearance on May 8. He had sent Angela Davis a note welcoming her to attend it with his mother and siblings. Davis agreed to come. Jackson believed she could be the revolutionary woman he envisioned as his life partner. He was determined to make Angela fall in love with him. When Angela entered the Salinas courtroom, she was amazed by the number of people who had turned out to support the Soledad Brothers in such a conservative community. Of course, almost all had been bussed or driven down from the Bay Area. The small percentage of black spectators offended her. Davis did not know Fay had tried to get Assemblyman Willie Brown to make a special appearance at the May 8 hearing on the Soledad Brothers' behalf.

Once again, the Soledad Brothers made their entrance in shackles and chains. This time Jackson marched proudly, beaming at his family and Angela Davis seated with them. As he had hoped, Davis was immediately taken with Jackson's bearing and beautiful smile. To George, Davis's presence was the only positive aspect of sitting quietly on best behavior as the attorneys once again wrangled with the hostile judge who held Jackson's life in his hands. Judge Campbell was clearly irritated by Fay's additional filings on the court's busy Friday morning calendar. These new papers meant only one thing — the Soledad Brothers' counsel were padding the record in an effort to get Campbell's decision reversed.

Fay first argued that the three inmates who testified before the grand jury may have been coerced. Fay next added testimony to support her challenge to the grand jury. The defense needed time to pore through new census data to analyze whether blacks, the poor and Spanish-speaking citizens were systematically underrepresented in the voting list used to select jurors for this case.

Judge Campbell had started the morning hearing in a testy mood. The prosecutor sensed he was winning and chose not to respond. Thorne convinced the reluctant judge to allow the defense to submit further evidence. All of the defense lawyers then explained why they needed three months to adequately prepare for trial. Judge Campbell had heard enough. After a five-minute break, Judge Campbell resumed the bench and made a lengthy statement explaining why he was denying a delay of the trial and rose to leave the bench. Thorne refused to treat the hearing as over without completing the record for purposes of appeal. He precipitated an argument with Judge Campbell who found Thorne guilty of contempt and fined him $75 on the spot. Court was in recess. They had made their record and caused the cantankerous judge to lose his temper. It might be possible to provoke Judge Campbell enough to render him unfit to conduct an impartial trial. Thorne was game to try.

THE SHAPING OF A REVOLUTIONARY HERO

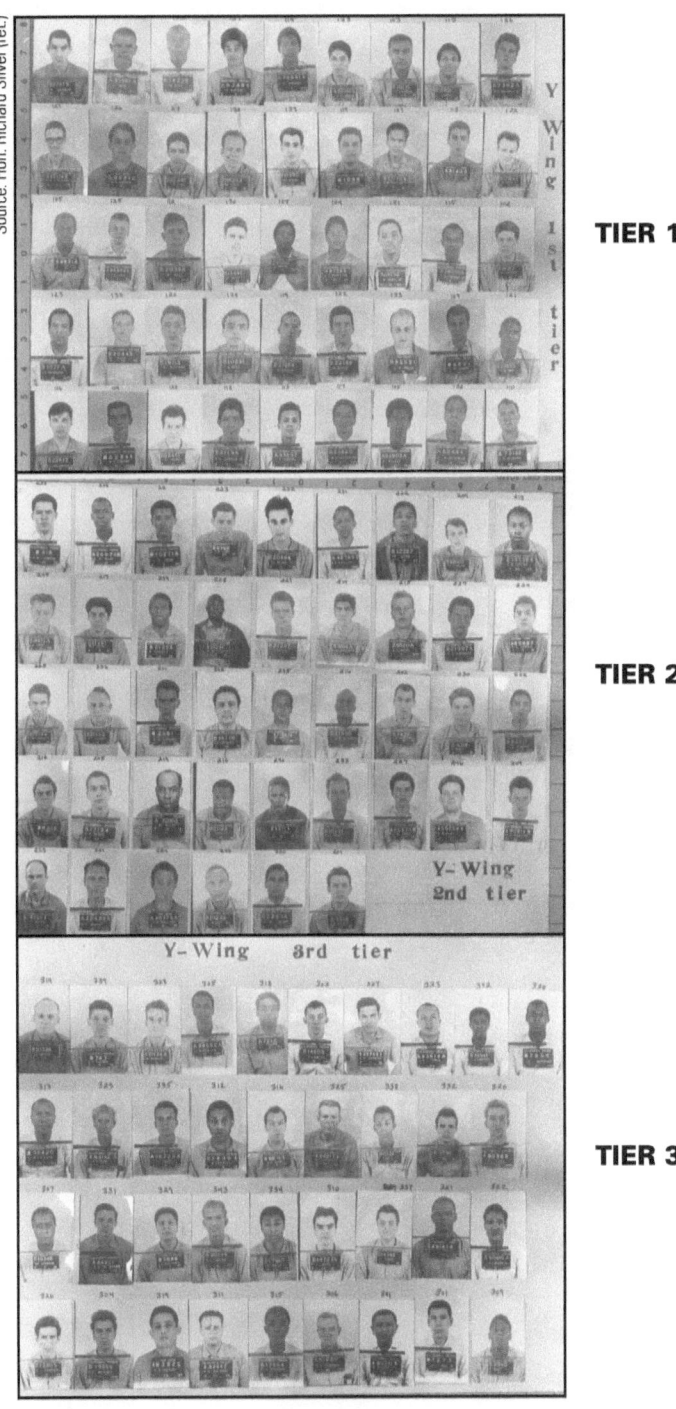

Inmates in "Y" Wing of Soledad Prison that the defense wanted a delay of trial to interview.

■ 7 ■
On a Roll

> *"Is your Honor collecting evidence that we are not supposed to see?"*[1]
> — FAY STENDER'S INQUIRY AT A SOLEDAD BROTHERS PRETRIAL HEARING

The following week a full house of spectators came to watch the next expected clash between John Thorne and Judge Campbell. This time, Thorne felt he had the ammunition he needed. Though the defense team had worked round the clock on more motions, Thorne's focus was simple — to force Judge Campbell off the case.

On Thursday morning, May 14, Judge Campbell woke up in a foul mood. He had set aside a full day for this case and read in advance all the motions and responses. Then, last-minute additional papers filed by the defense on Wednesday had forced him to stay up until past midnight preparing for the hearing. Judge Campbell counted a total of seventeen discovery motions. He began the hearing by scolding the defense counsel.

The defense team were looking to exploit any indication of bias from the bench. In rejecting one of Fay's arguments, Judge Campbell mentioned that Mills was the most popular prison guard at Soledad. Silliman jumped up to ask the source of the judge's information. The court reporter could barely keep up as Silliman and Judge Campbell repeatedly interrupted each other. After the exchange, Thorne echoed

Silliman's request that the judge disclose where he learned of Mills' popularity. Judge Campbell explained that he had read newspaper accounts earlier in the year. Other frosty exchanges followed as they worked through the pile of motions. The defense team then spent some time trying to convince the judge that he should order the county to pay for transcripts of earlier hearings. Costs were becoming a major issue. Except for a small amount contributed by Jackson's family, the defendants were not paying their lawyers. The judge delayed ruling on that request.

The real fireworks started after lunch, with the judge ejecting an unruly spectator. Even though Judge Campbell had already refused to postpone the trial date, Thorne raised the issue twice more. Judge Campbell scolded Thorne only to have Thorne announce that he wished to call the judge as an adverse witness and question him under oath.

This was Thorne's moment. He pulled out a copy of a letter that the judge had recently sent to the City Council. The presiding judge had requested an emergency ordinance to prevent crowds of radicals at the June trial. Television and radio stations had immediately broadcasted Judge Campbell's request, and it hit the front page of the local paper. Thorne then asked why the widely reported letter did not violate Judge Campbell's own gag order against pretrial publicity — the order expressly applied not only to all parties and their counsel, but to all officers of the court.

Chagrined, Judge Campbell defended his actions as an attempt to ensure a completely impartial atmosphere for the trial. Thorne asked permission to question the sheriff and the chief of police, which Judge Campbell denied. However, he handed the clerk copies of the newspaper clippings from his personal file that the sheriff had sent him and a memo to the judge from the Department of Corrections. Thorne asked that the documents be preserved for review. Judge Campbell saw no reason to do so, explaining that the documents would never have become public if Mr. Thorne had not asked what prompted the judge's letter to the city council. Before Thorne could retort, Fay interjected, "Is your Honor collecting evidence that we are not supposed to see?"[2] The judge became silent for a moment.

At the end of the day, Thorne asked the court to order the county to pay for a transcript of both May hearings. It was now apparent to both Judge Campbell and the prosecutor that Thorne planned to seek the presiding judge's removal for cause. All that was required was the appearance of bias. If it looked like the judge had his thumb on the scales of justice, that would be enough. And Campbell, in his outreach to the City Council to prevent unruly demonstrations at trial, had unwittingly played right into the hands of the defense. Judge Campbell voluntarily withdrew from further participation in the case.

* * *

The Soledad Brothers defense team did not really expect to fare much better with the newly assigned judge than they had with Judge Campbell. Anthony Brazil was a thin man in his seventies. He was of Portuguese descent. Like Judge Campbell, he had a reputation as conservative and old-fashioned, but fair. Judge Brazil often ruled from the bench based on his gut reaction to the issues. Fay remained skeptical. She suspected he was a closet racist. Yet, to her delight, Judge Brazil immediately granted them relief to resume pretrial publicity.

The second week of June, the Soledad Defense team cranked up their mimeograph machines. Volunteers ran off thousands of detailed flyers with a renewed attack on the criminal justice system. The flyers contained graphic descriptions of an uncaring government's slave-like treatment of the shackled defendants. Yet, almost at the same time, local papers focused on accounts of two other Soledad guards who had just been held at knifepoint by five prisoners. Where in Monterey County would the defense find jurors sympathetic to black militant inmates?

That same week, Fay filed the pivotal motion she had been working on: it requested either that the trial be moved to another county or that the defense be given a three-month delay of the trial. She cited a string of prejudicial newspaper articles and polls showing the hostility of county residents to Soledad inmates. The hearing on the motion was set for June 15, just a week before trial.

When that morning arrived, the air was thick with tension. The defense team approached the courthouse knowing their clients' lives depended on relocating the trial to another county. Fay ensured once again that the courtroom would be packed with bussed-in supporters. Hippies got new haircuts and conservative outfits to blend in with locals. This time the crowd was more racially diverse. Rumors spread that scores of Black Panthers had arrived ready to set the town afire.

The turnout impressed Fay. She knew that many in the crowd had to arise at six a.m. to arrive before nine, only to endure being photographed by deputy sheriffs and having the license plate numbers of their cars recorded. She became incensed when many of their followers were barred from the courthouse based on a brand-new fire department ruling that no more than 50 people, including court personnel, could occupy the third-floor courtroom at one time.

At the outset, all four attorneys angrily rose to question Judge Brazil about the source of the new rule. They pointed to benches with plenty of seating capacity. The judge was taken aback by their combative tone. He was as baffled as they were. He agreed that the courtroom could comfortably fit 85 persons and that he had seen as many as 200 accommodated on occasion. Still, he did not believe he was empowered to overrule the fire department. The limitation was based on the courtroom having only one exit. The attorneys pointed out that there were in fact two doors, including the one to his chambers. The judge insisted only one was a fire exit. Their repeated exchanges reminded Fay of a Kafka novel.

Fay and Thorne argued that Judge Brazil should order the fire department to send a representative to court to explain its action, but Judge Brazil refused. Fay then asked the judge's permission to test whether there was really only one exit, inquiring politely, "Do you mind if I see?" Judge Brazil was too surprised to reject Fay's request and replied, "Not at all."[3]

The door to Judge Brazil's chambers led to a rear corridor and a stairwell from which one could either leave the building or take the main hallway into the courtroom. Fay disappeared into the judge's chambers and returned by the front door, proving that the fire marshal was wrong — there were two exits to the courtroom. She was welcomed back with a burst of applause.

Judge Brazil had temporarily lost control of the proceedings and could not hide his frustration. He ordered the attorneys to proceed with their arguments without their clients. The attorneys did not know until that moment that the judge had ordered the prison not to bring the inmates to this hearing. The attorneys were stunned. They had never heard of a judge excluding defendants faced with the death penalty from attending any hearing in their case.

After reconsidering, Judge Brazil adjourned the hearing until one p.m. to allow time for the prisoners to be transported to the courthouse. As the judge was walking out, Fay and John Thorne rose to argue further, but he had disappeared into his chambers. Soon after the bailiff had cleared the courtroom, the attorneys were surprised to be called back in. Judge Brazil resumed the bench and said he had changed his mind. He curtly announced that trial would not proceed in Monterey. He granted the defense motion and agreed to send the case to San Francisco as requested. Judge Brazil then declared the court in recess. The defense team was ecstatic. They had won! Moving the case to San Francisco not only gave them a far better jury pool, it automatically meant at least a three-month delay of the trial. After losing so many hearings before the parole board and in court, Jackson was greatly impressed. Writing that same day to a woman admirer, he called the victory in that round: "The people — on the march."[4]

Fay assumed that her team's amazing success in the heart of Reagan country would convince Jackson to cooperate with their trial defense strategy once the case was transferred to San Francisco. This was just the first major step toward winning his freedom. The delay would also allow them to edit and publish his book of letters, establishing Jackson as a revolutionary hero. Fay counted on the favorable publicity it would generate to stymie the prosecutor's efforts to send Jackson to the gas chamber.

Fay took great pride in the unorthodox approach that the defense team had used. She told a group of Leftist law students later that summer, "If somehow an angel had given the defendants' families $100,000 and they had gone to a straight establishment lawyer, who would have done an honest job of the case — but as a non-movement case — he would never in a million years have gotten the change of venue." She credited their success to large numbers of spectators who acted as a "single instrument" to support their cause, including long hours behind the scenes making calls and mimeographing and distributing flyers.[5]

Despite Fay's self-effacement, everyone involved realized that she deserved the lion's share of the credit. With a second extraordinary court victory only three weeks after the reversal of Newton's conviction, Fay headed back to Berkeley having just proved herself to be the hottest Movement lawyer in the country.

■ 8 ■
Collision Course

*The possibility of us, as persons,
misunderstanding each other will always
rest on the fact that I am an alien.*[1]
— GEORGE JACKSON TO FAY STENDER, JULY 28, 1970

Jackson retained little faith in the judicial system even after the case was removed to San Francisco. While Fay and Thorne focused on how to win his acquittal, Jackson continued to plot his own exit strategy. Meanwhile, the three defendants increasingly quarreled among themselves, particularly Clutchette and Jackson. For motivation, Jackson kept a picture of Angela Davis in his cell. He had begun corresponding with her in late May, addressed in successive letters as "Dearest Angela" and "first among the equals."[2] She had quickly become his largest donor and his most powerful stimulus. He told her that her photograph made him feel inebriated and that she was constantly in his thoughts.

Davis wrote back that George had "smashed through the fortress erected around my soul." She, too, fantasized about the two of them side by side in revolutionary combat.[3] Davis suggested Thorne as their go-between. Thorne had no problem saying that Davis acted as his legal assistant. Prison officials took a dim view and denied access to the avowed Communist.

Jackson knew that his letters were read by prison staff. Still, he poured out his heart to her. He described his Marxist philosophy and righteous anger at Big Brother and black collaborationists. He sent Davis the same blunt message that he had earlier written Fay: "My credo is to seize the pig by the tusks and ride him till his neck breaks."[4]

By June of 1970, Lester Jackson realized how much other black inmates and prison reform activists admired George for his refusal to let prison life beat him into submission. His son's ordeal brought Lester's own suppressed rage to the surface. He did not want George's spirit broken like that of many African-American ex-cons Lester knew. George, for his part, came to value how hard his father had always worked for his family — sixteen hours a day with little to show for it — and how loyal Lester remained in his love for him and his younger brother Jonathan.

At George's suggestion, Angela Davis became closer to the Jackson family. She started tutoring Jonathan, who had been a gifted student and popular junior varsity basketball player in high school before he dropped out. Davis talked the teenager into returning to his classes. She bought guns and, at George's suggestion, used Jonathan as her personal body guard. When the Jackson family visited George in prison, much to his parents' consternation, George often took his younger brother aside to have private conversations. He considered Jonathan his alter ego. By June of 1970, Jonathan had become as single-minded as George on plans for his escape.

* * *

On June 17, just two days after the successful motion in Salinas for change of venue, Fay received a visitor who had just flown in from Manhattan — Gregory Armstrong, the editor for George Jackson's book of prison letters. The shaggy-haired, Harvard graduate was in his late thirties and at the height of his career. The Jackson assignment both excited and intimidated him. At dinner, Fay introduced Armstrong to Elizabeth "Betsy" Hammer of the Soledad Defense Committee.

Armstrong impressed Fay with the intensity of his interest. He found himself attracted to Betsy, a beautiful teenager in fatigues and combat boots whom Jackson had addressed in correspondence as "Z." Armstrong was not surprised to find that both Fay and Betsy Hammer were in love with Jackson. A radical woman friend in New York to whom Armstrong had shown Jackson's letters also found herself irresistibly drawn to the revolutionary author.

On Thursday morning, June 18th, Betsy Hammer drove Greg Armstrong from Fay's home in Berkeley to Thorne's office in San Jose. Thorne had arranged to visit Jackson that day at Soledad, bringing with him a new "investigator." The prison authorities had no idea a book was in the works or they would not have permitted the visit. Fay offered Armstrong the use of her tape recorder to interview Jackson, but Armstrong bought his own.

Armstrong had never before entered a prison and was pleasantly surprised to discover that the desk sergeant greeted Thorne with respect. Armstrong was simply asked to display his driver's license and sign in. He and Thorne were then escorted to the captain's office in another building in the compound and told that Jackson would be joining them shortly. When Jackson arrived in shackles, it surprised Armstrong as much as it had startled Fay back in February.

Jackson again poured on the charm. His magnetism enveloped Armstrong as Thorne reported on the current status of the case. As soon as an opportunity arose, Jackson turned to Armstrong and brusquely asked when the book would come out and whether any parts of it would be cut. Armstrong forgot Thorne's warning that the captain's office was bugged and replied that he expected it to be completed in September. Armstrong reassured Jackson that the book would only strengthen his message with explanations of events mentioned in the letters. The meeting immediately grew tense as Jackson jumped to the conclusion that Armstrong intended to eclipse Jackson's voice with editorial comments. Armstrong had to work hard to regain the inmate's trust. Midway through the meeting, guards escorted Drumgo and Clutchette to meet with the new "investigator" while Thorne had a private conversation with Jackson. Armstrong arranged to return the next day.

After they left Soledad, Thorne drove Armstrong to meet with radical tax lawyer Harry Margolis. Fay and Thorne had hired Margolis to set up an overseas corporation that would receive all the royalties from Jackson's book and prevent prison officials from collecting their usual twenty-five percent. Jackson had agreed that his book proceeds would be tapped for defense expenses.

Armstrong spent that night at Betsy's mother's upscale home in San Jose and returned on Thursday to the prison to meet with Jackson alone. He was relieved when the muscular inmate greeted him with a warm embrace. Armstrong had remembered to buy several packs of cigarettes and more candy, which Jackson appreciated. George smoked nonstop as he talked of his early life, his gratitude to Fay Stender and John Thorne, and the beautiful revolutionary women who had just entered his life.

Jackson confided to Armstrong that he had recently been visited by Betsy's mother Joan Hammer, another of the women visitors who found him irresistible. Prison officials had forbidden her from returning after she had been caught in Jackson's arms. Jackson had been philosophical: "She wants to be my mama, you know, and I can't stand that."[5] Jackson also sounded Armstrong out on his views of revolution. A pacifist by nature, Armstrong weighed his answers carefully, sensing the barely suppressed rage inside Jackson. As the interview progressed, Armstrong realized that Jackson was courting his help to break out. Jackson told Armstrong pointedly that there would be nothing a man wouldn't do for a guy who helped him escape.

Armstrong could not suppress a similar thrill of hurdling racial and class barriers that Fay experienced: "For me, identifying with George was like having a second self. I think it was like this for many of the people who knew him. George's power was our power. . . . We possessed him. . . . We even felt we had the right to live through him."[6] As heedless as he acted, Armstrong was frightened to be left alone with such a violent man. The tension between his excitement and fear would never be resolved. Later, Armstrong reflected: "What we all want from George is to be made an instrument of himself. To be made as real as death, as fateful as murder. The one thing George wants above all else is freedom. We can't give him that. We won't help him escape."[7]

Within a few weeks' time, all three Soledad Brothers were transferred from Soledad to San Quentin prison, north of San Francisco in San Rafael, where the trio occupied cells in the Adjustment Center, home to its most dangerous prisoners. Jackson did not mind. He wanted to reinforce inmates' belief that he was the "baddest mother in the joint."[8]

Jackson saw inmates still wasting their energy on gang feuds. He enlisted Fay's aid in forging an alliance among prisoners of all races to pursue common demands. Fay grew more strident in her speeches, suggesting revolutionaries in prisons could organize Movement activists on the outside to take to the streets. She met with the leader of the Aryan Brotherhood in "O" Wing at Soledad and offered to supply them with a wish list of books if the neo-Nazis joined in a united stand with black inmates against the prison administration. The incredulous white supremacist assumed she must be a Communist. Actually, Fay was headed toward a major break with Communist volunteers on the Soledad Brothers Defense Committee.

By the time of Jackson's transfer, the defense team had made arrangements to rent the second floor of a large San Francisco home in the Potrero Hill district to serve as its headquarters and communal living space. In late June, a wave of publicity brought so many new volunteers they could not fit under a single roof. The members often came to see the three prisoners in person since San Quentin had a policy of opening, inspecting and reading most mail. The guards made no secret of their special disdain for the infamous trio. Drumgo complained to Silver that Drumgo's newspaper arrived each day with "Mills" scrawled across the front page.

The Soledad Committee members saw their clients often. The main visiting room held rows of tables and benches with inmates on one side and visitors on the other. A guard on a tall chair constantly surveyed the room, but the participants could lean forward with their heads almost touching and no one paid much attention to what went on under the table. Jackson exuded animal magnetism. As at Soledad in the last few months, he asked almost every woman he saw for sex. Members of the defense team were entitled to use a private conference room in their role of investigator, paralegal or lawyer. Once inside the room, Jackson found he could evade suspicion if he stood with his back to the conference room window feigning nonchalance, with a cigarette visible in one hand. One enterprising visitor bragged to Greg Armstrong that she stood on her briefcase to have sex with George without getting caught.

Fay encouraged women on the committee to shower affection on the Soledad Brothers any way they could. She had long since sacrificed her own sense of decorum to prove the depth of her love for Jackson. Fay once brought along a Cal professor eager to meet the revolutionary for an interview. When the guard left the three of them in the private conference room, the professor stood for several minutes uncomfortably staring at the floor as Jackson, still in chains, embraced Fay and rubbed himself against her for relief. The two visitors later drove back to Berkeley in silence, her colleague still shocked by her behavior.

* * *

After George's transfer to San Quentin, Jonathan Jackson became increasingly obsessed with saving his brother's life. In the spring, Jonathan had left hearings in Salinas in tears. At high school, he had started a radical newsletter and challenged those who thought him too preoccupied with his brother's plight: "What would you do if it was your brother?"[9] As summer approached, Jonathan lost his prodigious appetite. In June, he told his mother, "Mama, if I die, I want you to know that I died the way I wanted to die."[10] His parents did not know George had given Jonathan instructions for an elaborate escape plan. It involved three teams of Panther guerillas and the fantasy that they could somehow hijack a San Francisco jet to escape with hostages to barter for the freedom of the Soledad Brothers.

* * *

Fay remained on a high throughout the remainder of June and into July as she welcomed her son Neal back from his year away. Yet soon Fay's life returned to a whirlwind of activity. Sacrificing home life was the price Fay felt that committed members of the Movement had to pay. Her prestige was at its peak. Decca Mitford had just helped her arrange a national fund-raising appeal with the same mailing list the Chicago Seven had used. The first week of June, Fay and Charles Garry chaired an event in San Francisco headlined by comedian Dick Gregory and actress Jane Fonda. Fay's speech garnered underground newspaper coverage of her description of the horrors of "O" Wing at Soledad, which she described as "the Dachau of the world."[11] Yet even with the Hollywood draws, they raised just $1,775 — the cost of a few days' trial transcripts.

The next weekend, Dr. Bernard Diamond, Garry's favorite expert witness, invited Fay to be the commencement speaker at the School of Criminology at Berkeley, where Dr. Diamond was then the acting dean. The following week, Fay moderated a panel on "The Movement Lawyer" for the Bay Area members of the National Lawyers Guild. The event featured Leonard Weinglass, one of the lead lawyers in the Chicago Conspiracy case, as well as upcoming Panther criminal conspiracy trials in Los Angeles and New York.

Even Fay's mother was caught up in the excitement. It pleased Fay to see Ruby gradually become liberal in her politics. Fay eagerly shared news clippings of her successes. Ruby avidly followed Fay's press coverage and contributed flea market items to help raise money for the Soledad Brothers defense, proud of her renegade daughter's extraordinary accomplishments. Fay reciprocated Ruby's admiration, exclaiming to a reporter that her mother was "more aware of movement problems than most people her age who are not part of the Old Left."[12]

In a lengthy interview with the *Berkeley Barb*, Fay claimed discomfort with the spotlight and the star system of media coverage. She used the opportunity to extol the virtues of legal collectives working together to change the status quo. Collaborators on the Soledad Brothers case consciously avoided the traditional hierarchy of lawyer, law student and secretary. Asked about the future, Fay embraced the need for social revolution. She recognized people might die, but rationalized: "People are dying all the time. The important thing is that they die in the right cause."[13] That belief would haunt Fay in her last days.

As Fay completed the flurry of June activity, Ann Ginger asked both Fay and Marvin to participate in a special series of lectures for

By June 1970 Fay Stender attracted international attention as a top Movement lawyer. This photo for the Berkeley Barb's June 16–25, 1970, issue was taken in her office on Telegraph Avenue in Berkeley by Gary Freeman.

radical law students that Ginger planned to tape-record and turn into a how-to-book. Dubbed the "Tom Paine Summer School of 1970," the ambitious program featured thirty accomplished Leftists whose topics ranged from war crimes to injecting politics into criminal trials, to representing radical labor clients, to addressing legal needs of the poor, to institutionalized racism against blacks and Latinos, to class actions, to prisoners' rights and tax avoidance. The program also included practical advice on how solo practitioners committed to social change supported themselves with other paying cases.

Apart from Ginger, Fay was only one of three women lawyers who addressed the students. The speakers included her husband Marvin, Charles Garry and two of his partners, and tax guru Harry Margolis. The resulting book, *The Relevant Lawyers: Conversations Out of Court on Their Clients, Their Practice, Their Politics, Their Life Style*, would inspire thousands of socially conscious college students to turn to careers in the law.

At the program in July, Fay enthralled her audience with details of the Soledad Brothers case as she explained how Movement supporters had effectively teamed up to achieve the venue change. Her mellifluous voice and earnest manner were compelling. Fay revealed that in the past two years, her identity had become almost anti-professional. She had abandoned the traditional lawyer-client relationship because it interfered with building her revolutionary clients' trust. Instead, she considered Newton and Jackson close comrades with a shared goal.

Fay told the students that she was so immersed in prison work that she no longer enjoyed cars, clothes or vacations. Ginger could not resist pointing out that she, in contrast, had never indulged in such bourgeois pleasures. Fay ignored the criticism. She informed the students that she felt more energized — more human — these days talking to prisoners than when she had appeared in the nation's highest court.

Fay shared her strategy for the upcoming Soledad Brothers trial. She did not believe that the defendants' antics in the recent Chicago Seven trial were appropriate in San Francisco, where they hoped to seat a persuadable "people's jury." Instead, Fay and John Thorne planned to appeal to the jury by shining the light on "O" Wing at Soledad through

Ann Fagan Ginger, Director of the Meikeljohn Institute for Civil Rights in Berkeley, conducted a seminar in the summer of 1970 for law students viewing the law as an instrument of social change. Thirty lawyers participated in "The Tom Paine Summer School of 1970." Among them were Fay Stender, three partners in her firm and her husband, all pictured below.

Ann Fagan Ginger

THE RELEVANT LAWYERS

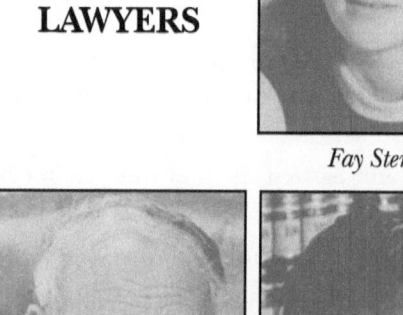

Al Brotsky

Fay Stender

Francis McTernan   *Charles Garry*   *Marvin Stender*

THE RELEVANT LAWYERS: Conversations Out of Court on Their Clients, Practice, Politics and Life Style by Ann Ginger (Random House 1972) inspired thousands of socially conscious college students to seek law degrees. Between the summer of 1970 — when Fay Stender was interviewed for the book about her revolutionary clients Huey Newton and George Jackson — and the fall of 1972 when the book was published, Fay had been fired by both clients and Jackson was dead.

a series of inmates called to court to tell their compelling stories. Fay hoped that exposure of atrocities at the Salinas prison would force the closure of that facility and others like it.

Fay kept well-hidden from the students at the summer school the deep anxiety she harbored about the pitfalls the defense still faced: they were running desperately low on funds; due to hurdles imposed by the Department of Corrections, the lawyers would not come close to interviewing all of the inmates before trial. Of primary concern was the risk that Jackson would not cooperate with their defense strategy. Though he never fully confided in Fay, he sent her a message in late July that tried to convey his state of mind:

> The secret things that I hide from almost everyone, and especially the people who are sweet and gentle and intellectually inhibited from grasping the full range of the ordeal of being fair game, hunted, an alien, precludes forever a state of perfect agreement. Don't mistake this as a message from George to Fay, it's a message from the hunted running blacks to those people of this society who profess to want to change the conditions that destroy life. These blacks are still in doubt as to whether those elements across the tracks want this change badly enough to accept the U.S. being physically brought to its knees to attain it. I dig them [the Weathermen], and love you.[14]

As trial preparations continued, Jackson advanced his own elaborate plans for escape. Another San Quentin prisoner, James McClain, was scheduled for jury trial at the Marin County Civic Center starting on August 3, 1970. McClain faced charges he stabbed a guard. Through his brother Jonathan, George planned to have outside collaborators bring weapons to the Marin courthouse. They would then arm McClain and other inmate witnesses, and take the judge, prosecutor and some of the jurors hostage. The assumption was that the hostages' lives would be valuable enough that the police would let the kidnappers go. Later, they would offer the hostages back in exchange for the Soledad Brothers.

Jonathan Jackson helped make arrangements through Black Panther Deputy Defense Minister Elmer "Geronimo" Pratt. An ex-Green Beret, Pratt headed the Panther Party's Los Angeles chapter after "Bunchy" Carter was killed in early 1969. Pratt was secretly planning to head up to the Bay Area with several other Panthers, all armed with weapons stolen from Camp Pendleton. The Panthers Pratt was bringing had little to risk — they already faced lengthy prison terms or death on pending criminal charges.

* * *

On July 22d, Fay must have breathed a sigh of relief that the Jackson case was no longer in Salinas. News broke that another Soledad guard had been killed, allegedly stabbed by black inmates near a shed in the prison yard. For the time being, Fay focused instead on arrangements for Newton's release from the Men's Colony. On July 24th, best-selling author Mark Lane published an article that Fay had likely arranged. Over the Fourth of July weekend, Lane had accompanied Charles Garry to visit Newton on the pretext of helping Garry prepare for Newton's retrial. Lane conducted three days of interviews of "America's authentic revolutionary." At the end of his article, Lane accused the government of targeting Newton for death upon his release. Lane urged that Newton's safety be assured: "For those who love peace and those who crave justice, Huey's leadership is crucial. He represents America's last, best hope for social change with a minimum of violence."[15]

On the same day that the court of appeal issued its order sending Newton's case back to the Alameda County Superior Court, Fay showed up in the trial judge's chambers inquiring how he wished to proceed. The judge suggested that Fay seek an informal agreement with prosecutor Lowell Jensen. Fay headed straight upstairs to Jensen's office. The dealings between the two adversaries were cordial. Though Jensen could have forced further delay he saw no reason to do so. He did not intend to dispute Newton's right to freedom on bail. Jensen also showed some flexibility in waiting for Garry to finish pending trials before setting the date of Newton's retrial. Fay reported back to Garry how pleasant and cooperative Jensen and the judge had been.

In the dark predawn of Monday, August 3, officials at the Men's

Colony turned Newton over to two Alameda County Sheriff's deputies, who drove him to the Alameda County jail. On the way north from San Luis Obispo, Newton felt overwhelmed just taking in the passing landscape. Newton did not believe he could live up to the expectations of the hordes of new recruits across the country: he was not the African king depicted in the Black Panther newsletter and on posters, nor was he ready for the revolution he espoused. Newton also knew he faced dissension from rabid followers of Eldridge Cleaver and threats by an unknown number of infiltrators.

Newton had two days to decompress in the Oakland jail as he awaited the August 5th hearing. It went smoothly, without any of the extraordinary security precautions that had surrounded the 1968 trial. Judge Hove set bail at $50,000. After two years of isolation, Newton was ambivalent about regaining his freedom. Fay and Garry convinced him how important his immediate release was to his followers, but Alex Hoffmann understood Huey's reluctance. Prison had been a safe haven where Newton could receive adulation and issue orders without accountability for results.

Fay ran off to post bail early that afternoon. Newton then walked out of his tenth-floor cell, joined by his friend David Hilliard, Huey's sisters and brothers, and the lawyers. Reporters shouted questions at Newton as he boarded the elevator. Outside, police warily observed the large crowd of Huey's fans who had begun gathering early in the day. For hours, the assemblage had been shouting over and over chants of "Free Huey," "We want Huey," "Where's Huey?" When they spotted him leaving the building, their cries switched to, "Huey's Free! Huey's Free!" Surrounded by a human shield, Newton, David Hilliard and Platt clambered atop the small roof of Hoffman's VW Bug to address the crowd. There, Newton tore off his shirt in the hot sun and gave photographers a great shot of his superb physique. He then yelled, "Right on! Right On! Power to the People!" and punched his fist in the air. The gesture drove the crowd to a fever pitch.

Newton exhorted the group to help free the Soledad Brothers and Bobby Seale in New Haven. Then he drove off with Alex Hoffmann to dress for a press conference in San Francisco. Hoffmann's souvenirs

Outside the Alameda County Courthouse

August 5, 1970. Huey Is Freed

Press conference in San Francisco later that day. Fay Stender is just behind Huey Newton to his left. Charles Garry is to Huey's right. Alex Hoffmann is crouched by the table further to Huey's left. By the time of Newton's release, Fay Stender had left Garry's firm to become a partner at Peter Franck's new law office in Berkeley.

from the media event were permanent dents in the roof of his car from the weight of the three Panther leaders.

Hoffmann brought Newton to his new temporary home, the apartment in Berkeley Alex shared with Elsa Knight Thompson. There, Newton donned a new outfit and Hoffmann drove him to Garry's office in San Francisco. This time, most of the reporters came from underground newspapers and magazines. Newton and Garry handled friendly questions and posed for photos with Huey's legal team, family and supporters. Fay sat just behind Huey, radiating her delight. Newton then got a ride to the Panther's new West Oakland headquarters and strolled through his former neighborhood greeting his well-wishers with Panther salutes.

That very day, Newton reportedly issued his first orders since his release. Huey had been told of George Jackson's plans for Pratt to bring a squadron of Panthers to invade the Marin Civic Center just two days later in a joint assault with Jackson's brother Jonathan. Huey worried that COINTELPRO already knew about the risky scheme and the Panthers would walk into a trap. Newton needed time to assess the best course for the Party's future. He stopped the Panthers from joining in the August 7 kidnapping and directed that word of the abrupt change in plans immediately go to George Jackson. Pratt and his cohorts were advised to disappear. They jumped bail and headed for Alabama where the fugitive Panthers created a satellite military encampment.

That evening, the Soledad Brothers Defense Committee celebrated the opening of its San Francisco headquarters. When Newton showed up at the festivities, he was overwhelmed with people vying for his attention. Among them was Jonathan Jackson, whom Newton had not met before. When an opportunity arose, the intent teenager took Newton aside to discuss details of the August 7 attack. To Jonathan's utter disbelief, Newton told him that he had called it off.

Later in the evening, intoxicated Panthers at the Soledad House party declared that Newton needed to make up for lost time and suggested Fay as Newton's prize for winning his freedom. The two were ushered into a bedroom and the door closed behind them while others continued their revelry. Fay later bragged to women colleagues at the

Guild about the Panthers arranging for her to have sex with Newton at that party. Some were aghast. Fay used it as proof the rank-and-file Panthers and their leader recognized her as a true comrade. To the contrary, Huey Newton was proving to the Panthers that the lawyer who won his freedom was just another woman he could use and keep close or discard at his whim.

* * *

Though aware no Panthers would join him, Jonathan Jackson persisted in his plans to free his brother. Just as Huey suspected, more than a hundred law enforcement personnel were already hidden near the Marin County Civic Center driveway. The only surprise for the COINTELPRO team was the small number of kidnappers. They were expecting a major confrontation with the Los Angeles Panthers. Like San Quentin guards, the Red Squad from Los Angeles operated under instructions to shoot to kill, regardless of any hostages. After the bullets stopped flying, the kidnappers' van was opened to find four dead bodies: the judge, Jonathan Jackson and two inmates. Deputy District Attorney Gary Thomas was among the wounded, shot by police and permanently paralyzed from the waist down. The sensational story was immediately picked up by the media.

Phil Ziegler was at work in his office, adjacent to Fay's, with the radio on in the background. When he heard that Jonathan Jackson had just been killed in a shootout at the Marin Civic Center, Ziegler ran into Fay's office. He interrupted her paperwork to tell her the devastating news. Fay shouted, "Oh no." More than thirty-five years later, Ziegler still vividly recalled her shocked disbelief. At San Quentin, George Jackson listened intently to the news and could not sleep. He blamed Newton for calling off the Panthers, but did not cry for his lost baby brother. George had tried to talk Jonathan out of the courthouse invasion when the Panthers withdrew their support. He was bursting with pained pride at the sacrifice: "I want people to wonder at what forces created him, terrible, vindictive, cold, calm, man-child, courage in one hand, the machine gun in the other, scourge of the unrighteous

— an ox for the people to ride."[16] George himself would never have attempted the kidnapping with so little back up.

Fay called George's mother and sister Penny and members of the Soledad Defense Committee with the tragic news. She offered her home as a gathering place that evening to absorb the shock and mourn Jonathan's loss. Fay made immediate arrangements to visit George at San Quentin on Saturday, together with his family. His parents were devastated. George's own complicity made it difficult for him to face them, knowing how hard they had tried to keep Jonathan from following his lead. He was grateful for Fay's presence. A few days later, he told Greg Armstrong, "She really helped them to understand. I don't know what I would have done without her."[17]

Georgia felt differently. She deeply mistrusted the legal team and resented Fay's intrusive role in George's life. The solicitude of white people like Armstrong and Fay, who commiserated with the Jackson family's years in "the ghetto," made Georgia angry. Her family lived where the poor people lived. These parasites had no way of sharing her anguish at the loss of her youngest child. As pained as she was, Georgia Jackson spoke at a press conference on Tuesday, August 11th. She tearfully announced that she probably would have helped Jonathan, if she had known. Georgia had reached the same conclusion as her younger son: "A black man doesn't get justice in the courts. If you can't get justice one way, you take it another."[18]

* * *

Prior to August 7th, COINTELPRO had already been tailing Angela Davis. They reportedly knew where she was on Friday when she heard the news of the shootout, that she made four telephone calls, and then flew from San Francisco to Los Angeles, where she disappeared. On Monday, August 10th, the police identified Davis as the registered owner of the shotgun, carbine and two of the pistols Jonathan had brought with him to the Marin Civic Center. The FBI immediately put her on its most wanted list.

Meanwhile, Fay visited Newton frequently at Alex Hoffmann and

Thompson's two-bedroom apartment. Fay was well aware, as Newton was, that their movements were being watched by the FBI. A suspicious-looking telephone repairman perched high up on a pole across the street for four days in a row. Hoffmann gave up his bedroom to Newton and now slept on the living room couch. He kept track of Newton's schedule, including his renewed love life. One of Alex's tasks was to avoid having the three women Huey was then seeing visit the revolutionary at the same time. Fay had no expectations of having the Panther leader all to herself, but reveled in both being his trusted advisor and having similar access to the buff militant's bedroom as his fiancée did. She did not see the abrupt turn in their relationship coming.

For his part, Newton continued to make the transition from prison with difficulty. Followers who heralded his freedom demanded that he inspire them with powerful speeches. Newton resisted. He was well aware that his high-pitched delivery could not match Bobby Seale's and Eldridge Cleaver's dynamic speaking skills. Huey much preferred conversing with individuals or addressing small audiences, who often found his lectures mesmerizing. But the revolutionary leader had no real choice in the matter. Newton decided to give his first talk to a large audience on laying the groundwork for a new socialist state by establishing a revolutionary "intercommunal framework." He left most of his audience cold.

* * *

On August 12th, Greg Armstrong visited Jackson at San Quentin, offered his condolences and brought him the manuscript of *Soledad Brother*. Armstrong suggested that Jackson write a new dedication for his brother. Jackson caressed the bundle. He had never seen the full, edited manuscript before, only a partial draft hidden among legal papers. Jackson skimmed through the manuscript that night and rededicated the book to "the man-child . . . who died on August 7, 1970, courage in one hand, assault rifle in the other; my brother, comrade, friend, the true revolutionary . . . " and to his mother and Angela Davis. He ended the dedication "to the destruction of their enemies I dedicate my life."[19]

The next day, Jackson told Armstrong he thought some of the

private communications were better left out, including some early bitter letters to his parents and some lascivious passages in his love letters to Davis. He noticed a passage where Fay had cut out something he had written. It greatly amused him because he knew her well enough to guess why. Another edit made him extremely angry. Armstrong owned up to having made that particular change himself and Jackson regained his composure.

The following day, the prison confiscated the manuscript, but Thorne convinced the warden to give it back. That night Armstrong's car was broken into and he found his copy of the manuscript strewn all over the trunk. Uniformed and plain clothes policemen raided the defense team's headquarters in San Francisco where Armstrong was staying. Though they had no search warrant, the police herded all of the staff into one room at gunpoint and thoroughly searched the premises.

Armstrong did a quick check of his belongings and panicked when he discovered the police had confiscated his taped conversations with George Jackson. Armstrong immediately contacted Fay, worried the case might be severely compromised. Marvin promptly followed up on Fay's request for help in demanding the return of "investigator" Armstrong's confidential client tapes. To Armstrong's great relief, Marvin got them back with assurances from the police that they had not listened to any of the tapes.

On Saturday, August 15, thousands of Panther supporters turned out for Jonathan Jackson's funeral service at St. Augustine's Episcopal Church in Oakland. Armstrong accompanied Drumgo's mother, Inez, whom he was now dating. Jonathan's casket was covered with a black and white Panther flag. Newton eulogized him as a fallen hero. Yet whispered accusations were already spreading that Newton had thwarted Jonathan's mission. Georgia Jackson had trouble containing her anger.

The FBI chronicled the growing fissures between Jackson and his followers, both in and out of prison, and Newton's Black Panthers. From its ongoing phone tap at Panther headquarters, the FBI noted a phone call from Fay just after ten p.m. two days after the funeral. Fay was in obvious distress. She asked for help in addressing a constant barrage of reporters' questions and needed the Panthers' advice on her responses.

Fay's worries went far deeper than figuring out what to tell the media. In Jonathan's death, Fay saw the shadow of George's. So did his mother. When Georgia had made burial arrangements for Jonathan, she bought an adjacent plot for her first-born son. With his younger brother martyred and his ideal revolutionary woman on the run, George Jackson would be hell-bent on a renewed, and inevitably doomed, escape attempt. Fay still held out one hope to save her death row client from himself and win his acquittal — redoubling her efforts to turn Jackson into an international cause célèbre. She had no time to lose. Trial was scheduled for September 21, less than six weeks after Jonathan Jackson's funeral.

■ 9 ■
Blood in His Eye

> *Sometimes I think this whole world*
> *Is one big prison yard.*
> *Some of us are prisoners*
> *The rest of us are guards.*[1]
> — BOB DYLAN, "GEORGE JACKSON"

In the last half of August 1970, Fay stayed constantly on the move: she visited George at San Quentin to reassure him of her progress, interviewed potential inmate witnesses to Mills' murder, saw Newton in Berkeley, generated favorable pretrial publicity, and, catch-as-catch-can, tended to her children's needs. She felt guilty about how little time she devoted to Neal and Oriane, then ages twelve and ten-and-a-half, but she loved Newton and Jackson as much as her family and told friends she would be willing to die for them. It had taken years of agonized soul-searching before she reached the conclusion, "Everyone's going to die sometime. Once you have these perceptions you have to act. You either exist in terrible conflict with yourself or do what you think is right."[2]

With the trial date a month away, Fay focused on jury selection in San Francisco and prepared a writ to the California Supreme Court attacking the composition of the Salinas grand jury that had issued the indictment. Meanwhile, through her friend Elsa Knight Thompson, Fay arranged for Pacifica radio to air interviews of the Soledad Brothers and to conduct interviews of their lawyers and parents. On Thursday,

August 20, Fay received welcome news — playwright Jean Genet would write the preface to *Soledad Brother*. In the spring of 1970, it had been easy for Fay to recruit Genet to the Soledad Brothers Defense Committee. The feisty ex-convict was already an avid Panther supporter. The existentialist praised the manuscript as a "striking poem of love and of combat."[3] Both Fay and Greg Armstrong realized that Genet's blessing gave Jackson status as a cult hero even before the new publication hit the stands. Huey Newton added his own endorsement of George Jackson, "the greatest writer of us all."[4]

After accompanying Fay for two frenzied days, Armstrong proved himself a keen observer. He noted in his diary: "The case is her whole life. She doesn't seem to care about anything else. No small talk. No diversions of any kind. Just a constant stream of meetings, hearings, phone calls to other lawyers, interviews with reporters. She literally can't keep still. She seems to be afraid of silence or the absence of frenzy. Long-fingered, long-armed, always moving, always coming at you, always reaching for you."[5]

Fay's attention had just switched from promoting Jackson's book to a pretrial crisis. Bertram Young, the assistant district attorney from Monterey County, was still assigned to prosecute the case after its unexpected move from Salinas. In the wake of the Marin County shootout, Young turned the tables on the defense. He argued that the San Francisco community was now so polarized that the Soledad Brothers case should be sent to San Diego.

In response, Fay and her co-counsel argued that what was needed was just a delay of the trial until the furor cooled down. They pointed out that the bad publicity from the Marin County shooting was not merely local, but statewide and even national. Fay provided the judge with articles from *Life* ("Slaughter in San Rafael"), *Time, Newsweek, Jet* and *U.S. News and World Report*.[6] But the trial judge agreed with the prosecutor and ordered the murder trial of the Soledad Brothers sent to San Diego. It might as well have been a death sentence. Too far for supporters to travel, the conservative Navy town would be a worse place to try the case than Salinas had been. Fay set to work challenging the unprecedented order, knowing that the Soledad Brothers' lives once again depended on her success. The court of appeal would unanimously rule that the prosecutor had no right to remove the case from San Francisco. Fay did not have to argue for a three months' delay of the trial; the appeal had already taken that long.

* * *

As Fay became increasingly absorbed in the Soledad Brothers' case, Newton began distancing himself from her. Once outside prison walls he wanted to dispel any notion that he was beholden to her for his freedom. It did not fit his macho image as a Party leader. The most celebrated Leftist in America now had many beautiful women — including Hollywood leading ladies — vying for his favors. He also had just begun courting singer Elaine Brown, an ambitious Party member from the Los Angeles branch newly returned from a tour of Communist countries with Eldridge Cleaver. At the next Panther celebration in Oakland, Huey pointedly left Fay standing by herself, while he socialized with others. Fay was deeply humiliated. She would never forget the embarrassment she felt at that moment.

One of the issues that had come between them involved Newton's plans to move to a downtown penthouse. Newton wanted more privacy and security. The Panthers located a penthouse apartment in a high-rise with a doorman and its own garage on the south edge of Lake Merritt near downtown Oakland. Wealthy donors were happy to foot the bill. Most prominent among them was Newton's hedonistic new buddy, Hollywood producer Bert Schneider, flush from his hits *Easy Rider*, *The Last Picture Show* and the television show *The Monkees*. Newton moved into the penthouse at the beginning of October 1970.

The living room and dining room faced the lake and the courthouse where he had been jailed during trial proceedings. Sliding glass doors led out to a terrace where Newton liked to focus a telescope on his former cell. The new apartment had high ceilings and was sparsely, though elegantly, furnished. Newton also had a den for his revolutionary library, where the "Servant of the People" could prepare position papers with help from others. Fay believed that these luxurious accommodations sent the wrong message to Party faithful, many of whom considered the arrangement a misuse of Party funds. Soon mainstream press mocked the new location as "the throne" and Newton's "plush penthouse." Newton would be under close FBI surveillance there, too, under direct orders from the Attorney General.

* * *

At first, Fay's young law partners had been excited by her rock star Movement clients, and awed when Huey Newton visited their firm. Then the office was broken into twice, and someone (they assumed from the police) rifled through the Soledad Brothers files. The partners started holding firm meetings at a secretary's home, for fear the office was bugged. Then came hordes of volunteers for the Soledad Brothers who traipsed in and out all summer. Patti Roberts, a Boalt law student on the Defense Committee, practically became Fay's shadow at the office.

By September of 1970, Fay's non-paying revolutionary clientele had put tremendous strain on the firm. Franck had lucrative entertainment clients, including Country Joe and the Fish. Hill had a money-making practice defending drug dealers. Ziegler was particularly resentful of sharing his income from a steady stream of well-to-do parents trying to keep their sons from being inducted.

The partners did not have a traditional profit-sharing policy favoring the lawyers who brought in the most money, but an agreement to distribute income on the Marxist principle — from each according to his ability to each according to his need. Some now openly questioned the disparity between the money they brought into the firm and their take-home pay. They also debated with Fay whose work was more important to the Movement. Peter Franck preferred investing energy in working with unions, not militant inmates. Franck thought prisoners were the last people one might expect capable of implementing societal change. Ziegler quit precipitately and started his own solo practice. Overwhelmed by draft dodging clients, Ezra Hendon, Fay's best friend at the firm, soon abandoned law practice to bake bread instead.

Fay appeased the partnership with the promise that her mounting unpaid fees would come from Soledad Brother's book royalties. The publishing companies had hush-hush plans for an outdoor champagne reception in front of the post office near San Quentin's gates in mid-October. Armstrong arrived from New York with advance copies of the book and distributed them excitedly to Jackson and his family. When the Stenders' telephone rang at six a.m. on October 14th, Armstrong was already awake and answered the call. He immediately recognized the despondent voice of Georgia Jackson: "Those people who put the book together ruined everything."[7] His heart sank.

Georgia had hoped the autobiographical collection would help vindicate George. Instead, she read George's boast that he had been a brigand all his life to imply he was capable of murder. Actually, George's original letters contained far more damning vitriol. Fay, like Georgia Jackson, viewed his rage as induced by the prison environment, a byproduct of prolonged isolation. Before submitting his letters to the publisher, Fay had removed all of Jackson's many cries for armed revolt and reprisal in an effort to paint a portrait of a proud innocent the system sought to destroy.

Georgia mistakenly felt that her son had been betrayed by whites ripping off blacks yet again. She knew all the defense funds were gone and blamed the attorneys for enriching themselves at her son's expense. Georgia threatened to go on radio and describe the book as blatant lies and distortions. Petrified, Armstrong said he would see George in a few hours and tell him of her plans. Armstrong reached San Quentin as soon as it opened. Jackson reacted with disbelief and anger. He told Armstrong to let his mother know he would never speak to her again if she attempted to carry out her threat. Armstrong took no chances on delay. He called Georgia from a telephone booth at the prison. She had to face the reality that it was her own son who wanted to broadcast an angry, militant image to the world, even at the risk of increasing the likelihood he would wind up in the gas chamber.

Early the next afternoon, Soledad Defense Committee members gathered at the San Quentin post office across from the visitor parking lot. They were joined by a select group of sympathetic media representatives and avant-garde authors, Decca Mitford prominent among them. To their relief, word had not gotten to the prison staff about the plans for the radical chic reception. At Fay's instigation, Armstrong stood on the post office steps before roughly one hundred and fifty attendees downing champagne and cookies. He read from a hastily prepared speech:

> This is a victory celebration. The publication of *Soledad Brother: The Prison Letters of George Jackson* is a victory over San Quentin, over Soledad Prison, over the entire California prison system which ten years ago set out to silence George Jackson. Inside the California prison system, George is known as a teacher. His subject is truth, the truth about the prison system in America and the truth about the society that created it.... There have been over twenty attempts on his life set up by the prison officials. The publication of this book is absolute proof that they have failed to silence him.[8]

Armstrong was surprised when his emotional delivery met first with silence and then a caustic question: "What are you going to do with all the profits from the book when you go back to your fancy New York office?"[9] Armstrong disavowed any personal stake in the publishers' profits and assured his audience that the royalties were all earmarked for defense costs. He called Jackson's writing "dynamite" and insisted his editing had been kept to a minimum: "George speaks with his own voice."[10] Armstrong suddenly recalled that arrangements had been made for Jackson to be in the San Quentin visiting room where he might see them. Armstrong led the crowd to the prison gates chanting: "Free all prisoners! Free the Soledad Brothers! All prisoners are political prisoners."

Afterward, Fay turned to Armstrong with amusement and asked, "Is that the first speech you ever gave?"[11]

Upon its release, *Soledad Brother* immediately created enormous excitement. *The New York Times* reviewer called it "one of the finest pieces of black writing ever to be printed ... the most important single volume from a black since *The Autobiography of Malcolm X*." *Look Magazine* praised the letters as "the raw stuff, ragged and bleeding, or proudly refusing to bleed ...." Fay was probably most gratified by

Source: San Quentin website at
http://www.cdcr.ca.gov/Visitors/Facilities/SQ.; html - http://www.cdcr.ca.gov/Visitors/images/aerialShots/SQ_8x10.jpg

Aerial view of San Quentin Prison

Fay Stender at release party outside San Quentin in mid-October 1970 for Soledad Brother: The Prison Letters of George Jackson. *Random House editor Greg Armstrong is partly visible to her left, toasting the release with a paper cup filled with champagne. The attendees believed George could see them from the visiting room window.*

The Washington Monthly's proclamation that "Jackson picks up where Cleaver left off.... Where Cleaver throws you back on yourself because you're not black, not oppressed . . . Jackson draws you in through your shared humanity — and that . . . has a far greater value."[12]

The publisher in England was eager to pay to have Fay and George's sister and mother fly to London for a few days' media promotion of the book. British Leftists, like their counterparts worldwide, raced to read the compelling story of a revolutionary hero "who had suffered the worst kind of degradation and humiliation, yet somehow managed to speak straight to his audience." This saga of one man's ability to rise from society's rejects and reconstruct himself beckoned to Leftists "to look to America's prisons as a new 'revolutionary front' when they had previously been viewed as 'a liberal side-issue.'"[13]

Yet as Georgia Jackson feared, a different and equally strong view was taken by prison officials. One circulated a confidential memorandum among his colleagues throughout the state:

> This book provides remarkable insight into the personality makeup of a highly dangerous sociopath who sees himself not as a criminal but as a Revolutionary dedicated to the violent destruction of existing Society.... It is imperative that we in Corrections know as much as we can about his personality makeup and are correctly able to identify his kind.... I recommend that *Soledad Brother* be placed on the must reading list of every employee in the Department of Corrections.... This is one of the most self-revealing and insightful books I have ever read concerning a criminal personality.[14]

The state corrections system already considered Fay a painful gadfly for focusing lawmakers and media on prison conditions in Salinas. Still, nothing had prepared its officials for the intense, negative spotlight Fay engineered with the publication of *Soledad Brother*. Jackson's meteoric rise to international celebrity attracted unprecedented press coverage of California prison life. Guards seethed at being characterized as barbarous and cruel racists. They already despised violent felons, particularly any who attacked, let alone killed, a colleague. In their view, Jackson was worse, the vile leader of a revolutionary alliance: "the head of a movement both inside and outside the prison, which had done more than any reform effort in the history of prisons to undermine the immunity of the guards and to destroy the sense of value that had gone with the job."[15]

Only three days after the book came out, police arrested Angela Davis in New York, disguised with a wig and registered at a motel under an alias. Davis was unarmed and surrendered without incident. A reporter shocked Fay by calling her at home with the news of Davis's capture. Fay declined to give an interview and referred him to Thorne, who had previously represented Davis. Armstrong was still visiting the Stenders at the time. The news demoralized him. He could not understand why Marvin and Fay remained in such a festive mood. They entertained friends on the defense team that evening with their wedding china, crystal and table linens.

When the wine kept flowing, Armstrong got drunk and asked Fay to explain all the gaiety. He was not persuaded when she told him they wanted to show Davis's arrest did not affect their celebration of the book's success. He drew the conclusion that Davis posed difficulties for the committee the same way Georgia Jackson did, by interfering with Fay's control. "Her blackness gave her a moral authority that made her impossible to deal with." Armstrong assumed that Davis "must have made it very hard for liberal white ladies to function in all their grandeur."[16]

Armstrong likely misread Fay, Marvin and their guests if he thought they acted from self-serving motives. It seems far more likely that they had George Jackson's survival first and foremost in their minds. With Angela Davis on the loose, Jackson had been bent on futile plans for escape. With Davis safe in jail awaiting her own trial, Jackson might finally cooperate with the defense team. (Indeed, Fay rejoiced when Davis later won her own acquittal and walked free.) The Stenders celebrated the success of Jackson's book release for an obvious, straightforward reason — the cost of defending George Jackson and the other two Soledad Brothers would now be assured by royalties. They believed that George's acquittal was achievable and that winning the case at trial was his only real chance to emerge from prison. If so, then the reason

Fay brought out her grandmother's fine china was that she assumed the Feds had just helped save George's life.

Fay visited Jackson two days later in one of the small visiting rooms at San Quentin's Adjustment Center. She brought work with her, by then accustomed to San Quentin's practice of making visitors sometimes wait hours for entry. Upset about the book, the guard who brought Jackson into the visiting room on October 20 treated Fay with blatant rudeness. Jackson could barely hold himself back. The following day, he told Armstrong he was resigned to Davis's situation, but if Fay were mistreated by a guard again, he would jump him. Armstrong concluded that Jackson had to "show Fay how much he is willing to risk for her. There was no way he could save Angela and he has to save someone."[17]

By early November, Fay's publicity strategy had taken off. Jackson became so sought-after for interviews that the warden restricted reporters to one visit each. At the same time, the warden banned *Soledad Brother* from the prison library, which Fay immediately challenged with a lawsuit. *Life* magazine offered to print a lengthy piece on the Soledad Brothers if Jackson would agree to a publicity gimmick — posing for a photo of himself holding *Life's* September 11, 1970, issue with a cover photo of Angela Davis.

Shortly afterward, Fay excitedly told friends that *Time* magazine wanted to run its own cover story on Jackson if he provided its reporters with an exclusive new angle. Fay told the reporter, "George and I know that we'll hate what you print, but we'll do it for the cover."[18] To Fay, this was the pinnacle of success — no one would dare execute a man who had been featured on the cover of *Time*. Mike Wallace also inquired about a possible on-camera interview of Jackson after Fay nailed down commitments from British and Canadian television to send their crews to San Quentin.

In the late fall, two different women reporters featured Fay in long newspaper interviews. She talked of her admiration for her militant clients and her special rapport with them, recognizing that women's liberationists might not view her relationship with Jackson and Newton as that of equals. Fay told reporter Susan Berman that her interaction with the two men was "more flowing, more natural" because she was a woman, adding, "It might also be because they know I regard them as brothers and believe in them."[19] Fay characterized the court's role as an "instrument of war against the oppressed" viewed by downtrodden classes as a "naked bayonet" despite the marble façade that provided a quasi-religious "mask of legitimacy" for the Establishment's ongoing power struggle with the Movement.[20]

Fay shared with both reporters her desire to promote socialism, but professed not to understand economics well enough to answer whether she considered herself a Marxist — Stanley Moore's tutorials notwithstanding. The truth was that she and Marvin, among the rare radicals then in their mid-thirties, were caught between generations of Lefties. Fay neither wholeheartedly agreed with the Marxists of the Old Left, nor ascribed fully to the Maoist tenets of the New Left.

Oriane interrupted one interview when she arrived in her mother's office after school. Almost eleven, she was still more than a foot shorter than her mother. Still known as Fifi, at that stage of her development she still resembled Marvin more, though her brown hair, eyes and heavy eyebrows favored Fay. As Fay embraced her daughter in obvious delight, Fay explained to the reporter that her round-the-clock commitment to the Soledad Brothers case took priority over her family. On Halloween, Oriane had surprised her parents by wearing a specially made costume. A family friend had made a black-and-white, prison-striped tunic and tights with "STENDER" printed in block letters on the front hem of the tunic and "FREE THE SOLEDAD BROTHERS" on the back. Fay was greatly amused. She proudly shared photos of Oriane in prison garb when she visited George Jackson, as well as sharing the pictures with her co-workers and friends.

In November, Fay and her co-counsel filed a pioneering federal action, *Clutchette v. Procunier*. They challenged the constitutionality of state prison disciplinary hearings where inmates were routinely denied written notice and defense counsel. The successful outcome of the lawsuit ultimately benefitted all California prisoners facing disciplinary hearings, not just the Soledad Brothers. It would be the first such ruling in the nation. In December of 1970, the legal team filed a more sensational suit charging that the Soledad Brothers defense was being sabotaged by prison officials, the Monterey District Attorney and the Attorney General's Office. The suit claimed that these government agents all threatened the lives and parole eligibility of inmates wishing to testify for the Soledad Brothers, intimidating potential witnesses into silence.

At first, Jackson was elated at all the favorable publicity, then overwhelmed as a steady stream of underground reporters beat a path to San Quentin, eager to interview the acclaimed revolutionary. He asked Fay to purchase new eyeglasses for him in the style Jonathan wore. When the glasses arrived in early December, George wore them constantly, convinced they made him resemble his deceased younger brother.

It did not take long after reading *Soledad Brother* carefully from start to finish for Jackson to grow incensed. He reflected on his brother's sacrifice as he realized how much of his thunder Fay had edited out of the published letters. Jackson had told Angela Davis months before that he and Fay did not share the same political strategy because "we are viewing things from very different levels of slavery. Mine is an abject slavery."[21] At that time, he had been convinced to defer to Fay's judgment. No longer.

Yet, if Jackson were honest with himself, he had deliberately misled both his mother and Fay to believe in his innocence. He had similarly courted other devotees with the remnants of his humanity. He wrote to one, "I just breathe people in."[22] The difference with Fay was her insistence that Jackson could only go free if he followed her advice to temporarily suppress the warrior within him. That was not going to happen.

In mid-November of 1970, Joan Hammer came to see George and let him know that her boarder, Mabel "Micki" Magers, was pregnant with his deceased brother Jonathan's child. Hammer was caught violating San Quentin's rules by sitting too close to Jackson in their private conference room. She witnessed guards forcibly remove Jackson and told Greg Armstrong that George was then beaten senseless in the hall. Afterward, George appeared increasingly delirious and more committed than ever to escape. Jackson's supporters worried with good reason that he might try something foolish.

In late October, Jackson and Jimmy Carr had in fact plotted another hostage-taking scheme. Carr arranged for George to be listed as a character witness for his cousin's upcoming jury trial on charges of assaulting a guard. Carr figured George could find a way to escape. The plan fizzled when the judge declined to permit Jackson to appear at the trial.

Throughout the fall, Jackson increasingly relied on Carr and Fred Bennett, the head of the Black Panther Party's East Oakland Branch, who served as the liaison to the Soledad Brothers Defense Committee. George created a new inner circle of supporters. He dubbed them "The August 7th Movement," named for Jonathan Jackson's day of sacrifice — day one of the revolution. In late December, Carr complained to Jackson that he needed more money for paramilitary training in the Santa Cruz mountains. Carr had asked Fay for a share of the book royalties for "living expenses," but Fay had refused. Carr reported that Fay also said she could no longer work with the Black Panthers. Jackson suggested that Carr approach Thorne about having the Panthers take control of the Soledad Defense Committee and the book royalties.

Soon, Jackson was in open rebellion against Fay just as he had been against his overly protective mother. He wrote reporter Eve Pell that "Fay cut so much material away from [*Soledad Brother*] that it turned out more her than me. There were several hundred pages of remedy left out."[23] Jackson felt it was time to spread his message to "seize the pig by the tusks and ride him until his neck broke." He told Fay the prison would never let him out alive and refused to cooperate with *Time* magazine. Instead, he feverishly undertook work on a second book, *Blood in My Eye*, which he also dedicated to Jonathan. The title derived from a postscript in a letter from his father. The new book would be a soulless, revolutionary training manual containing all the unbridled rage Fay had masked in his first book.

Jackson was still willing to be interviewed by Decca Mitford to promote sales of *Soledad Brother* through a *New York Times* book review. Jackson trusted Decca and told her what books he had read in prison and the revolutionary authors who most influenced him in developing his theories and strategy. He explained his efforts to build his vocabulary during long hours of solitary confinement. Decca wanted to know if he was given an opportunity to review the edits and correct his galleys as authors on the outside routinely did. Did he make decisions on which letters should be omitted? What were the reasons for selecting some and not others? Jackson told her that officials limited him to blunt pencils as writing implements to guard against him using a pen or sharp pencil as a weapon. He worked only in a poorly lit cell and never revised anything: "I write strictly off the top of my head. I don't go over it because I haven't time."[24]

Investigative reporter Jo Durden-Smith later put Decca's concern into a more succinct question to Fay's colleague Eve Pell, "How much of *Soledad Brother*, in the end, was Jackson's?"

Eve answered: "Well, not much of it was his . . . and he was madder than hell about it. The irony in the end . . . was that the book was sold all over the world, and attracted all kinds of people, thousands of them to the defense committee. They put their money in the hat, organized meetings, and made him a hero. And yet the guy they were doing it for wasn't George."[25]

Jackson was now asking everyone whom he trusted to help him escape. In early February, when Armstrong next visited San Quentin, Jackson drew a rough map with a sketch of a tool shed on the premises where he thought Armstrong might hide guns. Armstrong refused. Jackson then burned the sketch to ashes. When the guard saw the burnt paper he threatened to cut off all of Armstrong's future visiting privileges.

Jackson also asked Fay to bring him a gun to aid in his escape. She refused, too. It was crazy and could only end in Jackson's death. She also would not agree that all royalties now go to the Panthers for weapons for the revolution instead of defense costs. Though she remained on his defense team, Fay was totally demoralized. Thorne still kept telling everyone, "We've got a winner,"[26] but Fay admitted that chances of getting Jackson off were now dim.

Fay realized that, unlike Huey Newton, Jackson would make no effort to convince a jury of his innocence. Rather, with Jonathan already sacrificed, Jackson wanted to go public with his private boast: Jackson had already told a number of people that he had killed Mills in revenge

Source: Hon. Richard Silver (ret.)

FAY STENDER

SOLEDAD DEFENSE COUNSEL

Speaking On

SOLEDAD BROTHERS

"THE TRIAL OF SOLEDAD PRISON"

FRIDAY, FEBRUARY 19, 8 p.m., HUB BALLROOM

FREE ADMISSION

The FBI kept close track of Fay Stender's speaking events for Huey Newton, the Soledad Brothers and the Prison Law Project. At the time of this talk at the University of Washington in Seattle on February 19, 1971, Fay and George Jackson were already wrangling over her plans for handling his defense at trial.

for the execution of his friend and mentor Nolen in the prison yard. Armstrong had first learned the truth when George blurted it out unintentionally in their tape-recorded second meeting in June of 1970. The admission could be heard by listening closely to one of the tapes the police had seized in August and returned soon afterward at Marvin's demand.

On January 16, 1970, the day of Mills' murder, when almost all other black inmates had fasted in protest of the whitewashing of sharpshooter Opie Miller's conduct, Jackson had gone to dinner. He declared, "A warrior doesn't starve himself before going into battle."[27] Jackson then seized the first opportunity in which he found a guard alone, and Mills was the hapless victim, just as the prosecutor claimed, an eye-for-an-eye. But George was adamant that Yorke's claim that he witnessed Mills being grabbed was a lie: "Now listen man, he didn't see my face until later on when I dropped the guy." Drumgo and Clutchette weren't involved at all. Jackson was prepared to confess at trial, if necessary, to save the pair from execution: "I didn't need them. They would have gotten in the way."[28]

Still loyal to Jackson, Armstrong panicked when he learned that a reporter writing a book on the case might have uncovered evidence of Jackson's guilt. Armstrong frantically left word for Fay to call him, only to hear her deflated response that he should contact Thorne instead. Fay was thinking of leaving the case: "I've done all that I can do." Armstrong was incredulous. Fay was irreplaceable — she provided all the sound and fury of the defense. But Fay had no fight left in her: "Anyone can do it now. Besides, I'm not getting along very well with George. I'm just so tired of the whole thing."[29]

Fay had just returned from one last anguished visit to Jackson at San Quentin, a futile confrontation in which she tried once more to dissuade her client from pursuing a suicidal course. Jackson instead fired Fay from his legal team and told her he wanted nothing more to do with her. After their heated exchanged, he stood at the window of the small conference room, furiously banging on it to signal that the meeting with his attorney had come to an abrupt end. He wanted to be escorted back to his cell. Seeing how distraught she was, the guard reached out to comfort Fay, who was grateful for the show of unaccustomed empathy. A few days later, Jackson was remorseful. He asked a friend to call Fay and tell her, "George said he loves you no matter what."[30]

At the end of February, Huey Newton and Eldridge Cleaver split the Panther Party asunder in a public feud. At the same time, Fay formally withdrew as Jackson's trial counsel, citing her client's refusal to cooperate. Privately, she shared with a few friends George's demands that she help him escape instead of going to trial. Yet rumors circulated among members of the prison movement that Fay was a "sellout" and might herself be working for the police. Someone anonymously sent Fay a razor blade in the mail.[31]

Until that point, Fay had worked virtually nonstop on Jackson's behalf for more than a year. Armstrong was among those who held out hope that Fay and Jackson would somehow reconcile: "I think of George and how much he depends on her. . . . They are locked in the case together. Just the same way he is locked in his cell. . . . I think of how caged George will feel without her. When I close my eyes, I can see him throwing himself against the bars of his cell, tearing away at them and bellowing with pain."[32]

Jackson soon developed a new plan of escape that counted on his friends on the outside to ambush the van full of guards taking him to his next pretrial hearing in San Francisco. He wrote a will in March giving the Panthers his estate, including the lucrative royalties from *Soledad Brother*, which, the prior June, he had authorized Fay to use for defense costs. The ambush, like so many of Jackson's schemes, did not happen, but at his next hearing, he got into a fight with one of his guards, jumped up and yelled, "Power to the People. Death to the pigs."[33] Several supporters then got into a fight with police summoned by the judge's push of an emergency button. Jackson went back to San Quentin; his friend Jimmy Carr was among three spectators arrested and charged with assault. Fay would have represented Jackson at that hearing had they not had their falling out. It was likely where Jackson had anticipated she could slip him a gun.

Later in April, four months after his mysterious disappearance, Fred Bennett's charred remains were found at the Panther's Santa Cruz guerilla training site. *The San Francisco Examiner* then broke the story that an undercover agent had talked with an eyewitness to Bennett's murder. The caretaker of the site said he observed Jimmy Carr execute Bennett in early January after accusing Bennett of being a police informant. Officials soon made repeated visits to Carr at the San Francisco County Jail to pressure him to turn state's evidence against George Jackson and Huey Newton.

From the extraordinary high Fay had experience for much of the prior year, she started to sink into depression. Both revolutionary clients had fired her; both were seemingly hell-bent on behavior that would undo everything she had done for them. Yet working for them had opened her eyes to thousands of mistreated minority inmates who deserved a champion. Who better than Fay?

■ 10 ■

The Dragon Lady Reigns

Some day the Awakening will come, when the pent-up vigor of ten million souls shall sweep . . . out of the Valley of the Shadow of Death, where all that makes life worth living — Liberty, Justice, and Right — is marked "For White People Only."
— W.E.B. Du Bois, 1903

It could have been predicted that on some distant tomorrow prisoners would rise up in the name of their own humanity. Tomorrow is now.[1]
— The Prison Law Project, 1972

Back in the spring and summer of 1970, Fay had traveled to several California prisons to interview nearly 150 inmates who had been at Soledad with Jackson. A few inmates wanted nothing to do with the thirty-eight-year-old activist or the Soledad Brothers. Notably, Fay's efforts were rebuffed by those tattooed with Swastikas. Most inmates were far more interested in finding a receptive audience for their own grievances than in helping Jackson. The work was intensive and draining. Only a handful could be interviewed each day. The anguish left Fay's throat swollen.

Few men had any useful knowledge regarding Mills' killing, but all shared stories of the horrors of prison life. Fay encouraged them to write to her. Her tomboyish new companion, Boalt law student Patti Roberts, often worked alongside her, both listening intently to the miserable details of the inmates' treatment. Word of the woman lawyer with her overall-clad assistant quickly spread among felons at all twelve California men's penal institutions. Fay Stender had freed the legendary Huey Newton; she just might accomplish something for them as well.

Hundreds of hand-written letters addressed to "Mrs. Stender," "Fay and Patti," "Comrades" or "Dear Sisters" poured into the post office box for the Soledad Brothers Defense Committee each month. Some inmates had not had anyone to correspond with in years. The deluge of mail came from conservation camps for low-risk offenders as well as medium and maximum security California prisons. Some even arrived from out of state.

The prisoners complained of physical conditions or lack of access to medicine or psychiatric counseling. They described unfair isolation for their political views. They asked for help in getting paroled. They sought reading material denied them by prison officials. Some needed a lawyer after winning reversal on appeal. Others asked Fay to contact their family or become a pen pal. Many were desperate for at least occasional female companionship.

A poem by Michael McCarthy while at Soledad illustrated the men's pent-up sexual desire:

SOMETHING ABOUT PRISON

There just aint
no
tenderness
in
fucking your
fist
or
        a cotton-soft
tee shirt.[2]

Of the 24,000 men then held in California prisons, nearly half were black or of Mexican descent, far exceeding their percentages in the general population. Fay decided to focus on the 600 inmates in state Adjustment Centers, who received the worst treatment from prison staff and parole boards. More than three-fifths of these men were minorities. Fay learned that Adjustment Centers were originally intended as an enlightened replacement for dungeons, to be used sparingly for the most violent and unmanageable prisoners. Instead, inmates who served indeterminate sentences were disciplined for a wide variety of infractions by being isolated for long, dehumanizing periods in what the inmates still called "the hole."

Fay found a surprising ally in Dr. Frank Rundle, the new chief psychiatrist at Soledad. Rundle had been appalled when he first saw its Adjustment Center, a row of "dark, dirty little cages" filled with "the most concentrated human misery" to which he had ever been exposed. The inmates were either rattling "bars and screaming obscenities" or "lying on the cement floor as though in a stupor."[3]

Dr. Rundle rejected his predecessor's instructions to avoid the violent men in the Adjustment Center. His colleague had warned Dr. Rundle "always keep a table between you and the inmate, be prepared to shove it hard to pin him against the wall." Instead, Dr. Rundle saw men consumed by "torturing loneliness and yearning to meet another human being on equal terms." He agreed with Fay's assessment: the men "were hungry to be listened to seriously, to be believed, to be respected, to be cared about, to be liked, to be dealt with honestly."[4] (Dr. Rundle would last only five months in constant battles with the warden until he was fired. He then hired Fay to represent him in a wrongful termination suit.)

Fay recruited volunteers to help her respond to pleas for assistance. Most who joined her crusade had already been visiting the Soledad Brothers. Some were committed solely to organizing prisoners politically. Officials at Soledad were soon talked into permitting most of its 1600 inmates to join nearly 5,000 family members in celebrating their first "Family Day" at picnic tables set up in a warehouse at the prison. With donated food and rock group entertainers, the upbeat event would be hailed by all as the "beginning of a new era."[5]

The inmates courted any women who expressed interest in them. With few exceptions — like lesbian Patti Roberts — the women responded like besotted rock star groupies. One guard confiscated a nude picture of a paralegal. Women legal assistants or attorneys had rarely before visited prisons. They surprised the wardens when they used private conference rooms for trysts with violent felons. The guards soon became more vigilant in enforcing the no contact rule. Fay sensed the outrage of prison personnel toward her staff and attributed it to a visceral reaction to displays of affection across racial and class boundaries.

From the wardens' perspective, prohibited sexual encounters were only one example of Movement activists flouting prison rules. A new California law in 1968 permitted inmates to receive any subscription that was not obscene or incited violence. Wardens interpreted the law to permit *Playboy* but not *Ramparts, The Berkeley Barb* or *The Black Panther* newspaper. Radicals ignored the law and frequently sought to deliver contraband communiqués and publications.

In the spring of 1970, Fay had helped Decca Mitford obtain a contract with the ACLU to write a magazine article on prisoners' rights, the byproduct of media interest in the Black Panthers and the Soledad Brothers. One criminologist told Decca to publish a blank piece of paper because prisoners had no rights. Instead, Decca addressed the prison system's lack of basic human dignity for the occupants. Copies of Decca's article were passed from hand-to-hand among inmates. By August 1970, Decca took Fay up on the suggestion that she consider a book exposing American prisons. Fay introduced Decca to Dr. Rundle and San Francisco State Professor Robert Minton, who taught the writing class at Soledad that Michael McCarthy had taken. Minton was then completing work on an anthology of inmate essays and poetry.

As Fay received more and more mail from inmates filled with heart-rending accounts of callous and arbitrary treatment, she realized there was another book in the making. She recruited freelance reporter Eve Pell from the Soledad Brothers Defense Committee, who had written the introduction for Jackson's book. Prison reform was the cause du jour, a rallying point for liberals and a subject of surprising attention at the top levels of government. That spring, Chief Justice Berger had called the nation's prisons "the most neglected, the most crucial, and probably the least understood phase of the administration of justice," while President Nixon described the prison system as a "crime university graduating more than 200,000 hardened criminals a year."[6]

Student interest also ran high. In January 1971, Fay agreed to teach a seminar at Boalt Hall on prison law — one of the first of its kind. When Fay was in law school, she could not recall ever hearing the word "prison." Fay had plenty of material for the syllabus and considered including a field trip to San Quentin. Boalt Hall was no longer the stodgy law school she had quit after a week. Fay began to realize that most high-ranking law schools had also begun to offer a course in prison law. Many were developing clinical programs through which instructors could oversee students visiting prisons to address inmates' legal problems. Fay decided to form a separate "Prison Law Project" together with third year student Patti Roberts and free-lance reporter Eve Pell. Like a more focused Council for Justice, they would coordinate the representation of inmates in challenging some of the most egregious practices in California's prisons.

Fay began recruiting lawyers to volunteer in their spare time. She assumed correctly that many would now want to pursue groundbreaking prisoners' rights cases to help build on prior successes of the ACLU. The chance to establish new case law benefitting inmates was more psychologically rewarding than their paying clients' work. For a while, Fay continued operating out of the Franck, Hill office space she still shared with her old partnership. On April 1, staff arrived to find a bullet hole in the window, shot through a poster that urged community control of Berkeley police. That night the collective held an emergency meeting off-site, still worried the office was bugged. They decided against calling the police to report the shooting. What would have been the point?

That spring, acting like a woman possessed, Fay pressed many friends into service to represent one or more prisoners without pay in their own field of practice — divorce, probate of estates, whatever the inmates' needs were. She transformed one reluctant downtown San Francisco lawyer into a zealot when officials callously ignored his requests for their assistance in tracking down his client's missing prescription eyeglasses.

How could prisoners learn respect for law and order if their meager belongings were so often confiscated with impunity?

Although often gone long hours, Marvin was fully supportive of Fay's new mission. However attenuated their relationship had been at times over the years, he had always delighted in encouraging her to focus her legal talents on Movement causes. Fay even inspired him to help launch a prisoners' union at the Men's Colony in San Luis Obispo. Marvin then headed the Lawyers Guild office in San Francisco, which became the prisoners' bargaining representative on a list of demands ranging from fair wages to better-equipped law libraries. Shortly afterward, Folsom inmates followed the lead of the Men's Colony and issued a manifesto listing 29 demands. Prison officials saw Fay's superhuman efforts behind the tidal wave.

Fay and her recruits began negotiating with prison officials to improve conditions or bring suits, sometimes just assisting inmates who represented themselves. As the project grew, Fay applied for several grants and turned to the local office of Congressman Ron Dellums for help. Upon his election to Congress, the district's first black Congressman was deluged with letters from minority inmates and their relatives. Fay offered assistance from the Prison Law Project in responding to these demands. In turn, Dellums' young staffer Lee Halterman put the clout of the Congressman's office behind Fay's requests for funding from federal agencies and private foundations.

Fay drew up a formal proposal for the Prison Law Project with a goal she thought would sell to funders. If 95 percent of felons eventually returned to society, why treat so many of them like caged animals during their incarceration? Jail time only turned amateurs into professional criminals and hardened others to a life of crime upon being released with no job skills or legitimate employment opportunities. By late spring, Fay had raised half the money she needed to launch the project at its own site in north Oakland. When she moved, her former partners immediately noticed how quiet their office became.

While Fay obtained start up costs for the Prison Law Project, the Soledad Defense Committee funding ran dry. Some, like Georgia Jackson and her daughter Penny, blamed the attorneys, arguing that they had all grown rich off of the case. Particular venom was reserved for Fay. The Jackson family never understood that the high cost of the three inmates' criminal defense largely paid for hearing transcripts, experts, depositions and travel reimbursement. Little found its way into the lawyers' pockets. By May of 1971, when Betsy Hammer Carr had been in charge of the committee office for several months, some other volunteers surmised that the missing money had instead been used by Betsy's husband Jimmy Carr for military training in the Santa Cruz mountains (as George had authorized over Fay's objection).

At the Soledad Brothers next pretrial hearing on June 11th, more than a dozen sheriff's deputies were stationed in the courtroom. The judge then delayed the trial until August to permit installation of a bulletproof glass partition between the spectators and the participants. The defense team worried that the extraordinary precautions would make the jury prone to convict their clients. Thorne asked the judge to permit Jackson and Angela Davis to confer for trial preparation. Escorted by an armed guard and draped in chains, Jackson soon accompanied Thorne to meet Davis and her attorneys in the dining room of the Marin County Jail. Thorne attempted to shield the couple from the guards' sight as the two embraced. The lawyer-client conference went forward with Jackson fondling Davis in his lap. The guard reported it as "a lovers' petting party."[7]

Thorne remained in dire need of money for trial. Still frustrated and suspicious of Fay, Georgia Jackson and her daughter Penny raided the Soledad Brothers Defense Committee's headquarters, smashed furniture and confiscated its financial accounts, convinced they would find evidence that Fay had misappropriated funds necessary for George's defense. Shortly afterward, Armstrong returned to San Francisco to edit George's second book and visited Fay at her home. Though it was midday, she greeted him in her bathrobe with a Nero Wolfe mystery in her hand. He attributed Fay's somber mood to her ouster from Jackson's defense. He told her that Jackson asked to see her again. Fay reacted with fear: "I'm not going alone. I'll take another lawyer with me."[8]

Among others on the defense committee, talk still centered on the Soledad Brothers' missing funds. Armstrong thought the gloomy focus had a different meaning:

> My own sense is that people talk about money but what they really mean is Fay. Without her there is no center. Quiet hopelessness has taken possession of everyone.... Without Fay it must seem to George as if reality itself has disappeared — the reality of intense struggle that Fay, his mighty mouthpiece, had brought to the case with her uncompromising need to defeat her enemies... with the sense of momentum she brought with her, the sense of frenzied activity, the sense that she was always locked in mortal combat and that she wouldn't accept defeat, the endless number of activities that she initiated, the breathless battlefield reports — all that is gone. With her withdrawal, it must be as if death itself has entered his cell prematurely because everything suddenly must be so quiet and musty.[9]

But it was just the opposite. It was not Fay who had abandoned a central role on the defense team, but Jackson, the uncompromising warrior, who had decided to become a dead man walking. The despair of his family stemmed from the recognition Jackson no longer wanted to be defended, and their desperate need to have someone else to blame.

Fay relegated Jackson's fate to the back of her mind as she occupied herself setting up the new Prison Law Project. The group of ten agreed that everyone — lawyers, law students, paralegals and administrative assistants — would start out with the same full-time take home pay of $300 per month, just above subsistence level. No one objected when Fay, as head of the Project, took over one of the two bedrooms as her private office. Fay frequently invited all her co-workers to potlucks with her family and also spent many evenings at the Oakland North Street house where Patti Roberts lived. Roberts considered Fay the most remarkable, charismatic woman she had ever met. She was overwhelmed by Fay's intellect, high energy, intensity and vision. The two were having an affair which Fay managed to keep from her family, though it was an open secret at the Project.

Fay asked Decca Mitford to write letters of support for her fund-raising requests and told her the unique aspects of the Project that Decca could emphasize. The Project reached out to all inmates regardless of race or politics, well beyond the traditional legal focus. The staff answered every request for assistance and, in an emergency, promised a lawyer within 48 hours. The Project also had an ongoing media campaign. They spoke at churches, medical schools, community centers, law schools, colleges and high schools. They interacted with the ACLU, the NAACP, groups of ex-convicts and bar committees. Decca was leery of Fay's bias and blind spots: Fay credited inmates with telling the truth almost all the time; she also claimed to speak for all inmates with clashing political views, despite her recent bitter falling out with Jackson.

Fay extolled the collective's efforts to improve the public image of prisoners, to reconnect prisoners with their families and to refer them to other needed assistance. The project had already accumulated a data bank which functioned as a resource center for other researchers. Fay had also helped launch the Prison Lawyers Association and served on its first board, using it as a platform to lobby for prison reform. More than 50 attorneys now made prison law their full-time practice when less than a decade before there were only a handful who occasionally took a case.

Fay was proud, too, of her project's aggressive anti-professionalism. She told Decca that, unlike traditional legal help, the uninhibited manner by which her staff reached out to inmates was therapeutic for both groups, crossing class barriers. Yet Decca was aware of the unhappy outcome of Fay's own relationships with Newton and Jackson. Decca remained skeptical of this Project. From the outset, she had observed internal dissension at the Project, whose members held excruciatingly long meetings seeking to achieve consensus between two warring factions. The young radicals, Roberts included, wanted to overthrow the system; others, led by Fay, wanted to work on reforms. The radicals also wanted everyone to rotate in their jobs, seeking to wrest control of the Project from Fay.

The landmark decision in the case Fay had filed for the Soledad Brothers the previous November came out in June, declaring inmates had a constitutional right to written notice and counsel for probation violation hearings. It prompted introduction of a bill in Sacramento to codify those rights. Despite Fay's high hopes, the bill died. Decca told friends how much jollier it was to investigate funeral homes. It astonished her how prison work completely consumed Fay. Decca had already concluded that "the whole history of prison reform is the co-option by prison administrators of well-meaning reforms. . . . [D]o-gooding suggestions of whites about improving the lot of Blacks are pretty much doomed to failure — because only the Blacks themselves have the real insight to formulate their own program."[10]

At year's end, Fay herself realized the enormous power the Department of Corrections wielded with the Legislature: all of the 175 prison reform measures introduced that year would fail. By mid-summer of 1971, the Prison Law Project remained extremely low on money. Fay traveled extensively to fund-raise and publicize their efforts while the others did the grunt work. Staffers' resentment mounted. Meanwhile Eve Pell worked on publishing *Maximum Security*, culling the most effective letters out of the thousands Fay had received mostly from militant men of color. Just telling their stories in public put the inmates in jeopardy of harsh retaliation. Pell refused to filter their voices in any way, not even to correct spelling or grammar. The lawyers at the Project expected the book to expose biased indeterminate sentencing as a cross between the nightmarish world envisioned by Bohemian novelist Franz Kafka and *Catch-22*, Joseph Heller's satirical novel on the bureaucratic quagmire of American army regulations. For men made to feel like animals with no self-worth, radical political ideas gave new purpose to their lives.

* * *

Fay had not yet divorced herself entirely from work for the Panthers. Garry still expected her to help as Newton's second trial neared. He himself had just completed several punishing and financially draining months in Connecticut on the Seale and Huggins murder trial, which ended with a deadlocked jury, mostly favoring acquittal. All charges were then dropped against the pair. Seale arrived in Oakland amid much fanfare — the first time he was reunited with Huey Newton since the summer before Newton's October 1967 arrest on murder charges.

In June, David Hilliard went to trial for his role in the police ambush that Cleaver had attempted in April 1968 that resulted in Bobby Hutton's death. Hilliard was convicted and sentenced to Folsom for one to ten years. (He would serve four while Fay represented him on appeal.) Now it was Huey's turn. With the death penalty no longer an option, Newton's retrial was far less of a draw than his first prosecution in 1968. Some controversy was generated when, on the eve of its commencement, Ed Keating published *Free Huey!* promoted by radicals as the true story of Frey's murder. Keating claimed the murder was perpetrated by a midget who fled the scene and was never caught.

On June 28, Garry started Newton's manslaughter trial, without Fay sitting in the second chair. Though she agreed to help out behind the scenes with some motion work, Garry knew that Fay and Newton were no longer on friendly terms. The rift proved what Garry already knew — emotional involvement was an impediment to effective lawyering. The trial lasted until the first week of August, observed by a far smaller coterie of loyalists than in 1968.

After the passionate closing arguments, Newton's mostly female jury deliberated for six days through a blistering heat wave. The panel returned to court to announce an eleven-to-one deadlock for conviction. "It's what I expected," Newton told the press, assuming, wrongly, that it was the lone black woman on the panel who had held out for acquittal. Prosecutor Donald Whyte marched out of the courtroom "tight-lipped and grim," without talking to reporters.[11] Before the afternoon was out, District Attorney Lowell Jensen promised a third trial to avenge the death of the fallen officer. Meanwhile, Newton remained released on $50,000 bail.

Two weeks earlier, as the Soledad Brothers' August trial date approached, the three remaining lawyers on that case had met with Jackson and his co-defendants for final preparations. Jackson's only interest at the meeting was in obtaining another continuance, which the lawyers considered impossible to obtain. Decades later, Silver recoiled as he pictured Jackson that day. George displayed more anger than they had ever seen, slamming his fist on the table, insisting, "I need more time."

The first day of trial was coincidentally set to occur the day after the Newton verdict was reached. On the morning of August 9th, Thorne surprisingly accused the assigned trial judge of race bias for belonging to two clubs that allegedly discriminated against blacks. The judge was taken aback but treated the motion as Thorne's one free opportunity to recuse a judge without cause and promptly disqualified himself. He rescheduled the case for trial at the Hall of Justice on August 23 before a different judge. Jackson got his wish.

The San Quentin prison staff were already on high alert. On Sunday August 1, 1971, George's sister Delora and her two children had driven up from Southern California to join her sister Penny and her son in a visit to George. At the metal detector, guards confiscated toy guns and a .22 caliber starting pistol they had strapped under the clothing of George's niece and nephews. The two women were barred from further visits. The prison officials then stopped permitting any investigators to visit Jackson as of August 14.

Back in May George had written a new will that left most of the royalties from his second book to his newborn nephew Jonathan Jackson, Jr. — Micki Magers' son. In early August, George changed his will once more to devote all of the proceeds of his books to the Black Panther Party. George now wanted the proceeds to pay for weaponry for the revolution. He had almost finished writing *Blood in My Eye* by August 7, 1971, the first anniversary of Jonathan's death. The following week, Jackson sent his manuscript to Armstrong, with a cover letter: "I'm not a writer, but all of it's me, the way I want it, the way I see it."[12] Jackson's detailed instructions left Armstrong with the strong sense that Jackson did not expect to live to see the book published.

Envisioned as his last revolutionary will and testament, his second book claimed that "the power of the people lies in its greater potential violence" not "to outshout [an opponent] with logic [but to] slay him, assassinate him . . . shooting from four hundred yards away and behind a rock. Suffocation, strangulation, crucifixion. . . ."[13] On the morning of August 21st, George wrote another letter to Greg Armstrong stating that it was a good day to die.

That same afternoon, Fay took rare time off with eleven-year-old Oriane and joined tourists shopping at San Francisco's Ghirardelli Square. Shortly after Fay returned home, the phone rang. Thorne had received a call from the warden at San Quentin late in the afternoon just as he, Silver and Silliman had been hard at work preparing for trial the following Monday. Had Fay heard about George? She instantly knew he was dead. Fay turned on the news as the airwaves erupted with reports of another Marin County bloodbath. George Jackson was killed in the courtyard at San Quentin, allegedly trying to escape. She invited grieving colleagues to her home just as she had after Jonathan's death.

The reports were that Jackson had overpowered guards with a 9mm automatic pistol as he yelled "The Dragon has come." He then freed a number of other inmate co-conspirators before he was cornered. Six guards had their throats slit, three had died. Two of the dead guards also had bullet wounds in their heads. Two inmates besides Jackson had died and others were wounded — the worst episode of violence in the prison's history.

Jackson's only visitor that afternoon was twenty-nine-year-old attorney Stephen Bingham, a housemate of Patti Roberts and Doron Weinberg. Bingham had taken Fay's place that spring at the Franck law collective and had been added in June to Jackson's list of visitors after Thorne asked Bingham to handle a civil action for Jackson. The police wanted Bingham for questioning, but he disappeared the night Jackson died and was a presumed fugitive. Another person who unsuccessfully sought admission to see Jackson at the prison that morning, a black woman investigator from Black Panther headquarters named Vanita Anderson, had gone missing as well.

At a press conference that evening, Associate Warden Jim Park grimly announced that seventeen to twenty men had been involved in an attempted breakout that afternoon, with six fatalities and numerous grave injuries. When asked whom he held responsible for the aborted escape effort, Park retorted sharply, "I blame it on the bullshit talk of dilettante revolutionaries, on people who emptily advocate murder from the safety of outside the walls. . . . You can lay some of the blame for these six deaths at the doorstep of some of these radical attorneys who come in here and encourage the men to do this sort of thing."[14]

Mystery enshrouded the episode. Jackson himself had told a *New York Times* reporter in April that the only way he would leave prison alive was escape. The story was printed at the beginning of August. How could forewarned officials not have been prepared to prevent Jackson from carrying out his plans? They appeared either grossly incompetent or, worse, complicit in the bloodbath. Either way, their explanation of the way Jackson wound up shot to death in the yard raised more questions than it answered.

On August 28th, exactly one week later, the Weathermen responded, setting off explosives at the Department of Corrections that caused extensive damage in retribution. That same day, Jackson's funeral was held at St. Augustine's Church in Oakland. At the service, Jackson's family members were grim. The waxen-faced revolutionary lay in an open satin coffin surrounded by shotguns. He was dressed in a pale blue turtleneck, Chinese tunic and black beret. (His reluctant "revolutionary mama," as George had recently taken to calling her, had honored her namesake's emphatic wish that when he died he not be buried in a suit and surrounded by flowers.) When Jonathan died, she had swallowed her tears. Now, behind her dark sunglasses, no one could see if Georgia wept as she pumped her fist in the air to join in a militant salute to her elder son.

Fay was subdued as she sat through the lengthy tributes. She had not been surprised as much as saddened and frustrated by the tragedy. For her the situation was compounded by the Jackson family's open animosity and the awkwardness of her estrangement from the Panthers. Huey Newton gave the principal oration again, having just returned from Lake Tahoe where he had reportedly been vacationing with Bert Schneider and Schneider's girlfriend Candace Bergen. As Newton spoke of his fallen hero, Black Guerilla Family members bristled. They knew that George Jackson's best friend Jimmy Carr blamed Newton for abandoning Jonathan to certain death by aborting the Panthers' role in Jonathan's invasion of the Marin County courthouse. George's sister Penny also blamed the Black Panther Party for not coming to George's support in his efforts to escape.

The audience was more receptive to tributes from James Baldwin and Jean Genet. Congressman Ron Dellums decried the "horror and brutality of the prison system" and offered his assistance to the bereaved family.[15] Angela Davis sent a message from jail, calling *Soledad Brother* "a stirring chronicle of the development of the highest form of revolutionary fortitude and resistance . . . a primer to captured brothers and sisters across the world. . . .[T]his volume, perhaps more than any other, has given impetus and shaped the direction of the growing support movement outside the prisons."[16] Like the *Panther* newspaper's lengthy tribute to Jackson, Angela Davis did not in any way allude to Fay's pivotal role in getting Jackson recognized as a revolutionary hero through publication of his letters.

Jackson's death reverberated internationally. The morning after his death, inmates at Attica Correctional Facility in upstate New York had eerily shown their homage to the deceased icon by either donning black ribbons or arm bands. Officials were astonished at this concerted action among so many prisoners in separate cells with no known method of communicating to each other so quickly. On September 9th, one thousand Attica prisoners rose in rebellion, taking more than thirty guards hostage. Governor Rockefeller refused to negotiate and ordered the prison stormed. Eleven hostages and thirty-two inmates were killed, ten by state troopers.

The following month, the Prison Law Project erupted in open warfare over its mission and leadership when murder indictments were issued against a half dozen of the surviving inmates of the August 21 bloodshed. The San Quentin Six included Fleeta Drumgo and Hugo "Yogi" Pinell, who had also been transferred from Soledad. The district attorney charged attorney Stephen Bingham with complicity in murder. The radical faction of the Prison Law Project assumed that the Project would be front and center in the defense of the San Quentin Six. Yet Fay had no stomach for orchestrating supporters for the San Quentin Six as she had for the Soledad Brothers and argued that their own time was better spent in class actions. This was the last straw.

Pell later recalled, "We regarded the Six as righteous political

```
FD-122 (Rev. 11-22-71)

UNITED STATES GOVERNMENT
Memorandum

TO      : Director, FBI (Bufile-                    ) DATE: 3/15/72

FROM    : SAC, SAN FRANCISCO (100-49931) (P)

SUBJECT : FAYE STENDER, aka
          SM - NEW LEFT
               COMMUNIST                            (b) (7) (C)

Re: San Francisco report of SA ▮▮▮▮▮▮▮▮▮ dated 3/15/72

Recommend: [X] ADEX Card   [ ] ADEX Card changed (specify change only)   [ ] Subject removed (succinct summary attach
```

Name				
FAYE STENDER				
Aliases Ethel Abrahams, Fay Ethel Abrahams, Fay Stender, Fay Abrahams Stender, Fay Ethel Stender, Mrs. Marvin Stender, Mrs. Marvin Edward Stender.		[X] Native Born [ ] Naturalized [ ] Alien	Tab	[ ] Category I [ ] Category II [ ] Category III [ ] Category IV

```
[ ] AWC        [X] COMMUNIST       [ ] PLP     [ ] PRN     [ ] SNC     [ ] SWP
[ ] BNT        [ ] JFG             [ ] NOI     [ ] FPA     [ ] SDS     [ ] SPL     [ ] WWP
[ ] BPP        [ ] MIN                         [ ] Miscellaneous (Specify)
```

Date of Birth	Place of Birth	Race	Sex
3/29/32	San Francisco, California	White	[ ] Male [ ] Female

Business Address, Name of Employing Concern and Address, Nature of Employment, and Union Affiliation, if any.	Residence Address
Attorney Prison Law Project 5406 Claremont Avenue Oakland, Calif.	2210 Grant Street Berkeley, Calif. ALL INFORMATION CONTAINED HEREIN IS UNCLASSIFIED DATE 3/13/02 BY SP4 BJA/CB

```
Key Facility Data

Geographical Reference Number _____        Responsibility _____

(2) - Bureau (RM)
 1  - San Francisco                          SEARCHED ___  INDEXED ___
SDA:jc    S=2                                SERIALIZED ___  FILED ___
(3)                                             MAY 15 1972
                                             FBI — SAN FRANCISCO

                                             100-49931-159A
```

FBI Vol. II March 1972 description of Fay Stender's "aliases": Ethel Abrahams, Fay Ethel Abrahams, Fay Stender, Fay Abrahams Stender, Mrs. Marvin Stender, Mrs. Marvin Edward Stender

Source: FBI Freedom of Information Act request

brothers who'd been singled out for persecution by the fascist prison system.... For us, it was an intense emotional identification with them as heroes, as lovers, as comrades."[17] The radical faction abruptly quit Oakland to join Patti Roberts in forming a new Prison Law Collective in San Francisco to offer legal support to the San Quentin Six. To Fay's fury, the new competing collective was invited to set itself up in the Lawyers Guild building in San Francisco. The departing staff had kept a key. They used it to enter the Prison Law Project the next Sunday and grab half of the typewriters to install in their new location. As they competed for scarce funding, the feud worsened. Some members would never speak to Fay again.

* * *

After George's funeral, the Jacksons had flown with his body to a private family ceremony in East St. Louis before the family arrived at his burial site next to Jonathan's in a cemetery in Mount Vernon, Illinois. The paparazzi were waiting at the cemetery. Georgia irately accused them of taking advantage of her dead son. The family's Panther escort then smashed one of the photographer's cameras. Following the minister's short sermon, Georgia Jackson made a speech of her own, ending with the emotional pronouncement, "My son was one of the greatest human beings who ever lived."[18] Greg Armstrong accompanied the entourage from Oakland as he had done the year before. Last time, Georgia had been comforted by his bear hug. This time, when he attempted a similar embrace, she recoiled and snapped, "I blame you, Greg. I blame you more than any of the others."[19] But this was not true. Georgia still reserved special anger for Fay.

Back in the Bay Area a week later, Georgia and Penny Jackson once again began badmouthing "the Stenders and that bunch." They complained that none had called since George's death — not that their calls would have been welcomed. Both mother and daughter shared the view that those "money grabbing creeps" were only putting up a front before, but "now they are showing their true colors."[20] What upset Georgia and Penny anew was an issue that Fay had just raised concerning the ownership of his book royalties. Fay did not believe George had the power to transfer them by his new will. To represent the family in settling George's estate, Angela Davis's attorney Howard Moore recommended a young lawyer named Ed Bell who had worked with Moore before as a summer clerk at SNCC. Bell had no idea what he was getting into.

Meanwhile, Leftists rallied behind the Jackson family's call for a United Nations investigation of George's death. Knowing she could be of great help, Fay contacted Ed Bell. She offered the Jackson family attorney her assistance in drafting the paperwork. Bell was already impressed with what he knew about Fay's skills from reviewing Jackson's legal files and readily accepted Fay's offer. Bell and Penny Jackson brought a hurriedly drafted action item before the Berkeley City Council to seek its support in filing the U.N. charge.[21] Fay's analysis got them the backing of the Berkeley City Council by a six to one vote.

Congressman Dellums also demanded an official inquiry, not only to resolve questions of whether Jackson was deliberately set up and cut down, but to try to find Bingham and bring him home alive. (Bingham, afraid for his life, had fled to France, where he lived under an assumed name for thirteen years before returning to win acquittal on all charges.) Though Georgia and Penny Jackson remained hostile to Fay, Ed Bell was grateful to her. She had undertaken the daunting task of drafting the United Nations petition with detailed quotes from San Quentin inmates' affidavits. Bell would have had great difficulty on his own, but Fay quickly gathered descriptions of the stripping and beating of prisoners on August 21, 1971, after Jackson died; of black inmates from Soledad being fed feces and food mixed with ground glass; and the circumstances of the sharp-shooting deaths of the three inmates in the prison exercise yard on January 13, 1970.

Ed Bell mailed the extensive documentation to the National Conference of Black Lawyers in New York. The group had recently formed to represent black militants and had agreed to get the petition printed and submit it to the United Nations. When the petition emerged in final form, Bell was surprised to see his name plastered all over it. He had done none of the writing. The booklet made no mention of any contribution by Fay, its principal author. Bell felt badly.

Fay intended to cite the petition as an example of her work in seeking much-needed funding for her Prison Law Project. Bell assumed that the affront to Fay was Georgia's doing and felt powerless to correct it.

Despite this setback, Fay optimistically prepared to address a special federal judiciary subcommittee meeting in San Francisco focused on prison reform. Its nine committee members had just completed a tour of San Quentin, Soledad and Santa Rita. One compared Santa Rita's shocking "tiger cages" to the South Vietnamese prison cells he had visited two years earlier. Among the group was Chicago Congressman Abner Mikva (whom Fay and Marvin had campaigned for in the '50s). A federal study already recommended closing the nineteenth-century prisons at San Quentin and Folsom. It suggested modern replacements be built closer to the communities they served, that they focus on rehabilitation, have brighter walls, allow conjugal visits and offer inmates higher wages. This was extraordinary progress.

Buoyed by the new direction in which Congress was headed, on October 25, 1971, Fay and Marvin arrived at the hearing and listened with delight as the Chairman opened the proceedings with the observation that improvements were sorely needed. Prisons were a national failure in achieving societal protection and rehabilitation. Eleven witnesses would speak that day. Among them, Fay was the only woman. Department of Corrections Chief Procunier spoke first. He considered himself a centrist who saw both sides of the issue. (Fay already knew that. A few months earlier Procunier had become surprisingly chummy with Decca Mitford over drinks at a national conference of correctional officials. He then confided, to Decca's amazement, that he personally held Fay in high regard despite the bitter animosity she engendered in his colleagues.)

As Fay hastily scribbled notes on her program, Procunier testified that he was proud of innovations already in place and acutely aware of the system's shortcomings. Procunier agreed that further reform was necessary. "No one in the field of corrections believes a prison is [currently] a place to send people for rehabilitation."[22] To make progress, he suggested that "Extremists on both sides of the question ought to just shut up."[23] He castigated both those who would lock a man up and throw away the key and others who wanted to free all prisoners. Procunier favored reduction of recidivism through smaller prisons built closer to the communities from which the inmates came — an idea that would not gain traction in California for decades.

When Fay was called upon, her soft-spoken putdown was devastating, "I'm always interested in hearing Mr. Procunier — he sounds so good, and yet it just isn't like that in prison, it just isn't true." Fay submitted to the committee letters received from inmates, which described the system of terror resulting from "total powerlessness."[24]

The most strident speaker by far was Moe Camacho, the President of the California Corrections Officers Association, the guards' union. Camacho accused radicals of starting all the trouble by engaging in a conspiracy to destroy the penal system. Camacho urged that "we recognize the cold hard facts" and hold its perpetrators accountable. He named as the culprits "a small percentage of inmates, professional people and lay citizens, as well, apparently, as a few members of our legislature."[25] Camacho particularly blamed radical attorneys for providing an "ideal pipeline" between militant prisoners and outside sources. He called for an investigation of the National Lawyers Guild, California Prisoners Union, California Rural Legal Assistance and individuals such as Fay and Marvin Stender: "If found subversive and revolutionary-oriented, as we suspect they will, they should answer criminal charges including charges related to prison murders which may have resulted from their influence on revolutionary inmates."[26] The Chair quickly reminded Camacho that this was not a HUAC hearing called to identify subversives.

When Marvin had his turn at the microphone, he charged that the guard's union was itself lawless. Fay spoke up again. She urged that all inmates be afforded full constitutional rights in disciplinary and parole hearings. She denied that lawyers had instigated or directed prison uprisings and compared the treatment of inmates to "Jews in the Warsaw ghetto." Fay concluded that violence in and outside prison "begins with the treatment of the prisoners in these Dachaus of America. And it will not end until those controlling them are replaced by people and a process subject to the guarantees and restraints of due process of law." As she finished, all but a handful of the 50 attendees gave her a standing ovation.[27]

Procunier and Camacho were astounded at Fay's warm reception. Jackson was now dead, nationwide the Panther branches had been decimated by COINTELPRO, and Newton was facing his third trial for the death of Officer Frey. The Attorney General's Office had accused Fay the year before, in a brief to the state's highest court, of threatening the lives of prosecution witnesses and, today, the head of the guard's union called Fay a likely co-conspirator in murder. It was widely known that Fay's own Prison Law Project had just split asunder. Yet the stunning court victories Fay had achieved on Newton and Jackson's behalf had invigorated a nationwide prison reform movement. The dragon lady seemed unstoppable.

ACT THREE

■ 1 ■
Bitter Fruit

"No good deed goes unpunished"
SIGN GIVEN TO FAY STENDER FOR HER 40TH BIRTHDAY

A few days after the San Francisco hearing, Moe Camacho had his revenge. The Board of Corrections released an emergency study commissioned by Governor Reagan to address "the unlawful designs of self-proclaimed, revolutionary forces operating both within and without prison walls." The report concluded that the key to quieting the chaos inside San Quentin, Soledad and Folsom was to heighten security and curtail access to violent offenders by "radical elements" on the outside, including the inmates' lawyers and their staffs.[1] To this end, wardens now limited visits of attorneys, required investigators to be licensed, and banned inmates' receipt of radical underground newspapers that urged violence and revolution.

The timing of the report ensured a rapt national audience. Sensationalized trials of black militants were all over the front pages of newspapers: Angela Davis, the remaining Soledad Brothers, and Huey Newton for the third time. The analysis ordered by Governor Reagan was designed to show how radical inmates had been stirred up to commit mayhem by "outside lawyers," among whom Berkeley attorney Fay Stender figured prominently. One warden interviewed on CBS radio called militants in his Adjustment Center "Fay Stender's gang."[2] The report blamed the unholy coalition of inmates and their attorneys for a year and a half of escalating bloodshed: Soledad in January 1970, the Marin County courthouse shootout in August 1970, an unsuccessful strike at Folsom in November 1970, and the August 1971 San Quentin attack.

Before issuing the report, the Board had held seven days of public hearings, which critics assumed were just for show. The Board agreed that the catalyst for the violence was the shooting death of three black inmates in the Soledad exercise yard on January 13, 1970, but characterized those killings as a tragic incident. The Board focused blame for the next two years of prison violence on George Jackson and his radical supporters. The report accused outside agitators of inciting the retaliatory murder of prison guard John Mills and blamed the Soledad Brothers Defense Committee for painting the three accused killers as victims of systemic racism.

Officials linked Fay's glorification of the Soledad Brothers to prisoners who later stabbed two other guards. The report also claimed that Fay publicized false charges about inmate mistreatment, brought baseless lawsuits and maligned the corrections system to state and federal legislators, citizens' groups and college audiences. The bad press for the prison that followed was credited with encouraging disruptive inmate behavior at other facilities, including hunger strikes at Folsom. The report also rebuked the San Francisco National Lawyers Guild chapter headed by Marvin Stender for publicizing the Folsom hunger strike and pressing similar demands at the Men's Colony in San Luis Obispo.

The Soledad Brothers Defense Committee members were criticized for acting as go-betweens to help form revolutionary groups throughout the correctional system. Officials correlated radical legal activity with both Jonathan Jackson's attack on the Marin County Civic Center and the last bloody episode at San Quentin in August of 1971. Fay's name was then linked with two other women for whom the administration reserved special venom — radicalized actress Jane Fonda and Communist Angela Davis. The report also noted that SDS founder Tom

Hayden worked with Fay Stender to galvanize radicals to focus on prisons as "the birthplace of revolutionary leadership."[3]

The report relied on half-truths. Jackson clearly would not have posed anywhere near the same threat if no one had rallied a network of supporters to treat him as the next Che Guevara. However, the study left out the role of COINTELPRO in the August 1970 Marin County shootout that left Judge Haley among the dead. It made no mention that the government knew of George Jackson's plans for escape well ahead of time. Authorities should have easily been able to avoid the August 1971 bloodbath at San Quentin. The report also omitted any evidence of the wretched prison conditions that underlay the Soledad Brothers' following. Cruel and inhumane treatment at the Soledad Adjustment Center had been documented back in 1966 by an outraged federal judge. Prison officials exacerbated the situation by failing to implement his mandates. Even the most hardened criminals deserved better than to be caged like mistreated zoo animals left abandoned in their own stench.

At the same time as the California report issued, former Attorney General Ramsey Clark hit the best seller list with his controversial book, *Crime in America*. It found that overcrowded, uninhabitable prisons constituted crime factories. Clark characterized inmates as victims of barbaric practices and proposed a prisoners' bill of rights, including health care, vocational training, and jobs. Clark noted that alcoholism alone created an enormous, unnecessary burden on the criminal justice system. The Corrections Department's findings were intended to promote the opposite result: to ensure that public fear of felons would reach an all-time high.

* * *

When Fay learned that George had left his royalties to the Panthers, she felt obligated to speak up. She wanted to make sure that the two young lawyers still working to free Drumgo and Clutchette would get paid. Fay wrote a letter in early September 1971 raising the issue with Thorne, Silliman and Silver, as well as tax guru Harry Margolis and Greg Armstrong. Margolis and Armstrong had collaborated the year before in putting George's royalties outside the prisoner's personal control. It took courage for Fay to raise objections to the Panthers getting Jackson's royalties. She knew she was playing with fire, but not how badly she would get burned.

Fay then still possessed the original handwritten letters included in Jackson's book, together with many other letters from George written after *Soledad Brother* was published. She intended to use them to bargain with Huey and the Jackson family to ensure payments to Silliman and Silver as well as Micki Magers, the mother of Jonathan Jackson's posthumously born son. Fay had to delay talking to Huey face-to-face to resolve the issue. She had to wait for Huey to return from a trip to China as a guest of Chairman Mao — months before President Nixon's historic restoration of diplomatic relations with the Communist country. Ever the showman, Huey returned with great fanfare in early October 1971 and went straight from the airport to a press conference with Charles Garry. There he announced the Panthers' solidarity with all oppressed people of America.

The day before Newton's third trial was set to start, Fay visited Huey Newton in his penthouse to negotiate the Panthers' claim on Jackson's estate. She urged Huey to put a stop to the criticism of his indulgent life style by moving to a less ostentatious home. It was undermining his standing in the Movement. Huey angrily rebuffed her. She wanted too much control. Huey insisted that the Panthers get George's royalties. Fay left in tears. Two days later, at San Quentin, Fay ran into Bell, the Jackson family attorney. He indicated that the family was anxious to settle quickly without a court battle if they could get some money.

* * *

Though Fay appeared totally in command at the Congressional subcommittee hearing on prison reform in the last week of October 1971, she was in fact battling severe depression. The recent reduction in the number of prison inmates statewide was more than offset by one million persons in city and county jails, mostly awaiting trial. The typical man held in a county jail was black, in his early twenties, held a

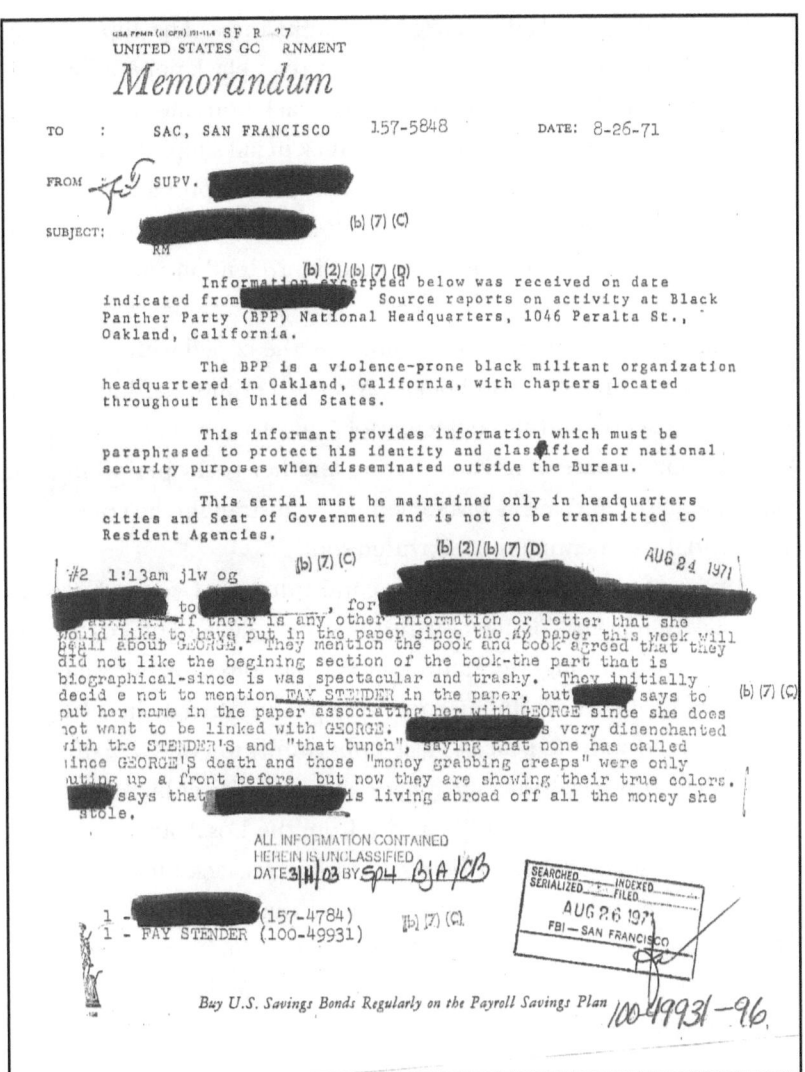

FBI Vol. II file notes, August 26, 1971, on wiretap of Black Panther newspaper staff preparing a tribute to the late George Jackson: "They initially decided not to mention FAY STENDER in the paper but [deleted] says to put her name in . . . since she does not want to be linked with GEORGE. [Deleted] is very disenchanted with the STENDER'S [sic] and 'that bunch', saying that none has called since GEORGE's death and 'those money grabbing creeps' were only putting up a front before, but now are showing their true colors."

low-paying job and faced a charge of drunkenness. The flip side was that California and other states with large urban black populations had in the last decade doubled the number of black households headed by women. The majority of arrestees were stuck in jail simply because they could not afford bail. Most would ultimately receive probation or a fine or a short jail sentence limited to time already served. Fay was grateful that she had talked her former partner Ezra Hendon into giving up baking to join her Prison Law Project. There was so much more to do.

That year Fay gained twenty pounds as she coped with all her setbacks: Jackson's rejection and death, Newton's rebuff, her bitter break with Patti Roberts and the defection of half of Fay's staff — all while Fay and Marvin were barely weathering another rocky period in their marriage. Ezra felt that Fay was sometimes so distraught, he considered her suicidal — an empathetic, tortured soul.

Fay reached a low point when confronted by George Jackson's Marxist prison friend Michael McCarthy in her Oakland office that fall. McCarthy was no longer grateful that Fay had saved his life when he was en route to being "disappeared" by prison officials in 1968. He was looking forward to a face-to-face opportunity to give Fay a dressing down. McCarthy was livid that Fay had refused to deliver his messages to George and put McCarthy's life at risk from the Los Angeles Panthers when they suspected him of being an FBI mole. Jackson's sisters had come to his rescue by smuggling a message from George in solitary that McCarthy was "cool." McCarthy also deeply resented Fay's removal of his name from correspondence published in *Soledad Brother*. He later prevailed on George to order his name restored in the best-selling book's next edition.

McCarthy had not recognized Fay when he attended George Jackson's funeral service. On this trip to the Bay Area, McCarthy was determined to investigate the circumstances of George's death. He suspected Huey Newton of complicity. There were a handful of staff present when McCarthy strutted into the Prison Law Project in Oakland in late 1971 looking for Fay. When he identified himself, Fay rushed him into her office and closed the door. Then she surprised him by throwing both of her arms around his neck and sobbing uncontrollably. Fay begged

Michael to forgive her. She was sorry for what she had put him through. She had thought their phones were tapped when he had called her the year before. All her efforts had come to naught: "Nobody will have anything to do with me anymore." McCarthy was startled and unable to deal with her emotional appeal. He turned on his heels and fled.

In December, Newton was still arguing with Fay over the rights to the Jackson papers in her possession. By then, Huey proclaimed that Fay was officially no longer recognized by the Party. She did not participate in the defense of Newton's third trial for the death of Officer Frey. Yet Garry made good use of her earlier handiwork. Garry picked a mostly middle-aged and female jury. None were African-Americans. He repeated his usual courtroom theatrics. Garry again produced witnesses to Frey's racism and put a medical expert on the stand to explain Newton's impaired condition after being shot.

On Saturday afternoon, December 11, 1971, the jury deadlocked six to six, all convinced Newton had shot Frey, but divided on whether he was conscious of firing the gun. At the end of the day, another mistrial was declared. Newton looked tired. A crowd gathered inside and outside the building. Twelve television crews were stationed in the press room as reporters and scores of Newton supporters grabbed seats in the courtroom. Jensen visibly trembled as he rose to speak. He said that after searching his conscience, he reluctantly concluded another trial would be futile and requested dismissal even though it would be "a frustration of justice,"[4] meaning not "in furtherance of justice," as the law contemplated.

Judge Hayes then granted Jensen's motion and, fifteen minutes after the hearing began, Newton was a completely free man. Despite Garry's pleas to join him in a press conference, Newton stopped only briefly before descending the stairs out of the courthouse. Newton uttered a clipped "No comment"[5] to the gathered reporters and raised his fist to those waiting to cheer him outside. Garry held forth at the press conference, praising Jensen as "a perfect gentleman and a worthy adversary" whom he had misjudged as not having "the intestinal fortitude to dismiss a case like this."[6] But Garry once again bashed the justice system for forcing Newton through long trials on charges which

Garry claimed never should have been brought in the first place. Fay, of course, was nowhere to be seen. Her pivotal role in securing Huey's ultimate freedom went unmentioned in the banner press that accompanied the anti-climactic dismissal of the trial of the century.

At the beginning of February, *Maximum Security* came out, the book of inmates' letters Eve Pell had edited the summer before when still working at the Prison Law Project. Consumer tastes ran to star power and no George Jackson or Eldridge Cleaver emerged from its haunting prose. Instead, the book focused on the rage of more ordinary violent men whom society had long since abandoned.[7]

The New York Times called the book "sickening" and "powerful" in its condemnation of the "Chinese water torture" of indeterminate sentencing. It was far less polished and "less ideological than *Soledad Brother*, less rhetorical, it doesn't bludgeon like Jackson . . . it pricks and bites and makes your skin crawl." The warden's office at Soledad had admitted to the reporter that maybe only a quarter of the men had warranted "massive, depersonalized lock-up," but inertia had taken over. One guard told him, "We're all prisoners here."[8] Yet, despite the forcefulness of the book's message, the public was no longer interested. Prisoners came largely from underprivileged backgrounds and had no constituency with any clout.

* * *

By Fay's fortieth birthday in March 1972, she was feeling her age. She had begun routinely wearing reading glasses and had more visible gray hairs in her dark mane. As a present, a friend gave her a wooden sign reading, "No good deed goes unpunished." Fay kept it on display in her home ever after. Jackson's dramatic death had enhanced interest in the ongoing murder trial of Fleeta Drumgo and John Clutchette. It had also spiked international sales of *Soledad Brother*, the rights to which were still hotly disputed.

Georgia Jackson came with her lawyer Ed Bell to meet lawyer Howard Berman at Garry's office to try to resolve the Panthers' competing royalty claims. Fay's efforts to pay Silver and Silliman had already been rejected. Georgia would not tolerate having any further profits from her son's book go to attorneys. She felt just as outraged when Fay sought money for Magers to help raise Jonathan's baby. Georgia demanded that Fay return George's boxes of tapes and letters. The still-grieving mother wanted nothing to do with Magers or with the middle-aged blonde's biracial baby.

Bell remained anxious to obtain royalties for Georgia, which would be the source of his fee. He had received nothing to date after several months of accompanying Georgia throughout the country on a speaking tour before gatherings of SNCC, the Urban League and the NAACP. Georgia had always been feisty and plain spoken. She had become increasingly formidable as she rose to enormous prestige among radicals as the mother of two revolutionary martyrs.

As they sat in Garry's law office waiting for Huey Newton to arrive, the telephone rang. Huey invited them to come instead to his Oakland penthouse. They drove over in Bell's car. He had not been to Huey's suite before and was impressed by its furnishings, as well as the gorgeous women the Panther leader had at his beck and call. The meeting began with Huey paying homage to Georgia. He hoped to convince the matriarch to work on her own autobiography and to share the proceeds with the Panthers. When the meeting ended, Huey asked Howard Berman to stay behind. Ed Bell asked how Berman would then get back to San Francisco, and Huey suddenly went ballistic, screaming, "Don't cross-examine me." Hearing his boss raise his voice, a bodyguard with an AK-47 emerged from a back bedroom. In response, Georgia pulled a handgun from her purse. The absurdity of the situation struck Bell and he started to laugh. He thought to himself, "What in the fuck was she going to do against an assault rifle?" Huey's anger dissipated. Georgia Jackson and Bell got in the elevator and left.

The decision on George Jackson's literary rights was made. All royalty checks for *Soledad Brother* would go to Georgia Jackson through a new foundation. The Jackson family would split with the Panthers the proceeds on George's second, less widely sold book. When Bell delivered the first royalty checks to Georgia, she told him she thought he should now get paid for his efforts. Bell looked up in anticipation and then shocked disbelief as Georgia withdrew a couple of one-dollar bills from her purse. He left the insult on the table, amazed at the depth of her animosity toward his profession. Bell never received a dime for his efforts, still marveling thirty-five years later at how militants believed the only way lawyers could demonstrate commitment to their cause was by working for free.

■ 2 ■
Spent

> *"Since 1971, Fay Stender and her associates have made exceptional inroads, both overt and covert, in the process of radicalizing the state penal system. . . . The demise of [the Prison Law Project] is viewed more in the context of its having outlived its usefulness than the claim of financial problems."*[1]
>
> — FBI AGENT TO STENDER FILE, SUMMER 1973

Fay took twelve-year-old Oriane with her on Fay's first grant-seeking trip to New York in January 1972. The two had lunch with Bob Richter, who was then working with Walter Cronkite at CBS. Bob noticed how much the shy young teen now resembled Fay.

In the early spring of 1972, Guild member Don Jelinek talked Fay into granting him a lengthy personal interview. In his spare time, Jelinek, under the pen name Argus, wrote for the *Freedom Press,* a local Bay Area underground monthly newspaper. Jelinek brought along a photographer and spent a day and a half with Fay and her family. He stayed at their home and followed her to her office and on errands. Jelinek had met Marvin first and only became acquainted with Fay in early 1970, when she spoke at a fund-raiser for Huey Newton's appeal. At the time, Fay knew that Jelinek had worked closely with Stokely Carmichael in Alabama in the mid '60s and had been among the last whites to be kicked out of SNCC. Fay quickly recognized a kindred spirit and began advising Jelinek on his high-profile criminal cases. A newcomer to the Bay Area, Jelinek appreciated an insider's guide to effective local strategies. By 1971, Jelinek had already written several articles on Newton and now wrote a five-page paean to Fay — "this much-maligned East Bay attorney."[2]

Jelinek covered Fay's work for Huey Newton and George Jackson and her creation of the Prison Law Project. They chatted about Fay's unhappy childhood as a middle-class musical prodigy in Berkeley, her college and law school years and family life. The omissions were telling. Fay never mentioned Marxist professor Stanley Moore, who had been her most significant early adult influence. For his part, Jelinek ignored all the recent political developments that made Fay so controversial among his readers: Fay's falling out with Newton after gaining his release from prison, the circumstances of her being fired by Jackson, and the bitter split in the Prison Law Project in the fall of 1971, which resulted in the competing Prison Law Collective.

Don had promised Fay she could read the draft before it was printed, in case he let slip some comment that could endanger her physically or politically. When Fay had read it and called him, Don thought she would be pleased that the article was so complimentary and avoided all the land mines. Instead, she was angry. Jelinek had mentioned in passing that one does not go to the Stenders expecting "culinary delights" because they "don't knock themselves out for meals." He described dried-out steak, defrosted peas and instant mashed potatoes prepared by their twelve-year-old daughter from a box. Fay was most irate about his description of Oriane's contribution. Jelinek promised to change it. When the article was printed, he left in the gibe at the cooking, but called her daughter's mashed potatoes "the highlight of the meal."[3] Fay fumed for days.

* * *

Later that month, Fay had a real public relations nightmare to address that dwarfed her silly reaction to Jelinek's article. *Esquire* magazine planned to publish a feature on Angela Davis. The editor shared it in advance with Greg Armstrong to verify some of its sensational charges. Armstrong was immediately alarmed and sent copies to Fay and to Davis's defense attorneys, putting them in an uproar as well.

Davis was still on trial for conspiracy to commit murder arrising out of the Marin County shootout involving Jonathan Jackson in 1970, and faced possible life in prison. A mistrial could occur if the jury somehow got wind of this article. The article implied that Davis and Jonathan Jackson had been lovers. It repeated hearsay that the two had gone to Jimmy Carr for help in sawing off the shotgun later strapped to Judge Haley during the ill-fated kidnapping. It also described, in salacious terms, Davis being fondled by George Jackson at their joint meeting with defense counsel at the Marin County jail in the summer of 1971. Though true, that pretrial conference took place a year *after* the Marin County events. Armstrong considered the article racist and "a sleazy journalistic smear."[4] *Esquire* agreed to delete all the passages to which Armstrong and Davis's lawyers objected.

Fay had her own concerns to address. The *Esquire* article could easily torpedo future grants for her Project. It stated that in forming the Soledad Defense Committee, Fay had turned primarily to the Black Panthers and Communists for financial assistance, including the woman who became the Defense Committee's chief fund-raiser. Black militants had already fallen out of favor among New York's Liberals. Fay denied that a Panther loan funded the defense team's headquarters in San Francisco. She also disputed the extent of Communist participation in the Soledad Brothers Defense Committee. Only one or two of the people Fay had initially contacted were known Communists. They put her in touch with a fundraiser, who turned out also to be a Communist. *Esquire* accepted all of Fay's corrections; the changes were unlikely to reassure skittish donors.

Fay continued to walk a fine line between the Left-leaning establishment to which she turned for cash and the Movement radicals she sought to motivate. In the spring of 1972, the *Buffalo Law Review Symposium* printed an article that Fay co-authored on "The Prison as Lawless Agency." Fay ordered extra copies she could autograph and distribute. Marxist philosophy had figured prominently in her co-author's analysis: "The prison system is . . . [a] central element to American society, it has been shaped, and in turn reinforces and supports the perpetuation of a status quo characterized by racism, inequity and exploitation."[5] The article concluded with a plea that reflected Fay's soulful touch: "The prisoner movement [is] still in its infancy; prisoners are only just now coming to an informed sense of identity and a consciousness of the possibilities of collective action.... Support from all of us [on the outside] is needed, and must be forthcoming, not only for prisoners' sakes, but for our own. For the prison indeed oppresses not just those who are locked behind its bars. It reaches out to every one of us."[6]

* * *

Fay's schedule that spring involved a whirlwind of activity across the country. She spoke at universities and negotiated resolution of an inmate strike in Tucson, Arizona. She received accolades from all quarters. The Director of the Board of Corrections in New York wrote that her projects ought to be duplicated in every state. All spring, Fay kept one eye on Sacramento. She and other reformers had rejoiced when the Department of Corrections planned to replace the antiquated San Quentin Adjustment Center as unfit for habitation. But she did not trust their intentions. Preliminary planning for the new units was secretive, but word had spread that the buildings would cost $12 million each and be worse than before.

Fay realized that she and Marvin were again spending little time together. She had been on the road almost every weekend for months. During the week, Marvin rose at 6 a.m. to prepare for trial and returned home each night exhausted. He rested a short while, ate and devoted more time to work he had brought home. Fay told her friend Elsa, "We are leading our usual lives. I guess we must like it, or maybe we don't like what happens when we don't do it."[7]

Fay was preoccupied with keeping the Prison Law Project afloat. They had nearly thirty cases challenging corrections policies on their own docket and four more planned. They also assisted on hundreds of other cases brought by students, attorneys and prisoners. In the summer of 1972, Fay focused volunteers on exposing misuse of the correctional system's inmate welfare fund. Her staff found that inmates on work furlough had their accounts charged each day for food at five times the actual cost of providing it; the administration pocketed the profits. Another new area of concentration was a class action for inmates' right to medical treatment. Where could Fay turn for new money? Her sister Lisie and her husband Don agreed to lend their names. Fay proudly listed Lisie among the Prison Law Project's cooperating professionals, both as a physical therapist and as President of the San Mateo League of Women Voters, following in their mother's footsteps.

In mid-June of 1972, Fay was invited to join other civil rights activists at a forum on law and justice sponsored by the newly formed Congressional Black Caucus. The caucus included Berkeley's Ron Dellums. With thirteen African-Americans elected to the House in 1970, critical mass had just been achieved to form a voting bloc to pursue its own ambitious agenda to address race discrimination, the death penalty and bail reform. As that historic forum met in the nation's Capitol, in Oakland Black Panthers Bobby Seale and Elaine Brown donned suits and started glad-handing residents in their quest for local elective office. Civil rights leaders — even Coretta Scott King — endorsed their fourteen-point program for Oakland's improvement.

To register voters in the flatlands, the Panthers arranged for truckloads of free groceries and shoes. Doctors and nurses operated a free clinic, testing for sickle-cell anemia. Newton, meanwhile, inspired renewed support by working with Dr. Herman Blake to complete a book of revolutionary essays, *To Die for The People*. Random House threw a champagne and fried chicken celebration at Newton's apartment. Decca and Bob Treuhaft were among the invitees, but not Fay. Decca had originally hoped to finish her own book on the prison system by the spring of 1972, but she found the project difficult to get her arms around. Who, if anyone, belonged in jail for public protection? For how long? What criteria should be used for putting them in custody? How should they be treated if they acted violently?

Fay and Marvin sometimes joined the Treuhafts with other friends at dinner or for drinks before their fire. One evening in the summer of 1972, personal experiences with assault came up. Bob mentioned an injured client who showed up at his office long after his tort case had settled for a large amount of money. The ex-client accused Bob of taking too big a fee. He then menacingly waved a letter opener in the air. Bob called the police and demanded the man's arrest, afraid the man would follow him home and harm his family. The responding officer was likely much amused in having to explain to a Lefty constitutional law expert that the man had not yet done anything that justified taking him in.

Fay described the pervert who had four years earlier accosted children at the local park where Oriane and her friend played. Fay had obsessed about helping the police identify the culprit and having him arrested before he killed a victim. Decca reacted with derision. The man's misconduct had been nonviolent. It did not sound much worse than the "willy-waver" her daughter Dinky had once seen on their street. Decca thought parents like Fay unnecessarily alarmed their children by exaggerating the risks. Fay retorted that, even if the man had posed no serious physical threat, shouldn't her children be free to play in a public park unmolested? Decca doubted that imprisonment of the man was the right answer. They reached no conclusion, but Decca wrote a friend afterward, "I am beginning to note that Fay has, if anything, less of a theoretical grasp of this dire subject than I have."[8]

Fay had a new client that summer keeping the Prison Law Project in the public eye. She represented Julia Cappenberg, a nineteen-year-old German who had become infatuated with a death row inmate named Robert Duren at San Quentin. Cappenberg had corresponded with him every other day while hospitalized with a long illness. When Cappenberg arrived in the Bay Area in June of 1972, with a ring in her nose and her hair in an Afro, the San Quentin warden's office refused the German teen entry. She did not qualify for visiting privileges because she had never met Duren before. Fay invited Cappenberg to stay at the Stender home while the Prison Law Project filed suit on her behalf. Fay then talked Drucilla Ramey, a new part-time hire of the Treuhaft firm, into helping out. The petite brunette, then in her mid-twenties, was six months out of Yale Law School and had not yet passed the California Bar. She came West at the recommendation of her friend Hillary Rodham, who had been a law clerk for the Treuhaft firm the summer before — still one of the rare law offices to welcome women.

Dru had no background in criminal law, but at Fay's insistence, the Radcliffe graduate swallowed her apprehensions and drove to San Quentin to interview Duren. When she read the inmate's jacket detailing five horrific murders, she was scared witless. She asked herself what she, a middle-class Jew from Bethesda, Maryland, was doing signing into a maximum security prison and attempting to gain the confidence of a violent felon from the streets of Los Angeles? Dru swore she would, under no circumstances, agree to handle another prison case. It seemed like chutzpah for her to offer empathy across such a class gulf. Fay could scoff at Dru's timidity, but it never occurred to Fay to ask herself a similar question. Her extraordinary ego did not permit her to consider that her race and middleclass upbringing might interfere with her acceptance as a spokesperson for incarcerated brothers from the hood. Having a sense of boundaries might have saved Fay's life.

Fay relished the opportunity to argue to a judge that the 500 letters Cappenberg and Duren had exchanged qualified them as long-standing friends. She claimed they had become soul mates and put Cappenberg on the stand to swear that she had traveled 7,000 miles to marry the "person I love most in this world."[9] The state's attorney dismissed the trip as a publicity stunt to market Duren's letters. He was not far off the mark. Cappenberg told reporters she viewed Duren more as a comrade devoted to a common cause than a love interest and only planned to wed him to qualify for conjugal visits. Privately, Cappenberg told Fay of her ambition to return to the United States to attend law school and follow a career like Fay's.

By the end of July, Fay had convinced the judge to grant the pair two weeks of visitation before Cappenberg's return to Germany. As Cappenberg headed for New York on her way back to Hamburg, Fay tried to arrange a press conference in Manhattan and interest *Ms.* magazine or a publisher in the German teen's story. Meanwhile, a more significant court battle was going on in California over a new prison policy of opening all prisoner mail, including correspondence with counsel. In his brief to the United States Supreme Court, California Attorney General Evelle Younger named Fay Stender and John Thorne among the chief offenders whose conduct justified invading the attorney-client privilege — more bad publicity.

Fay then had another setback that put her in a political quandary. At the end of August, she had taken a short vacation with Marvin to Aspen, Colorado. While she was away, the Prison Law Project was burglarized and three of its typewriters stolen. The staff debated what to do and decided they should report the loss to the police. Within days, 35-year-old Donald Leroy Barnes was arrested in Sparks, Nevada, carrying a pawn ticket for the typewriters. Barnes was a former client of the Prison Law Project — their very first inmate to be released on parole.

When a subpoena issued for Fay to testify against Barnes, Fay panicked. She asked a co-worker to put the Stender family up at her home in Berkeley for several days so Fay could elude the process server. The maneuver was silly: the process server could find Fay at the Prison Law Project. In the end, Fay accepted the subpoena. She showed up for the preliminary hearing with Bob Treuhaft as her lawyer before Judge Jackie Taber, only the second woman judge in Alameda County. Taber was a no-nonsense Democrat who grew up in poverty. She did not know Fay personally but thought highly of her at the time as a fellow pioneer.

Fay took the stand and then shocked Judge Taber by refusing to answer if she had given Barnes permission to take the typewriters. Judge Taber informed Fay she was risking contempt and called a quick recess of the proceedings. She then summoned Fay into her chambers and demanded to know "What the Hell is this all about?" Fay had no communication with Barnes that related to the burglary — she had been out of state on vacation when it occurred. The Prison Law Project had been the victim that had reported the crime. When Fay still refused to testify, Judge Taber held her in contempt and fined her $500. The exasperated judge then dismissed the charges against Barnes for lack of proof the typewriters were stolen. Taber shook her head in disbelief at Fay's stubbornness. Would it not have been a good lesson to other Prison Law Project clients not to bite the hand that feeds them?

Fay, of course, felt she had acted on principle to protect her radical credentials. She was a diehard prisoners' advocate even if a client stole Prison Law Project property needed for the benefit of other inmates. Decca Mitford thought the episode showed muddled thinking. Why did the Prison Law Project report the loss in the first place? If the culprit had not been a client, would Fay have testified? The police were astounded. To them, Fay was no different than her scofflaw clients. Judge Taber felt the publicity the incident generated was embarrassment enough for Fay and did not finalize her contempt finding, allowing it to be dismissed.

It was quintessential Fay that, as this awkward incident played out, she obtained the highest praise of all for her prison work. A New York professor had visited the project several times while researching a book. In October 1972, he called her project the "single most important agency working in the free world for inmate welfare."[10] Fay used that letter to support an ambitious grant application to review California's 80-year-old indeterminate sentence law. She told foundations that prison reform was "the social problem of the decade."[11]

By November 1972, the Project was woefully short of cash. Fay had just been forced to cut back two attorneys to half-time for lack of funds, leaving herself and Ezra Hendon as the only two full-time lawyers. Fay and Hendon took home the same $432 per month salary as the other remaining staff and used the rest of their salaries to fund expenses. Hendon leveraged his impact by working with outside volunteers to produce a jailhouse lawyer manual for inmate self-help. As the future of the Prison Law Project grew more precarious, the Treuhafts threw another party to celebrate the publication of Ann Ginger's how-to book, *The Relevant Lawyers,* and to honor all the Movement lawyers featured in the book, including Fay and Marvin.

In early December of 1972, the Prison Law Project achieved an historic victory against indeterminate sentences. The California Supreme Court held that a potential life sentence for indecent exposure violated the defendant's constitutional rights. Marvin told Fay, "Be careful what you wish for." Most criminal defense lawyers represented low profile arrestees who wound up serving only a few years of indeterminate sentences. These lawyers feared that the indeterminate sentence law would be replaced with far longer fixed terms for all inmates. Those misgivings would prove well-founded, but Fay gave them no credence. (In 1972, there had been 22,000 prisoners in the entire system. Four decades later, lengthy mandatory sentences would incarcerate many times that number. By then, California's prisons were filled beyond capacity and the cost of maintaining them severely compromised the state's ability to fund its schools and other vital public services.)

During the Prison Law Project's first two years, Fay had obtained a total of $125,000 in seed money from three national foundations headquartered in New York. That turned out to be two-thirds of all the money she ever raised. By 1973, no major funding source appeared on the horizon. Fay hinted heavily that Decca should share some of the proceeds from her upcoming book with the project. Decca ignored her. She had grown tired of Fay's self-importance. When Fay met potential donors she was routinely introduced as the "Dear Fay" in George Jackson's published letters, the author of the introduction to *Maximum Security* and head of the Prison Law Project. Decca's sister had coined a term for irritating friends: "frenemies." Decca decided Fay was the personification of a frenemy. Decca and her old friend Dobby Walker watched and waited for the axe to fall on Fay's Prison Law Project.

Decca realized that public interest in prisoners' issues was a fad that had passed before her own book made it into galleys in the spring of 1973. Decca had thought long and hard about the "prison business". Fay had told Decca that "most prisoners have an intense human value system, loyalty, respect, love and gratitude for those who care for them as human beings."[12] They had far less hypocrisy in their own relations than in outside society, but less impulse control, which Fay attributed to their harsh struggle for survival. Fay could only bring herself to estimate that perhaps five per cent of Adjustment Center prisoners were truly dangerous.

In the introduction to her own book, Decca criticized both Fay's rosy view of prisoners and the view of an administrator at San Quentin that maximum security inmates were inferior human beings, who exhibited stunted development. From her own research, Decca herself had come to the conclusion that prisoners and ex-convicts represented a cross-section of society whose imprisonment often resulted from happenstance. But Decca also concluded that conditions inside prison exacerbated criminal tendencies and took needlessly cruel and inhumane turns like "volunteer" participation as medical research guinea pigs in human experiments that would never have been approved outside of prison walls.[13] Decca noted how much more money was being spent on prisons under Governor Reagan and concluded that "the crueler the conditions of custody the more expensive it gets." Solitary confinement was costing Californians more than three-and-a-half times as much as minimum security.[14]

Decca's book was effusive about "the dimensions and dynamics of what has come to be called the 'Prison Movement.'" She called it an "amazing . . . new phenomenon on the American scene. It comprises legislators, newspaper men and women, lawyers, academicians, students, citizens from all walks of life and of a variety of political persuasions. . . ." Although it began with ex-convicts and radical activists, "it is fast acquiring astonishing breadth." Decca credited as Fay's "single most important contribution . . . to pry ajar the massive door to that closed world . . . to supply ammunition and momentum for the popular movement for change."[15]

Yet by February 1973, Decca and Fay were openly quarreling. In April, Fay exhausted herself vainly seeking new funding in New York and then wrote a letter to all of the Prison Law Project's clients and supporters announcing that the office would close its doors on June 30 for lack of funding. Fay was actually relieved to move on. She told Marvin that all but one of the men whose release they had obtained on parole later returned to prison. One had violently attacked a girlfriend. The problem was overwhelming. In the past, Fay had often quoted psychiatrists who concluded that conditions in "the hole" could drive the average male insane. Yet she had been slow to internalize that knowledge. The bitter truth Fay finally learned was that regardless of how salvageable they may have been before they went to prison, most of the men she cared so deeply about as victims of the system were no longer capable of productive lives on the outside without extraordinary support society simply did not provide.

Fay later confided to a colleague that her maximum security clients all "had a screw loose somewhere. . . . People should understand that there was always a reason they were incarcerated." A few years later she heard that an inmate who knew her from her work with the Prison Law

Project had escaped and was headed to her for help on his way to the border. Fay panicked. She neither wanted to be prosecuted for harboring a fugitive nor be an instrument in his recapture. She contacted several old friends, and she and her family camped out at different homes for the better part of a month.

The San Francisco Chronicle compared the shuttering of Fay's office to the closing of a heavy prison door. In "A Grim Finale for Prison Inmates," a reporter noted the bleak outlook for prisoners. Fay told him the reason was simple: the lack of "plain old money."[16] The reporter pointed out the stark contrast between her reputation among state officials and inmates. She had been vilified as "a demon agitator and worse" and as "one of the greatest threats to security in state prisons." Yet "hundreds, perhaps thousands, of inmates" viewed her as a "heroic figure" and "almost a legend in places where women once were seldom seen."[17]

The spokesman for the Department of Corrections acknowledged the bitterness prison personnel still felt toward Fay and the Prison Law Project staff. Yet he volunteered that Fay's project largely deserved credit for the re-examination that had just begun of inmate rights. The article noted the backlash as well: recent pressure for tougher sanctions, fewer inmates released on parole, and ever-increasing state funds for more and bigger prisons and staff.

The Prison Law Project had achieved remarkable results on a shoestring budget. Fay had charged on after Newton's humiliating rejection. The Attorney General's accusations and the enmity of corrections personnel only emboldened her. She weathered Jackson's firing, his death and his family's disparagement, fueled by hundreds of prisoners' letters each month begging for her assistance. But Fay had to admit defeat when faced with public antipathy toward sustained funding for prisoners' issues: the irresistible force had met the immovable object.

The FBI did not believe Fay's explanation for closing the Prison Law Project. Anyone with perspective on prisoners and parolees' issues knew that the complex problem required enormous resources to address over a long period of time, starting with the socio-economic conditions that predestined so many minority men to lives behind bars.

The best that any one small office could do was to draw public attention to the problems, to persuade the courts to expand the scope of constitutional rights afforded prisoners, to create a specialty bar focused on prison law and get mainstream lawyers to volunteer their own time and resources, to interest law students in prisoners' rights and induce law schools to sponsor clinical programs, to empower jailhouse lawyers with increased resources, and to precipitate meaningful legislative reforms.

Fay led the way in all of these directions. If she had looked at her project as the FBI did, the Prison Law Project had accomplished more than it could reasonably have hoped to do by igniting a new focus on prisoners' rights and galvanizing other organizations and institutions to carry the baton forward. But "reasonable" was not a word in Fay's vocabulary.

Just as the Prison Law Project closed its doors for good, Decca went on tour to promote her new book, *Kind and Usual Punishment: The Prison Business*. Meanwhile, as a tonic for Fay's emotional and physical exhaustion, Marvin suggested she sign up for a two-week trip to Cuba — the first delegation of American lawyers to the Communist country.

```
                    PRISON LAW PROJECT
                    5406 CLAREMONT AVENUE
                    OAKLAND, CALIFORNIA 94618
                                              Telephone: (415) 658-8969
                    BUDGET 3-15-73 - 3-15-74

Personnel Items
    Salaries and Wages
        Due Process Litigation and Project Administration
            2 litigative attorneys (Hendon & Stender)        $24,000
            1 non-litigative attorney                          9,600
            2 legal secretaries                               12,000
            1 administrator (Cornet)                           9,600
            law school student researchers                     3,400
            1 receptionist, correspondence screener,
                    and Project secretary                      6,000
                                                              64,600

        Parole project and Medical proposals
            1 parole/social service co-ordinator*              6,000
            2 litigative attorneys **                         24,000
            2 legal secretaries**                             12,000
            1 non-litigative attorney-researcher**             9,500

                            TOTAL SALARIES AND WAGES         116,200


    Additional Payroll Costs
        State Unemployment taxes (3.8%)                        4,415
        State Disability Insurance (1%)                        1,162
                                              TOTAL           5,577

    Consultant and Contract Services
        Certified Public Accountant                             600***
        Consulting attorneys (for emergency cases
                    where necessary)                          1,200
        Tax Attorney                                            600***
        Investigators ($25/day- very sparingly used
                    occasionally necessary)                     600***

                    TOTAL CONSULTANT AND CONTRACT SERVICES    3,000
                           TOTAL PERSONNEL ITEMS            124,700

Non-Personnel Items
        Rent and Utilities                                    3,840
        Telephone (including acceptance of collect calls      7,200
            from inmates in emergency cases, and conversations
            with attorneys and prison officials)
        Transportation (to and from prisons;conferences)      3,000
        Printing and Duplication                              2,000
        Postage                                               2,400
        Office Supplies and Equipment                         2,500
        Legal Fees (transcripts, depositions, etc)            1,300
        Professional fees and memberships                       600
        Insurance                                             1,000
        Inmate welfare (books, newspapers, writing materials)   600
                            TOTAL NON-PERSONNEL ITEMS        24,740
 * funded through 6/73 by Abelard Foundation  TOTAL BUDGET: $ 149,517
** funding requested from Robert W. Johnson Foundation
*** at present services are volunteered
```

The last budget Fay Stender prepared for the Prison Law Project before announcing its closing. The San Francisco Chronicle *compared the announcement to the slamming of a heavy prison door on "hundreds, perhaps thousands, of inmates" [who] viewed her as "almost a legend in places where women once were seldom seen." (Tim Findley, "A Grim Finale for Prison Inmates," May 25, 1973, 6).*

■ 3 ■
Cuba

> *The boat rocks at anchor by the misty island.*
> *Sunset, my loneliness comes again . . .*[1]
> MENG HAO-JAN, "MOORING ON CHIEN-TE RIVER"
> TRANSLATED BY GARY SNYDER

If, in the spring of 1973, any cause had even less appeal to foundations than the Prison Law Project, it was the Center for Cuban Studies in New York. Eight months after it opened in 1972, its director barely survived a bomb planted by counter-revolutionary exiles that blew the office to smithereens. Less than a decade since the Cuban Missile Crisis of 1962, an economic embargo continued. Not one foundation was willing to contribute seed money. The director was Marvin's and Charles Garry's good friend Sandra Levinson. She had been the star witness at the 1961 "Black Friday" trial in San Francisco and moved to Manhattan in 1965.

Sandra maintained her old Leftist connections in the Bay Area after she moved to Greenwich Village. Once there, she worked to complete a doctoral thesis on urban racial politics while she ran the New York branch of *Ramparts* out of her apartment. During the late 1960s, Sandra had co-led international fund-raising for Eldridge Cleaver, and her home then became a Panther gathering place — Garry's frequent get-away destination during the Bobby Seale trial. In the spring of

1970, at Fay's request, Sandra had conducted negotiations on George Jackson's behalf for the publication of *Soledad Brother*.

Sandra began making annual trips to Cuba in 1969 as a founding member with Jerry Rubin of the Venceremos Brigade. In the spring of 1973, she arranged for an all-expense paid invitation from the Cuban government to a select group of American lawyers. As Director of the Center, Sandra would choose the delegates interested in learning about the Cuban socialist legal system. Some would also share with their Cuban hosts what they knew about the no-fault divorce laws recently adopted in New York and California. The lawyers who came would meet with Cuban lawyers, receive a tour of the country and report back what they learned to interested colleagues in the states.

Both Fay and Marvin were highly curious to know more about how the Communist country actually operated. Fay's history of achievement as a Movement lawyer would undoubtedly make her a highly welcome addition to the tour. Fay would be the most senior traveler. Sandra's brother David was going as well. He had worked with Marvin as a young lawyer and only knew Fay slightly, but the breadth of Fay's knowledge and achievements impressed David. He had relied heavily on her materials when handling selective service cases in his first few years of practice.

The six members of the travel group met on June 3 in Mexico City, where officials processed their visas for the following morning's flight to Havana. Emily Jane Goodman, one of the two New York Guild lawyers, eagerly started a diary. The 1968 Brooklyn Law School graduate was the only other woman on the tour. She found Fay surprisingly subdued. Michael Krinsky, a new member of the New York Bar and its Lawyers Guild, had the most interest in Cuban legal affairs. His firm had carved out a specialty in representing foreign governments, including Cuba. He would later become Cuba's General Counsel in the United States.

Fay and Emily were immediately taken aback when the entourage at the Mexico City airport was ushered onto a Cuban prop jet by stewardesses in miniskirts and makeup. When the plane arrived in Havana, a small welcoming committee of four women and one man met the Americans and arranged for drinks and coffee while they went through customs. The travelers were photographed and had all their shoes fumigated before they were permitted to leave the airport. Receiving a smallpox vaccination affronted Goodman. The message was loud and clear that no preferential treatment — as Americans received in other countries — applied. Members of the group brought packages from Cuban-American friends and relatives in the United States to loved ones still on the island. Goodman carried with her several publications Sandra Levinson had asked her to deliver to acquaintances in Havana. Each traveler was also relieved of any packages and letters, without explanation, presumably for review by censors.

It was early evening when they arrived at the impressive grounds of the Hotel Nacionale de Cuba, once one of the most luxurious hotels in the entire Caribbean. The setting was magnificent. It surprised the Guild members to be housed in such a palatial, Spanish-style villa — until they got inside. Then, everyone noticed that the hotel had fallen into serious disrepair. Following the revolution, locals had carted off the toilet seats and waste paper baskets from nearly every bathroom.

The first night, the Cuban government held an elaborate multi-course dinner in the American lawyers' honor, featuring filet mignon with white and red wine, champagne and plenty of rum and brandy. Fay held her own among the drinkers. A group of musicians serenaded them at their table, playing several classic American tunes they had mastered years before to please wealthy American corporate executives and tourists.

The six visitors could not help but note the strained quality of that evening's festivities. Their hosts made only light conversation and deflected pointed inquiries. Fay was among those who assumed the emerging Watergate scandal was a topic of great interest to the Cubans, but they appeared incurious about the political situation in the states. Goodman chalked it up to a natural reserve upon meeting strangers. It crossed her mind that if the trip continued in this surreal vein, the experience would chill her to the core.

Early the next morning after breakfast at the hotel, they began their tour at the law school. At the dean's office, a photo of Che Guevara immediately drew their attention. The group would soon discover the photo was ubiquitous. So was tobacco smoke and the offer of strong

Source: http://centerforcubanstudies.org courtesy of Sandra Levinson

In 1973, Sandra Levinson, Director of the newly opened Center for Cuban Studies in New York, arranged for the Cuban government to invite the first delegation of American lawyers to learn about the Cuban socialist legal system. The Center's blue, red and white brochure cover was designed by famed Cuban artist Raul Martinez. Currently, Marvin Stender is chairman of the board of the Center for Cuban Studies, which Sandra Levinson still runs.

The Hotel Nacional de Cuba, where the lawyer delegation stayed in Havana in 1973.

coffee, which their hosts drank heavily sugared. The visitors learned from professors that after the revolution few lawyers remained. Pursuit of that occupation was initially considered irrelevant and undesirable. With state ownership of property, what did they now need lawyers for?

By 1969, in all of Cuba only eleven individuals were enrolled as law students. Later, the state realized lawyers did have limited uses. Although law students could indicate job preferences after completing their legal studies, they invariably chose to go where the revolution needed them. Few were women. The Cuban government had started day care centers to encourage women to work outside the home, but many had decided to stay with their children. Female judges were rarer still. As a woman lawyer served the group coffee, their male hosts explained that women were most likely to be found as translators or legal secretaries.

The visitors were curious about how criminal defense operated. In practice, most defendants chose not to have counsel. They appeared before lay judges in panels of three to whom a professor explained the law. The lay judges then imposed the sentence by majority vote. Execution for capital crimes was by firing squad in front of "el paredón" — the wall where so many Batista supporters had been executed at the time of the revolution. The Americans had their interest piqued to learn that a high percentage of criminal offenses were committed by blacks. Having started with the worst living conditions before the revolution, they still often committed crimes for self-support. What about prisoners' rights? Fay already knew that Eldridge Cleaver's private meetings with discontented ex-convicts in Havana had precipitated his expulsion from the country in 1969.

The meeting ended in time for the group to return to the hotel for their mid-day meal. After lunch, the Americans discovered that even with their room keys, they could not return to their hotel rooms without first obtaining a pass from the front desk. That afternoon, their hosts showed great reluctance to accommodate the visitors' requests to see particular points of interest. Their principal liaison was a rather dull functionary who frustrated them with superficial answers to their questions. The government had planned a museum tour for the Americans on the night of June 5, but the group declined in favor of attempting to contact people they had been asked to look up on arrival. Connections proved difficult to make. Meanwhile, their hosts offered more touristy entertainment.

The most famous traditional nightclub in Havana was the Tropicana, long since considered the highlight of local nightlife. After the revolution, the new government made access widely available. Ordinary Cubans saw it as a symbol of success in eradicating elitism. The cabaret attracted a mostly male audience, who enjoyed endless rum drinks while ogling thousands of scantily clad exotic dancers. The extravaganza included a spectacular light show. When their hosts offered to take the small group to the Tropicana, it was meant as a special treat. Both Fay and Emily politely declined, revolted by the sexist entertainment. The only taker was David Levinson. He had a great time and felt honored that he was seated at a table near the front with their female interpreter and driver. The two were treated to a plate of sandwiches and constantly refilled rum drinks.

By the time his hosts brought David back to the hotel, around two a.m., David could barely navigate the hallway to his room. He was startled to find Fay sitting, reading a book outside his locked door. With a look of disgust at his condition, she brusquely asked how he could attend a show so demeaning to women. He was setting a terrible example. Through the fog of his hangover, David felt her reprimand was unfair. He told Fay he thought it was good manners. Besides, he wondered to himself, how she could question his commitment to equality. He was in a law partnership with two women, when most male practitioners would never consider such an idea.

The next morning, and for several days afterward, Fay and Emily treated David frostily. Both women felt strongly the group should convey their total opposition to women's exploitation — not reinforce misogynistic behavior. On June 9th, the group headed out on a bus tour of the island. En route, they passed many sexist billboards used to convey political messages. Yet major advances impressed the Americans. Education was universal as was health care. People generally seemed welcoming. One adult school instructor explained, "We are friends of the American people, but not of the system."[2] Yet the travelers noticed with growing frustration that, wherever they went, questions about any problems encountered in the new society met with a party-line denial of any difficulties whatsoever.

In addition to visiting farming collectives, their hosts offered the Americans a tour of a traditional cigar factory to see how Cubans transformed the best tobacco in the world into its finest cigars. The factory was indeed a throwback to an earlier age. All the cigars were handmade. To alleviate the tedium, it was customary to have a senior employee stand and read a novel or newspaper aloud to his co-workers. Though the Castro government used the readings for cultural education, the practice dated back more than a hundred years. Fay observed that the men had all of the best jobs. She was told it was because women only started working at the factory after the revolution, but Fay was skeptical. That was more than a decade ago. Surely, some women could have mastered the art of hand-wrapping cigars in ten years' time, had they been offered training.

Word had arrived in advance that the small group touring the factory included George Jackson's attorney. The workers were all familiar with the American revolutionary and his fate. Fay was asked to please say a few words. Caught by surprise, she agreed and was introduced, to thunderous applause. As the room quieted, Fay managed a few innocuous remarks that were then translated into Spanish. Her male companions considered the honor bestowed on Fay dramatic praise for her work for the martyred revolutionary. Fay no longer took pleasure in such accolades.

The group grew disappointed in the trip's lack of meaningful activity. Emily stopped attending the factory tours. All six became tired of being offered heavy, uninspired food and grew less tolerant of each other's foibles. Back in the Cuban capital, Fay had an opportunity for an impromptu visit to the former Jewish neighborhood in Old Havana. Ironically, it occupied streets named for Catholic saints and the Inquisition. It was sad to view the now-dilapidated synagogues and cemeteries where a once-vibrant community had been active.

Jews and Jewish converts to Catholicism had played a major role in developing the Cuban economy and its government. Fidel Castro's father was a Sephardic Jew. Unlike Ashkenazi Jews of Eastern Europe who stayed mainly in Havana, the Sephardic "turcos" or "syrios" often assimilated after they spread across the island. It probably amused Fay that the Cubans called all the Ashkenazi "polacos" — whether they came from Poland, Russia or other Slavic countries. Most arrived in the '20s after World War I when renewed pogroms prompted them to flee. By then, the United States had adopted stricter immigration laws. Had Fay's Polish ancestors left Brest-Litovsk 15 years later, they could have wound up in Cuba.

By 1959, many Cuban Jews had become successful entrepreneurs. After the revolution, they became targets of the new Communist regime, which was bent on nationalizing private enterprise. Long before Fay's visit, more than 90 per cent had fled, mostly to the United States. By 1973, no rabbis were left. Less than three months after Fay's trip to Cuba, Castro officially broke off diplomatic relations with Israel — yet another aspect of the revolutionary government with which Fay could not identify.

In Havana, arrangements were made for the American visitors to meet with newspaper editors. The subject of censorship came up, resulting in a heated discussion about freedom of speech. Fay was outraged that rock and roll was not played on state radio stations, or even the Beatles' music. She was eager to get home. Fay now had a new mission. She had endured more than she could handle of mini-skirted Cuban stewardesses, macho billboards, job discrimination against women and night clubs featuring chorus girls in scanty outfits. Fay had finally begun to realize that someone needed to address the arrogant sexism of revolutionary men.

■ 4 ■
The Barb

I'm beginning to wish I had never opened this can of worms.[1]
— FAY STENDER

Fay still involved herself from time to time on issues of prison law reform, including the prestige of serving as chair of the American Bar Association subcommittee on Offenders' Rights. Yet the demise of the Prison Law Project weighed as "a terrible pain and anguish."[2] In the fall of 1973, Fay took Marvin up on his offer to join his practice. Fay had to have misgivings about working with her husband in a small office when they often did not communicate well at home. Fay had no interest in rising at dawn with Marvin for an early start across the Bay to his San Francisco office and did not get along with his partner Gordon Lapides. She also bore a grudge against the other new partner, Marvin's young Guild protégé Doron Weinberg. Fay took over the cramped firm's library, while Doron camped out in an adjacent cubicle.

When Doron had first met Fay at the beginning of the '70s, he had found her incredibly charismatic, driven and strong-willed. As a volunteer on the Soledad Brothers Defense Committee and, later, at the Prison Law Project, Weinberg considered Fay's achievements amazing. He thought she created the prisoners' rights legal movement "almost out of her desk." Weinberg tried without success to steer clear of the clashes between his housemate Patti Roberts and Fay. Yet he still incurred Fay's wrath when the two factions split. Fay became incensed when he allowed the Prison Law Collective office to share space with the San Francisco Guild. That anger did not totally dissipate even after the demise of both prisoners' rights projects.

Weinberg expected to interact little with Fay as he focused on his criminal defense practice and Guild activities. (He would become the Guild's National President in June 1974.) To his dismay, Fay soon tried to involve everyone in their small office in a nasty court battle that deeply divided long-time members of the San Francisco Guild.

Fay started out enthusiastic about building her own practice. She reported to Marvin she had filed two petitions in paying cases in two weeks, "first the Court, then the world (e.g. some money)."[3] Marvin then handed Fay a case he thought she might find of special interest — clueless that it would destroy old friendships and wind up splitting the Leftist community in Berkeley down the middle.

Earlier that year Marvin had begun representing Jane Peters Scherr in a successful child support action against their old friend Max Scherr, the publisher of the *Berkeley Barb*. Bob Treuhaft was then representing Max, but had since handed the defense of that case to his partner, Dobby Brin Walker, an old friend of Marvin's. A veteran trial lawyer in her fifties, the feisty Marxist had become the first woman President of the National Lawyers Guild three years earlier. In 1972, Dobby and Marvin had worked together on the headline-grabbing Angela Davis conspiracy trial. Dobby had been co-counsel for Davis, and Marvin a defense witness.

Marvin and Fay knew Max Scherr far better than Jane. Max's parents were Yiddish-speaking Russian Jews who emigrated to Baltimore shortly before the turn of the century. After obtaining his law degree in Maryland, Max practiced labor law for a few years before serving in the Navy in World War II. It was unlikely any of his fellow recruits would recognize him any more. Now in his late fifties, Max resembled a revolutionary Santa Claus: overweight and out-of-shape, a bespectacled, jovial soul in wrinkled secondhand clothes, with long

Berkeley Barb logo copyright © Berkeley Barb 2018 (www.berkeleybarb.net)

Left: *Max Scherr, publisher of the Berkeley Barb, with Jane Peters Scherr, participating with other activists laying claim to People's Park on Sunday, April 27, 1969.*

Below: *Max Scherr with his wife Estela and three young children around 1950. Sergio was the oldest, then Raquel born in 1947, and the baby in the stroller was David. Raquel recalls the family being very happy back then.*

Doris "Dobby" Walker, first woman President of the National Lawyers Guild, represented Max Scherr in Fay Stender's palimony suit on Jane Scherr's behalf. People *magazine described* Scherr v. Scherr *as "a furious clash of two high-powered feminist lawyers over the rights of an 'unofficial wife.'"*

Harry Margolis was profiled, along with Fay Stender, in The Relevant Lawyers. *He helped keep George Jackson's royalties from government claims. In* Scherr v. Scherr *he helped Max keep Jane from the* Berkeley Barb's *proceeds. Fay felt betrayed.*

graying hair and a straggly, salt-and-pepper beard. But that was far from what he looked like when the Stenders met Max in the mid-1950s. They first encountered Max while he was still a clean-shaven commuter to San Francisco, wearing suits and ties as he edited textbooks for the legal publishing giant Bancroft Whitney.

Back in his commuting days, Max had been married for more than a decade to a medical student he met in 1942 on a trip south of the border. Juana Estela Salgado had been in the forefront of independent-minded Mexican women when she embarked on a new life with Max in California's East Bay. Estela Scherr was well-read but spoke only broken English. She stayed at home raising their four children while Max earned a master's degree in sociology at Cal and went to work as a legal editor. In 1958, Max bought The Steppenwolf Bar in Berkeley, which had become a popular watering hole for students and beatniks. For entertainment, the hangout booked well-known folk musicians. It was while running the bar that Max took to dressing in jeans and sporting a long scruffy beard. Estela and their children helped out regularly in the bar.

Max met Beatrice J. "Jane" Peters when she was a politically naive Cal undergraduate who frequented The Steppenwolf Bar. Jane was nearly twenty years his junior. She told Fay that Max had separated from Estela before he moved in with Jane in 1960, but that he continued to pay Estela regular monthly support. Max told Jane that he considered his marriage to Estela invalid due to a technicality of Mexican law. He and Estela had kept their marriage a secret at first to allow her to continue her medical studies because the school had a policy of not permitting married women to attend.

Within the first few years they lived together, Jane and Max had two daughters — Dove and Apollinaire — whom Jane stayed home to raise. Meanwhile, Max sold The Steppenwolf Bar in the summer of 1965 and used the proceeds to launch *The Berkeley Barb* in their living room. Fay and Marvin knew that the birth of *The Barb* was highly controversial. Max had used cut-throat tactics against a new Movement paper, *The Citizen*, after Max was passed over to become *The Citizen*'s original editor. The first edition of *The Barb* (designed "to stick a barb" in the competition) was appallingly amateurish. No one but Max would try to hawk it on the streets, even at ten cents per copy. But using the *Village Voice* and *Los Angeles Free Press* as models, *The Barb* soon rose to national recognition and forced *The Citizen* to fold for lack of funds.[4] At its peak, *The Barb* would have a circulation upwards of 100,000.

Max benefitted from shrewd timing. He launched *The Barb* when global attention focused on the Free Speech Movement and Vietnam War protests on the Berkeley campus and in Oakland. The uncensored paper attracted many volunteer and underpaid Leftist reporters. In 1966, *The Barb* introduced highly profitable ads for massage parlors and sex clubs. By the spring of 1967, *The Barb* outgrew Max's colonial home and moved into space in the same four-plex as Fay and Marvin's friend Peter Franck, where their Council for Justice had previously operated.

Before Max and Jane split up in 1972, the Stenders had often seen the petite brunette accompany the legendary underground newspaper publisher at Leftist social gatherings. They were regulars at the Treuhafts' parties. Though Jane used Scherr as her last name and Max often referred to her as "my old lady," Jane Peters and Max were never married.

Until she represented Jane, Fay considered Max a great ally who supported all the same causes Fay championed. Max liked to boast that *The Barb* was the first newspaper to feature stories about Huey Newton and Bobby Seale back in 1966, before anyone else had heard of the pair. *The Barb* later lavished praise on Newton as a Movement hero in its coverage of his 1968 Oakland murder trial. More recently, it had published an exposé of conditions at San Quentin prison while Fay led the fight for inmates' rights. But if Max had done Jane wrong, Fay was game to take him on. Jane immediately took a liking to her aggressive new lawyer.

After Marvin got Jane the child support order from Max, Fay suggested the then novel idea that Jane should claim a half interest in *The Barb*. Fay was new at promoting women's rights. In 1964, when Betty Friedan's *The Feminine Mystique* became a best seller, Fay remained disengaged. Nor did she become interested in women's liberation two years later when the National Organization for Women ("NOW") was founded. Fay's focus at the time was civil rights and the anti-war movement. Until the late '60s, Fay had been critical of feminists. "At first

I thought if they'd just get down to work like me and stop complaining everything would be fine. But then I realized I was taking the position of a Negro in the 1940s who went to Harvard."[5]

By the fall of 1970, Fay could see how one movement helped launch another. Starting that year, feminists had begun successfully lobbying for women's studies programs in colleges, using as their model the recent creation of ethnic studies departments across the country. The Black Panther Party was credited with a major role in instigating that effort. Prominent in the Party's ten-point platform were demands for education that teaches "our true history" and "our role in the present-day society." Women wanted that, too.

In January 1972, feminist icon Gloria Steinem cofounded *Ms.* magazine with African-American activist Dorothy Pittman Hughes. By March, women's groups convinced Congress to send the (ill-fated) Equal Rights Amendment to the states for ratification. Shirley Chisholm, the first black Congresswoman, was then running as both the first black presidential candidate in either party and the first female to seek the Democratic Party's nomination. Fay now embraced women's rights as the new frontier.

In 1973, Dru Ramey talked Fay into joining San Francisco's ACLU board to give it a strong feminist voice and open the door for others. With the ACLU's national office now promoting women's rights, the San Francisco Board had just invited Dru and her young feminist colleagues to form their own committee, without realizing that their goal was to dismantle the old boy network. (By 1978, the ACLU Board's direction would change so dramatically that Dru's selection as its first woman chair was uncontroversial.)

So when Marvin handed Fay Jane's case in the fall of 1973, Fay was eager to break new ground with claims against Max for the couple's twelve years together. At first, Fay and Marvin assumed that Max had few assets to go after. He dressed poorly. His home was large, but not well-maintained and sparsely furnished with scuffed, secondhand furniture, mattresses with no bed frames or box springs, and orange crates for tables. Jane surprised the Stenders by claiming Max was perpetrating an elaborate charade to fend off demands for raises from his underpaid staff.

By 1969, as Fay and Marvin knew, thirty employees and freelancers who called themselves "The Red Mountain Tribe Collective" staged a revolt and marched on Max's office, demanding to see the books. The Tribe members were then fired or quit to establish their own competing paper. Jane said that the unhappy employees were right. Secretly, at his instructions over the years, Jane had deposited hundreds of thousands of dollars from *The Barb* into his bank accounts. By 1973, Jane assumed *The Barb* was worth at least half a million dollars.

Still, one could understand why the first attorneys Jane consulted in 1972 showed little enthusiasm for pursuing her claims. Jane had no money to pay their fees. The prospect of any substantial recovery from Max looked highly doubtful. Historically, unmarried women living with men had no rights in California except for the rare instance when the couple had established a common law marriage in another state. Otherwise, cohabitation without a license violated California's strong public policy against "meretricious relationships." Judges refused to enforce salary sharing agreements between men and stay-at-home sexual partners.

Until 1970, even spouses could lose rights on divorce if they were found to be at fault. Photos of a spouse caught cheating could prove extremely costly. The new law Fay had reviewed for her trip to Cuba — The Family Law Act of 1970 — drastically changed the ground rules for terminating marriages. Since its passage, dissolution was based on irreconcilable differences, not fault, and marital community property was now split 50-50.

Just as Californians were beginning to absorb the new ground rules for no-fault divorce, in late September 1973, a case called *Cary v. Cary* created shockwaves. The Carys had held themselves out as husband and wife. They raised four children and lived as if they were a married couple, except for the lack of a marriage license. After they split up, the court of appeal ordered an equal division of the Carys' property.

Marvin had alerted Dobby Walker back in the summer of 1973 that Jane intended to follow up her child support action with a suit claiming a half interest in *The Barb*. At the time, Walker had asked Marvin to hold off on filing suit to see if the case could settle. When Marvin handed Fay the *Scherr* file in early October 1973, he told her that he had seen Dobby at a Guild meeting a couple of days after the *Cary* case hit the newspapers. He took the opportunity to give Dobby the clipping. Marvin assumed it would convince her to recommend to Max a sizeable settlement. But the next time Dobby saw Marvin, she instead invited him to sue and take his best shot.

Fay immediately began researching all the theories under which Jane might obtain recovery against Max. The first obstacle was his marriage in Mexico to Estela. To Jane's knowledge, Max had never sought a divorce. Fay found a helpful case involving a woman who recovered money from the estate of a man she had lived with but never wed. At the time of his death, the man remained the legal husband of another woman.

Fay spent more time in the library and uncovered a line of cases dating back to the early 1930s involving sharing agreements between unmarried couples. Like any other partnership, such agreements could be enforced upon proof the couple intended to pool their resources while living together. Still, Fay could find no case where the court allowed an unmarried woman compensation for staying home to raise children. A 1952 decision equated the performance of homemaking services with being a "concubine."[6] Such cases hardly reflected contemporary mores in the 1970s. The law was ripe for change.

Fay wrote an article for the ACLU newspaper on how the *Cary* case represented "one of the most important court decisions in the emerging field of women's rights."[7] The ACLU showed no interest in getting involved. As Fay knew, the ACLU had actually defended Max Scherr in a criminal prosecution for obscenity back in 1969 over a *Barb* photo of a couple apparently engaged in sex.

Fay considered her best bet for a half share of *The Barb* to be the new *Cary* decision. This was still an uphill battle. Unlike the Carys, Jane and Max had never held joint bank accounts or filed joint tax returns. Fay asked Jane to gather evidence that Max referred to her as his "wife" or "spouse," including lists of friends and acquaintances who believed they were married. Fay also requested that Jane detail all her efforts to help launch *The Barb* as a joint project.

While Fay drafted the complaint, she heard rumors that Max was preparing to sell *The Barb* and permanently leave the country. Fay hurried to have the pleadings ready to file in early November 1973, only to discover that Max had just left for an extended trip to Europe. Both Fay and Marvin were furious. They were convinced that Dobby used her friendship with Marvin to lull him into delaying suit on Jane's claims so that Max could hide all his assets in Switzerland.

Fay readied for combat on Jane's behalf. Max had turned out to be one revolutionary she had no compunctions in challenging head on. No theory of recovery was left behind as Fay drafted a suit claiming $250,000 for a half interest in *The Barb*. Fay arranged to have Max subpoenaed the day he returned in January 1974. She then obtained a temporary order preventing him from selling *The Barb*. Walker immediately filed her opposition. War between the parties had begun.

Marvin and Doron resisted Fay's efforts to get involved. Both complained as Fay consumed more and more of the small firm's resources on her non-paying case. Fay had brought into the tight quarters on the Embarcadero a new young secretary, Joanne Schulman. Schulman was a loyal staffer who had stayed to the bitter end of the Prison Law Project in June 1973. While still an undergraduate at UCLA, Schulman had revered Fay from afar, like thousands of other student radicals awed by George Jackson's lawyer. When Joanne transferred to Berkeley in 1972, the shy twenty-year-old volunteered at the Prison Law Project. She was surprised at her first glimpse of her idol up close. Fay's slip was hanging out and she had a run in her stocking. But Joanne would also see Fay transform herself into a stunning beauty to impress potential funders.

Fay now commuted to work in San Francisco with Schulman in Marvin's Mercedes. As she sped deftly through traffic, Fay constantly vented her spleen, complaining bitterly that Marvin focused too much on profits rather than furthering political causes. Schulman thrilled at all the time she got to spend with her mentor, even when it meant bracing herself in the car as Fay raced the wrong way down San Francisco's alleys. Fay often preferred to work out of her home where there was far more room and no recriminations. Though Joanne listened sympathetically to Fay's complaints, she admired Marvin's ability to keep balance in his life better than Fay did.

Fay used a similar political strategy in the *Scherr* case as she had for Huey Newton and George Jackson: an all-out effort to create a climate of public acceptance that would convince the court to rule in Jane's favor. In December 1973, Fay alerted a local reporter that she intended to file an extremely important women's rights case.[8] With her sights on national media coverage, at the end of January 1974 Fay sent out a flurry of letters to newspapers and magazines. She solicited a law student at U. C. Berkeley's Boalt Hall to write an article and notified a local television station about the case.

Fay explained to her media contacts that the case had "obvious implications for all women, particularly for minority women who have lived in family common law relationships."[9] In her zeal for publicity, Fay did not mention that, in this particular case, Jane Peters Scherr was not a member of any minority group. As Fay also knew, Max Scherr's pre-existing marriage to an Hispanic immigrant had yet to be challenged in court. Even if Max's Mexican marriage was ruled void, how could Fay assume Estela's common law rights were inferior to Jane's? It was easy to paint Max in an unfavorable light. Beyond that, the sympathy factor might not exactly favor Fay's client.

Fay sought help generating favorable publicity from fellow ACLU Board member Marilyn Hall Patel, who was general counsel for NOW and a member of the NOW Legal Defense Fund's Board of Directors. (Patel would later become the first woman Chief Judge of the local Federal District Court.) Since its founding in 1966, NOW had become a leading voice in the country for women's rights. Patel arranged for a press conference on the eve of the court hearing.

Fay's outreach to the media bore immediate fruit with favorable articles in two prominent local dailies. By mid-February, a popular weekly paper, *The Pacific Sun*, used the *Scherr* case as a hook for writing a general article on the impact of the growing feminist movement: later marriages, two-career families, and the new trend toward lifelong retention of maiden names. To Fay's delight, one expert credited the Women's

Movement as "the biggest impetus for change in the marital structure."[10]

The week of the March hearing, *The Sun* followed up with another favorable article, predicting, "If Stender wins this one, it will set a significant precedent for a future in which a lot more love matches will start coming apart at the seams."[11] In late March, Fay excitedly watched a family law professor at U. C. Davis tout the *Scherr* case on a morning talk show as one of the first of its kind.

Dobby Walker knew as well as Fay the value of favorable press. The first woman President of the National Lawyers Guild had credentials that also impressed reporters. She began publicizing her own view that the *Scherr* case had no women's liberation angle. "Either you're making your own independent situation or you're looking to the courts to protect you as a poor, weak woman. I don't get this business of coming in years later and claiming the benefits of a relationship you did not enter into."[12]

As the *Scherr* case proceeded toward trial, Fay realized that Dobby Walker was a "a hell of a good lawyer." Still, Fay felt confident that she herself was "no slouch."[13] By April 1974, *The Wall Street Journal* had its interest piqued and wanted to do an article on relationships like the Scherrs'. *People Magazine* contacted Fay and Dobby Walker for interviews. NOW activist Marilyn Patel worked with Fay on another press conference. At Fay's instigation, CBS News also expressed interest, but Walker would not agree to another interview until after the trial was over. Marvin suggested that Fay "let it go."[14]

That spring, to Fay's great dismay, a law review article severely criticized the *Cary* case for using the wrong theory to divide the couple's property evenly.[15] Fay encouraged a woman law student to draft a response. Meanwhile, she was now deeply embroiled in unraveling the complex international transactions by which Max Scherr had transferred ownership of *The Barb* in the fall of 1973 to a charitable trust.

Walker had collaborated with tax attorney Harry Margolis, the same expert Fay had asked to put George Jackson's royalties beyond the reach of prison officials. As part of the deal transferring *The Barb* to the trust, Max received the promise of an annuity for life. That maneuver would make it difficult for Jane to collect much, if anything, from Max even if she won. Fay and Marvin were fuming. To add insult to injury, one of the trustees was Fay's Soledad Brothers co-counsel, John Thorne. To set aside these transactions, Fay needed to prove that the trustees — her old colleagues Margolis and Thorne — knew that Max intended to defraud Jane out of an interest in *The Barb*.

Fay's health was now her foremost concern. She wore a neck brace from a recent car accident. What concerned her most was a growth on her finger which her doctor could only diagnose by performing a biopsy. If cancerous, the finger should be amputated. Fay begged Marvin to promise that, under no circumstance, would Marvin authorize her finger to be cut off. Marvin was aghast. He refused to make such a promise. Fay became furious, precipitating one of the worst fights of their marriage over her vanity about her beautiful hands. She brought a friend to the hospital to ensure that her wishes were honored. Marvin could not believe she would rather die than live with a minor deformity. Fortunately, it was a benign growth requiring only that the medical team scrape the tumor from her tendon and bandage it. Greatly relieved, Fay went back to work.

In August 1974, *People Magazine* printed "Split: An Unofficial Wife Wants Her 'Rights.'" Both Fay and Dobby Walker bristled at its description of *Scherr v. Scherr* as "a furious clash of two high-powered feminist lawyers, both with impeccable radical credentials, over the rights of the unmarried 'wife.'" The woman reporter contrasted the two "hard-edged lawyers" with "quiet and hesitant" Jane Scherr. Several pictures accompanied the two-page spread, including a tranquil shot of Jane watching her two daughters playing violins in the small cottage they now occupied. This picture infuriated Dobby, who had gotten Fay's agreement that the two girls would be kept out of any publicity. An irate exchange of letters followed. Walker asked for a court order to restrain Jane from allowing reporters access to her daughters. The paper trail Walker was creating incensed Fay, who accused Dobby of not acting in good faith. Fay scrawled a note in the case file that summed up *Scherr v. Scherr* — a "can of worms."

To Fay's delight, Marvin managed to find spacious new quarters for their firm just off Washington Square in San Francisco that allowed her an office of her own. Gordon Lapides would stay behind, while Weinberg made the move with the Stenders. By then, Joanne Schulman, inspired by Fay's example, had left to attend law school.

In February, *The Oakland Tribune* featured the *Scherr v. Scherr* case in an article, "'Free Love': It Can Be Costly." Fay's elation dissipated quickly. Bob Treuhaft published a reply accusing the newspaper of bias. He demanded a retraction of defamatory statements against Max. Treuhaft had represented Max in a prior lawsuit over *The Barb* from a failed attempt to sell the paper in 1970. In that suit, Treuhaft noted that the court recognized Max as *The Barb's* sole owner, not a co-owner of the paper with Jane. Treuhaft then questioned the reporter's good faith for ignoring Max's wife Estela in Berkeley and "possibly also, the good faith of the petitioner and her lawyer [Fay] if they failed to mention it."[16]

From then on, the Treuhafts stopped inviting the Stenders to the popular gatherings at their home. Fay, in turn, studiously avoided the Treuhafts and Walker at Guild events. Al Brotsky told Fay that she and Dobby were both being childish, but Fay wouldn't listen. Surprisingly, Decca criticized her husband's and Walker's role in defending Max's behavior. She sympathized with Jane Scherr's position. Other mutual friends of Fay and Dobby in the Lawyers Guild refused to choose sides.

With Fay's partner Doron the current National Guild president, the feud proved particularly awkward. In fact, since 1969, many local Guild members disliked Max for his poor labor policies. *The Barb* staff was also split in its allegiance. Many reporters and former staff members were furious about how much money Max had extracted from the paper over the years while pretending to be broke. Others were concerned the lawsuit might jeopardize the paper's future.

The Barb had already become a sore subject for feminists because it profited from sex parlors and pornography. After a prostitute who advertised in *The Barb* was murdered, someone painted "Max Murderer" on Max Scherr's house. Max was appalled. He had misgivings about the sex ads, which had grown to dominate the paper. They had begun as an expression of anti-establishment sexual freedom, but were now just seen as exploitation of women for profit.

As the trial grew near, Max complained publicly that his former

Leftist friends were unfairly ostracizing him because of Jane's suit: "I am turfless in Berkeley. Fay has turned a family squabble into a political cause."[17] Max was taken aback by feminists who viewed him as a chauvinist pig. He had fully supported Estela's educational aspirations and treated his daughter Raquel as co-equal to her three brothers when growing up. Max had strongly encouraged Raquel throughout her pursuit of a Ph.D. at Cal. She considered herself a feminist, too. (In 1977, she would co-author the Spanish edition of the ground-breaking 1971 book on women's health, *Our Bodies, Ourselves*.)

A new twist then developed to the fight over women's exploitation in *The Barb*. Soon after Max sold his interest in *The Barb* to the new trust, it stopped running the sex ads. (They would reappear a couple of years later in a spin-off weekly adult magazine *The Spectator*, which featured stories about bondage, sadomasochism, and other kinky sexual practices. It would far outlast *The Barb*.) When *The Barb*'s profits plummeted following the decision to forego sex ads, Jane asked Fay what she could do to prevent the paper's continued revenue loss. Fay knew from past experience that Harry Margolis had a reputation for draining the profits out of businesses until they collapsed. *The Barb* appeared headed toward bankruptcy.

Fay took aggressive action, asking the judge to appoint his own receiver to run the underground paper while the lawsuit remained pending. As proof of bad management by the trust, Fay cited its decision to stop running the lucrative sex ads — hardly a persuasive reason for the court to take over the paper. The motion was denied. *The New York Times* then ran a lengthy article on the bitter court fight being waged in an Oakland court that provided "insight into the life-styles of an important element of Berkeley's radical society."[18]

With her adult daughter Raquel acting as an interpreter, Estela finally told her own sympathetic story to the press. She claimed that *The Barb* started from proceeds of The Steppenwolf Bar, which had only been kept solvent through her own sweat equity and that of her children. It was Jane who exploited Estela's family by making competing claims against Max. Estela had confronted Jane at one point as Jane pushed a baby carriage on a Berkeley sidewalk. Estela told her to find a man her own age — Max was married "with me" and had children. Jane remained with Max. Though Max continued to provide Estela with support, Estela and her children had been devastated by Max's lengthy extramarital relationship with Jane.

On the eve of trial, Max called a former *Barb* reporter who now worked for an extremely sleazy Los Angeles tabloid called *DYNAMITE*. Like *The Barb*, *DYNAMITE* covered Movement issues, but the graphic child pornography in its ads would have put the ACLU to the test to defend on grounds of redeeming social value. *DYNAMITE* printed Max's absurd claim that Jane bought trial witnesses with sexual favors. Worse still, the paper crudely exploited the illness of one of their daughters.

Before going to press, Borin called Fay for her response. Fay filled his ear with her own charges that Dobby Walker had conspired with Max to move *The Barb*'s assets out of the country to avoid the lawsuit and then fraudulently backdated the documents. Borin sent Fay a copy of the next issue of *DYNAMITE*. It now included in the explosive, multi-page article all of Fay's accusations as well as Max's. Fay was livid. She believed she was just providing Borin with background information to forestall the printing of Max's claims.[19] Fay wrote back that she was "appalled and truly horrified" at the coverage. The media wars were over. The case was now in court.

Originally, Marvin had asked Fay only to handle pretrial work. They both expected Marvin to try the case himself, but he was now busy with paying cases. It would be a fifteen-day court trial in which Marvin feared Fay would be seriously overmatched. She lacked any significant civil trial experience and faced Dobby in her element. Media coverage was guaranteed for this pioneering palimony case pitting Leftists against each other. But Fay's ego was on the line and she felt ready for the challenge.

Reporters had another angle to cover. The scarcity of women trial lawyers made it extremely unusual for a major case to have high-powered women attorneys on both sides. At forty-three, Fay looked the part of an aging '60s radical, her dark hair with wisps of gray held back in a ponytail, earrings dangling. Walker was equally resolute, dressed in more conventional business attire. Despite being almost a generation older than Fay, Walker's closely cropped hair remained mostly brown.

THE BARB

The diminutive old war horse was all business.

To Fay's dismay, Max and Estela had apparently reconciled. Estela came to court to sit each day behind her husband. She now had her own highly regarded attorney to pursue her interests against the trust that had purchased *The Barb*. Still not facile in English, Estela was represented by bilingual Oakland City Councilman John Sutter. Fay believed Max put Estela up to hiring an attorney. Yet Fay herself belatedly recognized that Estela had a valid claim against Max.

As Dobby would show at trial, Max Scherr had actually maintained two Berkeley households for a number of years. The one he established first was with Estela and their four children. The second, out of which he launched *The Barb*, was with Jane and their two daughters. There had never been a clean separation from Estela as Fay believed at the outset. On nights that he was not home with Jane, Max had at least sometimes stayed with Estela. In her anger at Max for refusing to pay child support to Jane and later manipulating *The Barb*'s assets, Fay had not thought through Estela's likely rights.

Mid-trial Fay sought to reconcile the competing claims of the two women and their children. She proposed a settlement in which both families would be recognized as having ownership interests in *The Barb* — Max, Estela, Jane and Max's five surviving children by both mothers. Walker wasn't interested. She had Max and Estela's Mexican wedding certificate and plenty of proof that Max's marriage to Estela remained ongoing, including conjugal visits while living with Jane. Walker felt she was on the verge of an all-out victory. Fay soldiered on.

When the trial ended, Judge Robert Kroninger took the case under submission for a month before issuing his opinion. At the time, the California Supreme Court had the exact same issue under submission. The celebrated *Marvin v. Marvin* case involved claims against Oscar-winning actor Lee Marvin by his live-in girlfriend Michelle. But Judge Kroninger did not want to wait for that ruling to come down. When he issued his opinion, Fay found that she had both succeeded in convincing the judge that palimony cases were viable and lost this case.

Judge Kroninger had been impressed by Fay's presentation but found that Max had a lawful wife the whole time he lived with Jane.

He noted evidence that in some parts of the Berkeley community, Max Scherr still held himself out as Estela Scherr's husband. The judge concluded that Jane Scherr had no reasonable expectation that she would share in Max's earnings as an "ostensible wife" when she knew Max continued to support his pre-existing family.

After some post-trial skirmishing, Walker offered $50,000 to settle the case if Fay would drop all further proceedings. It was the same amount Dobby had been prepared to offer at the outset before both sides spent so much money on legal expenses. Fay reluctantly accepted. Six months after Jane's case settled, the California Supreme Court put *Cary* to rest for good in its landmark decision in *Marvin v. Marvin*.[20] The high court was unanimous in recognizing for the first time that the large increase in unmarried couples living together marked a radical change in society. The parties in such relationships could now have their reasonable expectations enforced in the courts, including the value of household services.

Though Fay did not win the *Scherr* case, she played a major role in focusing public attention on the rights of co-habiting couples. That publicity helped change the political climate in which the Supreme Court considered its milestone *Marvin* ruling. If it was any consolation to Fay and Jane Scherr, when the *Marvin* case was retried, Michelle Marvin could not prove her claim against Lee Marvin either. For much of their relationship, the actor was still married to Betty Marvin, which proved a similar insurmountable obstacle.

Fay could not forgive Bob Treuhaft or Dobby Walker for the way they handled Max's defense. She never spoke to either of them again. She was convinced that she took a strong feminist stand and was stabbed in the back: "The left betrayed me."[21] Yet Fay herself had marginalized Estela Scherr while championing Jane's interests. Fay failed to realize before trial that Estela not only had a competing claim for a share of *The Barb*, but one on superior legal ground. Ultimately, the judge ruled that Estela and Max remained husband and wife the whole time Max lived with Jane. How could Fay believe Jane's claims took precedence? In the view of Estela and her children, Jane's lawsuit smacked of racism. Fay's blinders never permitted her to appreciate their perspective.

Marvin and Doron had been right about the case involving a huge amount of uncompensated time. When it was over, Fay increasingly wrapped herself in a cocoon of women friends and feminist projects. Meanwhile, she tried harder to figure out how to earn a decent living practicing law. By June 1976, Doron Weinberg left to start his own firm.

Fay's problem was that she found herself always drawn to causes with complex problems and little money at their disposal. The Women's History Research Center was a good example. At first, Fay was delighted to join its Board. By 1975, WHRC had gathered 2,000 articles on "herstory," women and the law and women's health issues. Its founder, Laura X, employed Jane Scherr in cataloguing her own case. WHRC developed an ambitious distribution plan plunging the avant-garde organization into an unfamiliar world of business red tape and copyright concerns. By the spring of 1977, Fay tendered her resignation and told Laura X that what WHRC really needed was its own in-house counsel. For once in her life, Fay had reached the conclusion she was overextended. This was, indeed, a milestone.

Whenever she took a new case, Fay wanted to believe she was on the right side. She had some fun representing kindred spirits in a losing effort to elect a maverick slate to take over the board at KQED, the award-winning, San Francisco-based educational television and radio station. On the Board of California Women Lawyers (CWL), Fay achieved greater satisfaction. In 1974, Dru Ramey had urged Fay to join Dru and others who had just launched CWL as a statewide organization. CWL's first elected president, Dean Judith McKelvey, of Golden Gate Law School, credited Fay with ending a debilitating rift between its Southern and Northern California Board members shortly after it first got off the ground. United on common goals, CWL soon emerged as a powerful advocate for women appointees to the judiciary and other government offices as well as for women's rights in society at large.

Fay herself developed an ambitious proposal for CWL involving lawyers, psychiatrists and psychologists who promoted non-traditional child custody arrangements. She obtained a grant for a year-long project she then codirected, reconnecting with Patti Roberts to help push for lesbian custody rights. Together with other new studies, the CWL report

Fay coauthored helped reshape custody decisions in California.

In the meantime, CWL's annual dinner at the State Bar quickly became a highlight of the State Bar's annual convention. In September 1977, Fay shared in CWL's proudest moment. Board President Louise Renne (later the first female City Attorney of San Francisco) presented their keynote speaker to a packed house — CWL member Rose Bird, newly appointed as the first woman Chief Justice of the California Supreme Court. Three years later Chief Justice Bird would be among the mourners at Fay's funeral.

As Fay increasingly associated with mainstream practitioners in the late 1970s, her spirited defense of the rights of violent felons still sometimes perplexed them. One night, Fay invited two fellow CWL board members, law professors Judith McKelvey and Herma Kay, and their husbands to dine with her and Marvin. The three couples had been enjoying a lovely meal when Herma Kay's spouse, psychiatrist Carroll Brodsky, brought up his outrage at a recent newspaper article in that day's paper about a black inmate just released on parole.

The former physician had murdered his unfaithful wife by throwing acid on her. He won his freedom on the condition that he would leave the country to volunteer his medical skills in China or Korea, where he had no need of a license. Fay surprised her guests by responding, "I'm the one who got him out." Dr. Brodsky could not contain his anger as Fay adamantly defended her action. The circumstances that prompted the murder would not likely recur. His skills were needed. Why wasn't his exile to a Third World country a beneficial solution? Not that long in the future, Fay herself would live in exile, deeply troubled by where all her empathy for violent black men had gotten her.

■ 5 ■

Reflections in the Mirror

"Is F.S. C.P.?"
GEORGE JACKSON'S SMUGGLED NOTE TO HUEY NEWTON (SUMMER 1971)

"She's only a liberal, that's all she is." [1]
UNIDENTIFIED BLACK PANTHER RECORDED BY FBI (FALL 1970)

Fay was like many '60s activists who had recently shifted their efforts to working within the system now that the Vietnam War was drawing to a close. She and her friends looked on with dismay at the misguided new white radical group calling itself the Symbionese Liberation Army. The SLA had evolved from a splinter group of Venceremos. The SLA shocked the Oakland community and the nation in early November 1973 by murdering Marcus Foster, Oakland's highly popular first black superintendent of schools. Their rationale was that Foster had implemented tightened security on school campuses — in the SLA's view, a fascist move. In early February 1974, the SLA struck again in Berkeley, kidnapping newspaper heiress Patty Hearst. Soon Hearst stunned the world by taking the name "Tanya" and joining her captors in a series of bank robberies. Most of the SLA's leaders died in a fiery confrontation with a Los Angeles SWAT team on May 16, 1974, while "Tanya" remained still in hiding.

On August 1, 1974, Fay received a phone call from her old client and friend Jerry Rubin, who had just returned to the East Bay. He asked Fay to help Eldridge and Kathleen Cleaver negotiate with local prosecutors to put his 1968 parole violation to rest. Eldridge Cleaver had recently undergone a religious conversion, disavowing revolution and socialism. He wanted to bring his family back to the United States. Before Fay signed on to help the Cleavers, she checked with Charles Garry to gauge Huey Newton's reaction. Just two days earlier, the newspapers reported that Newton had been rearrested at a downtown nightclub after an altercation with police. As usual, Garry would be representing him. Fay was not proposing to get herself caught in any ongoing Panther disputes, glad to have successfully avoided their internal warfare in the past.

By 1974, Newton had invested considerable effort pursuing greater respectability for the Panthers. Though their paths seldom crossed these days, Fay had recently seen Newton at a community gathering to dedicate a new youth educational institute. In 1973, Bobby Seale and Elaine Brown had won many thousands of votes in their unsuccessful bids for city office, wooing residents of the flatlands with health clinics and an alternative learning center in East Oakland that opened in the fall of 1973. Newton then promoted Elaine Brown to a Party leadership position and helped her gain considerable influence with the state's new Governor Jerry Brown and the Democratic Party. But, at the same time, the Panthers engaged in deadly turf battles with other black militant groups. Like a Mafia capo, Huey strictly controlled his followers with brutal repercussions for infractions. His disciplined minions regularly shook down black business owners and retaliated viciously against those who refused. The Panthers were prime suspects when arson destroyed a major Oakland theater in 1973 and when the corpse of a Berkeley bar owner was found stuffed in the trunk of his own car.

Garry told Fay that Newton's response to her assisting the Cleavers was unpredictable. Newton exhibited increased paranoia these days as he sank more heavily into cocaine use and drunken rages. The Party's central committee had just witnessed a major falling-out between Newton and Party co-founder Bobby Seale, who had since quit the Party and moved East. Fay wrote Newton a letter telling him she wanted to help the Cleavers unless he objected. Newton did not write back. He had far greater concerns. The following week, Newton was arrested on two felony charges: shooting a seventeen-year-old-black prostitute in the head and, shortly afterward, pistol-whipping a tailor. Fay did not envy Charles Garry when he showed up in Judge Jackie Taber's courtroom on August 23 without his client. Newton had just forfeited bond and escaped to Cuba, leaving Elaine Brown in charge of the Panther Party.

Four months later, Fay learned that an acquaintance from *Ramparts*, Betty Louise Van Patter, had gone missing. Van Patter was last employed as a bookkeeper at the Black Panther community school in East Oakland. The last place Van Patter was seen was meeting with a couple of Panthers on December 13 at the Lamp Post bar, a favorite Panther hangout part-owned by Huey Newton. In mid-January, Van Patter's bloated body was found floating in the San Francisco Bay south of the city, off the coast of the peninsula, her skull fractured. Leftists in the East Bay community absorbed the shock in stunned silence. A rumor circulated that the Panthers had killed Van Patter to prevent her from exposing financial irregularities at the school. The police never solved the murder.

On Sunday, June 8, 1975, one of Fay's allies in the prison reform movement, Wilbert "Popeye" Jackson, was executed gangland style along with a female companion as they sat in his car in San Francisco's Mission District. A message from underground radicals two days later claimed that Jackson, an ex-felon who headed the United Prisoners Union, had been killed for turning police informer. *The San Francisco Examiner* reported that the hottest lead police possessed was a gang called "Tribal Thumb," of mostly white revolutionary ex-convicts with ties to the SLA.

The leader of Tribal Thumb was a former Black Panther, Earl Satcher, whom Fay knew well from Soledad. Satcher had witnessed the sharp-shooting death of George Jackson's mentor W. L. in the prison courtyard on January 13, 1970, and had afterward orchestrated a number of inmate hunger strikes. Though police were not supposed to share their theories with reporters, they mentioned the possibility that Popeye Jackson's assassination was the work of militants associated with the August Seventh Guerrilla Movement. George Jackson had founded the August Seventh Movement with his friend Jimmy Carr in honor of Jonathan Jackson's fatal Marin County kidnapping attempt. Carr himself had been assassinated in April of 1972 outside the home of his mother-in-law Joan Hammer, but his name had come up again in the pending trial of the San Quentin Six.

Fay's old mentor Charles Garry was among the lead lawyers in the marathon San Quentin Six trial. He represented Black Panther Johnny Spain on assault and murder charges for his alleged role in the bloodbath surrounding George Jackson's death. The case had dragged on for nearly four years of pretrial proceedings before the trial started at the end of July 1975. Fay had no desire to be involved.

As was his trademark, Garry produced a surprise defense witness, Jimmy Carr's brother-in-law, Louis Tackwood. Tackwood offered to testify that he had previously been an informant for COINTELPRO. His final assignment before quitting was laying the groundwork for the assassination of George Jackson. Tackwood said the plans included smuggling in useless weapons Jackson was expected to use in a doomed escape attempt. Garry accused Jimmy Carr of being a double agent secretly working for COINTELPRO. Vigorous objections prevented the jury from hearing most of Tackwood's hotly disputed confession.

Fay counted herself lucky to be safe on the sidelines. When an inmate who knew her from the Prison Law Project escaped, Fay panicked at the thought of a prisoner on the lam calling at her door. If she assisted him in any way, Fay faced prosecution. Nor did she want to be blamed for helping the felon be recaptured. She contacted several old friends, who took turns putting up the Stenders for a few weeks.

That summer the grueling San Quentin Six trial set a record for length, not ending until August 12, 1976, with the acquittal of three of the six defendants. Only Charles Garry's client, Johnny Spain, was convicted of murder. As the legal spectacle ended, Fay sat in the safety of her arm chair, reading a new book she was asked to review that focused on the August 1971 San Quentin debacle. Fay had been interviewed a couple of years earlier by its author, British investigative reporter Jo Durden-Smith. An activist sympathetic to revolutionaries, Durden-Smith had journeyed from London to California intent upon writing an exposé of how Jackson was set up and murdered by prison officials. After extensive interviews with almost everyone involved, including some harrowing encounters with underground radicals, Durden-Smith ultimately concluded both sides were to blame: Jackson was gunned down attempting to escape. Fearing for his own safety, Durden-Smith fled back to England where he wrote a different book than he had originally intended: *Who Killed George Jackson? Fantasy, Paranoia and the Revolution.*

In her review for *The San Francisco Chronicle*, Fay noted that the book contained insights into its revolutionary subject that, for various reasons, never surfaced in the just-completed San Quentin Six trial. Fay praised the perceptive portrait of "an enigmatic, powerful man, about whom cluster lawyers, friends, lovers, enemies, conspirators and dangers from right and left." She observed that Durden-Smith did a good job examining "[t]he personal talent and literary brilliance of Jackson, the persecution complex, grandiosity, tunnel vision, the sweep to destruction, the difficulties others faced in communicating reality to Jackson, isolated by ten years in prison." Fay considered the book "essential reading for those seeking to understand the relationship of prisons to black revolution and radical movements in the Sixties and early Seventies. . . . It provides convincing analysis of why the failing momentum of the civil rights and peace movements led the Left to believe that prison revolts would constitute a vanguard of general revolution, when in fact assisting prisoners from the outside was either reformist or adventurist. . . . " She concluded that although the book suffered "from some lack of information and speculation," it provided an "honest, level-headed assessment of events little understood and still reverberating in the Bay Area."[2]

Fay might have had in mind not just the San Quentin Six trial, but also the murder of Popeye Jackson. Durden-Smith had himself started a tally of related deaths starting from the killing of the three black prisoners in the yard at Soledad on January 13, 1970. The next 27 months saw multiple related deaths at Soledad, the Marin County Civic Center, and the San Quentin Adjustment Center, ending with Jimmy Carr being gunned down in San Jose. Durden-Smith figured there were, in addition, "uncounted . . . beatings, stabbings, tear-gassing and consignments to illegal isolation cells," all in the same causal chain.³

Violence begot violence. Durden-Smith pointed out that one could actually trace all of the related deaths back further to the racial killing in the Soledad exercise yard in April of 1968 of two black prisoners. One could also add on the other end the deaths of eleven hostages and 32 inmates in September of 1971 at Attica when the prisoners erupted in response to George Jackson's death. That brought the interconnected killings to 64 so far, without including Popeye Jackson. As Fay contemplated the ongoing ramifications of George Jackson's bloody saga, she surely had no inkling that the list of tragedies would include herself before the decade was out.

Fay's review caught the eye of East Bay author and activist David Horowitz, while he was still reeling from his friend Betty Van Patter's death. The former *Ramparts* staffer had only met Fay in person once when fund-raising for his magazine in the early 1970s, but she had helped him gain access to Huey Newton at the California Men's Colony when Horowitz was writing a book about revolutionaries. After Newton's release, Horowitz had worked closely with the Panthers in their community outreach. It was Horowitz who was the principal fund-raiser and creative force behind the Panthers' community school in the Oakland flatlands that opened to great acclaim in the fall of 1973. Horowitz was now riddled with guilt. In his zeal, he had turned a blind eye to the Party's violent propensities. It was Horowitz who had recommended Betty Van Patter as a bookkeeper, only to face the horror of Betty's murder a few months later.

Horowitz had the sense from reading Fay's review of Durden-Smith's exposé that she shared his disaffection. When Fay answered the telephone Horowitz spoke guardedly about how Durden-Smith's book sounded troublingly authentic. Fay replied, "Everything that is in this book that I know about from my own experience is true." When Horowitz asked to meet with her, Fay refused. She did not want to be interviewed, but added, "I will tell you one thing: I don't defend prisoners anymore."⁴ To Horowitz, that statement spoke volumes.

Newton returned from his self-imposed exile in Cuba in 1977 to face trial for the beating of the tailor and death of the prostitute. Neither resulted in conviction. Newton was a free man once more. Meanwhile, freelance reporter Kate Coleman was asked to do an updated, in-depth article on the Black Panthers for the avant-garde magazine, *New Times*. Truth trumped politics. She and her co-author sent shock waves through the community with "The Party's Over" — the first time a member of the Movement wrote an exposé of the Panthers' history of violence.

Coleman had spoken at length with David Horowitz about the murder of Betty Van Patter and also tried to interview Fay for the piece, but Fay shook her head. She was disgusted with Newton but did not want to be quoted. Not long afterward, Newton threatened Kate Coleman's life. In May 1978, several weeks before her article hit the stands, Coleman had heavy bars installed on the first-floor windows and doors of her Berkeley home. Coleman then fled to Japan for two months, taking the risk of returning only after the hoopla created by her article had died down. By then, Huey had himself headed to U.C. Santa Cruz with his body guards and started working on a Ph.D., focused on FBI persecution of the Panther Party. Fay steered clear of Newton these days, which was easy because he now spent much of his time in Santa Cruz.

Fay told a close friend she was despondent over money worries and considering suicide. Fay and Marvin had renewed talk of divorce, but their only asset of value was the house. Fay could not bear the thought of selling it. That was where she wanted to remain into old age, entertaining grandkids. She blamed Marvin for not saving enough money and being too generous with clients behind on their payments. At work, Fay tried to relieve her frustration by bringing an organ into the office to pound on when her work day was over. It did not help much.

As Fay focused on how hard it was to make her law practice profitable, it dawned on her that she was far from alone. Many women and minorities hung out their own shingle more by necessity than by choice. Most of the state's lawyers were solo practitioners. Yet they had no voice in the Board of Governors of the State Bar of California, which had made policies for all lawyers in the state over the past fifty years. Marvin hated to see Fay depressed. When she set her sights on becoming the second woman ever to sit on the State Bar Board, he encouraged her to go for it.

Fay quickly accumulated hundreds of endorsements from former colleagues at the ACLU and CWL and lawyers who volunteered to take cases through the Prison Law Project. She decided to focus her campaign on bread-and-butter issues for solo practitioners, such as affordable insurance. Fay worried out loud about the balance between cultivating paying clients and volunteering for good causes. "What happens to the lawyer who does ten years pro bono and wants to send his kids to college?"[5]

In her quixotic campaign, Fay had tough competition — a popular past president of the San Francisco Bar. *The San Francisco Examiner* would label the race "Mr. Inside" versus "Ms. Outside." Bob Raven, then a leading anti-trust lawyer at one of San Francisco's top firms, had a compelling life story. The son of Midwestern sharecroppers had worked during the Depression on Detroit's assembly lines. In World War II, he flew 33 bombing missions and returned a hero. As a young lawyer, Raven became a pioneer in getting downtown firms to welcome Jewish lawyers and then women and minorities, while helping transform the San Francisco Bar into one of the most socially conscious in the nation. (Later, as President of the American Bar Association, he would get it to embrace free legal services for the poor, earning him the nickname "revolutionary in pinstripes.)"[6]

Fay was undaunted by Raven. She eagerly glad-handed anyone who might be persuaded to endorse her to speak up for solo practitioners. One day, she had coffee with her old friend Ying Lee, who now sat on the Berkeley City Council. Ying had begun running a mile three times a week to keep in shape and invited Fay to join her. Within two months, Fay was running twice as much as her old friend and also began lifting weights. A year later, Ying concluded that Fay's new physical fitness regimen was probably the reason she survived the attempt on her life.

By June of 1978, Fay was in excellent health and great spirits. Among the many envelope stuffers for her campaign literature was Mario Savio, now a burned-out activist with his own family to support. Fay's maverick campaign also excited feminists. One recent graduate from Golden Gate Law School fell in love with Fay at first sight. Katherine Morse had been a grade school teacher in Kansas. In law

REFLECTIONS IN THE MIRROR

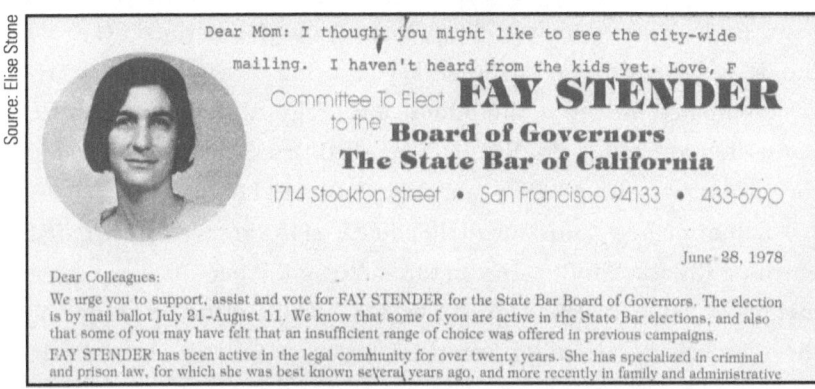

Ms. Outside
Fay hoped to become the second woman ever elected to the State Bar Board and the first to represent struggling solo practitioners.

Mr. Inside
Bob Raven (pictured in 1976 with his wife Leslie-Kay Raven) was a senior partner in a top San Francisco firm known for his Progressive views. As a young lawyer, Raven prodded downtown firms to start hiring Jewish lawyers. He then championed the hiring of women and minority associates and helped transform the San Francisco Bar into one of the most socially conscious in the nation. Later, as President of the American Bar Association, Raven convinced the ABA to embrace free legal services for the poor, earning him the nickname "revolutionary in pinstripes."

1978 Candidates for a seat on the Board of Governors of the State Bar of California school, the newcomer in her mid-thirties stood out, a five-foot-eight extrovert in loose overalls leading a coterie of self-described dykes. At the debate she witnessed between Fay and Bob Raven, Katherine felt Fay dominated the room with intense electricity. After passing the Bar, Katherine worked for Dru Ramey. She asked Dru's advice about taking the summer to work on Fay's campaign. Dru told her, "Go for it."

Katherine began working night and day at the Stender office doing anything Fay asked for to assist in the campaign. When the two women met at the Hyatt Regency for drinks, Fay borrowed the piano during the musician's breaks and mesmerized Katherine with a lively Gershwin melody. Katherine quickly became Fay's constant companion. Fay was petrified of the potential impact of her new secret lover on her career and family relationships.

Raven had been so cordial throughout the campaign that Fay had grown to like him. She praised her opponent for promoting women like CWL co-founder Joanne Garvey to positions of power in the Bar. To Fay's embarrassment, Garvey endorsed Raven. But Fay's pitch was: "It is still important that women, non-whites, non-corporation lawyers, people who have spent time in the dungeons of the prisons, the non-traditionalists, the public lawyers be represented."[7]

After Fay held a campaign party at her home to get out the vote, she told Katherine she had two dreams. In the first, Fay won the race; in the other she lost. Katherine said, "Maybe you are of two minds. You want both." Fay refused to consider losing an option. When Fay attended traffic school for yet another speeding ticket, she chased a lawyer in the same class down at a break only to have him tell her, "I already voted for you, Fay."

Moments like this reinforced Fay's belief that local practitioners did not pigeon-hole her by her past as a radical lawyer for black militants. Fay confided in Katherine her disdain for what Newton had become and resentment of how he treated her after all she had done for him. When Katherine saw Newton pass by in a red Mercedes on the highway in Oakland one day, she could well understand Fay's original infatuation. Even to a confirmed lesbian, the man was a "good-looking hunk."

When voting by mail had closed, each candidate sent a

representative to watch the vote count. Katherine's heart sank when she had to call Fay with the results: two to one for Raven. Fay took the loss hard. Once again, despite nonstop preparation, she had not made the cheerleading squad.

Fay took time to relax with family on the patio of her sister's home in San Mateo in September 1977. Lisie is on the lounge chair with her daughter Lora seated behind her. Fay had grown estranged from Lisie in the 1960s, but bonded with her sister starting in the mid–1970s when Fay began embracing feminism. Ruby Abrahams is seated on the right, closest to the camera, with Fay seated behind her. Their relationship always remained prickly.

*Sketch of Huey Newton on trial in Oakland in 1978
by Don Juhlin, reproduced courtesy of the artist*

Katherine Morse saw Newton in a red Mercedes in Oakland in 1978 and understood Fay's prior infatuation. Even to a confirmed lesbian, the man was a "good-looking hunk." Fay had last been in touch with Huey by letter in the summer of 1974 to see if he objected to her assisting estranged Panthers Eldridge and Kathleen Cleaver return to the U.S. from Algeria, where they had lived in exile since 1969. Newton did not respond. He had other concerns. After driving Bobby Seale from the Panther Party and leaving it in Elaine Brown's hands, he fled to Cuba in August 1974. Newton returned in the summer of 1977 to face still-pending 1974 charges of assaulting a tailor and murdering a prostitute. Represented by new high-powered defense counsel, he was acquitted of the assault charge and got the murder charges dismissed after two hung juries.

■ 6 ■
Temps Perdu

> *"One runs away to find oneself
> and finds no one at home."*[1]
> — JOAN DIDION

Earlier in the summer of 1978, Fay's high school friend Hilde had invited Fay to accompany her on a three-week vacation in late September in Greece. Hilde was now a philosophy professor in Massachusetts. The two had kept up over the years; their children sometimes joined each other's family on vacation or stayed in the other's home. Hilde's daughter had even worked at the Prison Law Project. This European trip would give Fay a much-needed break. Marvin encouraged her to use the opportunity to decide once and for all whether she wanted out of their marriage.

Fay was no longer worried about financing Neal and Oriane's further education. Marvin's father planned to leave all his money to his grandchildren. Oriane seemed undecided about college and Neal, at twenty, was taking a year off in France to find himself. On the eve of Fay's trip to Europe, Fay broke off her relationship with Katherine. She said Marvin insisted on it if Fay wanted to keep alive the possibility that they might reconcile. Still, Fay left Katherine with the hope of getting back together again if she and Marvin divorced. Fay thought she might spend another month or so in Europe after Hilde returned to the states. That would give Fay the opportunity to reflect more fully on the future of her marriage, her sexual orientation, her career — all now up in the air.

Before she left California, Fay arranged to meet Hilde in France. Fay's first priority was hooking up briefly with her son Neal, who was already in Paris. Fay then headed off with Hilde to Provence on September 27th to stay with Hilde's British cousin near Cannes, on their way to Italy and on to Greece. Hilde's cousin worked for Amnesty International, which intrigued Fay as a possible alternative career. She received no encouragement from Hilde's cousins, who were offended by their brash houseguest's radical feminism.

As they headed to Italy, friction developed between Fay and Hilde, who was eager to reach Greece, the ancestral home of Western philosophy — Hilde's whole reason for the trip. Fay convinced Hilde to spend a day touring Florence, where Hilde had already been. To make up time, the two friends spent only two hours in Rome between trains, dining at a restaurant next to the railroad station, before they boarded the overnight milk run around the boot to Brindisi, sleeping in their seats.

Throughout Italy, the two women had argued each time they got off the train whether to pay porters to carry their baggage or lug it themselves. When they arrived at Brindisi, the dilapidated seacoast town struck Fay as a drearier version of Tijuana. Fay wrestled her suitcase from a porter at the station to avoid a fee, then clambered after Hilde to the docks only to learn that the only boat that day to Patras would be a twelve-hour wait. They settled in a nearby, grimy café from which Fay eyed the hundred other weary travelers also taking the cheap route to Greece — students carrying backpacks and middle-aged people on tight budgets. She had already realized that the rich flew from Rome to Athens, and if she had done so, too, she could have seen the sights of Rome instead of being stuck in Brindisi.

The two friends' mutual irritation, like that of sibling rivals, came pouring forth as they passed the time until their departure. Fay wanted to relax and be pampered on this vacation, Hilde wanted to experience life much as the locals did and soak up the culture. Fay thought they cleared the air and reached an understanding. Hilde began to feel this trip was cursed.

As they pushed and shoved their way through the crowd toward the boat in the light rain, clutching their tickets, exhaustion and annoyance overtook Fay once more. She snapped at a fellow American who compared the rope that harbor police used to hold back the tourists to one he had seen recently at Dachau, used to herd Jews at the prison camp. Fay had known that being Jewish would affect her European experience, but was surprised how her feelings bubbled so quickly to the surface. At home, she only felt the weight of her Jewish heritage on rare occasions; being abroad intensified her sensibilities. It dawned on Fay how much she had turned into a prototypical ugly American as she barked in English at the ship's porter. The poor man was just doing his job, trying to load her luggage, while she demanded to know how much he would charge.

After Fay sailed through customs, she looked back to see Hilde singled out by one of the Italian officials, studying her German passport. Fay recalled how Hilde's family had fled to escape the Nazis in the 1930s. Frightened for her friend, Fay shoved back through the crowd and urged Hilde to take back her documents and keep moving. Fay was proud that her instinct was to stand her ground at Hilde's side, as the irate man yelled at Fay in Italian and tried to push her away. Finally, he waved Hilde through. Neither woman later spoke of this incident, but Fay wondered whether if the stop had been random or because Hilde fit a disfavored profile.

Once on board, Hilde settled in the cabin and studied her Greek phrase book. Fay headed for the ship's bar, where she ordered cognac and opened up a novel. That evening, they made friends with an Italian-Swiss couple. The husband admitted he did not usually much care for Americans. The next day Fay and Hilde endured a long bus ride to Athens. What struck Fay most on arrival was the city's squalor, men ogling foreign women and the vendors in the plazas who tended not to give back the right change. Oriane had warned Fay that hashish was everywhere in Greece, but Fay saw no obvious signs of its use. To her relief, the hotel Hilde had booked was clean, comfortable and not overpriced, with helpful middle-aged clerks who spoke some English.

That first night they dined at a terraced restaurant on a promontory near the Acropolis, joined by the Italian-Swiss couple they had met on the ferry. As they shared several bottles of wine, Fay was startled to look up at the rocky hillside to see it overrun by feral cats. Hilde tingled with joy, awestruck that she had reached her destination. She announced her plan to visit the ancient ruin early in the morning before the crowds came. Fay preferred to sleep in.

The next day, long after Hilde had left their room, Fay made her own way over to the Acropolis. By midmorning, the monument was swarming with organized tours of Europeans and Americans, bi-lingual guides and cameras. Adjacent to the Acropolis was the Theatre of Dionysus, the reputed birthplace of the world's first tragedies staged in the sixth century B.C. Fay realized how much her appreciation for ancient Greece had dissipated since she was a freshman at Reed. Now, she wondered about the slaves who built the temples and why her professors had never credited ancient Jewish culture with any lasting influence on Western tradition. The experience clearly did not speak to her soul as it did Hilde's, or so she thought. A year later she would identify completely with Greek tragedy as a metaphor for her life.

What Fay found instead at the time she visited the Acropolis in 1978 was an overwhelming urge to reaffirm her own heritage. It was almost the High Holy Days. Fay had attended Kol Nidre services on Yom Kippur every year since her father died almost a dozen years before. When Fay spied an American tourist at the Acropolis wearing a Star of David necklace, the young woman obligingly inquired of her guide if there was a synagogue nearby. Fay thought the Greek woman grimaced as she indicated she did not know. Later that day Fay talked Hilde into canceling an excursion to the Peloponnesus to join Fay at services. Fay appreciated her friend's sacrifice, realizing Hilde harbored no similar yearning.

Neither Fay nor Hilde knew what the current Jewish situation was in Greece. Reportedly, no Jews were left after World War II ended. The tourist map did not indicate any synagogues. The obvious place for the pair to ask next was at the front desk of their hotel, but instinctively,

The Parthenon in 1978

Fay and Hilde toured the World Heritage site of the Acropolis shortly after arriving in Athens in September 1978. On the south side of the Parthenon was the Theatre of Dionysus, famed through the ages as the birthplace of tragedy in the sixth century B.C. – predating the Parthenon.

they both felt uneasy at the prospect. Instead, Fay made an excursion to the high-security El Al airline office in Athens, which phoned the Israeli Embassy. It turned out that the synagogue was near their hotel. The two friends still had no idea if it was walking distance. Still nervous, they simply asked the concierge where the street was located. He immediately realized they wanted "the Israeli church" and had been too self-conscious to say so, despite having peppered him with questions for the past couple of days for other information. He was happy to point the way.

Fay and Hilde gave themselves ample time to walk in the early evening light. When they came upon the synagogue there were several policemen milling around outside. As the two women entered the building, they noticed that only men filled the pews and none were welcoming. Fay sized the group up as lower middle class and provincial, but definitely Jewish, unlike most men she had seen on Athens' streets. Where were the women? The caretaker's wife took pity on the befuddled pair and ushered them to a stairway. This time, roles were reversed as Fay soaked up the atmosphere. Hilde barely concealed her anger that women and young children were shunted upstairs to a stifling balcony, where they sat with few prayer books, no direct line of sight and no official role while the self-important men paraded in their prayer shawls below.

Most of the chants were unfamiliar. Hilde's few phrases of Greek helped as the two assisted one Greek mother with a restless four-year-old. It occurred to Hilde that the men likely heard them whispering and dismissed all the women as gossips. It made her even angrier. Fay was glad to see three American girls attending the service. She also spoke with a well-dressed American woman, who confided that her son had been killed six months before.

Fay felt a kinship with everyone there. She wanted to stay until the rabbi blew the shofar to signal the end of the service. It held special meaning for her as a ritual her father had captured in a painting that she had hung in her office. But after three long hours Fay took pity on Hilde. Actually, the Greek service did not inspire Fay like the far shorter Kol Nidre service at the orthodox synagogue in her own

Source: https://commons.wikimedia.org/wiki/File:Etz_Hayyim_Synagogue_(Athens)_03.jpg, (© dafniotis)

Etz Chaim Orthodox Synagogue Athens

While visiting the Acropolis, Fay felt an overwhelming urge to reaffirm her own heritage. Fay had attended Kol Nidre services on Yom Kippur every year since her father died in 1966. She kept in her office a painting of a rabbi her father had done. On the eve of the High Holy Days, Fay talked Hilde into attending services at one of the few remaining synagogues in Athens.

Sketch of Orthodox rabbi by author's mother, Amalia "Mali" Pearlman, in author's collection.

Berkeley neighborhood she attended at home. This one left Fay with a flat feeling. Her strongest ties were to friends and family, not rituals. As they left, Fay had no intention of fasting, as observant Jews would now do through the following day. Instead, Fay rewarded Hilde's patience by taking her out to dinner.

The next day they left for the island of Crete. Fay envisioned several days on the warm beach by a white-washed villa, reclining in wooden lounge chairs, each with a book and cocktail in hand. Hilde had no such luxury in mind. She wanted to trek through the island's rich trove of antiquities. The Minoan culture, named for its legendary first king, Minos, dated back to 2600 B.C., the very origin of Greek civilization. The myths surrounding the island provided an abundant resource for the tragic plays Fay had studied in college. Minos was semi-divine, the son of Zeus and Europa, for whom the European continent was named. King Minos took as his queen Pasiphae, the daughter of the Sun. Legend had it that Pasiphae mated with a bull, producing the Minotaur — a monster with a man's body and a bull's head and tail. King Minos kept the Minotaur in a labyrinth where the half-man, half-beast was later slain by Theseus. Among the children of King Minos and Pasiphae was Phaedra, who married Theseus after he became king of Athens. Though these stories had once held Fay in thrall, unlike Hilde, Fay was now focused on creature comforts, not ancient history.

Fay despised the dingy hotel Hilde had booked and spent evenings looking for alternate accommodations. They rented a car to explore the mountainous terrain. Hilde drove too slowly for Fay, who took over the wheel and frightened Hilde with her recklessness. Hilde found that her phrase book again came in handy when asking directions. She wondered how Fay would have fared without her.

The original plan had been for the two to use their Eurail passes to travel on to Istanbul from Athens, take another train to Rome and then fly back to the states. Hilde knew Fay might stay longer in Europe to attend a United Nations conference on children and the law in Stockholm in early November. Just before she left, Fay had worked on a law review article on joint custody and told Hilde she might represent California Women Lawyers at that historic gathering in Sweden.

Palace at Knossos

Hilde wanted to visit ruins from the Minoan era on Crete – the origin of Greek civilization during the Bronze Age, circa 2600 B.C.–1400 B.C.

Grecotel Creta Palace, Missiria, Crete

Fay wanted to pamper herself at a luxury hotel on the beach.

By the time they arrived back in Athens from Crete, Fay had developed a bad cold and decided not to accompany Hilde back to Rome. Instead, Fay planned to fly directly from Athens to Geneva to visit friends on her way to Stockholm. Hilde felt abandoned. It was out of the question for Hilde to take the train by herself to Istanbul. Turkey and Greece were then on such bad terms that Turkey did not even appear on Greek maps. Hilde booked a train back through Yugoslavia instead. Even in a first-class car, a Greek man carrying a gun made a pass at her.

Fay had no idea how furious Hilde was at her as Fay spent the next day-and-a-half in an Athens airport hotel. Fay spent that time nursing her cold and reading newspapers and novels, only emerging for quick meals in its dimly lit restaurant. Fay felt liberated, having the chance to rest her aching feet from so much walking. She saw a lame three-year-old Gypsy girl begging in the streets and was halfway tempted to take her along when she left Athens, but stopped herself. Fay went back to reading the papers, offended to discover that Qantas, the airline she had taken to Europe, had recently agreed not to book any Jewish passengers on flights through Syria. Fay vowed to boycott Qantas from then on in protest.

Fay's reaction to the Qantas announcement reminded her of how distanced from others in the New Left she felt over the troubled Middle East situation. She did not see many of her Leftist colleagues at the Guild criticizing the lack of social justice in Arab countries. Instead, though mostly Jews themselves, they condemned Israelis as "pigs" and elevated Palestinians to the pedestal the Panthers formerly occupied. Fay agreed the Palestinians deserved their own homeland, but so did the survivors of the Holocaust. From afar, Fay had more difficulty understanding how Jewish-born radicals developed such antipathy for their own.

Once in Geneva, Fay had only planned to stay for a night with Congressman Dellums' former aide, Lee Halterman, and his wife Roberta and her small son from a prior marriage. The young couple had just arrived in August for a six-month stay while Lee clerked at the headquarters of the International Commission of Jurists. Fay had engineered this plum opportunity for Lee to work on human rights issues by writing a glowing letter of recommendation earlier that year to its Secretary General, whom she had met through her prison reform work. Only two days after the Haltermans moved in, their new landlady had reproached them in alarm at the hippie she found parked on the bench outside, who had asked in French for the American couple. It was Fay's son Neal, whom the Haltermans then hosted for a week, appeasing the landlady with three francs per day for the extra burden on the utilities. Lee Halterman was even happier to show his gratitude to Fay herself.

While traveling to Geneva, Fay became preoccupied with a recent exchange of letters with Marvin. It greatly upset her that he was pressing for a decision about their marriage. She did not realize how exhausted and bedraggled she felt until she reached the Haltermans' clean, homey apartment and they put their son on the couch while offering her his room. From the apartment, she made an emotional transatlantic call to Marvin, reaching no resolution. She needed more time. Observing her anguish, Lee and Roberta invited Fay to stay longer. Though Fay did not feel comfortable confiding all of her troubles to her young friends, she told them in general terms of her new feminist perspective, fueled by her anger at the lack of appreciation she received for her prison work, especially from Huey Newton.

The Haltermans knew that Fay's feelings on black militants were complicated. Two years' earlier, Fay had given them as a wedding present one of her cherished letters from George Jackson. Now, they lent sympathetic ears as she angrily bemoaned how she had sacrificed her family life for so long to work for Newton's freedom night and day. She shared the deep humiliation she felt when Newton suddenly gave her the silent treatment, broadcasting his ostracism of her at a Panther party shortly after his release. They realized there must have been more to such a bitter memory of an eight-year-old slight, but they did not wish to pry. Roberta ended up playing hostess for the next week, taking Fay sightseeing and shopping, before driving her to the train station, reinvigorated by their warmth and generosity.

After leaving Switzerland, Fay stopped for three days in Paris. The side trip was not to see Neal — who was now enjoying life on a French farm, milking goats — but to visit an old Leftist friend, who had lived abroad for 30 years in an inter-racial marriage. Fay enjoyed once again being pampered. When the conversation turned from family updates to politics and religion, she tried not to offend her hostess by arguing too passionately about the Palestinian question. Fay had in fact reached the conclusion that the very lives of her children and unborn grandchildren depended on Israel's continued existence. Fay's friend also obligingly took her to a pub that had a piano bar. Fay had confided that she was exploring the idea of returning to Paris to work there as an entertainer if she changed her mind about returning to California after the conference in Stockholm.

Fay then headed for uncharted territory. She took the train through Germany in a couchette shared with five other people. When they stopped in Köln after midnight to let two German men off, Fay wondered if it was the same station Hilde's family had passed through in the '30s with their jewels and money sewn into their five-year-old's teddy bear. The train continued by ferry to Copenhagen where Fay spent a day. She checked out a piano bar there as well and dined with a polite, fashionably dressed divorcé, who said he was a house painter. It surprised Fay somewhat when he pulled a mezuzah from his pocket that he intended to affix the next day by the front door of his latest client. He assumed Fay was Jewish, too, and she nodded. On the train to Stockholm, Fay had a whole day of staring out the window at the Danish and Swedish countryside to ponder the question of both her ethnic and sexual identity. She thought once again of Katherine, to whom she had penned four letters and posted none.

Fay had been traveling just over a month by the end of October when she settled into her second-floor room at the Hotel Karlaagen in Stockholm. Soon she learned how to navigate the city's subways, but enjoyed the warmth and solitude of her room better than the gloom and cold of Stockholm. It generally turned dark at 3:30 p.m. Sometimes the sun did not shine for days. The prices also surprised her. At a bar, she paid as much as $7 for a mixed drink and $3 for a beer. Even coffee was $1.25 and, unlike at home, one got no free refill. Her funds would not last long if a moderate dinner out with wine and dessert cost $20 to

$25. Fay took to eating in her room. She would have to find a job if she were to stay more than a couple of weeks longer.

Fay soon made connections with several Swedish feminists who spoke fluent English. The women greeted her warmly, but Fay felt oddly isolated. Every feminist she met was an avowed Marxist. They had all just participated in demonstrations against the historic Camp David Accords negotiated between Israel and Egypt by President Carter. They were young and mostly married. Their spouses helped with childcare and household chores; their biggest issue was women's employment outside the home. Fay joined in a torch-lit demonstration through downtown Stockholm one cold night on behalf of a woman being tried for killing a rapist. Back home in California the year before, Fay's feminist friends had supported Inez Garcia's successful effort to win acquittal in a similar high-profile murder case. But Fay made clear her disagreement with her new Marxist acquaintances about the situation in the Middle East. Swedish dinner parties were by formal invitation, even among radicals. Fay began receiving fewer of them.

After attending the Children and the Law Conference, Fay redoubled her efforts to find a job playing in a piano bar. Most required singing, which Fay could not carry off, but she did not want to go home yet. The wintry beauty of Stockholm suited her mood as she contemplated her long-term and immediate future. She found a job playing piano and switched to an efficiency apartment on the thirteenth floor of another hotel. She settled into performing at the bar in the evenings and spending her days mostly holed up in her room, trying to write. Fay had assumed that lack of time had previously kept her from putting her ideas to paper, but, with hours on end at her disposal, she often had a mental block. Her room felt like a prison cell, albeit one she could walk out of any day and go home.

Fay was reminded of George Jackson as she began exercising vigorously until she could do 20 pushups in a row. Through diet and her daily regimen, she gained strength and delighted in watching years of accumulated bulge around her stomach disappear. At home, she still had all her files from the *Soledad Brothers* case. She considered whether she should write about George. How honest could she be about the delusional revolutionary? Fay had other ideas as well. She already had extensive notes for an ambitious history of English constitutional law and other notes for a study of primitive women and the origins of feminism.

Fay began to feel like an expatriate hovering between two worlds. Though she flirted with the idea of making a permanent home in Stockholm, she did not feel she had yet gotten a true sense of the Swedish people. It troubled her to read that Sweden had fallen under Nazi influence during World War II. She missed having someone like Hilde in whom to confide. Fay kept up with news from home with her new shortwave radio but wanted more insight than could be derived from that distance. The week before Thanksgiving came the startling news out of Jamestown, Guyana, of the mass murder-suicide of Jim Jones and his followers. Jones was a client of Charles Garry's. Garry had in fact been visiting the Jamestown compound at the time and barely escaped the carnage by fleeing through the jungle.

Fay found great comfort far from home exchanging letters and postcards with close friends and family, especially Lisie, who had just returned from a trip with her husband to Israel. Fay kept up correspondence with Marvin, remaining undecided about their marriage and when she would return. On Thanksgiving eve, Fay finally wrote a warm letter to Katherine describing her life in Stockholm, her circle of new acquaintances, but no true friends. Fay told Katherine she was still torn over her future direction, cautioning that nothing had changed since their breakup.

The following week, Fay had more shocking news from San Francisco. Mayor George Moscone and Supervisor Harvey Milk, the first openly gay member of the city's governing Board of Supervisors, had just been assassinated. Only a year before, Fay had joined in celebrating Milk's historic election. Fay wondered if the local community considered his killer a misguided lunatic who needed medical treatment or favored the death penalty for his hate crime. She was beginning to feel the pull to return to the Bay Area. Still, Fay shied from committing to an openly lesbian relationship with Katherine. What would her children think? Her sister? Her mother?

The only person in Stockholm with whom Fay felt no cultural or language barrier was a Swedish literary editor she had just met, who had taught for a semester in Texas. Though he was politically conservative, their intellectual interests overlapped. Fay learned something new about herself, that she could be passionately attracted to a man whose politics she abhorred. He shared with her his experience in the American South where the blacks he met all seemed subservient, unlike the African blacks he knew. Fay tried to discuss with her new lover her conflicted feelings about Israel and the Palestinians, only to be rebuffed by his view that all the Jews he knew were too touchy on the subject to address it dispassionately. Fay decided to stay in Stockholm until mid-January, hoping that, by then, she would gain clarity on her future.

Meanwhile, Fay spent more time reflecting on her own identity. What it meant to be an American — appreciating the benefits of freedom of travel, of individual expression, of informality, self-confidence. She contrasted that with what it meant to be female in a world where women were traditionally subservient, and, what preoccupied her most, what it meant to be a Jew. She started a diary about her overseas trip. Her very first thoughts were about how her religious heritage colored all her observations. She expressed the self-revelation as one that slowly dawned on her: "It is not clear to me what stirred my knowledge that being Jewish would bring a different daily consciousness to me when traveling in Europe. But I did know it, dimly at first, and it was no surprise to me when it resonated."[2] Reflecting on recent political arguments with her new Gentile lover, Fay noted the paranoia of being a Jew, "which feeds on the gas oven reality and . . . endless more subtle reminders, which haunt the most trivial dinner conversations and can shadow the most intimate friendship."[3]

One day buying a ticket for the subway, Fay struck up a conversation with an English-speaking Finnish girl, Oriane's age. The girl wore a feminist button. They met several times afterward for coffee. The teenager shared her aspirations for the London stage and offered to take Fay on a hike to her favorite local destination, a small island on the outskirts of Stockholm. It reminded Fay somewhat of a special hillside view in Marin County she liked to share with visitors. As they sat talking over tea and cookies, Fay made a point to tell her young friend she was

Jewish, in case that might alter her offer of companionship. Fay was touched when the teenager wept copiously to think that should make a difference.

Fay was invited to attend another international seminar in Warsaw on children's rights in early December and decided to represent CWL at that event as well. She wanted to take the opportunity to find out more about her roots. From the capital, it would be only a short side trip to her father's home city of Brest-Litovsk. She made her way one snowy day at the end of November to the Russian consulate in Stockholm to secure a visa and learned to her surprise that she need only make arrangements at a tourist office.

Fay had read of the Warsaw uprising and researched her ancestry on her father's side before leaving for Europe. Nowhere in the tourist literature she now perused could she find reference to the former Jewish ghetto in the capital city — the largest one established during World War II by the Nazis. The absence of any information on the ghetto was especially noticeable because sites of former Nazi concentration camps were marked by small notations on the map.

Upon her arrival in Warsaw, Fay signed up for a city tour. She wanted to see the monument erected after the war to honor the poorly equipped Polish Jews who rose up against Hitler's final solution in April of 1943. Fay empathized with their story. She had been in her late twenties when American author Leon Uris wrote his best-selling novel *Mila 18* about the Polish Jewish resistance fighters. But the tour bus made no stop at the memorial to the ill-fated uprising. It made Fay angry to have the Polish capital's ugly past glossed over. Everyone should know how the Warsaw ghetto started with nearly half a million people in 1941 — 30 percent of the city's population — but dwindled in two years' time to 37,000. Visitors should learn how the Nazis decimated the Warsaw Jewish population by herding residents onto trains bound for extermination or hard labor, and leaving others to battle starvation and disease. After the uprising in mid-May of 1943, only a few stragglers survived.

It also bothered Fay to see no recognition of the vibrant Jewish culture that had flourished for centuries alongside Catholic neighbors before the Russian pogroms and the Nazis ended it. Impoverished Polish peasants reportedly received two pounds of sugar from German officials for each Jew they killed. Now, when Fay attended the Warsaw Symphony, she was anguished by the absence of any musicians who looked even faintly Jewish. Fay recalled that, when she was young, she wondered whether Christians were right that Jews had brought persecution on themselves by some internal flaw. Now she scoffed at the self-loathing Jews among her Leftist colleagues. Fay saw Jews targeted for hate and oppression through the ages similarly to blacks brought on slave ships from Africa. Societal forces were to blame, not the victims.

Fay felt a special kinship with Jews who clung to their identity even as they were herded into concentration camps. Acutely sensitive to her ethnicity, Fay also realized she was the lone American at the second joint conference of attorneys from Western European and Eastern socialist countries. Simultaneous translators facilitated discussion among those speaking Polish, Russian, English and French, but culture clashes were still evident. Westerners were more argumentative, criticizing Marxist suppression of religion while freely admitting the West's own failures; socialists only reported successes, rigidly adhering to the Communist Party line.

Earlier that year Fay had published a review of the memoir *The Romance of American Communism*, by Vivian Gornick. Fay had been struck by the similarity between the original social justice appeal of Communism and the ancient Talmudic quandary: "If I am not for myself, who will be for me? if I am only for myself, what am I? and if not now, when?"[4] Fay had long since concluded that the Communist promise of human salvation that Stanley Moore had bought into so many years ago, turned out to be a Faustian bargain with the devil, characterized by sexism, rigidity and unyielding self-importance.

Fay's eyes had been opened to a reappraisal of Communism by reading a book by a former Communist criticizing her, mostly male, ex-colleagues. Fay considered the book to have been written "with love, absolute honesty, critical acumen, and shrewd psychological analysis."[5] It made Fay wonder, "Will feminism ever be as blind to human oppression as the CPUSA was to Stalinism?" Fay now considered herself to be following a "better-lit pathway," one in which she had the freedom "to question and to say no to the inhumane command, no matter its source." In contrast, Fay had written a dismissive review of Jessica Mitford's *A Fine Old Conflict* as a disappointing celebrity memoir, despite Mitford's ability to make her laugh out loud and Mitford's unparalleled "eye for the distinction between the hip and the dreary."[6]

Back in Stockholm, Fay decided that clinging to Marvin and her rocky marriage was premised on fear of the unknown. She was now willing to trade safety for new adventure, believing she had come to terms with her prior bouts of self-doubt. Neal was headed back to Berkeley to finish up his undergraduate work at Cal. Her daughter Oriane, her sister Lisie and her mother would all provide a support network along with her many friends. Fay felt she could make it on her own.

Fay finalized her plans to return to the United States in January 1979. She would first dissolve her law partnership with Marvin and then spend the next year writing, expecting Ruby to loan her the money. Fay had already drafted an outline of a paper on the origins of female subjugation. She wanted to do more thorough research on exactly why men dominated the marketplace and culture of almost all societies from the very beginning of civilization. Fay also intended to write more literary critiques for the new feminist magazine *Chrysalis* and the *San Francisco Review of Books*, where she was now on the editorial board. Perhaps she would try her hand again at teaching law. She wrote to Katherine that she was headed back to Berkeley but again cautioned she did not know yet what might happen between them.

Fay booked a flight to New York in late January and wrote to Hilde to meet her there, excited to share her new philosophical views with her old friend. Fay also wanted to get Hilde's reaction to a new review Fay had prepared for *Chrysalis*. Fay remained oblivious to how angry Hilde had been when they parted in Athens, and had no clue about Hilde's later harrowing experience on the train ride back through Yugoslavia. But Hilde realized that one could not stay friends with Fay all these years without a high tolerance for her self-absorption.

Hilde gamely came down from Massachusetts to meet Fay in Manhattan. Fay had lost a lot of weight since Hilde had last seen her and was now down to a trim 125 pounds. Fay shared her feminist writing with Hilde. As a disciplined scholar, Hilde was unimpressed. Fay also confided in Hilde her torrid affair in Stockholm with a conservative intellectual. She and Hilde had a long philosophical discussion on the proper relationship of politics and sex. Fay had always been most attracted to forbidden sex with radicals. When she thought she broke her own political taboo in Sweden, it had not yet dawned on Fay that, for the past four years, she had actually been on the path to renouncing her Leftist politics.

Fay wanted Hilde's input on another idea. Though Fay had told friends and family she was headed back to California, she still wavered. Fay had fond memories of prior visits to New York, including one excursion with Bob Richter to the Waldorf Astoria, where she had spied Cole Porter's piano on display in the lobby. Fay had sneaked over and begun to play the historic instrument before the bellman jumped up to remove her. He had then stopped in fascination at the beauty of her performance. Fay enjoyed the effect she had on people like that bellman and on Katherine, like Bob Richter's fellow prisoners long ago in Tucson and the intimate, cocktail-sipping audiences she had attracted at the piano bar in Stockholm.

Fay asked Hilde to accompany her to check out piano bars in New York. If she could afford it, Fay could easily imagine giving up her law career and starting life anew in Manhattan. The Duplex, a cabaret and comedy club on the west side of Greenwich Village, was particularly well known for helping launch the careers of Woody Allen and Dick Cavett as well as Barbra Streisand. Several others were a possibility, though not if they required her to sing in accompaniment. She knew she lacked a professional singing voice. If an opportunity presented itself to support herself as a piano player, Fay thought it would be fun — to entertain people, like Billy Joel did, and "forget about life for a while." This would mean not only divorcing Marvin, but telling Katherine good-bye as well. But with a few notable exceptions — like Bobby Short at the ritzy Carlyle Hotel on the Upper East Side — most pianists in Manhattan made little money. Not realizing that her life might hang in the balance, Fay boarded a plane headed back to California.

Fay likely sent this photo to her sister from Stockholm in late 1978. Lisie kept it on her desk for the rest of her life.

■ 7 ■
Death Comes Knocking

"La fille de Minos et de Pasiphaë"[1]
— Jean Racine

Fay had delayed her return from Europe well past January 5th, her 25th wedding anniversary. That symbolic act of indifference greatly relieved Marvin. During Fay's lengthy stay in Europe, Marvin had moved to San Francisco, starting a new serious relationship with Dru Ramey. Dru dreaded having to tell Fay. But Fay's response when she heard was, "Better you than some bimbo." Marvin told Fay he wanted to begin divorce proceedings right away so he could marry Dru.

Only then did Fay reach out to Katherine Morse, who could not wait to shower Fay with affection. Fay was full of energy and ambition, proud to have lost 35 pounds since she met Katherine the summer before. Fay was also bursting with ideas now that her mother had agreed to finance a sabbatical from her law practice. Katherine took Fay on double dates with other lesbian friends. She read with great interest Fay's feminist writing. Fay still worried about her children's reaction, but they were fine with it. At times, Katherine got along better with Oriane than Fay did.

Katherine sometimes spent the night at Fay's home, usually bringing along Daisy, her Sheltie-Keeshound. Katherine was delighted that Fay had a grand piano in her living room — it had been a gift from

Fay's mother. Fay played when the mood struck her or when Katherine asked her to, taking delight in showing off how her ability to improvise. In turn, Katherine clucked at Fay's lack of domestic skills; she was happy to don an apron and tidy up. Katherine asked why Fay locked up her stereo in a closet. Fay explained that they had once had a burglary. Since then, they had their household window vents redesigned so no one could climb through them again. Katherine wondered why Fay bothered. The front door still just had a curtain over a pane of glass.

Fay's cat Puddin' was the only one unhappy with the new situation. The family had never owned a dog. Though Fay tolerated Daisy, she was not that fond of dogs. Growing up, she and her sister had once wanted a collie, but, as an adult, Fay was a confirmed cat person, enjoying their combination of affection and independence.

Accustomed to far more organization, Katherine had to adjust. Life with Fay was a whirlwind of spontaneous activity. They often made last minute decisions to go to a movie or concert or college gymnastic performance. Yet Katherine noticed that Fay could be devastated by the most trivial things. When Fay backed into a parking space and dented the bumper of her Toyota, she obsessed about the incident for hours. Usually, Katherine put up with Fay's impetuosity without protest, but not when Fay insisted on dropping in unannounced at the home of a former Prison Law Project volunteer. The single mother was overwhelmed with grief, struggling with a new baby and coping with the death of her mother. When they left, Katherine and Fay engaged in the biggest argument they ever had about Fay's thoughtlessness and insensitivity to others.

Given what Fay revealed of her prior complicated love life, Katherine had reason to doubt their relationship would last. There was a part of Fay she just did not fathom. But now, for the most part, life was exhilarating. Like Fay, Katherine was then focused on public interest work. She had landed a full-time job assisting the elderly poor with their legal problems. This gave Fay hours on end to focus on her writing. Sometimes she took a break for a spirited game of racquetball with Katherine.

Fay happily pursued several projects at once. She sent board members of the ACLU her suggestion to rethink its position on the First Amendment in the wake of Jonestown, concerned that the ACLU was being exploited by cults misusing freedom of religion. Fay had a number of friends in Berkeley whose children had become Moonies. She felt there was no time to lose in the battle against brainwashing. The appalling People's Temple example of mass murder-suicide was still fresh in everyone's mind.

Yet Fay's primary focus was pursuit of a teaching career. She crafted an outline of a law school course, "Overall Strategy in Socially Significant Cases," which Fay thought could also be adapted for college or graduate students outside the law. This ambitious course would recap her own career as a Movement lawyer. Fay thought of starting with the Sacco and Vanzetti trial, whose outcome had outraged her in college. From the McCarthy Era, she wanted to include both the Rosenberg espionage case on which she had worked in law school and Smith Act loyalty oath trials. She added the 1964 legal challenge to the Mississippi Democratic delegation at the end of Freedom Summer, the Caryl Chessman "Lovers Lane bandit" case that engendered worldwide support through his best-selling books on death row, the coalition to end the death penalty, and representation of conscientious objectors to the Vietnam War.

Fay also made a list of recent high-profile cases in which she and her Guild colleagues figured prominently: the 1968 Newton murder trial, the Soledad Brothers, the Angela Davis trial, the San Quentin Six trial, the Scherr palimony case, and the Inez Garcia murder trials for killing the man who raped her. (Charles Garry had lost the first Garcia murder trial; a new attorney won on retrial.) To these, Fay added abortion rights, gay rights and human rights cases — a category that included her own prison law class actions.

Fay felt compelled to add as well the lessons to be learned from "nightmare" situations like the Jonestown debacle and Newton's 1977–78 felony prosecutions, the defense of which furthered no Movement cause and ended under a cloud of witness intimidation. Fay wanted to explore the role of law in bringing needed change, the conflicts that lawyers faced when representing clients, and the difference between educating the public and engaging in propaganda. She intended to draw in part on her own experience in discussing the occupational hazards of high-profile cases, their limitations and potential benefits. Students might be aghast to learn that Oakland police used Fay's picture for target practice, or the repeated death threats Charles Garry received while representing the Panthers.

Fay wanted students to realize that the best interests of a particular criminal defendant or civil plaintiff sometimes conflicted with attempts to further an overall cause. To add to the mix, Fay wanted to discuss government harassment and sabotage and intra-group rivalry. She was intimately familiar with all of these subjects. Fay figured this could be a long-term project for which she might eventually prepare a textbook. But the first year she could simply make use of materials from the Meiklejohn Civil Rights Institute library that Ann Ginger had assembled, and Laura X's Women's History Research Project. Recent autobiographies could also be included. Garry had just co-authored his own life story in 1977, *Streetfighter in the Courtroom*. Fay planned to gather an array of guest speakers, including journalists, counsel and clients. She had enough material for several courses.

Meanwhile, Fay also spent time analyzing the work of a feminist scholar and historian for her own ambitious essay on the subject of feminist oppression. Katherine was anxious to introduce Fay to South African author, Professor Diana Russell, who taught at Mills College and lived in Fay's neighborhood. Dr. Russell had dedicated her career to writing about violence against women and, like Fay, contributed articles to the new feminist magazine *Chrysalis*. When Katherine told Dr. Russell about the wife-murderer whose freedom Fay had won, Dr. Russell thought, "Some feminist!" Her first reaction was reinforced when they met. Fay impressed Dr. Russell at first sight as a highly self-centered dilettante in search of admirers. It annoyed Dr. Russell that when Katherine introduced them in Fay's home, Fay proceeded to carry on a nonstop conversation while inviting them to follow her as she walked to her bedroom and stripped to her underwear to change clothes, obviously proud of her trim physique.

Like Hilde, the Harvard Ph.D. had spent years studying, writing and thinking about her field. Fay had only spent months and barely scratched the surface. A confirmed lesbian herself, Dr. Russell also noticed Fay seemed out of her element. She assumed Katherine was Fay's first woman lover and pegged Fay as a lifelong heterosexual indulging in a fling. In fact, Fay remained uncomfortable revealing her new choice of partners to extended family, neighbors and old friends.

That spring, Bob Richter made one of his periodic trips to California from New York on business related to one of his films. When he had arranged with Fay ahead of time to detour to see her again, he expected another romantic tryst. On his arrival, he was astounded by her aloofness. Fay introduced Richter to Katherine, who puzzled him by constantly staying at Fay's side when they sat down for coffee in Fay's kitchen. Slowly, as the awkward conversation progressed, Richter realized Fay's changed orientation since his last visit.

Meanwhile, Fay delighted in spending time with Lisie once again. The two made a date to meet at the San Francisco Museum of Modern Art to see "The Dinner Party," by feminist artist Judy Chicago. Both thoroughly enjoyed the gigantic, mixed media tribute to famous women throughout history. Chicago had created a triangular banquet table with 39 floral, ceramic place settings for women — both mythical and real — whom Chicago felt should be specially honored. The bold work with its overtly sexual imagery suited Fay's current world view. "We could not see so far, today in the women's movement, if we did not stand on the shoulders of our sisters. . . ."[2]

Katherine and Fay began attending events at Golden Gate University together, a test for Fay since Dru was still a member of the faculty and brought Marvin along. Dru confided to Dean Judith McKelvey that she felt funny about the complexities of the situation, but Fay seemed quite happy in her new relationship. Both Judy and her husband Stuart had, by then, become quite close to Fay. Stuart may have reminded Fay somewhat of her lifelong friend Pip, with whom Fay still corresponded while he taught Shakespeare in Cairo.

In April, Fay, Katherine and Judy McKelvey went on an outing to the Gold Country and ate a picnic lunch by the edge of a stream. Somehow, the conversation turned to people with disabilities. Fay emphatically declared to her two companions what she had already told Marvin — that she would rather die than live with any impairment. Her two friends were taken aback. They had no reason to suspect how soon Fay would face that issue.

As energized as Fay was, she had not settled on a particular future direction. She even considered returning to Europe. She invited Lisie to accompany her to London where Fay had arranged an interview with Amnesty International, only to discover that the organization paid too little for her to live on. That spring, Fay also gave some serious thought to creating a new feminist law firm with her young friend Barbara Price, who had worked with Fay on the *Scherr* case and in California Women Lawyers. Fay was upbeat in her conversations with Price, who already shared space in Marvin's San Francisco office. Yet Fay privately worried about how the finances would work.

When Fay ran into her old friend Penny Cooper at a church party, she made a point of probing Penny about how she had managed her own profitable criminal law practice. As the two sat together on a garden bench, Fay asked her, "How do you make a living at it?" Fay told Penny she was tired of having incredible passion for a case and never earning any money. Cooper shook her head at Fay. Cooper had never focused her practice on capital cases. She did accept the defense of homicides but largely made her living defending drug dealers whose cases often ended in a plea bargain. Penny told Fay that she had not started out interested in making money but soon learned to treat her practice as a business: "Listen, Fay, when you are practicing law you are plying a trade. You need a caseload of 50 to 75 cases and you cannot worry about each and every element of each client's case. They couldn't pay you enough for that." Penny realized Fay was too single-minded and relentless to have a clue how to take that advice. Fay only had an on-off switch, and "on" was full speed ahead. Penny suggested that Fay forget about private practice and instead look for a job like teaching or heading a nonprofit where Fay's zeal would not be a handicap.

By the beginning of May, Fay had taken in a young student boarder to help with the mortgage. Rand Miyashiro got along well with Neal and Oriane and liked to cook, letting Neal share the use of his wok. Fay

Future Hall of Fame criminal defense attorney Penny Cooper launched her successful practice in the spring of 1969 with arrestees from People's Park. Ten years later, Fay sought Penny's advice on how to make a decent living if she opened her own small law firm. Cooper's "bread and butter" in private practice came largely from drug cases. She was expert at challenging illegal searches and seizures. She told Fay, "When you are practicing law, you are plying a trade. You need a caseload of 50 to 75 cases and you cannot worry about each and every element of each client's case. They couldn't pay you enough for that." Penny suggested that Fay instead look for a job like teaching or heading a nonprofit where Fay's zeal would not be a handicap.

now enjoyed inviting her family and old friends to her home. She had a brunch for Ruby to celebrate Mother's Day and asked the family to mark June 3d on their calendar when she planned to hold a large family gathering at the house for Neal's twenty-first birthday. Marvin was coming, too, though Fay would be celebrating her new independence.

The following week, when Lisie came to stay overnight, Fay enthusiastically shared her plans for Neal's birthday with her sister as well. Lisie had just returned miraculously unscathed from a harrowing car crash on vacation with her husband in Canada. It delighted Lisie to be welcomed by Fay with a vase of fresh flowers by her bed. She very much looked forward to returning in two weeks for the birthday gathering.

In the meanwhile, Fay kept a busy calendar. On Friday, May 25, she attended a fundraiser at a restaurant in San Francisco's Chinatown. Despite repeated resolves not to immerse herself again in Leftist causes, Fay always found that a hard promise to keep. At the dinner, she insisted to an old anti-war colleague that her whole focus these days was on staying fit. She likely did not mention to him that she planned to host a political brunch on Memorial Day in opposition to the Moonies. But she did say something that would soon haunt her good friend: "I think if I were to lose my body health I would want to die."[3]

The next night, Saturday, May 26, Professor Russell and her African-American lover Donnis joined Katherine and Fay for dinner in Berkeley. Fay had not met Donnis before. When Donnis mentioned she was born in Chicago, Fay asked what part of "the African-American ghetto" she was from. Donnis bridled the same way Georgia Jackson had done years earlier. Fay's question smacked of condescension. Russell thought so, too, and noticed that Fay was oblivious to having offended Donnis.

On Sunday morning, Fay and Katherine shopped for groceries for Fay's new mission. The brunch she planned for Memorial Day was for friends as alarmed as she was about the Moonies' recruitment methods. Fay's Grant Street home already looked festive in preparation for Neal's twenty-first birthday the following weekend. Fay had begun decorating early, unable to contain her excitement.

The rest of Sunday, Fay and Katherine spent a quiet day at home preparing for the brunch the following morning. Neal took Fay's Toyota to spend the afternoon and evening with his girlfriend at a barbecue. On Sunday night, Oriane wanted to see the new hit movie *Superman* starring Christopher Reeve. Fay refused. She had no interest in the bulletproof cartoon hero. Unable to change Fay's mind, Katherine went with Oriane and left Fay behind. Neal came back past midnight and was the last to bed, stopping to chat with Oriane in her room just before he retired.

Neal was almost asleep listening to music in his bed when he heard the buzzer at the front door around 1:20 a.m. He pulled on his pants, not bothering to buckle the belt as he headed downstairs. He turned on the porch light and lifted the curtain of the front door to see a young, light-skinned black woman who looked like she needed help. When he opened the door to find out what she wanted, the woman uttered only a word or two before a gunman surprisingly emerged from hiding on the porch beside the door, telling them both, "Be quiet."

Neal did not see the young woman flee as the gunman commanded him to lie face down on the hall floor and demanded that Neal tell him if this was where Fay Stender lived. Neal said it was, but everyone was asleep upstairs. The gunman then demanded to be led to Fay and forced Neal to head up the staircase. Neal turned part way up to beg the gunman not to hurt his family. The gunman assured him he only wanted to talk to her: "Get going or I'll blow your fucking head off."[4]

At the top of the stairs, Neal turned on the hall light and knocked on the door of the master bedroom, waking his mother. When she asked, "Who is it?" Neal took a couple of steps inside the dark room and said, "There is a man here with a gun who wants to talk to you."[5] The gunman then followed Neal in and instructed Neal to sit in a chair on the far side of the room as he directed Fay to get out of bed. Katherine was still asleep and her dog Daisy lay at the foot of the bed.

When Fay arose naked, the gunman asked her to confirm that she was Fay Stender and ordered her to get dressed. She crossed to her closet and put on a nightgown. He then asked Fay if she thought she had ever betrayed anyone. Fay said, "No." He asked if she had betrayed George Jackson and she again said, "No." and offered to answer any questions he might have. Instead, the gunman told Fay to sit at her desk and take out a piece of paper to write a confession. By then, Katherine was awake and trying to act calm so Daisy would not sense grave danger and start barking.

The gunman instructed Fay to write "I, Fay Stender, admit I betrayed George Jackson and the Prison Movement when they needed me most." Fay replied: "I will write this because you have a gun, but it is not true."[6] He asked her for proof she was in fact Fay Stender and she showed him a credit card receipt with her signature, which he compared to the signed confession before he pocketed it. Then he asked them all for money. Neal offered the few dollars he had in his wallet and Katherine pointed to her jeans. From a pocket, the gunman extracted several dollars more.

Fay offered to fetch $40 she had in a kitchen drawer. The gunman then told Katherine to lie face down on the bed and made Neal take off his belt and tie her hands behind her. The gunman then yanked the cord from a bedside lamp and had Neal lie down beside Katherine. He used the cord to tie Neal's hands behind Neal's back. As the gunman left the room with Fay, he turned to warn Neal and Katherine, "Don't move, or I'll shoot you."[7]

Fay then led the gunman downstairs to the kitchen. When she started taking money from a drawer, he impatiently barked, "Come on, come on." Fay turned to hand him a $20 bill. She was just a few feet away when she saw him brace his right hand with his left. It was the Weaver two-hand stance the Panthers had adopted years before from a police manual. The gun man immediately started shooting. Fay felt each of five shots as she slumped to the floor. She remained fully conscious though two hollow-point bullets pierced her torso and one grazed her head. The loud sound echoed in the still of the night. The gunman forgot the money he had robbed as he bolted for the front door, leaving Fay bleeding profusely. No more than fifteen minutes had passed since Neal had answered the buzzer.

Neal heard the sickening sound of the gunshots. He waited a few seconds to be sure the gunman was gone before he went to the top of the stairs. After the front door slammed, Fay started crying. Neal shouted, "Are you all right, Mom?"[8]

Fay called back. "I'm shot. I'm dying. I love you."[9] His hands still tied, Neal ran to his sister's room, kicked open the door and woke Oriane up, shouting for her to call an ambulance. Neal ran down to the kitchen to find his mother on her back with blood all over her arms and chest. Fay moaned and clutched her sides. Neal urged her not to talk or grab her wounds and went out to wait for the paramedics to arrive.

Katherine came rushing downstairs to see Fay lying on the kitchen floor in a pool of blood and then ran into the street in her nightgown, shouting, "Fay's been shot."

None of the neighbors saw the gunman flee, but next door, Michael Magbie was startled awake by the rapid succession of loud gunshots. It was like nothing he had ever heard before — berrump, pause, berrump, berrump, berrump, pause, berrump. He and his wife had slept in a back room upstairs instead of their own bedroom because of construction work on an addition. It had been a warm night. The window was open. It felt like the shots went off right next to Magbie's ear. Not pausing to dress, Magbie jumped up and ran outside naked. Magbie did not know who Katherine Morse was, but embraced her as she repeated, "Fay's been shot."

Neal then came out of the open front door of the Stender home with his hands behind his back, still tied. Soon, the Berkeley police and an ambulance arrived on the scene as well as other neighbors awakened by the commotion. The police focused first on the large, naked black man standing in the street hugging a woman in a nightgown. One officer challenged Magbie with "Who the fuck are you?"

Magbie explained he was the next-door neighbor and told them he might have heard something on his roof. A rookie then directed Magbie to open his garage door. A set of stairs inside led to the flat roof. Magbie and the young officer approached carefully, thinking the gunman might be hiding up there. The officer drew his gun but appeared even more afraid than Magbie. "Wait a minute!" Magbie called out, "You do this. I'm not doing this." The rookie cautiously went in but found nothing.

Magbie crossed over to Neal and untied the cord still binding his wrists. Paramedics then wheeled Fay out of her house on a gurney. Miraculously, she still remained conscious, but she was now gurgling for air. The scene reminded Magbie of his searing experience watching a man be killed in Mississippi in the summer of 1965. When Neal joined his mother in the ambulance, Magbie retreated back inside to his wife and young children. Magbie was not alone among the neighbors in wondering where Marvin was. They had not seen him at the house in months.

Neal stayed by Fay's side as she was rushed to Herrick Hospital, near death with blood accumulating in her right lung and hemorrhaging in her liver. There, surgeons lost no time placing a tube in her chest, surgically removing a perforated section of her intestines and two bullets. One of the bullets had lodged in her right elbow and the other, of graver concern, remained near her spine. The doctors saw no damage to her spinal cord, but her legs were at least temporarily paralyzed. It was too early to know whether she would survive all her injuries. Fay was listed in critical condition and placed under armed guard, with three police officers stationed in her hospital room and six more downstairs.

Marvin was unreachable by phone and unaware of the horrific news, though it was the day's top story on both television and radio. Fay's friend Don Jelinek's housemates heard it that morning while Jelinek was taking a bubble bath. They gathered outside the bathroom door debating which one should tell him, knowing how hard he would take it. Jelinek himself had suffered for a long time from depression and had stopped doing prison work. His shock at the news was deepened by memories of seeking Fay's advice on handling his own death threat years before when he represented Attica inmates. Then, both assumed she spoke from the vantage point of someone who had navigated similar difficulties and emerged unscathed.

Marvin had not turned on the car radio while he and Dru were driving back late Monday afternoon from a relaxing weekend of mud baths at a resort in Napa County. When Marvin reached his home on Russian Hill in San Francisco around 5 p.m., his roommates ran out of the house to tell him that something terrible had happened and he needed to call the Berkeley police. As soon as Marvin learned where Fay and his children were, Marvin rushed straight to Herrick Hospital to be with them. From that evening on Marvin and Dru associated the

St. Helena spa where they had spent the weekend with the attack on Fay and could never bring themselves to go back.

The police kept secret where Fay was hospitalized and refused to share her gunpoint "confession" with the swarm of news reporters anxious for a scoop. Instead, a Berkeley Police lieutenant told reporters the obvious: "It's fairly evident that someone wants her dead, presumably . . . because of her political ties."[10] The police said they had no clues and no leads to potential suspects — the nature of the case barred the release of further information.

Many of Marvin's and Fay's mutual friends did not know that the two of them had separated long before she was gunned down. In fact, Marvin had only recently told his best friend Gordon Gaines about the impending divorce — well after the decision was made. Those who did not yet know treated Marvin as if he had just walked out on Fay and was somehow responsible for leaving her vulnerable to attack. Meanwhile, Marvin's only thoughts were for the safety of Fay and his children. He wasted no time in getting a gun, a .357 Magnum he wore openly in a shoulder holster.

Marvin went back to his old Grant Street neighborhood and knocked on neighbors' doors, asking them not to talk to reporters. He arrived unannounced at Michael Magbie's door, wearing the large gun over his three-piece suit. Magbie understood the message Marvin was telling the world: "Don't mess with my family." Marvin said he was moving around and asked Magbie not to let anyone know where Neal and Oriane were. Magbie had no idea anyway. Reporters combed the neighborhood for several days afterward, but the neighbors said nothing. No one in the family had returned to the house after the shooting, though they left behind their cat Puddin', which the neighbors fed.

Police listed Fay's assault as a case of armed robbery and attempted murder. A public defender speculated that it might be the work of an angry "splinter prison group"[11] arising out of the Prison Law Project in the early 1970s or Fay's representation of George Jackson. *The Oakland Tribune* drew attention to how Fay's criminal defense work had earned her the hatred of prison officials, noting that the chairman of the State Board of Corrections had criticized Fay "for fomenting trouble in state prisons" and linked her with actress Jane Fonda and Communist Angela Davis — two other women who "spurred on the 'revolutionaries' of the day."[12]

The *Tribune* also noted that Fay had once assumed that she risked death for her work in prison reform. The paper quoted her statement in 1970 that "[i]t's now dangerous to one's life to resist oppression. Those of us who believe the things we always believed are now in a position where we might be killed or jailed."[13] But, at the time, Fay feared vengeance from Oakland police who used her picture for target practice or prosecution on trumped-up charges that she conspired with her revolutionary clients — risks she considered the price for forceful advocacy of prisoners' rights. She had not then considered her life might be imperiled by someone she championed.

Following the shooting, Fay remained in critical condition. Marvin, Neal and Oriane were allowed to stay with her in her room. Security remained tight. By Wednesday, May 30th, the media were reporting the name of the hospital where she was being treated, that she had been shot multiple times with a .38 caliber gun and forced to write a note including the false confession.[14]

Some reporters had speculated that the note might have been a cover-up to a robbery attempt, but abandoned that theory when they learned the gunman had taken the note but left behind the $11 he had taken from Neal and Katherine Morse. In her short periods of consciousness, Fay had told the police the shooter was a stranger to her. The police changed tactics with the media, realizing they needed help from the public. Neal's and Katherine's descriptions were released: "a black man in his early or middle twenties, five feet eight inches tall with a medium build, a mustache and a two-inch natural hairstyle."[15]

The *San Francisco Examiner* reported that, a couple of weeks earlier, Oriane Stender had a conversation with a black militant outside a Shattuck Avenue restaurant in Berkeley, who told her some friends of his were looking for her mother. The reporters indicated only that Fay was acquainted with the man who spoke to Oriane and that he was not the gunman. In fact, Oriane's source was Soledad Brother Fleeta Drumgo, now out of prison. At the time, Oriane had not known what to make of his warning. No one in her family thought Fay still remained at risk because of her prior prison work.

The police made a list of recent parolees from San Quentin who might yield information on the motive. The newspapers reported that the police believed The Black Guerilla Family, then one of the largest prison gangs in California, was behind the assassination attempt, but the police refused to confirm that theory. Still, they told reporters that investigation into Fay's other activities provided no alternative motive and they were checking the whereabouts of known BGF members.

After Jackson's death, the BGF became infamous for ruthless contract killings, while still holding on to Jackson's revolutionary image as its founding father. Though Jackson was still affiliated with the Black Panther Party when he died, the BGF and the Black Panthers then mistrusted each other and were soon open enemies. The BGF characterized Jackson's former alliance as one that Newton had betrayed. In recent years, the BGF itself had focused far less on Jackson's call for fighting white oppression as it became more heavily involved in drug dealing.

San Francisco lawyer John Keker, who had negotiated Eldridge Cleaver's return from exile a few years earlier, had a different theory. Keker speculated that an angry ex-con shot Fay because he was one of the thousands of prisoners who vainly wrote to her wanting to be her "new George Jackson."[16] An ex-felon activist agreed — for every inmate Fay had helped, she had to turn down two or three. Other sources wondered if some inmate Fay had done work for was "pissed off" at her failure to free him from prison and tried to kill her through a pact with a friend on the outside.[17]

A spokesman for the San Francisco prisoners' union disagreed: "Fay has among the highest reputations of anybody in the land among prisoners in the state of California, black and white. I can't imagine who would be crazy enough to do something like that to Fay." He had not seen evidence of strife within the movement "in at least the last year or so. Things have been pretty low key."[18] Prison officials confirmed that the BGF had maintained a low profile in the past few years as systematic efforts were made to reduce its ranks by paroling leaders or isolating them from their followers.

One suspicious Movement lawyer downplayed the significance of the attacker's accusations. She cautioned: "It is important that people not take at face value what the gunman said.... So many things happen that turn out to be something else."[19] But Marvin was not alone in scoffing at this idea. Why would the gunman claim Fay had betrayed George Jackson in order to misdirect blame for her death? Yes, COINTELPRO sowed seeds of dissension among black militant factions a decade earlier. But why now? It made no sense when there was no longer a prison movement to discredit.

After giving police her statement, Katherine Morse had gone into hiding, frightened for her life while the perpetrator remained at large. But she knew not to jump to conclusions about the reasons for Fay's attack. When Katherine had done abortion counseling before *Roe v. Wade*, the Kansas agency she worked for sent women across the state line to a Missouri doctor, who wound up being murdered. Instead of a right-to-life group, it turned out that he was killed by a rival illegal abortionist.

By May 30th, the police had added to the prior description of the attacker to include a goatee as well as a moustache. *The San Francisco Examiner* wrote a long, front-page story outlining the theory that the shooting arose out of a dispute between Fay and George Jackson who had become angry at Fay, starting in late 1970, when she refused to agree to divert defense funds to the purchase of weapons.

Police shared with reporters a secret BGF "Manifesto" from 1974 which proclaimed that "Our support has been destroyed by the vultures who call themselves movement lawyers, with the help from their patron saint Huey P. Newton." It called for the exposure and punishment of those responsible "for such atrocious crimes against the revolution" and issued death warrants against them. Both Fay and Charles Garry were on that five-year-old list.[20] The assumption that a BGF gang member shot Fay fit with other information the police leaked, such as that the gunman had asked for Fay by name, without knowing what she looked like. Reporters noted that, in 1977, Fay told friends she feared an attack by associates of former clients. She had long since exhibited great care in giving out her ever-changing home phone number and had taken other security precautions for her home.

When interviewed in June of 1978, Fay had candidly admitted that there were people unhappy with her for quitting prison reform work, that some believed she had betrayed the prison reform movement, and that threats had been made against her. The *Examiner* reporters noted, "She said she wouldn't be surprised if someone took a shot at her."[21] But by 1978, Fay actually thought so much time had passed that the risk from black militants was negligible if she kept a low profile, which was why she had not cooperated with Kate Coleman's exposé of Panther violence in "The Party's Over."

The *Examiner* noted that Jackson and Stender's falling out preceded Jonathan Jackson's attack at the Marin County court house in August of 1970. An unnamed source claimed Fay and George Jackson were "mortal enemies when he died." One of her colleagues disagreed: "Jackson felt ripped off by a number of people, including attorneys, but Stender's name was not specifically mentioned," even though Fay and Jackson parted company over the use of his royalties.[22]

The *Examiner* published a related piece reviewing Jackson's 1970 affectionate letters to Fay from prison. The newspaper reported that on March 23, 1970, Jackson had written to Fay that he felt he had fallen into a garbage can on which the authorities had closed the lid for good. The paper quoted Jackson as writing: "Someone is going to be hurt, my friend, when it's over, someone's going to be hurting bad, and it won't be us. It won't be you. Be assured that your safety will always enter any defense move I make, your safety first always."[23]

Yet Jackson's unquestioned appreciation for Fay at the outset did not foreclose a bitter falling out between the two later on. The same day as the confusing *Examiner* stories surfaced, *The Oakland Tribune* reported that a prison union official who worked closely with Fay categorically stated, "I know there was no betrayal of George Jackson."[24] The evidence was enticing but inconclusive as to Fay's relationship with Jackson at the time of his death. It was an issue that would figure prominently in the upcoming trial.

About a week after the shooting, Magbie was out front while his kids were playing in the plum tree in front of the Stenders' house. Two young, aggressive blacks pulled up in a car and asked if he knew the

Stenders. He denied knowing them, but they did not believe him.

"Is Marvin here?" the two men asked.

"No, he's not," Magbie replied.

"You tell him we're looking for him," and they drove off. Magbie could not believe how brazen they were with such a heavy investigation under way. Marvin's fear was amply justified. Magbie himself did not want to live in the neighborhood another day if he could help it.

Fay's shooting cast a pall on the June 4, 1979, tribute at a Berkeley restaurant honoring Barney Dreyfus as the co-founder of the Bay Area National Lawyers Guild. Among the letters of praise in the evening's program was Fay's own loving description of her former mentor written just weeks earlier. The evening started out strangely. Guild members, as a rule, refused to cross picket lines. Yet, to attend the dinner, they had to walk past demonstrators protesting their evening's entertainer, Joan Baez, for her recent accusations of human rights violations by the North Vietnamese during the Vietnam War.

Guild members' unease only increased when Marvin rose to the podium to address the large gathering. They knew he had just joined the Garry, Dreyfus law firm as a partner, but he did not rise to toast his senior partner. Instead, Marvin reported that Fay's condition had improved and that she was taken off the critical list on June 1. She remained hospitalized under armed guard, in serious condition, her legs apparently permanently paralyzed. Marvin then announced that a $10,000 reward was being offered for anyone providing him or the Berkeley police with information about the crime. Police were preparing a composite sketch of the gunman from the descriptions provided by the three witnesses. The reward would be administered by the City of Berkeley. Anonymous informants would be eligible.

Such an announcement by a former Guild President marked an ironic and grim occasion. Many attendees were aghast at being asked to act as informers. For four decades, the Guild had championed the constitutional rights of those accused of crime — not aligned themselves with the police. Some, like Doron Weinberg, wondered aloud if different rules should apply if the victim was one of their friends. Others felt the brutal assault threatened them all and had no objection to Marvin's plea. They noticed Doron's hair had turned white almost overnight. The reputed head of the BGF, Hugo "Yogi" Pinell, now imprisoned at Folsom, had been Doron's own former client.

After the shocking assassination attempt, most radical lawyers grew far more cautious. They already knew how violent their clients could be in their own element — deadly gang rivalry, contract killings, robbery-murder, severely beating girlfriends and wives, disciplining errant gang members with mud-holing. All of these were quite commonplace, but turning on their lawyers added a whole new dimension. As one chastened lawyer put it, "Who's going to . . . [get] involved in a field of law where you can get murdered just because you piss somebody off? . . . I'm no hero!"[25]

Ironically, the District Attorney at the time Fay was shot was Lowell Jensen. When their paths had crossed years before in Huey Newton's first murder trial, Jensen had little respect for Charles Garry but held Fay herself in high regard. When news of the attack reached Jensen, he immediately swung into action. He did not want whoever committed this outrageous home invasion to get away with it. Jensen knew that most of his staff considered Fay Stender and Charles Garry charter members of "the enemy." Jensen was also keenly aware how much the Black Panthers hated him, his office and the police department. The Panthers had tried to have Jensen recalled from office for race bias after he pursued two retrials of Newton. The realization that Fay Stender might be equally mistrustful of him made Jensen doubly determined to obtain Fay's cooperation and bring her attacker to justice. To Jensen, rising above politics in carrying out his official duties was a matter of pride. He assigned the case to Howard Janssen, head of the D.A.'s Berkeley office.

Janssen was tall and handsome and low key by nature. The slim, blond prosecutor had started in the District Attorney's office as a clerk. He had worked on motions for the Newton trial back in 1968 but had no involvement in later Black Panther cases. Janssen had observed some of the "trial of the century," watching the aggressive courtroom antics of Charles Garry. He thought Garry had acted far beyond acceptable limits, stretching the law, pushing witnesses and the judge. Many of Janssen's officemates felt Fay Stender was no different.

Jannsen stood out from his more aggressive colleagues, who still fumed over Fay Stender's success in winning Newton's freedom on appeal. Janssen held a different view — that a vigorous criminal defense bar was absolutely essential to the judicial system. His job was to get the conviction, theirs to get an acquittal. Janssen assumed that was why Lowell Jensen assigned him the prosecution of Stender's attacker instead of his colleague "Mad Dog" Gilbert. Yet Janssen approached this high-profile assignment with substantial trepidation: if the prosecution were mishandled, the media would give his office a black eye.

Jannsen wanted to avoid what happened when the verdict against San Francisco Supervisor Dan White for killing Mayor Moscone and Supervisor Harvey Milk was returned on May 21, 1979 — just a week before Fay Stender was shot. In reaction to the lenient outcome, the San Francisco Gay community erupted in riots, smashing doors and windows at City Hall and burning a dozen police cars. Mayor Feinstein castigated the criminal justice system and ridiculed the defense. Coming on the heels of the Dan White case, the Stender shooting was drawing similar media coverage even though it did not involve any public officials.

Jannsen fully expected Fay to resist confiding in him. He had met her several years before when she ran the Prison Law Project, but never faced her in a major case. She gave the impression of hating the entire system, thinking all prosecutors were evil because they put people in prison. Fortunately, Jannsen was blessed with ample determination, compassion and patience. In his office, people often repeated the story about Fay's role as the uncooperative witness in the 1972 burglary of the Prison Law Project, forcing dismissal of the case. Janssen did not want a similar fiasco to happen on his watch.

Janssen's first priority was finding the shooter. Fortunately, Fay's family was being highly cooperative. Marvin had quickly volunteered to help gather evidence, convinced this was not the work of a lone crazy. Marvin said Fay had been hearing rumors for quite a while that Jackson's supporters were calling her a turncoat. On June 12th, the National Lawyers Guild issued a press release vehemently denouncing the attack. The same day, Marvin held a press conference announcing a goal of a $200,000 trust fund for Fay's medical needs and security.

Having devoted herself to so much pro bono and low-paid legal work over the years, Fay had no savings. "Friends of Fay Stender," co-chaired by Elsa Knight Thompson and Ying Lee Kelley, solicited contributions, with over seventy prominent people lending their names to the effort, Bob Richter, Jerry Rubin, Jane Fonda and Tom Hayden among them.

Doctors were concerned that Fay's wounds might become infected or she would develop pneumonia. "If those dangers are avoided, she's going to live." Marvin asked again for help in finding her assailant. He said that whoever shot his wife was "incredibly familiar with the minutiae of the prison movement."[26]

Fay was not only in great pain, but profoundly depressed. She feared she would never walk again. Both arms had suffered fractured bones and nerve damage; one arm remained in a cast, severely weakened. She wore a catheter; her sex life would be permanently impaired. She took so many painkillers she could no longer think clearly. She felt only bitterness and betrayal. Among the cherished letters Fay had saved for years was one Jackson sent her a month after she started representing him. It ended: "Stay out of harm's way. I need you — right on."

To find out she was on an official BGF hit list after quitting prison work was terrifying. Fay began to think of herself as a tragic heroine, punished for loving two younger men too much — first, by public humiliation and now by an unfathomable assassination attempt. When she stopped wishing that the gunman had been competent enough to kill her, Fay wanted to be avenged.

* * *

Los Angeles Times reporter Austin Scott empathized with Fay's plight. He had closely followed the California prison reform movement in its prime. Recognizing that the "confession" she was ordered to sign may have been "a decoy," he still felt that "the irony of its wording is beyond belief." He pointed out that, from 1969 until 1973, Fay Stender was "nearly consumed . . . by the prison reform movement." Earlier in the decade, Scott had watched with amazement as Fay worked long hours for little pay, mobilized lawyers to attack the correctional system in court and led a public relations campaign to get the public to care how prisoners were treated. "For her troubles, Stender was called all the customary nasty names reserved for people who adopt unpopular causes. . . . She didn't have to get involved. . . ."[27]

Scott said, "In her attempt to take on as many individual cases as she could, Stender left herself too little time for her family, for her friends, for her own piece of mind. This country is full of causes that eat people alive, as many burned-out . . . activists know . . . because too few care enough. And so, for those who do care, the workload of what needs to be done yesterday becomes discouragingly large. . . ." Scott understood completely why Fay had shut the doors of the Prison Law Project six years before, which made it extraordinarily "hard to accept the idea that, in the mind of some would-be assassin, pulling out just before she burned out is a sin punishable by the kind of lunatic brutality visited on her in the middle of the night in her own home."[28]

The police received a lucky break a few days later. On June 8th, a San Francisco beat cop saw three black men sharing a joint in broad daylight on a sidewalk in the Haight district. As three other officers stood nearby, he stopped just to give them a warning when one stocky man with a goatee pulled out a .38 caliber revolver and declared, "You're not taking me to jail."[29] After a struggle, the men were arrested. The one who had brandished the gun was Edward Glenn Brooks of Albany, California. He was charged with battery, carrying a concealed weapon, possession of marijuana and resisting arrest. He and his two companions were freed on $8,000 bail pending arraignment.

The police kept the heavy black leather satchel Brooks had thrown down when he was arrested, and found to their surprise another loaded gun, two bags of hollow point bullets, a stopwatch, wig and three pairs of surgical gloves. It looked like a robbery kit. They traced a $2 bill in the satchel to one reported stolen in a bank robbery by masked gunmen at the Bank of America on Telegraph and Russell in Berkeley on June 1 — coincidentally the same corner where the Franck law office had been located when Fay was a partner. A hidden bank camera at the bank photographed the synchronized robbery. The story was leaked to the press that one of the robbers appeared similar to the description of Stender's attacker. Then, ballistics tests matched the bullets of the .38 caliber revolver taken from Brooks with those recovered from Fay's wounds. They decided to stake out a Berkeley address listed in a notebook they had found inside Brooks' briefcase.

On June 14th, less than a week after the marijuana arrest, another bold, commando-style bank robbery occurred at a Berkeley branch of the Wells Fargo Bank. It was carried off with similar precision by men also wearing masks. The Wells Fargo robbery occurred the same day Brooks was to have returned to court on the charges stemming from the San Francisco arrest. He never showed up. The robbers fled the Wells Fargo Bank with over $5,500, taking two getaway cars. Police were summoned by a silent alarm and pursued the suspects to an apartment complex six blocks away at 1643 Prince Street — the same Berkeley address already under surveillance. Police immediately arrested three men on the street as they tried to flee from their car. The other three holed up inside the complex and held police at bay for an hour and a half before surrendering.

The six men arrested were all African-American: Charles Coleman, age 30, also charged with parole violation; Keith Lott, 26; Edward Moten, 27; Edward Glenn Brooks, 27; Roy Gant, 28; and William Lofton, 31. Coleman and Lott had Berkeley home addresses. Lott's was on the same street as Fay Stender, a few blocks away from her home. Brooks lived in Albany, Gant was from Oakland and Lofton, a paroled ex-felon, was from San Francisco. Coleman had been arrested and released on June 2nd for a different robbery. Soon, the police discovered that two others were state prison parolees, including Brooks, who had served several years at San Quentin.

The arrested men were jailed on the robbery charges. Two days later, the *Examiner* reported that at least four of the six were members of the Black Guerilla Family — Coleman, Gant, Lofton and Brooks. Officials could not confirm that report, but Gant was with Brooks when he was arrested in San Francisco, and Coleman had been linked by ballistics evidence with the .38 caliber revolver used in the Stender shooting. Brooks and Coleman were also acquaintances of Fleeta Drumgo, who visited Coleman in jail.

While the investigation began to bear fruit, Fay remained at Herrick Hospital, where she was upgraded to fair condition. Lisie had been calling Fay daily. Ruby was equally concerned. Yet when Ruby and Lisie came to visit, Fay shrank from her mother's hand as Ruby reached out to soothe her brow. The nurses could see how tense Fay became and thought Fay's feelings extended to both her mother and sister. But Ruby was the real target of her bitterness. It seemed as if Fay could see "I told you so" in Ruby's eyes and feel it in her gestures. Fay could not forgive her mother for being right.

But Ruby was hardly alone. Dru Ramey was among those who felt similarly. The assault on Fay reminded Dru of her own instinctive fears seven years before when Fay talked her into interviewing convicted killer Robert Duren at San Quentin to help German student Julia Cappenberg obtain visitation rights. Dru felt out of her element: "At some level, I always thought they'd come back and kill you."

Fay refused to see much of her mother or talk with her. Lisie felt caught in the middle as Fay unfairly blamed Ruby for her predicament. Fay now regretted the entire career path she had followed. She felt it was Ruby's fault she had rebelled as a teenager instead of pursuing a safe career as a concert pianist. Perhaps Fay could have been an internationally acclaimed virtuoso, like Van Cliburn. Of course, Fay had fought as much back then with her father. It was unfair to blame either parent for her rejection of a career as a pianist.

One of the few visitors to draw out a spark of Fay's former zeal was Jane Scherr, who brought her elder daughter Dove to see Fay in the hospital. The high school senior had just been admitted to Harvard, though with no scholarship because Harvard insisted that her father could afford tuition. Fay immediately dictated a letter to the financial aid office, castigating Max as a heartless skinflint, detailing her bitter court battle and the lengths to which he had gone to deprive Jane and his daughters access to his assets. It got Dove her scholarship.

Since Memorial Day, Oriane and Neal had not gone back home even to fetch clothes. Marvin told Ruby and Lisie his family would never return there. The two women then volunteered to pack up the Stenders' possessions. The house had been left as it was when the shooting occurred — with the decorations for Neal's intended coming-of-age celebration still in place. By the guest bed Lisie had slept in on her visit in May still sat the vase of flowers, now long-since wilted. Lisie and Ruby packed up the china Fay had inherited from her grandmother and left Puddin' to the neighbors' kindness.

After the arrests, Katherine Morse came out of hiding. Two weeks of seclusion had given her plenty of time to wonder why Fay had never taught her children not to let strangers into the house, especially in the middle of the night. Though still traumatized, Katherine made several trips to see Fay in the hospital. When Fay complained her hands constantly hurt, Katherine massaged them and took dictation from Fay of letters to friends. There was little else Katherine could do to help. By July, Fay would tell her not to visit any more. What was the point? Fay's overwhelming needs were far too much for Katherine to handle. She could not make Fay feel safe, as Marvin did. Fay felt her only hope was to win Marvin back.

On June 18th, the six suspects were brought from Santa Rita to a hearing in Berkeley. Police had taken extreme security precautions beforehand, including sharpshooters armed with rifles, ammunition clips and binoculars on a nearby rooftop. A dozen policemen patrolled the courtyard below the second-floor courtroom. The hearing had been set for 2 p.m., but it was 3 o'clock before it began. All spectators were thoroughly searched. Many others were denied entry to the jammed gallery. Then the guards force-marched the shackled defendants awkwardly into the room.

Freelance reporter Eve Pell, who had quit Fay's Prison Law Project to join the Prison Law Collective seven years earlier, was among the press covering that hearing. Though she found Fay's injuries appalling, she still viewed the court proceedings through the lens of a prisoners' rights advocate. She gaped as the suspects were brought in, "chained in line like slaves from *Roots*,"[30] referring to the popular book and television miniseries about an African-American family's long struggle to gain freedom from servitude. The prisoners then complained to the judge that they were given no shoes or underwear and lacked access to showers for the four days since their arrest. When the judge said she was given no evidence of their claim, the prisoners each angrily lifted one of their two bare feet.

All six suspects were charged with armed robbery of the Wells Fargo Bank branch on June 14th. Only Brooks was charged with the shooting of Fay Stender. Judge Dawn Girard was told that eyewitnesses to the Stender home invasion had identified Brooks from photographs. Brooks muttered "bullshit" twice as the judge read the charge of attempted murder against him.[31] Tensions were running so high that the judge sensed a security risk if she proceeded. She called a halt to the hearing, but the suspects refused to leave without being assured of better treatment.

Coleman yelled to his friends in the gallery to "get out" because things might have to "get down." Bailiffs formed a partial ring around the defendants. One tugged on their chain. Pell described the bailiff's efforts as trying to pull the prisoners out of the courtroom "like oxen."[32] Four defendants shouted out and leaped at the bailiff, their feet high in the air. Coleman grabbed a wooden chair, menacing bailiffs and police, who were quickly joined by officers stationed in the hall. The remaining two prisoners were dragged into the melee as the others fought nightsticks with fists and chairs, knocking one bailiff to the floor. After a few minutes, the defendants were subdued. Some observers were in tears; three spectators were detained by the police for questioning and later released with no charges.

Eve Pell reported her dismay at the "the full, awful circle" of events from when she had accompanied Fay to Salinas in 1970 to decry the Soledad Brothers' shocking treatment. "In that red-neck valley town, I saw those three accused chained up like beasts, jeered at as they walked across the town sidewalk to court, and given short shrift by the judge."[33] She recalled how Fay had used that very image to gain widespread support for Jackson's defense. Though Pell condemned the brutal attack on Fay and joined in fund-raising for her recovery, Pell appeared far more upset by the suspects' inhumane treatment — in Berkeley, of all places!

On Tuesday, June 19th, every suspect except Brooks was brought back from Santa Rita County Jail to appear once again before Judge Girard, now sitting in the far more secure Oakland courthouse. She issued an unusual order as the hearing began: requiring the men to be restrained "in such a manner as to preclude further outbursts and to insure the orderly progression of these hearings."[34] The men were then brought into court one at a time, each with his hands chained to his sides. But this time, they all had been provided with tennis shoes.

A Berkeley police sergeant told the judge he overheard one of the defendants boast that they planned to create a disturbance at every court appearance. For this hearing, most of the spectators present in the locked court room were actually plain clothes investigators from the District Attorney's office and detectives from the Sheriff's office. They had been admitted before the public to fill up seats and be ready to assist in case the prisoners were again disruptive. As a result, over twenty people wanting to attend the hearing were denied access.

All five men pleaded not guilty to the Wells Fargo Bank robbery, but their strategies differed markedly. One of the suspects, Coleman, sought permission to represent himself. Gant wanted a separate trial where the press would be excluded. His co-defendants welcomed all the publicity they could get just as Fay had done in the Newton trial and for the Soledad Brothers.

On June 21st, for security reasons, Brooks was brought to a separate hearing in Alameda County Superior Court. He was led into the locked courtroom wearing leg chains, his hands cuffed to a waist chain as the other five had been. Brooks pleaded not guilty to both charges: shooting Fay Stender and participating in the Wells Fargo Bank robbery.

The police were still investigating the possibility one of the other bank robbers conspired with Brooks in the shooting. It was hard to determine if Brooks was connected to the Black Guerilla Family. Members were sworn to secrecy under pain of death. The situation frightened Leftists more when Charles Garry and Marvin held a joint press conference the following week. Garry announced that police had been warned by an anonymous caller of a "hit list" of three prison reform attorneys that "the movement was going to get," which included himself and Fay.[35] *The Los Angeles Times* and *The New York Times* both sent reporters to cover the story. Garry accepted an offer of special police protection after the attempt on Fay's life. He told one reporter that he was not aware of anyone in prison he had ever had a problem with, but had no other explanation for the threats.

Marvin then told the press that, before his wife had left the prison reform movement, she had interacted with more than 4,000 convicts. She had only quit because funding for the project dried up. She maintained friendly contact with many former convicts but never returned to prison work after 1975. He voiced grave concern that the man who shot his wife "might try to come back" and revealed that he and their two children were hiding out while Fay remained under 24-hour police guard.[36]

Soon, all six defendants were back in court, minus the shackles but still clad in Santa Rita County Jail jumpsuits instead of the street clothes they requested. Observers were checked for weapons before they entered. The hearing was short and uneventful. The defendants remained quiet and subdued as charges were dropped against one of them and Coleman was granted permission to represent himself.

Meanwhile, the police doubted that Fay would really cooperate with the prosecution. Janssen met Fay as soon as she was able to see him and was amazed at her openness and candor. He wanted her thoughts on why she was shot. Obviously, the intruder had intentionally sought her out and knew where she lived. But that hardly presented a short list of black militant suspects. As noted by *The Berkeley Barb*, Fay's "extensive contact with inmates had made her dozens of friends inside California prisons — and, no doubt an equal number of enemies."[37] In the fourteen years the Stenders had lived at their Grant Street home, they held many fund-raisers for SNCC and the Panthers, gatherings for friends and family of the Soledad Brothers, and get-togethers for the Prison Law Project. Many militants had been to her home, including Huey Newton, with whom she was no longer on friendly terms. Any one of them could have given out her address.

Fay told Janssen that she thought the attack might well have been retaliation for her refusal to divert Jackson's royalties from the Soledad Brothers Defense Fund. Jackson wanted to arm revolutionaries, which she considered foolhardy. Fay believed Jackson had developed a warped perspective from ten years in prison. If he had followed her advice and gone to trial, she assumed he would have been acquitted like his two co-defendants Drumgo and Clutchette later were. Janssen agreed that Jackson might have gotten off if he had possessed the temperament to let court procedures take their course.

The dispute over the use of the funds, Fay's split with Jackson and his death left her bitterly disillusioned. Janssen became convinced Fay was deeply committed throughout her career to working within the law. His colleagues remained skeptical. She and Janssen still struggled with the motive: Why would someone take so much trouble to kill her when she hadn't even worked on prison cases in more than five years?

In the meantime, newspapers and magazines covered the creation of the fund for Fay's recovery as its own story and encouraged readers to donate. *The San Francisco Jewish Bulletin* also published an appeal for help for Fay. Though she was not a congregation member, she and her family had deep roots in the Jewish community. The *Bulletin* noted that, while better known for her activism in seeking prison reform and women's rights, she had spent time on her recent trip to Europe investigating records of Jewish settlements in Warsaw before the Holocaust.

While the attempted murder received heavy coverage in the mainstream media, it received none at all in *The Oakland Post*. The attack was mentioned only once in *The Black Panther* newspaper, which reminded its readers that Fay had acted as a "lawyer for the people" who had helped gain Huey Newton's release and represented George Jackson. The *Panther* reporter told readers that the shooting of Fay Stender must have been a police setup intended to falsely incriminate the Party and prison gangs. That claim fit with the Party's efforts to have readers contribute to the costs of a pending suit against the FBI and CIA. Before the next issue came out, it was public knowledge that Fay was cooperating with Brooks' prosecutor. While most media continued months of front-page coverage, the *Panther* newspaper dropped all reference to the assassination attempt, treating it as a non-event. Marvin later mused, "With friends like that . . . [who needs enemies?]"

■ 8 ■

Star Witness for the Prosecution

*May no trial however severe,
embitter our souls and destroy our trust.*
— JEWISH PRAYER FOR STRENGTH

Neal was the first to view a lineup and, with some hesitancy, picked out Edward Brooks. Next, Katherine Morse tentatively chose Brooks but gave serious thought to a couple of others. She told police she was unsure she could ever identify the assailant. She had not been wearing her glasses and the lighting was poor. Fay was too weak to attend a lineup so it was videotaped and shown to her in her hospital room. The defense vigorously objected to this relatively novel procedure. Fay picked out Edward Brooks as the man who most resembled the assailant.

Not surprisingly, Janssen planned to rely principally on Neal at the preliminary hearing in July. To the family's relief, Oriane was not asked to play any role since she slept through the home invasion. Yet it was Oriane who had the earlier warning from Fleeta Drumgo, which might have yielded a motive for the shooting. The police had not even brought Drumgo in for questioning, perhaps because Janssen figured that Brooks' lawyer would then demand access to Oriane for her side of their conversation.

Janssen also had no desire to muddy the case up with unprovable allegations against the Black Guerilla Family. So far, all he had was that Fay's name appeared on the BGF 1974 enemies' list, along with a number of other people who were never attacked. Meanwhile, Yogi Pinell published a statement from his prison cell at Folsom that denounced Fay's shooting as "tragic." He rejected "false rumors" that the six men arrested for the twin bank robberies were responsible and urged supporters to rally to their defense.[1] Like the Panthers, Pinell charged that law enforcement agencies or reactionaries were the true culprits, trying to divide prisoners from their progressive attorneys. The Stenders considered Pinell's denial self-serving. Even diehard radicals had to face the realization that Charles Garry accepted police protection after Fay's close call.

Though Fay did not want Neal to bear the brunt of proving the prosecutor's case, the slow pace of her recovery surprised her nurses, who had seen patients with worse injuries recuperate faster. But they did not appreciate the extent of her psychological damage. Fay was now just a shell of her former self — her belief system shattered and her sense of empowerment destroyed. She had begun to realize she would never walk again when, after a few weeks in the hospital, the neurological surgeon no longer included her on his rounds. It took two months before the cast was removed from her left arm and it still hurt. Looking at her future, Fay realized that she could not bear becoming utterly dependent upon friends and family and again wanted to die. She asked her friends to help her obtain enough sleeping pills to kill herself. Concern for Neal's and Oriane's grief stopped her, but only for the time being. Ying urged Fay to wait at least a year, as recommended by experts on trauma, before evaluating whether she could adjust to her new situation. Fay only felt motivated to live long enough to see her attacker convicted.

Fay's own $50,000 medical insurance policy had been depleted by the end of June. "Friends of Fay Stender" worked not only to raise the mounting costs of her continued rehabilitation and security, but to give Fay reason to live beyond revenge: "In the work she has done, Fay has acted for all of us. Now that she and her family must pay this awful price for her integrity, . . . your contribution means much more than [money] to Fay. It will be a validation, . . . an assurance that her work in the past and her chance to continue in the future are important to each of us."[2] Fay was uncomfortable with that message, unable to imagine volunteering for similar causes again. As money, telegrams and cards from well-wishers came pouring in, she became even more upset. After all she had sacrificed, the donors were almost exclusively white. Now she was so paranoid of black strangers that she cringed when she saw an African-American doctor in a hospital corridor.

Artist Judy Chicago expressed her admiration for Fay by sending a framed copy of a 13-line poem she had recently published. Entitled "Merger: A Vision of the Future," it began: "And then all that has divided us will merge, And then compassion will be wedded to power, And then softness will come to a world that is harsh and unkind." It ended: "And then everywhere will be called Eden once again."[3] Fay did not believe it. She had reached her late father's state of dying despair.

When Fay was released from the hospital on July 23rd, her new location was secret. However, it was widely publicized that she remained under 24-hour police guard, bedridden and permanently paralyzed below the waist. In fact, under an assumed name, Fay was then undergoing rehabilitation at a convalescent hospital on Castro Street in San Francisco. Katherine received police protection as Janssen did his best to keep her name out of the papers. Oriane and Neal were also in hiding, though Marvin had not taken up the offer of orthodox Hasidic Jews in Berkeley to conceal them.

On July 26, Janssen called Neal as the chief witness at the preliminary hearing against Brooks. Marvin came along for moral support but was excluded from the courtroom at the insistence of Brooks' attorney. The defendant had a right to keep Marvin out of the courtroom because he might later be subpoenaed to testify. Neal spoke nervously in a near whisper as he recounted the details of his ordeal on May 28. Janssen asked if he could identify the gunman and Neal pointed to the defendant.

When first arrested, Brooks had been assigned only temporary counsel. Few members of the local criminal defense bar were willing to consider defending Brooks at trial despite their sworn oath "never to reject . . . the cause of the defenseless" for personal reasons. Though they had represented clients accused of viler crimes, Fay was one of their own and they were uncharacteristically eager for a conviction.

The appointment was finally accepted by African-American Tom Broome, the former probation department officer who had testified against Newton at his post-trial parole hearing. Broome was only a few years out of law school, but was both diligent and capable. Janssen appreciated having a worthy adversary. From day one, Broome clearly put himself under pressure to do his best for a highly unpopular client under most difficult circumstances.

As his private investigator, Broome employed a former member of the Prison Law Project staff fiercely loyal to Hugo Pinell, who had quit Fay's Berkeley office in the fall of 1971 to join the rival Prison Law Collective. Fay's allies in the bar shunned both Broome and his assistant. She, in turn, viewed Fay and others siding with the prosecutor as turncoats. The percentage of minorities in California's inmate population had skyrocketed in the last ten years to sixty per cent — twice as high as when Fay first represented Huey Newton.

So far, in trying to provide a meaningful defense, Broome felt only frustration. He told reporters that facing Neal Stender on the stand was the first opportunity Broome had to talk to any witnesses. Broome questioned Neal closely about the sequence of events and got him to admit he had glanced at newspaper coverage of the story, which included a photo of Brooks. When the hearing continued, Janssen reported that Fay was still unable to testify. Observers might have wondered if she would ever be well enough to appear.

To cast doubt on Neal's identification, Broome then put two Berkeley police officers on the stand, who testified how they had prepared a composite drawing of the suspect from the eyewitness accounts. It had more facial hair than Brooks and had the wooden quality characteristic of composites. The videotaped lineup was reshown in court. One at a time, it flashed a front view of the heads of seven black men wearing a light blue knit cap like that worn by the attacker. Although Neal had quickly picked out Brooks, an inspector admitted that Neal had expressed some uncertainty about his choice.

Broome argued that Neal's identification was as shaky as that of Katherine Morse, which Janssen had decided not to rely on. Neal was near-sighted and had also not been wearing glasses at the time. Broome complained to the judge that his defense was hampered because "I don't know where the witnesses are." He demanded an opportunity to meet with Fay. Janssen retorted, "A good deal of expense and time has been put into getting her into an environment where she feels safe."[4] Instead, Jannsen offered to make Fay available by telephone, which the judge then ordered.

Broome was not satisfied. He wanted to wait until Fay was able to come to court. He also demanded access to both Katherine Morse and Oriane. The judge ordered Janssen to make both available immediately for Broome to interview, but backed off the following day when Jannsen produced neither witness and offered to rely just on Neal's account. Brooks was not helping his attorney out. One charge against him was theft of the piece of paper on which Fay had written the forced confession. During a heated exchange on this issue between Broome and Janssen, Brooks was overheard to comment, "I didn't take nothin."[5] Broome failed to get bail reduced from $75,000. The hearing ended with Brooks led out in handcuffs, facing multiple charges, including attempted murder.

Trial was still months away. A major concern was that after completion of rehab, Fay needed somewhere else safe to stay. Lisie and her husband offered their suburban home in San Mateo County. As an experiment, they invited Fay to spend a weekend there. Lisie and Don had their ranch-style house wired in advance for additional security. An ambulance picked Fay up at the San Francisco hospital and drove her to the peninsula. Don went along in his own car. They were joined by local police patrol cars and arrived at the quiet residential street in a caravan.

For the entire weekend, the police provided round-the-clock, armed protection. They stopped everyone who came to the Stones' front door. The living room had a pair of glass doors leading to the Stones' patio, which was also reachable by a gate from the street. The police considered it unsafe from invasion and wanted to post an officer inside the Stones' living room with a machine gun. The family declined. They preferred some semblance of normality, despite the enormous strain.

Fay confided in her younger sister her bitterness and suicidal wishes. The shooting was the "thanks" she got for all the years she had devoted to the prisoners' rights movement. She asked if Lisie could bring herself to let Fay die if Fay later became so overwhelmed that she took an overdose of sleeping pills. Lisie could make no such promise. Instead, she and her husband Don did their best to cheer Fay up. Don made suggestions for different pain killers and anti-depressants that might not make Fay feel so fuzzy-headed as the ones she had been prescribed. She declined. He also tried to convince Fay that her talents would make her a highly effective advocate for the disabled. Lisie sat her sister at their piano. Fay could play, but not use the foot pedals. To Lisie's ear, it still sounded quite beautiful. To Fay, her talent was gone.

Meanwhile, Marvin and Oriane stayed with Dru at her two-bedroom house in San Francisco's Noe Valley. It was dark outside when the lights suddenly went out. Dru realized the fuse box was outside. She and Oriane froze with fear, assuming "this was it" — imminent death from a home invasion. Dru urged Marvin to call the police, but Marvin saw no reason to panic. He assured them it was probably just a power outage. He phoned Pacific Gas & Electric, only to learn that no problem had been reported in the area. Marvin then called the local police, still matter-of-fact in his tone, his classic first response to most situations. Marvin mentioned to the dispatcher that there had been a prior shooting incident involving a family member and asked if someone could come by to check out what happened to their power.

The police saw no reason to hurry. The patrol car made another stop first. All of a sudden, the name Stender rang a bell to one of them. The two officers immediately alerted a SWAT team to descend on Dru's home. A week before, the BGF had taken credit for shooting out the window of the nearby Mission Police Station. The SWAT team turned up no intruder at Dru's home but did find broken glass and barbed wire. They could not determine why her power had gone out. The irate precinct captain could not believe no one had alerted him to possible assassination attempts in his own backyard. He told Marvin and Dru, from now on, he wanted to know "if you hear a twig snap."

Marvin realized that he could no longer afford to relax his guard anywhere. The reaction of the San Francisco police reconfirmed that the family remained at great risk from BGF gang members. Ruby received an anonymous threat in her mailbox: "We got your daughter, now we'll get you." She then hid out for a few days with Lisie and Don, but bravely returned to her San Francisco apartment after removing her name from the mail slot in the lobby.

Marvin obtained a permit to carry a concealed weapon and made sure the whole family took shooting lessons, Dru and Lisie included. Even Fay applied for a permit only to be turned down because she was physically unable to work the trigger. Dru was afraid of guns, so she asked for advice from a night law student at Golden Gate Law School, who worked in law enforcement. His suggestions were chilling: if confronted by an attacker, shoot to kill, putting him down like a dog. He also counseled her not to go home the same way twice.

Marvin brought the family several times to a gun and rifle range just south of Oakland in the city of San Leandro. The cars and trucks in its parking lot were plastered with reactionary slogans and signs. The noise at the range was deafening. Dru noticed some large Japanese men shooting off carbine rifles and other patrons wielding revolutionary war muskets and cannons. She found it traumatizing but came back anyway, equipped with ear muffs. When Oriane went back for further training with Katherine Morse, she looked around and said, "I know why we're here. Why are they here?"

The Stender family's fears were reinforced when their pediatrician's Berkeley office was broken into. The police said the only files pulled were Neal's. Marvin still had cases he needed to attend to, but he kept his legal work to a bare minimum. He was at a deposition when he received a telephone call threatening Neal and Oriane's lives. It was too easy to discover that Neal was staying at the International House on the Berkeley campus. Marvin abruptly left to find both Neal and Oriane.

Soon afterward, Marvin sent Oriane to stay with his former secretary, Joanne Schulman, who had moved to New York. Marvin decided to hide Neal until trial on the other side of the world — at a language school in Beijing, China. Marvin obtained the money he needed for tuition all in cash so it could not be traced, but wanted someone else to get Neal's visa. A number of friends turned Marvin down — too scared to help. Don Jelinek volunteered to pick up the money from Marvin's office to make the secret arrangements.

Guild lawyer Dan Siegel (of People's Park fame) wrote an article capturing what everyone around him on the Left was whispering: the attempted assassination of Fay Stender "drove yet another nail into the coffin of the prisoners' rights movement."[6] He noted that activism in that arena first gained momentum in 1967 with the "Free Huey" campaign, which united black militants and their families with radical students and Left-leaning intellectuals. Over the next few years, Beverly Axelrod and Fay Stender's close bond with revolutionary authors Eldridge Cleaver and George Jackson epitomized that alliance.

Siegel realized that, more recently, the prison movement, had become "hopelessly split" between those still championing prisoners' rights and those advocating revolution — oblivious to the reality that they had no chance whatsoever of overthrowing the American government. Siegel reviewed the doomed terrorist tactics of Tribal Thumb and the SLA, which "prompt[ed] more frustration and fratricidal violence, such as the 1976 murder of [black prison reform activist] Popeye Jackson . . . who, like Fay Stender, was accused of 'selling out.'"[7] In fact, if one connected all the dots, as investigative reporter Jo Durden-Smith had undertaken, Fay was the last in a chain of prison-related violence that started at Soledad a decade before.

Though the Stender family focused more on their immediate safety, they still lacked funds for the enormous anticipated expense of Fay's recovery. CWL joined Queen's Bench and Equal Rights Advocates in hosting a benefit. A popular stand-up comic also dedicated the proceeds of his "Salmon Show" to the Stender trust fund. It likely even raised a rare smile from Fay. Bob Carroll's routine followed the life cycle of a salmon mingled with political satire, advertised as "fish, George Jackson and multi-national corporations."[8]

Fay took little comfort when CWL's President then nominated Fay for a prestigious State Bar award created just three years before to honor the memory of Judge Loren Miller, an African-American champion of civil rights. At the State Bar's annual meeting in September, Fay would be chosen in absentia over eleven other candidates for her "impressive history" of demonstrated commitment to legal services for the poor — the first woman lawyer to receive the award.[9] Just a year before, Fay would have welcomed such recognition. Now, it came at far too high a price.

Meanwhile, Fay's friends met frequently to brainstorm on fund-raising. The appeal resonated nationally. By the end of September, they had sent close to three thousand letters out and raised $76,000. They increased their goal to $250,000 and began to consult professional fund-raisers. Advised to obtain a tax-exemption, they then formed a charity dedicated to public interest lawyers, whose work in the vanguard of fighting social injustice made them targets for assassination. Fay was still their only recipient.

Marvin and Dru scoured San Francisco for a safe location where Fay's friends could visit her often and improve her spirits. By October, they moved Fay to an expensive apartment off upper Market Street in San Francisco. It had a 360-degree view. The street entrance had a combination lock. Police installed cameras outside and a television screen in the apartment's front door. They provided Fay with a guard dog and 24-hour police protection. No one could surprise Fay with the stunt she had repeatedly pulled on her mother a few years back by bypassing security at her mother's apartment house entrance to arrive inside unannounced at the door of Ruby's San Francisco apartment.

Coincidentally, Hilde Stern had just received a grant to do research for a year at the Exploratorium in San Francisco. To Marvin's relief, when Fay was released from rehab, Hilde volunteered to be her roommate. Fay would also be accompanied by a trained nurse and Neal's twenty-year-old girlfriend Amy as an aide to assist Fay with showers and other daily tasks. Marvin thought the apartment was cheery. Hilde did not care for it.

On October 11, 1979, shortly after Hilde and Fay secretly moved into their apartment, Edward Brooks and another maximum security prisoner escaped from the Alameda County jail. The other inmate was facing the death penalty for a robbery-murder in June of an Oakland coin shop dealer. (The crime had just been reclassified as a capital offense in 1978 by California voters.) The two men cut through a half-inch steel bolt fastened to a grating over the jailhouse window. They then climbed down from the eighth-floor jail to the third-floor roof using a rope ladder fashioned from torn bed sheets and prison overalls. They were wearing civilian clothes, routinely issued to prisoners awaiting trial. Luckily, their plans went awry when an employee of the District Attorney's office saw them drop to the roof. The pair put up a struggle but were grabbed and manacled. The attempt made chilling headlines.

For added safety, Fay gave her new address and phone number to only a few select friends, who were asked to memorize the information and not write it down. Even though Elsa Knight Thompson remained hard at work as co-chair of the fund-raising committee, Fay refused to let either Elsa or Alex Hoffmann know where she was. The two were still on friendly terms with Huey Newton. It was not worth the risk he might discover her whereabouts. When visitors came, Fay found it painful to sit up for very long. Instead, she would lie stretched out on the carpet for hours. It became difficult to see people "because my posture is so boring."[10] Whenever Fay went out, she had a police car downstairs waiting for her. If Marvin took her somewhere, Fay insisted he bring his gun along. She carried one, too, in her purse, for comfort.

At first, Fay seemed somewhat happier, while Hilde adjusted to life as a semi-hermit. Hilde could not invite any co-workers home and had to take a circuitous route back from the Exploratorium every evening. Hilde's social life was also subjected to strict scrutiny. In the evenings, Hilde listened to Fay's complaints: she was upset against the black community for not rallying to her defense; she hated needing a catheter to pee; no matter what she ate, she now experienced constant indigestion; sitting was too painful; she would never have a sex life again; and her hands hurt too much to write to friends.

It was not in Hilde's nature to hover over Fay. She gladly left the nursing tasks to others, but she volunteered to act as Fay's scribe when asked to do so. One correspondent Fay wrote to herself was Katherine Morse. Since Fay had banned Katherine from the hospital in July, the two women had remained in touch. Though Fay found it hard to hold a pen, she sent Katherine a note in August that she was sorry to hear Katherine had been subpoenaed by Brooks' counsel. Unlike Fay, Katherine was still living in her own home. In September, Katherine received a death threat and, on the advice of the police, moved in with a friend.

Throughout the summer and fall, Fay was still obsessed with the idea of winning Marvin back. He was the only person who made her feel safe. Meanwhile, Katherine kept a low profile in the community and nervously awaited the trial, hoping that afterward she could somehow help Fay recover. Katherine cherished letters from Fay that left the possibility of reuniting open. Fay had written: "I know there was much beauty and dignity between us, and much love, from each of us, according to our abilities, but for all that limitation, real."[11]

As depressed as she had become, Fay managed to be on her best behavior whenever Howard Janssen came. He wanted to keep her spirits up, giving her updates on developments in the case against Brooks. Janssen also wanted to further explore possible motives for the shooting. When he learned that Fay could not comfortably sit for long, he volunteered to join her on the carpet, lying facing each other for lengthy conversations about his prosecution strategy. By this point, they had become friends. Janssen no longer worried about Fay changing her mind. She trusted him and clearly wanted a conviction.

Janssen shared with Fay how extensive investigation into the BGF angle had proved fruitless. Neither his office nor the police could establish a strong enough case against the amorphous prison gang, which had not been highly active of late. Some of the men who had participated in the bank robberies were BGF members, but others were not. Brooks was "a bad egg," but they had no proof the ex-felon was a member. Janssen had even met Brooks' family — nice people who came to Brooks' support and could not understand how he had gone wrong.

Janssen accepted Fay's theory that she was targeted because she quit working on the Prison Reform Project in 1973. From his own experience, criminal defendants who wound up in prison often bore a greater grudge against their own attorney than against the prosecutor who put them there. They figured the prosecutor was just doing his job; their own attorney took their money and betrayed them. Janssen guessed that Brooks wanted to join the Berkeley branch of the BGF but was quirky enough that its members were skittish. So Brooks was looking to prove himself when he came to Fay's home. Still, Janssen felt that Brooks could not possibly have been in on the planning stage. He was not smart enough and did not know Fay. Who suggested the execution to him? Why, after all this time since she had left prison work? Who was the young woman who led Brooks to the Stenders' door? Janssen hoped to win this case even though he had no answers to these questions.

Two days after Thanksgiving, Fleeta Drumgo was walking down a sidewalk in East Oakland around 3:30 p.m. when he was accosted by two other black men. One wielded a shotgun used for deer hunting, the other, a handgun. The man with the shotgun fired three blasts of heavy pellets at Drumgo's head, killing him instantly. Though it happened in broad daylight, the police had no suspects.

In early December, the police leaked to the local newspapers an aspect of the case they had been sitting on since June — a piece of evidence seized during the June 8 marijuana arrest of Brooks and his two companions. It involved BGF plans for an elaborate breakout at Folsom Prison, including an exchange of hostages for Hugo Pinell. By December of 1979, the police had reconstructed the bizarre plot from the contents of Brooks' confiscated satchel. It contained the names and home addresses of high level diplomats at the Swiss, West German, Japanese and Swedish consulates in San Francisco, whom the BGF apparently intended to kidnap. The director of the Kaiser Foundation Hospital in Oakland was also listed. Although the plans were at a preliminary stage, the police had taken the threat seriously and warned all the proposed targets.

The satchel also included an underground bomb-making manual, *The Anarchist Cookbook*, with chapters on "Electronics, Sabotage and Surveillance" and "Explosives and Booby Traps." Reporters already knew that Brooks' satchel included color photographs of a building. The police now identified that building as an electrical power plant near Folsom. Apparently, the conspirators planned to bomb the plant, disabling electrical security devices and lights at the prison to facilitate the breakout. It looked like an attempt to improve upon the plan that Jonathan Jackson had unsuccessfully sought to implement in August of

1970 at the Marin County courthouse. For the scheme to work, the BGF had to assume authorities would value the lives of diplomats far more than a judge, prosecutor and jurors.

Police attributed the plan to the Berkeley BGF cell. They figured that the Bank of America robbery was to help finance Pinell's escape and that the second bank robbery was to raise money for Brooks' escape after he shot Fay. Police had also discovered that both Coleman and Brooks were once imprisoned in the same prison wing as Hugo Pinell. An investigator told the press, "We think the Stender attack is just part of a much a larger picture." They believed Fay was the focus of "simmering hatred" by Jackson's convict followers. Her death "was intended to give new impetus to the prison gang, which had been faltering since Jackson was fatally shot."[12] Janssen still had no proof of such a conspiracy that he could introduce in court.

Accusing the BGF of orchestrating the shooting would also add a major complicating factor. In 1977, the Alameda County District Attorney's office had convicted several BGF members for the murder of a prisoner at Santa Rita. The case was currently on appeal before the United States Supreme Court because the prosecutor had removed all black panelists from the jury — out of concern that black jurors would likely be subjected to threats of retaliation by the BGF. If the BGF were brought into Fay's case, gang intimidation of jurors could potentially stymie the prosecution. Janssen concluded that the bank robbers "were just a bunch of thugs. The gang that couldn't shoot straight." Despite the execution-style cross pattern of the shots fired at Fay, Brooks was not an accomplished assassin. He had not even gotten rid of the gun. Under the intense glare of the media, Janssen thought it best to keep it simple and try the case without any reference to the BGF.

* * *

Fay's close friend Gene Pippin and his wife Karma were then living in Cairo, Egypt, where Pip had been teaching for the past fifteen years at the American University. Neither had heard about the Memorial Day 1979 home invasion. The shooting occurred about the same time as Pip was diagnosed with terminal lung cancer. The couple then left to return to Wichita, Kansas, where he was hospitalized near family. By October, Pip had heard sympathetic wishes from every one of his lifelong friends except Fay. He was disconsolate at her failure to get in touch with him.

Right after Fay moved in with Hilde in October of 1979, Fay tried to call Pip at the Wichita hospital but could not get through. A mutual friend obtained Pip's address so Fay could write to him. By early November, Fay had practiced using her right hand enough to print a letter to Pip explaining her situation. When Karma received Fay's letter, she decided not to share it with Pip. He remained gravely ill in the hospital and she feared it would break his heart.

By the beginning of December, after Pip kept asking why he had not heard from Fay, Karma relented. Only then did he learn Fay had "been shot by a 'revolutionary' black ex-convict and rendered permanently paraplegic." She was out of the hospital but depressed ". . . and neither optimistic [n]or motivated. . ." Fay wrote: "I hurt a lot — in the back, sides, and hands (nerve damage)." Fay inquired about the details of Pip's own condition and updated him on her children and her separation from Marvin, who remained "very supportive and helpful." Fay ended with: "I remember all those old Berkeley days and even the day we met — Love, Fay."[13] Karma thought Pip took the news better than she expected. He was visibly relieved to know Fay still cared deeply for him and had a powerful reason for not having been in touch sooner. Karma left the hospital and returned home. Not much later, she was on the telephone with a friend when the operator broke in with an emergency message — her husband had just died of a heart attack.

As the Christmas holiday approached, Fay wrote to Katherine. It had been a while since their last exchange of letters. Fay expressed her sympathy for Katherine's own situation since the night of the attack and shared her continuing indecision about committing suicide after the trial ended. She told Katherine of her constant pain, fear and depression. She could then only bring herself to see very few visitors — Katherine still not among them.

In an attempt to cheer Fay up, a large group of her friends held a cocktail party at Christmas time at a safe house in San Francisco.

Fay sat in a corner, very depressed, talking in a soft voice about what had happened. She saw no reason to try to get over the devastating blow. Marvin took her out to dinner a couple of weeks later with Judy McKelvey and her husband Stuart at a favorite Mediterranean restaurant in San Francisco, whose spicy food Fay realized would no longer sit well in her stomach. Getting her in and out of the car was a clumsy process which none of them were good at. Judy noticed that Fay lacked full control of her hands. Struggling with her purse, Fay revealed the gun she was unable to shoot.

* * *

Though Fay was overjoyed to see Neal back from Beijing, she worried about how he would handle the ordeal of the trial. Swallowing her terror, Fay made a special trip back to Berkeley to visit her neighbor Michael Magbie. Fay arrived in the afternoon with a burly policeman as bodyguard. The officer maneuvered Fay's wheel chair up the steps to her home and stood watch as Fay spoke urgently with Magbie. Honored by her call, Magbie was especially impressed that Fay defiantly sat on her own front porch in broad daylight. As they both vividly recalled, the last time Fay crossed its threshold was on a gurney in the dark of night when they both feared she was dying.

Their conversation struck him as otherworldly. Fay had always been on the go and was now wheelchair bound, with useless legs. She had been "Ms. Anti-Death Penalty," and was now urging her pacifist neighbor to get a gun to protect himself and his family. And Fay now spewed hatred, angrily swearing she would see the perpetrators who did this to her "taken off the face of the earth." But then Fay came to the real purpose of her visit. She pleaded with Magbie to come to the courthouse every day of the trial, particularly when Neal was there. Magbie had spent so much time helping to raise Neal, his friendly face in the gallery would likely make Neal feel more comfortable. Fay did not need to worry. Coming to the trial to support her and Neal was the least Magbie could do.

Key pretrial motions were set for January 9, 1980. The courtroom of Judge Harold Hove filled with many white friends and colleagues of Fay's, but also with supporters of Brooks, who were mostly black. It was the same imposing building on the shores of Lake Merritt where Huey Newton was repeatedly tried. Brooks had as his co-counsel a recently admitted woman lawyer as well as the continuing assistance of his investigator. For the past several months, the investigator had been designated as the principal defense liaison to Brooks in his jail cell, but her visiting privileges were suspended just before trial. Her known support for Hugo Pinell may have made police suspicious she was acting as a go-between. Fay knew how easy that was from her own many visits to Huey Newton in the Men's Colony.

One of the first issues to be taken up before the trial began was Broome's challenge to the identification Fay had made in June from her hospital bed. He argued that the police had violated standard procedure for conducting a lineup that led Fay to point to his client. Broome also claimed that critical witnesses had never been made available to him and asked to delay the trial so he would have more time to investigate. His frustration mirrored Fay's own indignant reaction when she had been in a similar position representing both Huey Newton and George Jackson years before.

Broome criticized both Janssen and Marvin Stender for thwarting his efforts to gain access to Fay and Oriane. By then, Marvin had asked Penny Cooper to represent him. If he were subpoenaed to testify, Marvin would rather go to jail for contempt of court than divulge Oriane's current whereabouts. Judge Hove ordered Janssen to grant Broome access in advance only to witnesses Janssen intended to call. Janssen announced that Fay would appear the following day.

A strong winter storm struck that night and heavy rains were expected during the day. Yet the heavily guarded courtroom was filled to capacity. Attendees were searched in advance by bailiffs furnished with hand-held metal detectors. Marvin sensed the deep hostility against Fay of the militants who came to show support for Brooks. Though the defense was based on mistaken identity, the expression on their faces was "the bitch got what she deserved."

Some friends avoided the trial. Jae Scharlin, a private investigator and longtime friend of Fay and Marvin's, was among them. She herself was an impassioned prisoners' rights activist who fell in love with a black prisoner on San Quentin's death row and ultimately married him when he was paroled. Scharlin thought that the same thing that befell Fay could easily have happened to her. They all knew that life in a cage affected the prisoners' psyches. Militant ex-felons who remained alive were often either drug-addicted or sent back to prison for parole violations, demonstrably incapable of handling life on the outside.

Lisie remained at home, too, though she had wanted to come to provide Fay with moral support as she confronted, face to face, the man Fay thought had tried to kill her. But Lisie was mindful of her husband Don's fear that Lisie might be followed home if she came. The family resemblance was so strong, it was a valid concern. Their address was still being withheld from the public. Lisie hoped that Fay had the strength to handle this ordeal without her and might still consider living with them when it was over.

While other observers waited inside the courthouse on the morning of the 10th, the press lined up outside to catch the first glimpse of Fay upon her arrival. Katherine and Neal were in the police van with Fay. As it pulled up to the curb, Fay spotted the photographers and panicked. Pictures of Neal could help target him for an attack on his life. She asked the police to disperse the photographers while the driver circled the courthouse.

As expected, the judge again excluded Marvin from the courtroom when witnesses were called because he was also going to be a witness. Marvin would be practically climbing the walls for the duration of the trial. Fay appeared nervous as she was wheeled into the courtroom by a plain clothes security guard. She was well-disguised with a gray wig under a large kerchief. As soon as court was called into session, Fay seemed to steel herself and become totally composed. This was what she had been waiting for. Brooks arrived after Fay did, smiling and raising a clenched fist salute to supporters. He glanced at Fay, who remained impassive and stoic. After wheeling her up to be sworn in, her bodyguard sat nearby in the empty jury box.

Jannsen had already explained to Fay that he was going to be brief, focusing only on the identification of Fay's attacker. This was a test run of her likely endurance as a trial witness. Janssen asked Fay if she was shot in the early morning hours of May 28, 1979. She said, "That's correct." Janssen then asked if she would recognize the man who shot her today. Fay was already wearing her glasses. She responded, "Yes, I can."[14]

"Who shot you?" asked Janssen.

Fay pointed with her right hand: "The gentleman at the end of the counsel table without the tie."[15] Fay added, "He is much more real to me in person than on the videotape."[16] Brooks, for once, showed no signs of emotion. Broome then had his first opportunity to cross-examine Fay. He spent an hour reviewing the process by which she had originally selected Brooks out of the videotaped lineup, hoping to weaken her identification. Broome focused on perceived contradictions in her first description of her attacker and lack of certainty when viewing the videotape at the hospital.

Fay said she had never seen Brooks before the attack and repeatedly insisted that she picked him out because "I thought he was the man that shot me."[17] As a trained lawyer, she had been cautious in the summer, but when she saw his "bouncy walk" when led into court that morning, it reinforced her recognition of the man who attacked her.[18]

As the bodyguard wheeled Fay out of the courtroom, a friend commented, "It's so good to see her behaving and talking like the same old forceful, confident Fay."[19] Both Neal and Katherine Morse then identified Brooks as the gunman who held them hostage in the early morning of May 28th. Trial was set to begin on Monday, January 14th, unless delayed by the court of appeal, as Broome had just requested by an emergency writ petition.

The trial started the following Monday. Questioning of potential jurors proceeded quickly. The first day, the defense excused eight, while the prosecutor challenged four. They completed their selections the following day, seating seven women and five men. The presence of so many of Fay's criminal defense colleagues as spectators added to the pressure on Janssen — a whole peanut gallery of second-guessers breathing down his neck.

Since Marvin was barred from watching, Dru made a point of

STAR WITNESS FOR THE PROSECUTION

Courtroom sketches reproduced courtesy of sketch artist Don Juhlin

Shooting Victim
Drama in Court —
Stender Testifies

By George Williamson

One-time prison reform attorney Fay Stender, looking remarkably strong in her wheelchair, appeared in court yesterday and pointed out the man she says shot her and left her for dead in her Berkeley home last Memorial Day.

The accused, Edward Brooks, 28, likewise displayed little emotion as he and Mrs. Stender eyed each other for only a split second.

It was the first time since the shooting that Stender had directly faced the man she thinks did it.

It was also her first public appearance since a night intruder fired six .38-caliber bullets into her after forcing her to write that she had "betrayed George Jackson and the entire prison reform movement."

"It's so good to see her behaving and looking like my strong, forceful, confident Fay," one woman said to a friend after a plain clothes security guard wheeled Stender out of court.

Stender remains under around-the-clock police guard at a secret location. Doctors say the shooting left her paralyzed for life from the waist down.

Authorities claim that Brooks connected with the Black Guerrilla Family, which George Jackson, a prisoner and symbol for the prison reform movement, organized before he was shot to death in 1971 by San Quentin guards.

Prison officials think the Black Guerrilla Family formed after Jackson's split with the Black Panther Party, is now a lone-knit "gang" with little of its initial political impetus.

Stender was sure one of Jackson's attorneys. She later was part of the defense team in one of Black Panther leader Huey Newton's trials.

Her appearance in court yesterday, even before jury selection has begun for Brooks' trial, was required because defense attorneys needed to review her initial identifications of Brooks made from a videotaped lineup.

Stender contends that Stender and two other persons in the house on the night of the shooting — her son, Neal, 21, and a friend, Priscilla Camp— were examined by police and by other factors; to single out Brooks from the lineup.

Stender's testimony yesterday was limited to reviewing her initial identification of Brooks, made after seeing a videotape from her hospital bed, and being asked if anyone in the courtroom was the man who shot her.

Both Brooks and Stender remained stoic as she pointed to him.

From her wheelchair in the courtroom, an impressive Fay Stender pointed to an equally impressive Edward Brooks

Stender's full account of the shooting will come during Brooks' full trial, which probably will begin next week.

When Stender first entered the court and waited for proceedings to begin, she appeared nervous. But when court was called into session and Brooks appeared, her composure changed dramatically and the veteran attorney was fully composed.

Yesterday's hearing was delayed 35 minutes because Stender, upon seeing cameramen awaiting her arrival, had the driver of her car circle the Oakland courthouse until authorities dispersed photographers.

A friend said her primary concern seemed to be that photographs of her son — who was with her in the car — might endanger his life.

from seven black men shown her on a videotape screened in her hospital room three weeks after the shooting. Stender, who has said she never saw Brooks before the shooting, never wavered yesterday in her assertion that thought he was the man that shot me.

Alameda County Superior Court Judge Harold Hove said he will rule on Brooks's motion today. Jury selection is expected to begin Monday.

Source: Alameda County District Attorney's Office website, www.alcoda.org

District Attorney Lowell Jensen had been impressed by Fay Stender's legal skills when she was on Huey Newton's defense team in 1968. After she got shot, he was determined to show her that he would spare no effort to bring her attacker to justice regardless of the animosity toward her still felt by many members of local law enforcement.

When prompted by prosecutor Howard Janssen, Fay Stender pointed to defendant Ed Brooks as her assailant. Fay Stender, her son and Katherine Morse had all been less sure of their original identification of the gunman before trial than they were when they saw him in court, where Edward Brooks' distinctive gait and appearance in the flesh triggered recognition and fear.

attending the trial most days. She was now driving Fay's Toyota Celica, repainted from its distinctive pink and reregistered under a fictitious name. One day on her way to court, Dru ran a stop sign coming off the freeway exit ramp. When the Oakland traffic cop who stopped Dru asked for the registration, she burst into tears and told him whose car it really was. He said, "Well, I guess even Fay Stender doesn't deserve to be shot in her home."

Broome's witness list puzzled the press. He included an astronomer and a dermatologist. In addition, he named Katherine Morse. In his opening argument, Broome outlined his defense: that the police had focused on the wrong man and convinced the witnesses to pick Brooks as the gunman. Broome would prove that it was a dark night, the lighting was poor, and that Fay and Neal had originally described the gunman as having a heavier beard than his client was capable of growing.

In his own forceful opening statement, Janssen said Fay and Neal "have no question in their minds that Edward Glenn Brooks is the gunman."[20] The shooting occurred at point-blank range. Janssen also informed the jury they would hear police testimony of the narcotics stop in San Francisco at which Brooks had been relieved of a .38 Smith & Wesson pistol that ballistics tests proved had shot the bullets retrieved from Fay's wounds.

The lead-off prosecution witness on Wednesday, January 16, 1980, was Neal. Brooks glared at Neal as he took the stand. Magbie had made good on his promise. He could be easily spotted among the crowd in the gallery because he was the only black seated on the prosecutor's side. On another day, Diana Russell — drawn closer to the drama by having been in Fay's home just the night before the shooting — would come with Donnis and notice the same phenomenon. Donnis was the only black that day among Fay's supporters. Seeing such polarization by race struck Russell as the most disillusioning experience in her life. The segregated audience in that courtroom starkly revealed to the South African native the hypocrisy of America's claimed superior race relations.

Neal spent the entire day on the stand. The jury listened closely as he described being wakened, donning his pants and going downstairs to answer the ringing doorbell around 1:20 a.m. the previous May

28th. "I looked out the curtains and saw this young black woman on the porch."[21] She slipped from sight as he answered the door and faced a male intruder wielding a gun. Neal identified the defendant Edward Brooks as the man in the blue cap who forced Neal to lead him upstairs to the master bedroom. After describing the ordeal that left him and Katherine Morse face down on the bed with their hands tied, Neal said his mother and the gunman went downstairs where he could no longer hear them talking. "Moments later I heard five shots and the slamming of the front door." I called "Mom, are you all right? I heard my mother moaning. She said 'I'm shot. I'm dying.'" After kicking open his sister's door and yelling for her to call an ambulance, Neal ran downstairs and found his mother on the kitchen floor covered with blood, crying and clutching her thigh.[22]

Neal's riveting direct testimony took only part of the morning. The rest of the day was spent in cross-examination. When Broome pointed out that local papers had printed Brooks' picture as a suspect before any identification was made, Neal insisted that after seeing Brooks in person, he had absolutely no doubt that Brooks was the man who forced his way into their home. Broome pointed out discrepancies between Neal's description of the gunman when interviewed by police in June and Brooks' physical appearance. He acted incredulous when Neal denied drinking any alcohol or consuming any drugs at the party he had attended that night with his girlfriend Amy. Neal admitted that he was near-sighted and was not wearing his glasses at the time of the attack. Though the house lighting was poor and he was frightened and upset, Neal still insisted that he got a good look at the gunman.

Fay heard how Neal had done and was extremely proud of him, though it distressed her greatly that he had to relive the horrific experience. Although Janssen did not consider the discrepancies in Neal's identification of Brooks significant, the prosecutor had some concerns about the jury's impressions. Jurors did not realize there were always some differences between people's recollection and what an attacker actually looked like. Unsure how much headway Broome had made with the jurors to doubt Neal's identification of Brooks, Janssen realized that Fay's testimony would make or break his case.

Following Neal, Janssen called two doctors to testify to the extent of Fay's wounds and permanent paralysis from gunshots inflicted at close range. Janssen then called a ballistics expert to testify that the gun found on Brooks when he was arrested on June 8th in San Francisco was the same .38 caliber revolver used to shoot her. With the stage thus set, Janssen called Fay as his star witness. She was dramatically wheeled into the Oakland courtroom on Friday morning, January 18, 1980 — the moment she had been living for since the shooting. Today, the crowded courtroom included Charles Garry in the front row. Fay also spotted her good friends Ying Lee Kelley and Bergie Mackey in the audience.

Fay's wheelchair was escorted in by four armed policemen. She wore a white jacket and a black blouse, with the same gray bouffant wig and kerchief. Reporters noticed how fragile and tired Fay looked compared to the week before, but Janssen was proud of how tough Fay was: "She sat in that wheel chair and I could see the color drain in her body as she was using every ounce of energy she could to fight to testify. She was in constant pain. She didn't want to take drugs." Janssen also knew that Fay remained frightened that the BGF would come after her and her children.

On direct examination, Fay spoke in a fast monotone as she described being awakened early on Memorial Day by her son Neal announcing a stranger with a gun. She relayed the gunman's accusation and the note he forced her to write that she had betrayed George Jackson. Fay had the rapt attention of the jury when she recalled protesting, "This isn't true, you know."[23]

Fay continued with her description of the ordeal. She led the intruder downstairs where she had $40 in a kitchen drawer and started removing the bills to give him. He became impatient and motioned with the gun, saying, "Come on, come on." She had a twenty in her hand: "I walked to about two feet from him and he shot me, he held the gun in his right hand and braced his wrist with his left hand. I'm not truly sure if he fired five or six times, I remember feeling five shots." The first bullet hit "in my abdomen or stomach, and I heard a kind of snap, and I thought it was a spinal cord kind of thing." She then felt another in her chest, two more in her arms and "one buzzing in my head."[24] The jurors winced at her description of the wounds. Charles Garry swallowed hard. Fay then told the courtroom she remained conscious as the gunman fled and looked up to see first her son and then Katherine and her daughter Oriane standing over her in the kitchen. "I said to everybody: 'I love you, I'm dying.' I think I also said: 'It hurts. Get an ambulance.'"[25]

Without betraying any emotion, Fay described how she suffered permanent paralysis from the waist down. She also described how the shooting caused her to have permanent digestive and intestinal problems, residual lung damage, substantially weakened arms and numbness in the hand. She suffered from chronic, pervasive fatigue. She told the hushed courtroom, "I can only be in a wheelchair for a few hours." To accommodate Fay, the judge took no afternoon break. As Neal had done in the trial's opening session on Wednesday, Fay swiftly and without hesitation identified the gunman: "He's the gentleman at the end of the counsel table with the Afro haircut."[26]

It was already mid-afternoon before Broome started his cross-examination. No matter how much he tried to get her to waver, Fay remained convinced that Edward Brooks, seated in the courtroom facing her, was the man who shot her. Broome moved on, focusing on Fay's relationship with George Jackson. He asked her whether they had a major dispute. Fay said, "I wouldn't put it that way. There was a time when he and I agreed that I would not be his counsel of record in the Soledad case, but that I would loosely represent him on other things." She insisted, "George Jackson and I were on the best of terms until he died."[27]

Fay was oversimplifying for the jury her conclusion that she and George remained friends. Her testimony surprised reporters who had already learned from some of her former colleagues how furious Jackson had been when he fired Fay from his trial team. The reporters also had access to reports from the Attorney General's office identifying associates of Jackson who were extremely unhappy with Fay. Some were now leaders of the BGF. The reporters knew that none of this was before the jury.

Observing the pained expression on Fay's face as she discussed George Jackson, Judge Hove interrupted to ask if a brief recess might be appropriate. Janssen was extremely solicitous of Fay and amazed at her stamina. He walked to her side and talked with her briefly, before reporting to the judge, "A recess would not be of any assistance to the witness — all positions are painful."[28]

Later, when Janssen saw Fay flagging near the end of the day, he stood up, obviously poised to ask for a recess until Monday. Fay waved aside his concerns. She was determined to get her testimony completed in one day. When Broome was finished, Fay was wheeled from the courtroom, exhausted but smiling. A number of friends tried to hug her as she exited; one clutched Fay's hand and burst into tears. Garry rose to follow Fay out of court, whispering to a reporter. "She was a good attorney and now, a perfect witness."[29] Friday ended on a decidedly upbeat note for the prosecution.

Janssen concluded his presentation on Monday, January 21, choosing not to call Katherine Morse as a witness. The next day, Broome began Brooks' defense. He explained to the jury that he did not plan to prove anything because "that is the duty of the district attorney." He argued that Janssen had failed to prove "to a moral certainty" that his client shot Fay Stender. Broome told the jury he would call several "hostile" witnesses aligned with the prosecutor's view of the case, including Katherine Morse and Marvin Stender.[30] Broome wanted to show that Marvin interfered with defense attempts to interview key witnesses. He planned to call an astronomer to establish there was no moon the night of the crime to undermine Neal's testimony that he first saw the gunman "in the glow of moonlight."[31] Broome concluded that, "[b]ecause of the horrible condition of Fay Stender, the witnesses have conspired to lay the blame on Mr. Brooks — we will show that he didn't do it."[32]

Broome then called Katherine Morse to the stand to prove his point. He expected her to sow seeds of doubt about Neal and Fay's identification. Both had said the overhead light was on in the bedroom. Katherine had already testified at the pretrial hearing that only the dim hallway light had been turned on before Fay used the desk lamp to write the note.

When Broome asked Katherine if she could identify the gunman, she surprised the courtroom, by pointing out Brooks at the defense counsel table and stating, "I recognize him as the man I saw in Fay's house."[33] It was obviously a heavy blow. Broome then got Katherine to admit she had earlier doubted she would ever be able to identify the gunman because "I wasn't wearing my glasses and the room was fairly dark."[34] She also agreed that she had been unable to give the police a detailed statement immediately following the attack "because I was hysterical, I was screaming."[35] Why then was she now so positive? She explained that originally when she viewed a lineup, "There were several persons there who seemed to generally resemble the man. I had a strong emotional response to number five (Brooks) that I would characterize as fear."[36] At trial, she no longer had any doubts because she recognized him when she saw him at the pretrial hearing, just as Fay had done. Broome dismissed her and called his expert witnesses.

The astronomer addressed the lack of moonlight. A dermatologist at San Francisco General Hospital testified that Brooks was incapable of growing a beard as dense as the one on the suspect the police artist had drawn at Fay and Neal's direction in the summer. The jury could see that Brooks currently had only a mustache and thin goatee. Broome considered the facial hair testimony critical. Yet the doctor diminished the impact of his testimony by mentioning that "light and many other factors can change the way a beard looks."[37]

Broome also called the police artist who drew the composite sketches from the witnesses' descriptions. Washburn described Neal as being surer the gunman had a goatee and mustache than he was about a beard. Washburn pointed to strong similarities between his drawings and defendant Brooks, but conceded there was no striking resemblance. "You don't get that kind of strong, psychological resemblance" in composite sketches.[38] Broome also called Neal's girlfriend Amy Fujishige to the stand to ask her how much alcohol Neal had consumed at the party they had attended on Sunday evening. Like Neal, she insisted neither had drunk any alcohol or taken any drugs.

Broome decided not to call Marvin Stender to the stand. He had also long since made the strategic decision not to call his own client. Broome concluded Brooks was better off invoking his right not to testify. First, Brooks had a felony record that Janssen would focus the jury on. In any event, Brooks' belligerence would not make a good impression on the jury. At one pretrial hearing, Brooks had called a police witness "A lying motherfucker." Even now, Broome barely had Brooks under control. Brooks had considered taking the stand to proclaim his innocence. He would have testified to being elsewhere at the time the shooting occurred. But he decided to follow his attorney's advice, concerned that his version of the events would implicate one of his friends from the bank robbery instead.

Janssen gave a compelling closing argument: the state had proven its case by "powerful, overwhelming . . . evidence."[39] The only reason it differed from a murder case was that the victim miraculously survived to describe what happened. Broome responded just as emphatically, in his closing arguments, that the state's case was "riddled with inconsistent testimony."[40] He told the jury that the witnesses had been led by police to focus on his client, and their increased certainty over time demonstrated "an organized effort . . . to change their testimony" to convict Brooks of the crime. They were "three nearsighted people without their eyeglasses in a dark room," more positive about the gunman's appearance at the trial than they had been at the time of the crime.

Broome characterized Fay's confidence in pointing out Brooks at the trial as "inherently unbelievable." He explained to the jury that Fay's criminal defense experience would have led her to recognize the importance of making a positive identification from the outset — if she had been certain of his identity. Broome also suggested that Neal may have become more certain because he was "unconsciously" feeling guilty for having opened the door to admit the gunman and wanted to ensure a conviction.[41]

Reporters could practically see steam on Janssen's glasses as the tall, blond prosecutor rose to respond. Janssen angrily ridiculed Broome's theory as "outrageous" and "uncalled for . . . There is absolutely no evidence of any conspiracy. His client attempted to take a life. He took her legs. He took her strength. Now they're trying to assassinate her character and reputation."[42] Janssen was contemptuous of the defense theory that any conviction would serve the Stenders, even if the man accused was innocent. This would still leave the perpetrator at large, capable of returning. Their interest was in seeing the guilty man taken off the streets.

Both sides had completed all of the trial testimony in just six days. Judge Hove instructed the jury Thursday morning, January 24th, for half an hour and then had them escorted to another room to begin their deliberations. They had barely chosen a foreman when the building was jolted by a 5.5 earthquake, one of the largest temblors to hit the Bay Area in years. Fortunately, it did no apparent damage to the Oakland courthouse and they resumed their discussion. At the end of the day, the jury sent Judge Hove a request to have part of Broome's cross-examination of Fay reread, signaling their concern that her testimony might be inconsistent and not credible.

On Friday morning, Judge Hove called the attorneys back into court as the jury focused once again on the strength of Fay's identification of Brooks at the hearing a week before the trial. In the afternoon, after more than eight hours of deliberation, the jury returned with its verdict. They had taken ten ballots, including two on the attempted murder charge before returning to the courtroom with a unanimous verdict. When the judge read the result, Janssen breathed a sigh of relief. They had agreed to convict Brooks on all counts — attempted murder, three robbery charges and one of burglary.

Broome asked to have the jury members polled individually. Brooks glared at them as they each confirmed their agreement with the verdict. The judge set the sentencing date for February 22nd to give time for the Probation Department to prepare a report and recommendation for Brooks, who was looking at a minimum fifteen-year prison term. Brooks interjected, "For what? I'm not going to talk to them about the case — I have nothing to say."[43] As he was led out by the bailiff, Brooks saluted three friends with his clenched fist.

The jurors had agreed not to talk to the press about their deliberations and quickly filed out of the courtroom after the trial ended. As they left, Janssen made no move to talk to them either. He was just happy it was over and that Brooks was convicted. He rushed from the courtroom to telephone the news to Fay, who was back in seclusion in San Francisco. Janssen hoped that she and her family could now gain some closure.

One juror broke their pact as soon as he saw a reporter outside the courtroom. They had found Fay Stender "convincing, honest, effective." Then another spoke up: a primary "concern" that took them some time to consider was the "lack of an apparent motive."[44] In closing argument, Janssen had argued that Brooks shot Fay so that she could not recant the confession she wrote that she had betrayed George Jackson. But that made no sense to the jury when the gunman left both Neal and Katherine Morse alive and both could attest that Fay had only signed it under duress.

Broome told reporters he planned on filing an immediate appeal: "My client was not surprised by the guilty verdicts. He didn't think he would get a fair trial." Broome said Brooks was innocent and did not take the stand because the jury would then have become aware of his prior prison record, which would likely have prejudiced them against him. Broome complimented the judge on his handling of the case and credited the jury with being "very conscientious."[45]

The press questioned Broome further about Brooks' connections to the Black Guerilla Family, which Broome rejected out of hand, "No way, it just isn't there." He is "absolutely not" a member of the BGF. Broome went on to state emphatically, "One of the biggest problems they have is determining if there really is a BGF." When asked why he believed the prosecution witnesses had conspired to convict his client, he responded: "'Why' is a good question. I'd rather not speculate."[46]

After telephoning Fay, Janssen also spoke with the press. He told them this was "the most powerful case I've ever tried." They asked why Janssen had not introduced the Black Guerilla Family issue into the trial. He told them the connection to the BGF was based on police speculation, but added, "in my mind, he (Brooks) probably is a member of the organization."[47]

When asked about Fay's reaction to the verdict, Janssen couldn't find the right words. She had simply said, "Thank you very much," but conveyed far more. Janssen said, "The trial of Edward Brooks might be over, but it sure as hell isn't over for her; she still has to live in her wheelchair."[48] But that was not all. With Brooks convicted, Fay would soon lose all police protection. How could she obtain closure when she still feared another attack on her or her family? Though Janssen did not mention this to the press, he thought Katherine had also turned out to be an extraordinarily good witness, and made sure to communicate that to her after the trial ended.

One troubled freelance reporter wrote: "The entire incident left those involved in the prison movement . . . with more questions than answers." Among them were "1) Why did the attack take place? 2) Was Brooks the attacker, and who else was involved?"[49] Lawyers who had worked alongside Fay defending radical prisoners were deeply divided about their future allegiance to inmates whose judgment was warped by harsh prison conditions. Who might be at risk next? As others pondered their own vulnerability, Fay and Neal went back into hiding.

■ 9 ■
Nowhere to Run

Everywhere the ceremony of innocence is drowned.[1]
— W. B. YEATS

Fay had been planning her own funeral for months, telling some close friends she was still suicidal but trying to avoid the topic with other friends and family members, including Lisie, for whom the thought was too painful. Ying told Fay she must not do it, she was too precious a human being, imploring her: "Live for yourself, live for us." In her nightly conversations with Hilde, Fay alternated between self-pity and self-loathing, castigating herself as "a crippled, lesbian Jew."

Fay knew exactly what she wanted — a traditional Jewish ceremony at Sinai Memorial on Divisadero Street. It was the same prominent synagogue in San Francisco where her father's service had been held thirteen years before and those of so many other family members she had attended. Her pro-Palestinian friends would likely be uncomfortable. That was their problem. Fay made arrangements for a burial plot at Salem Memorial Park in Colma, just south of San Francisco, where her father was buried and her mother also had a plot reserved.

Lisie had agreed to be the executor of Fay's will. In a morbid mood in January, Fay prepared several farewell notes she entrusted to her estate planner, lawyer Susan Bender, for future delivery. To her mother,

Fay was abrupt but suggested that her mother could take comfort from Neal and Oriane. Neal resembled Fay's father in some ways and Oriane reminded Fay a bit of herself. Fay wrote a sweeter note to Lisie, thanking her for her constant devotion. She asked Lisie to offer Neal and Oriane whatever financial support from the estate they needed and gave her sister strict instructions against medical intervention: "If by some disaster, I survive for God's sake, pull the plug."[2]

Family and close friends had made a concerted effort over the months since the shooting to interest Fay in the future: teaching, running a nonprofit or obtaining a judgeship, any of which could likely be arranged without much difficulty. Colleagues reminded Fay that Gary Thomas was now a judge — the prosecutor paralyzed in August of 1970 when Jonathan Jackson was killed in the parking lot of the Marin County courthouse.

Fay realized she had enough influential friends in the Brown administration that a judicial appointment was likely hers for the asking, but she could not imagine trying to pass judgment over criminal cases. She assumed she would be an easy target for revenge. Fay also shunned the idea of the Movement law course she had so enthusiastically proposed the spring before. Any and all other suggestions for activism sparked no enthusiasm, including one from a Jewish friend from the Guild, who thought Fay might make a great rabbi. Fay told friends, "I am tired of doing anything for everybody else." She still could not fathom why she had been singled out for revenge. Did BGF devotees really believe the world would improve for people of color if Fay were killed?

Fay remained frightened for herself and her family. The county had stopped providing her police protection in January. Fay now had two security guards paid for from private fund-raising. How long could she afford to continue? Yet Fay was not alone in assuming she risked reprisal if she returned to live anywhere in the Berkeley community. All her friends thought Brooks had acted under orders. From whom? The mere thought of navigating Berkeley streets on her own in a wheelchair terrified Fay.

Only one idea held some promise. Neal was back in Beijing, where he had recently found a job working for an American company. She could go to Hong Kong, where Neal could visit her frequently and she could try acupuncture treatments to see if they eased her pain. Fay's nurse, Sara Levine, and Neal's girlfriend Amy Fujishige would travel with her. Fay could rent an apartment there for six months, if it worked out, and then re-evaluate where she might permanently relocate. Suicide remained plan B.

* * *

A few weeks after Pip died, his widow Karma came out to San Francisco to visit friends. Marvin provided her with Fay's address and phone number on her solemn promise not to write them down. Karma then took a roundabout route to reach the secure hideaway to make sure she was not followed. Once Karma got past all the locks, Fay greeted her warmly. They reminisced about Pip, and Fay told Karma of her upcoming plans to travel, but also shared her continuing depression and thoughts of suicide. They promised to keep in touch.

Fay's mood improved. Amy cut her hair and Fay received more visitors. Fay now offered them presents. She had always enjoyed making spiritual connections with friends and family through special gifts. To Judy McKelvey, Fay gave a pair of long dress gloves. Fay had already given Bernie Bergesen, her close friend on the ACLU board, a flask inscribed to Bernie Burgleheart, which he would always cherish. To Bergie Mackey, she offered a rubbing from China that Neal had brought back with him. To Hilde, Fay offered a handwritten letter she had saved from George Jackson. This one missed the mark: Hilde had never shared Fay's fascination with the revolutionary prisoner and had no interest in the memento.

At Christmas, Fay had also sent Katherine Morse a rubbing Neal brought back from China, hoping to make partial amends for her prolonged silence since their last exchange of letters. Though Katherine had later accompanied Fay and Neal to the pretrial hearing in January, Fay still did not invite Katherine to visit her at her San Francisco apartment. Katherine knew Fay held out hope for reconciling with Marvin. By February, that was clearly a lost cause. Marvin was proceeding with the divorce. Nevertheless, Fay felt more upbeat since the trial ended. She told Katherine where she was located and invited her to visit. Now, when Hilde came back from work, she would often find them cuddled in bed together.

Yet Fay was unsure where her future lay. Fay wrote to Karma to let her know Brooks had been convicted and floated the idea of the two women living together when Fay returned from her six-month trip abroad. Fay realized they had engaged in little contact over the years, but she felt a strong connection when Karma had visited her that winter. Karma did not quite know what to make of Fay's fantasy.

By the second week of February, Fay felt self-assured enough to thank Elsa Knight Thompson for her extraordinary fund-raising efforts and, at long last, to invite her to Fay's hideaway. She could accompany Ying on an upcoming visit, if she would like. Fay was deeply mortified that over the past months Elsa and Ying had seen her in such a horrific psychological state. She felt increasingly resentful that Friends of Fay Stender had taken ownership of who she was and what she stood for. One anonymous client of Mal Burnstein's had just given $5,000. Fay no longer wanted to be considered a heroine or a martyr. Nor did she welcome the guilt that came with donors' expectations that, once recovered, she would resume working for Movement causes. Fay's frustration was not unlike that George Jackson and his family displayed at the packaging Fay had engineered when she controlled his public image.

Regaining some perspective and sense of irony, when Fay was with Katherine or other friends, she started telling them to "call me Phaedra." Fay had studied Racine's tragedy in college and now identified with the myth of the humiliated and suicidal Greek queen. Phaedra's own marriage to King Theseus was doomed by her unrequited love for her biracial stepson Hippolytus, son of Theseus and an Amazon queen. Walking through ancient ruins on the isle of Crete with Hilde less than eighteen months before had made Fay's connection to the primeval story all the more real. Fay worried that, as payback for her past mistakes, fate had even worse pain in store for her than she now endured.

* * *

Tom Broome remained as dedicated to his unpopular client as Fay had been in a similar position. Broome was, by no means, ready to concede defeat in January when the jury verdict was announced. Instead, he interviewed jurors and considered moving for a new trial as well as an appeal. Although the jurors had rejected Broome's claimed conspiracy to pin the attack on Brooks, Broome learned that three of the jurors did have some unease about Neal's lineup identification. The jurors also were troubled by Fay's original statement when she viewed the video from her hospital bed that Brooks only looked "most like" the man who shot her.[3] It bothered them that Fay never told the police she was sure until the pre-trial hearing.

For most of the deliberations, one juror had held out for acquittal. If that juror had remained firm, the case would have ended in a mistrial. Though the lone holdout still retained some doubts that Brooks was Fay's attacker, the juror finally yielded to pressure: "I just got tired. I couldn't fight them anymore."[4]

None of this information was a basis for overturning the verdict, but Broome was also told that some of the jurors read news articles on the case during their deliberations. If the jurors relied on what they read in the newspapers, Broome had the grounds he needed for obtaining a new trial. Broome immediately prepared a motion, supported by a sworn statement from a juror. Janssen countered with the statement of another juror denying any impropriety. Fay had to be greatly relieved when Judge Hove denied the motion. She could not imagine gearing up to go through another trial or forcing Neal to return from China again for such an ordeal.

Fay remained sequestered when Brooks was brought back for his sentencing hearing on February 22nd. Tom Broome asked the sheriff's office ahead of time that his client not be brought from jail in shackles. Both Janssen and the judge agreed that handcuffs were sufficient — no extra security precaution appeared necessary. At the start of the hearing, Brooks rose and told Judge Hove, "I have something to say" and started reading from a six-page handwritten statement: "And so the railroad continues and you have successfully convicted another innocent man . . . it doesn't surprise me because you have been doing it for so many years that you have become proficient at it."⁵

Brooks glared at the judge and reporters as he accused the system of racism and injustice and praised his attorney for bringing the conspiracy to convict him to light. Brooks then asserted that he was not the man who invaded the Stender home on the early morning of Memorial Day. Judge Hove quickly cut him off and invited Tom Broome to read the statement into the record instead.

Broome started up where Brooks had left off, "I chose not to take the stand because of the probability that the D.A. would misconstrue facts to attempt to do harm to myself and others in another case." Brooks was obviously referring to the Wells Fargo Bank robbery charge that had not yet gone to trial. Reporters' ears perked up. The man the jury had convicted of shooting Fay Stender was now asserting he had witnesses who could provide an alibi. Instead, it appeared that Brooks was about to implicate one of his friends arrested for the bank robbery. Broome continued reading Brooks' angry accusation that Fay perjured herself when she denied under oath that there was a rift between herself and George Jackson when Jackson died. Brooks believed Oriane Stender could have attested to that rift if she had been made accessible to the defense. Judge Hove had had enough. He shook his head and said, "I'm not going to sit here and listen to this."⁶

Judge Hove ordered Broome to file the statement with the court clerk instead of reading any more of it. He then denied Broome's request for parole and issued his sentence, fourteen years in prison — the maximum available — for the attempted murder of Fay Stender. The judge added three more years for the $11 robbed from Neal and Katherine Morse that had been left on the kitchen table. Brooks had already been found guilty of attempted escape from jail and faced an additional three years for that outbreak. It amounted to two decades in prison and Brooks had yet to go to trial on the bank robbery charge.

Brooks remained silent while the judge read the sentence. He then stood and turned to three women friends in the gallery and blew kisses to them as the bailiffs prepared to lead him out a side door back upstairs to the jail. Brooks then surprised everyone by quickly turning and bolting across the courtroom toward the front of the jury box where Howard Janssen was approaching the clerk to ask a question. The startled prosecutor barely had time to glimpse Brooks charging him before Brooks leaped on Janssen and began pummeling him, handcuffs and all. Janssen's glasses went flying off as he grabbed Brooks and the two wrestled on the floor.

Bailiffs descended upon the pair, hovered over them and swung their nightsticks at Brooks whenever they got a clear angle. More bailiffs arrived with shackles. Spectators left their seats to crowd around the struggling men. With help from some of the bailiffs, Janssen pulled Brooks off as other bailiffs hit Brooks repeatedly in the head with their nightsticks. Brooks was then dragged from the courtroom, bleeding profusely and kicking at the bailiffs. In the stairwell, another scuffle broke out before Brooks was subdued. His hands were then chained behind him as they completed the trip upstairs to the jail.

The cuts on Brooks' head required stitches, but other than that, sheriff's deputies reported back afterward that Brooks was now "calm and in good condition."[7] Janssen's glasses were broken. Shaken, but otherwise unharmed, he told reporters that the attack "emphasized the ridiculous, senseless violence we've seen and heard about throughout this case."[8] After the unexpected fisticuffs with Brooks, the first person who called Janssen to see if the prosecutor was all right was self-proclaimed streetfighter in the courtroom, Charles Garry.

Even among diehard radicals, few believed that Brooks was in fact railroaded. This was just more of the same rhetoric Garry and others had used on many occasions. Most militant followers assumed that Huey Newton had in fact killed Officer Frey and that George Jackson killed the Soledad guard, but considered these acts politically justified. Publicly, of course, they had proclaimed the men's innocence and supported their legal defense because that was how one played the game to secure their release or, in Jackson's case, buy time while he plotted his escape.

In the process of defending the two revolutionaries and other militant Panther Party members, Movement activists had lionized many violent felons despite their known proclivities. But they had done so in the name of a greater good, a more just society. The request of the

BGF to rally round Brooks had been a shocking moment of self-revelation. It fed suspicion that Brooks acted under orders from the BGF as a political hit. But most jaded radicals viewed the BGF more as a vicious racial gang than a credible champion of revolutionary change. Some whispered that Pinell was a psychotic cutthroat so volatile that George Jackson had even warned his own followers not to trust him.

Not even Pinell had tried to publicly justify Fay's execution on an ideological basis. But his call for support for the idea that the prosecution was simply an establishment conspiracy to convict yet another innocent black man gained no traction with white radicals. The evidence was too damning. Brooks had been found carrying the gun that crippled Fay, together with strong evidence implicating the Berkeley branch of the BGF in a scheme to free Pinell from Folsom. No one thought Fay would deliberately misidentify her assailant or that she had trouble distinguishing one black man from another.

At best, if one accepted Brooks' own version of events, one of his bank robbery cohorts shot Fay and later left Brooks holding the gun. Leftist reporters not only found themselves unable to condone the home invasion, but they also had to reexamine their own prior silence in the face of hideous truths like Betty Van Patter's murder. The real question they all faced with the BGF attack on Fay was whether to start reporting the facts accurately or to stop covering the prison movement altogether.[9]

* * *

There was one potential benefit from the "confession" Fay was forced to write when she was shot. With the help of his friend Gordon Gaines, who was now a workers' compensation judge, Marvin brought a novel claim on Fay's behalf, seeking disability benefits, physical therapy and attendant care. Because she had been forced to write that she betrayed George Jackson and the Prison Movement, they alleged that the brutal home invasion was a work-related injury arising out of her employment as a prison lawyer. If the novel claim succeeded, it would cover a substantial part of her anticipated future expenses. This would go a long way toward the cost of making her home handicapped-accessible and hiring a long-term attendant. A successful worker's compensation claim could considerably ease the burden on her family and on Friends of Fay Stender.

By the end of February of 1980, over 3,000 people had contributed more than $100,000 to Fay's recovery — including a wine and cheese fund-raiser by the prisoners' union. But the committee was still at least $120,000 shy of its goal. A poetry benefit was planned for the spring and a concert by singer Holly Near. The Golden Gate University's Women's Association offered the proceeds of their yearly talent show to the Fay Stender fund "to show our appreciation for all of her past work and efforts and also our support for her continuing courage."[10]

Elsa Knight Thompson thought the poetry reading might appeal to Fay the most. She had been working for months to make the arrangements with Beat poet Lawrence Ferlinghetti, who talked Fay's Pulitzer-Prize–winning fellow Reed alum Gary Snyder into joining in the benefit. Posters were prepared to advertise it widely to encourage a large turnout aimed at giving Fay a spiritual lift as well as raising additional funds. Ferlinghetti sought out African-American novelist and poet Ishmael Reed to join them, hoping to project a message of inter-racial unity, but Reed declined to appear.

Fay had reached the limit of her endurance as an object of pity from her white Movement friends. The poetry reading and Holly Near concert were to take place in San Francisco on April 11. Fay now planned to depart for Hong Kong at the end of March, just after her forty-eighth birthday. It made Fay angry that she felt she had no choice but to leave. Brooks likely had collaborators who remained at large.

At the end of February, Fay was gratified to see *The San Francisco Bay Guardian* publish, "Stender Shooting: How Did It Happen?"[11] Aside from Dan Siegel's article in 1979, it was the only Leftist coverage Fay saw that raised serious questions about the relationship of the attack on her to the current state of the Movement. The *Guardian* article mentioned that activists were whispering about a recently paroled gunman who was sent out with orders to kill turncoats in order to intimidate anyone with similar ideas from quitting their work for militant prisoners. The reporter wondered if that same mentality led to Fay's attempted execution. If so, it backfired as more former activists shied away from any further involvement with violent inmates.

* * *

At the beginning of March, Fay experimented with travel by taking a trip to Portland with Amy to visit an old friend. It went well. Fay sent Katherine a postcard for her birthday and arranged to spend the following weekend in Tiburon alone with Katherine, except for short visits from Amy to care for Fay's needs. Fay bought Katherine a book of Gary Snyder's poetry, *The Old Ways*, and inscribed it, "Here is to old times & new times (skipping middle times) F." It was as upbeat a note as Fay could then muster. It gave Katherine hope going forward.

When Ruby revealed to her daughters she had been diagnosed with breast cancer, Fay could not bring herself to contemplate her mother's mortality. She told Lisie that Ruby was exaggerating the severity of her condition to shift attention from Fay to herself. Fay must have realized that wasn't true. As the spring approached, Lisie was relieved that both her mother's and sister's situations appeared stabilized, along with that of her father-in-law, who was also gravely ill. Lisie and Don planned a much-needed spring vacation in Italy and gave Fay their itinerary to keep in touch. Lisie promised Fay she would join her in Hong Kong in the fall to help her pack up to return to the states.

Most friends also thought Fay was feeling better as she prepared for a long trip overseas. Yet Fay was methodically dismantling her prior life, with no vision of any viable future. She instructed Barbara Price to deliver every file from her office related to her prison work — boxes and boxes. Fay kept a constant fire going in the apartment fireplace. She fed every piece into the flames. Fay was particularly anxious to destroy anything to do with George Jackson, so the paperwork would not endanger her family. She was literally watching much of her career reduced to ashes.

When Lee Halterman's wife Roberta Brooks came by for a weekly visit, Fay was the first person Roberta told that she was pregnant. Fay asked her to wait while she rummaged in her closet and came back with a twenty-year-old maternity dress she had worn when carrying Oriane. Roberta was touched by the gesture, though she could not imagine ever wearing the faded garment. Fay said she no longer feared getting killed; she was only afraid of more pain. Roberta added her voice to those trying to encourage Fay to consider returning to work for the rights of the disabled.

Like Fay's other friends, Roberta was clueless as to Fay's destination. Most assumed she was heading to somewhere in Europe when she sent them postcards with a preprinted message, telling them they could write her at her old law office address in San Francisco. Barbara Price would forward the mail overseas. Most postcards ended with a handwritten "Goodbye for a while. Fay." Shortly before her departure, Fay spoke with Don Jelinek. She confided that she still planned to commit suicide. He told her that, under the circumstances, he agreed with her decision and would do the same if it had happened to him.

On Fay's birthday, March 29, both Katherine and Marvin joined Lisie and a few friends to see Fay, Amy and nurse Sara Levine off at the airport. It was a warm day and Fay wore shorts. She joked with Barbara Price that she was planning to start a "Jewish Lesbian Nearly Fifty Paraplegic Gun Club."[12] Fay's friend Wendy hoped Fay might take any inconveniences in stride and "find peace, excitement, distraction, romance and purpose" as well as many new friends.[13] Fay had no such expectation, but she enjoyed the sendoff; particularly glad Marvin spent the better part of a day with her, knowing their divorce would become final in a few weeks. Marvin was glad to hear her talk of the future and thought her emotional state much improved.

Fay did seem upbeat as she handed Katherine a note: "I'm glad we are re-connected at more levels and I love you very much. Come to see me when you can. . . . I don't want to lose you." Katherine did not yet know that Fay had written her another note three weeks earlier that Fay left with her attorney: ". . . Today I feel the certitude I won't come back from the far east — that I don't want life as it appears possible to me." Fay had the recurring "sense fate has shown me handwriting on the wall . . . You have been truly good to me, and not gotten much back. I tried to be honest, I've felt your love and loved you . . . Remember me with some joy as well as sadness."[14]

In Hong Kong, though they enjoyed milder weather than they had been led to expect, Fay, Sara and Amy had trouble at first locating an apartment. They stayed at the Imperial Hotel for the first two weeks before they settled into a comfortable, three-bedroom flat on the fifth floor of an apartment house on Robinson Road, a main thoroughfare of an upper-middle-class neighborhood. It was located just below the peak of the island and overlooked the South China Sea. Fay used her own name and made a few new acquaintances, confident no one there knew who she was. Even at home, only a handful of people had any idea where she had gone.

The first order of business after Fay's arrival in Hong Kong was to suspend future efforts of Friends of Fay Stender. For nearly a month, Fay had been composing a letter to Elsa to get her committee to stop its activities. Fay vividly recalled a humiliating battle of wills she had lost to Elsa back in 1970 in front of a roomful of Black Panthers. Elsa had flatly rejected a plea for radio publicity for George Jackson at a crucial time. Fay was determined that, in this confrontation, her own wishes would prevail.

With so much distance between them, Fay felt she could speak plainly. Whatever was left to her life — months or years — would have to be on her own terms. Fay would no longer tolerate being represented as "a fallen civil rights hero" or a worthy charity. She was thinking that she might make her future living as a tax lawyer. Having finally shed the last vestiges of Stanley Moore's radicalization, Fay yearned to be free to voice personal and political views inconsistent with those of her donors and fundraisers and "if I find I don't have the strength or employability, to die rather than live on a civil liberties' public subscription."[15] Fay had come to agree with the high value her father placed on breadwinners. She viewed her own prior dedication to serving others as a luxury and faulted herself for lacking the self-confidence to try to compete in the world. She confided in Elsa that her malaise was not the result of the shooting. She had felt this frustration for the past five years. Though she dreaded what friends and family might think of her, she considered it "neurotic" to obtain "self-esteem by continual service" to the under-privileged.[16]

Fay concluded, "I know how hard it is to want to give something which is rejected. I don't want what you & other friends now want to give now . . . I want to decide for myself whether to die or 'live' — and if I decide to live, to work for money in a straight job situation at the highest salary I can command. . . . Help me — don't fight me, Elsa — I'll write again. Love, Fay."[17]

The very next day was Good Friday. Fay noted it with grim irony. Crucifixion was on her mind. She prepared a note addressed to medical personnel: "No one has authority to consent to any medical treatment for me. I do not consent to any medical treatment." She wrote another suicide note to Katherine wondering if their souls would meet again. She asked Katherine to remain a lifelong friend of Neal and Oriane. "Know that I tried and, at times, with you almost thought I might make it, but I couldn't. Every moment of it hurt overwhelmingly — too deep, too pervasively — way beyond acupuncture — or psychotherapy." Fay told Katherine she took comfort from a line in the Hebrew prayer books she and Sara had brought with them. "We live on in the memories of those who remember and loved us."[18] But when it came down to it, Fay could not bring herself to end her life that day and did not mail the note.

Fay settled into twice weekly physical therapy sessions, including swimming. She remained in pain, disappointed to learn from her new doctors that acupuncture provided temporary relief like aspirin and she should not expect miracles. In some ways, like Socrates, Fay deemed life in exile worse than death. A letter from her mother cheered Fay up. It pleased her to realize Ruby must have written as soon as she had received Fay's own letter and that Ruby always stood by her, no matter what, like Lisie did. Fay fretted when close friends like Ying did not write and at the slowness of other correspondence, delayed both ways by being channeled through her old San Francisco office so no one would guess where her letters came from.

Fay delighted in telephone calls with Neal, who was planning to visit later in the month in conjunction with business he was conducting at the nearby Canton trade fair. Neal sounded so mature! Fay also took great pleasure in Oriane's frequent letters sent directly, care of Sara Levine, like that of other family members. That way Sara did not have to keep borrowing Fay's passport to retrieve them. Oriane enjoyed New York and was hard at work on an acting career, but was having no luck yet with relationships. Soon, Fay heard from Bergie and wrote back that her mood swung now between moderately cheerful and suicidal. The past year had been "without doubt the most horrible of my life."[19] In one of the first batches of forwarded correspondence from her office, Fay received a moving letter from author Kay Boyle. Boyle expressed her admiration for Fay's courage and convictions that Boyle had first observed close up more than a decade before when she covered the Newton murder trial. Herself a survivor of brutal blacklisting in the '50s, Boyle urged Fay to write her own life story for the sake of the public and for her children. Fay strongly disagreed. Particularly, for her children's sake, Fay thought it best to remain silent and not call any more attention to herself. Maybe then she would bring an end to this unfathomable vendetta.

Fay also did not believe that her story would benefit the public or herself. In T. S. Eliot's play *Murder in the Cathedral,* Thomas à Becket, the Bishop of Canterbury, grappled with a question Fay might have asked herself: "The last temptation is the greatest treason: To do the right deed for the wrong reason." Fay never realized how her preoccupation with personal glory might have interfered with the achievement of her laudable goals. Looking back, Fay only felt that she had tried to rescue a drowning man without the necessary skills. Fay was mindful that a drowning man is often irrational and might flail wildly — coming to his aid could easily drown an untrained Good Samaritan as well. She wondered whether her poorly thought out good intentions were worthy of anyone's regard. Fay drafted a quick reply that she forwarded to Barbara Price, but then had second thoughts. Boyle deserved a more thoughtful response. She asked Price not to send the letter to Boyle. She needed to think some more.

Fay looked forward to Neal's visit. It was easier to pass the time when she received letters from friends back home. Fay viewed them as teasing morsels of soul-to-soul contact — each one only made her anxious for more. Despite her misgivings, Fay must have enjoyed hearing about the final weekend of fund-raising. The April 11th poetry reading attracted a standing room only crowd of 700 to the Golden Gate University auditorium. It turned into an exuberant celebration of life. The event buoyed everyone's spirits with earthy humor and satire as well as lyricism, reported in the newspaper as "drawing thunderous applause and massive outbreaks of laughter."[20] Women friends attended an equally uplifting benefit that same weekend as Holly Near and Robin Flower staged a feminist bluegrass tribute to Fay with an all-women band.

Fay delighted as well in mail from Lisie from every stop in Italy from Milan on south, as she and Don headed to Sicily. Fay had surprised Lisie by writing so far ahead of time that her younger sister found a letter from Fay already waiting for her at each hotel. Fay suppressed her recurring unhappiness so as not to burden Lisie on her vacation. Instead, Fay filled her letters with lighthearted observations. She spoke of subscribing to *Newsweek* and asked for a supply of postcards from the Uffizi.

Amy was planning to leave for Japan the last weekend of April. Though Neal arrived before Amy left, Amy and Neal were obviously no longer romantically involved. Fay had predicted their relationship would end, thinking Amy too serious for her son. In any event, Neal reported that he had a new Chinese-German girlfriend, then visiting family in Europe. Fay hoped to meet her soon. Fay was impressed at how well-groomed Neal looked in his gray silk suit, clean shaven and with a stylish haircut. It relieved Fay to recognize that Neal remained her same son underneath and appeared unscathed by their shared ordeal. His several-day visit seemed all too brief, though he promised to be back again in two weeks. After that, Neal did not expect to be able to come more often than once a month. He liked his job and his young Australian boss, who had accompanied Neal to Hong Kong. Neal introduced the twenty-five-year-old Aussie to Fay and she agreed. Neal also told Fay he did not expect to be back to the states in years — which did not bother him at all, unlike his mother.

Fay looked forward to Oriane coming out in the summer. Fay wrote to Lisie that she would love to have her come visit as well, but not to plan to help her pack up to return to America, because Fay had no current return plans. Fay simply could not envision living in California again without all the same safety precautions, which she assumed her friends would no longer be able to tolerate. Fay wrote back again to Karma, reminding her of the suggestion they might eventually consider moving in together. She also sent an upbeat letter to Marvin, like the ones she had been writing to Lisie.

Sara's steady companionship helped keep Fay going, but, right after Neal's return visit the second weekend in May, Fay was again despondent. Communication by mail took ten days to two weeks, sometimes more. Whenever she had not heard recently from someone, she fretted. International phone calls were $3.20 per minute and could not be conducted with any frequency. Neal's job would not bring him back for at least four weeks. The weather was muggy and Fay missed having Amy as an attendant. Fay had a burn on her foot from accidental exposure to scalding water in the tub and could not go swimming until it healed. Most troublesome was a serious bladder infection that Fay had recently developed from fumbling repeatedly with the catheter. It was a task Sara flatly refused to perform. Fay focused on the upcoming anniversary date of the shooting and feared that her situation would only get worse. Still suffering from chronic pain, Fay spent most of her time every day in bed. Though she could distract herself with her color television and *The International Herald Tribune*, her thoughts always returned to despair.

Sara tried to cheer Fay up by buying her a stuffed kitten. Fay took it to bed with her, hugged it close and wept like a child. She felt emotionally bereft and unloved. The stuffed animal reminded her of losing her own pet cat Puddin', her home, her legs, hope and freedom. Cradling it in her arms, she bemoaned the irreparable damage to her life and family, forcing her to live apart from her children. The next day Sara brought Fay some candy to lighten her mood.

By mid-May, Fay realized that as much as she liked Sara, Sara was the wrong person to have brought along on this extended trip. Fay had made no effort to repress her suicidal feelings when talking to Sara as she did with Lisie or Neal. Sara found that burden increasingly difficult to bear up under. She had her own mood swings. Sometimes, Fay was up and Sara was down, complaining about repetitive cooking and housekeeping chores, although the apartment came with a young Chinese cleaning woman, who spoke passable English. Fay found Sara unwilling to host dinner guests anymore, increasing their isolation. Sara was feeling adrift, separated from her boyfriend, isolated and bored in a foreign culture. Whenever Fay tried to cheer Sara up, she sensed Sara bristling at too effusive a display of affection.

During one of her bouts of optimism, Fay planned ahead for Katherine to come visit her in mid-July, possibly overlapping with Oriane's trip. It would not be until then that Katherine would earn her first yearly vacation from her job. Katherine tried to reach Fay by telephone on May 12, to gauge her current mood and talk about the trip, but was unsuccessful. On May 18, Sara told Fay that she missed her boyfriend too much and planned to leave for the states by the end of June or sooner, if Fay could obtain a replacement nurse before then. Fay understood completely. She let Sara know that she appreciated how good her care had been and thanked her for being a devoted friend as well as a dedicated professional. Still, Sara thought Fay seemed on the verge of suicide. Sara promised not to abandon Fay. She would wait until Fay found a new caretaker. Fay wrote a short letter to Katherine, urging her to come on July 14, but said she did not blame Amy for departing or Sara for wanting to do so. Fay considered herself "so wretched and depressing to be with people escape when they can."[21]

Fay then entertained another fantasy. Perhaps she could move to Denver with Sara. They would only tell a few people where they were — Katherine and Lisie, Neal and Oriane and Sara's boyfriend. Fay thought that if she seriously applied herself to rehabilitation, she could make it work. It would mean getting operations on both hands, which were still often numb. That would take four to six months of recuperation. But then reality sunk in. If she had them both operated on at the same time, while waiting for her hands to heal, Fay would be totally dependent on a caretaker, which she dreaded. It also did not address Fay's bladder problem. Her urologist had just told Fay that the recurring inflammation was no longer treatable with antibiotics. Surgery and a pouch were strongly recommended. Fay did not doubt they were medically appropriate, but refused to contemplate that option.

Even if Fay could live with her health problems, she realized that the serene life she envisioned in Denver was a pipedream. Fay called

Neal and realized he was firmly committed to building his future career in China. In Denver, she would not see Oriane often either if Oriane was based in New York. Nor could Fay expect more than monthly visits from Katherine, who could not realistically quit her Oakland job and find another in Denver, where Katherine had no license to practice law. Despite what Fay told friends just before she left California, Fay was still frightened of being killed. If Fay returned to the United States, she expected to live under an assumed name because otherwise she would remain in constant fear of discovery. If Fay used an alias, how could she ever gain a law license in Colorado to support herself?

On Monday morning, May 19, Fay tried to reach Katherine by telephone. It was around 6 p.m. the evening of Sunday, May 18 in California, but Fay did not find Katherine at home. Fay then called her old neighbor Marling Mast to ask Marling to arrange for a mutual friend to come to Hong Kong to relieve Sara. Fay had already tried a couple of other options, including writing to the Finnish girl she had befriended in Stockholm in the fall of 1978, but her young friend was traveling and likely would not respond for weeks. Fay even inquired if Marling herself would fly out to attend Fay for a month. Fay probably realized that the idea was totally unrealistic. Marling had two teen-aged sons at home. Marling told her she would make the call to their mutual friend and get back to Fay.

Not wasting any time, Fay wrote Katherine another letter about her Denver fantasy and its unworkability. In her distress, Fay mistakenly addressed her lover by the wrong name. Fay held out a faint hope that she could still hold out until Katherine came to discuss her choices. Fay asked Katherine to move the start date of her visit sooner. Fay then thought some more and realized that her aim in inviting Katherine to come was to convince Katherine that suicide was the only viable option. Fay felt it only fair to advise Katherine of her thinking before Katherine paid her way out to Hong Kong. Fay then wrote her third letter to Katherine in two days. In her distraught state, Fay again mistakenly addressed Katherine by the same wrong name. Fay explained that she could only visualize a future if her life were safe, she was surrounded by people she loved and had a meaningful job. Her problem was in not being able to see how she could make that happen, which left her depressed and isolated. She urged Katherine to realize that future discussion of Fay's options had to include suicide or the two women would not be communicating honestly.

Fay had another task she felt she must accomplish. For the last month, she had been mulling over a more elaborate explanation to Kay Boyle of the reasons why Fay did not think her life story merited telling. Such a book would not benefit Neal and Oriane, who already knew what she had accomplished, her political point of view, her anguish and weariness. Her children remained her pride and joy. No, Fay would not write her own story, reliving her obsession with two black militants at the expense of her own beloved offspring. Fay could not get over her guilt that she had once considered Huey Newton and George Jackson equal in her affections to her family — the only two other people she had once been willing to die for. Now she was instead on the verge of taking her own life, unhealed from the psychic wounds of their dagger blows to her heart.

Fay had given a great deal of thought to her mistakes, which she still considered most analogous to attempts to save a drowning man without the proper skills. She had also focused repeatedly on why she had been singled out as the target of an execution attempt in punishment for her errors in judgment. She viewed the injustice of so many black men suffering inhumane treatment behind bars as a malignancy that one fought with every remedy available — compassion, lawsuits, publicity — whatever it took short of arming a revolution, which she refused to participate in.

Fay knew that George Jackson accepted the limits of her assistance, but his followers apparently considered her efforts an act of betrayal. Fay thought they should look in the mirror. She wrote Boyle that she fully expected Brooks' cohorts to make a second attempt on her life if she returned. Despite monetary support from the Guild and members of the prisoners' union, Fay was dismayed that neither organization demanded further investigation by authorities to determine who gave Brooks his instructions. How could she write about her experience with Brooks' co-conspirators waiting in the wings to take further revenge?

Fay wrote Boyle that she was grateful for the incredible display of love from her friends and from feminists, but dismayed by the dearth of Leftist political commentary. She confided that she no longer considered herself a Leftist and wondered what remained of the Movement. What hurt Fay more than anything was the absence of any meaningful outcry on her behalf from members of the black community. Fay could not conceive how anyone felt that targeting her for execution could achieve any progress whatsoever toward a more just society.

After describing to Boyle her unbearable pain at exile from her family, her home and her profession, Fay had reached the point of total despair: "If this is the world, I don't know any way to participate in it."[22] By then, she had crossed out April 4 on the suicide note she had previously written for medical providers and redated it May 19, 1980. Fay knew her cousin Hank Abrahams was then in Hong Kong, staying at the Mandarin Hotel. Fay wrote a note to Sara telling her to call him and her uncle Irving, who would be arriving the next day, so they could help Sara make arrangements for the return of Fay's remains for a Jewish funeral in San Francisco and burial near her father. Fay provided Sara with her sister's current location and asked Sara to call Neal and Oriane and tell them again "how much I love them." Fay did not feel she could have asked for a better care giver. "My problems resulting in this act started long before I met you & you did not contribute to them."[23]

Fay finished the note by wishing Sara well and apologizing for the burden she was about to place on her. Then Fay called to say good-bye to Oriane. It did not go well. Oriane quickly called back to offer to come out to visit her mother right away. Sara answered the telephone. She had just entered Fay's bedroom to discover Fay's slumped body, the open bottles of pills and Fay's suicide notes. Sara immediately called Fay's doctor and an ambulance, but it was too late.

Sara then called Marvin, who telephoned the hotel where Lisie and Don were staying in the seacoast town of Sorrento, Italy. Lisie was in shock when the staff summoned Don to the phone from the hotel restaurant for an urgent international call. Fay had been pronounced dead on arrival at the Queen Mary Hospital in Hong Kong. They immediately cut short their trip and returned to California.

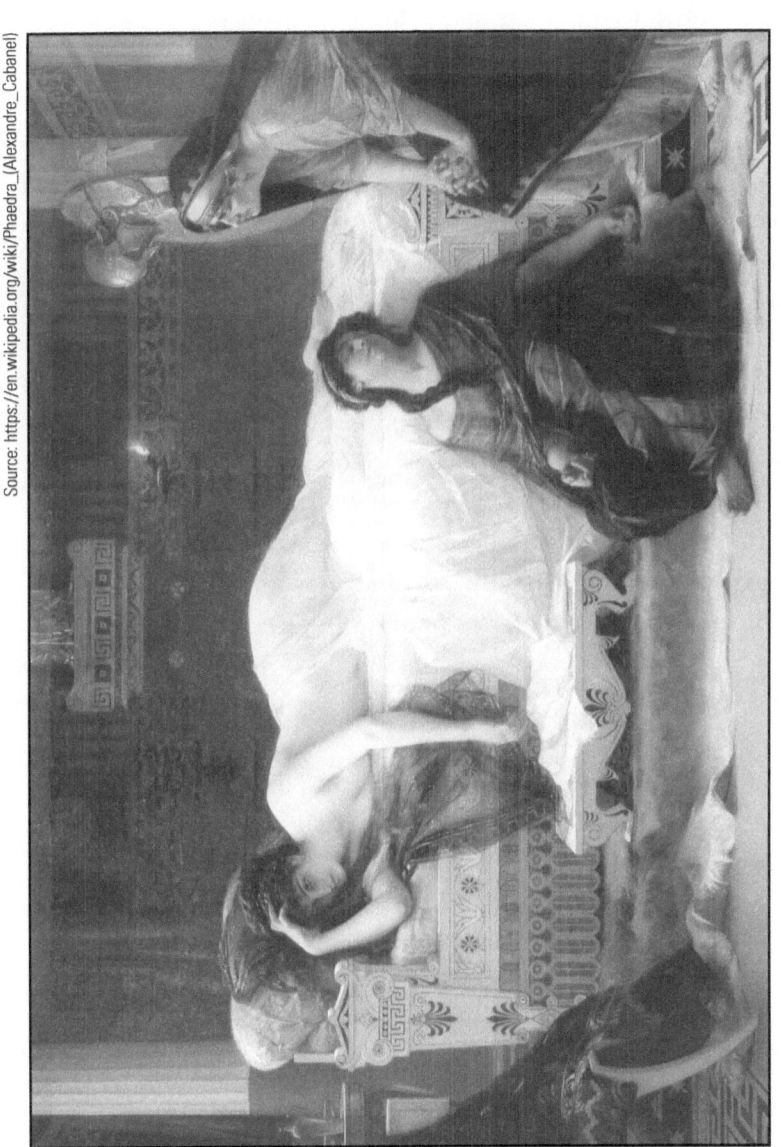

The Death of Phaedra — 1880 painting by Alexandre Cabanel.

By May 21, word of Fay's death was international news. For religious Jews everywhere, it was Shavuot — the festival celebrating the day the Torah was first given to the Jewish people. Fay's close friend and former colleague Ezra Hendon was now a devoted member of Congregation Beth Israel in Berkeley, just blocks from where Fay had been shot at her home on Grant Street. Ezra never forgot that it was Fay who had recommended Congregation Beth Israel to him.

On May 22, the second day of Shavuot, the rabbi and members of the congregation who had lost one or both parents recited the customary Yizkor prayers of remembrance, which they would repeat at Yom Kippur and twice more during the year. Supplicants offered charitable contributions in their deceased parents' names and requested that their souls be "bound in the Bond of Life" together with the souls of Abraham and other virtuous Jewish people in the Garden of Eden. During these prayers, everyone with both parents living was expected to leave the synagogue as a sign of respect. After Fay died, Ezra stayed each time the prayers were performed to beseech God to allow Fay's tortured soul to find eternal peace. For years, she would be the only person included in Ezra's Yizkor prayers.

* * *

In her instructions to Sara just before she died, Fay expressed her strong desire that Neal not endanger himself by returning to California for her funeral. Neal could not honor her request. He flew in from Beijing to accompany Fay's body back from Hong Kong. The plane did not leave for San Francisco until May 24. Transfer was delayed because the authorities first required an autopsy to confirm the cause of death was a drug overdose. Meanwhile, arrangements had been made for Fay's funeral to take place on Wednesday, May 28, a year to the day from the shooting. The night before, Ezra came over to see Marvin, who was at a total loss how to handle his role in the religious service and grateful for Ezra's assistance.

Several hundred people turned up for the ceremony. The casket was festooned with white gladiolas. As Fay anticipated, it felt incongruous to many of her radical friends. Mourners filled the balcony after overflowing the main floor. Television cameras recorded Chief Justice Rose Bird among the crowd. Both mainstream and Movement reporters mingled among the subdued mourners. When former prison psychiatrist Frank Rundle was introduced to Ruby Abrahams, he gathered her in a warm embrace. Eve Pell could not control her tears. Ying Lee Kelley whispered to Bernie Bergesen that she had counseled Fay against suicide. Bergesen had not taken any position on the issue, but he thought to himself that if it were him, he would have felt the same way Fay did.

Fay had asked that fellow ACLU board member Ephraim Margolin deliver the eulogy. Ephraim was known for his strong defense of Israel, which he represented in lawsuits. Fay thought Margolin's political outlook most closely mirrored her own of the past few years. In 1978, she had even asked Margolin if she could join his solo practice when she left her partnership with Marvin. Margolin had politely, but firmly, declined. Margolin focused on Fay's formative teen-aged years during World War II and guessed that they gave Fay a strong sense of identification with Holocaust victims and Jewish refugees. He said that Fay shared his own conviction: "I am a Jew, therefore I am in opposition to injustice." Margolin called Fay a real "mensch." The Yiddish term captured her essence as someone with a strong sense of right and wrong and willingness to act on those principles.

Bernie Bergesen took his turn at the microphone, focusing on Fay's passion for so many causes: civil rights, anti-war demonstrations, law reform, women's issues, gay rights and prisoners' rights. He preferred to remember Fay for the many unknown prisoners she had defended rather than her more famous clients. He wondered how many people became involved in working for causes because of her contagious enthusiasm and dedication to the struggle. Bergesen ended: "She is at rest. It is we who mourn."[24]

Ying Lee Kelley spoke, too, angry that someone of Fay's immense talent was cut down at the height of her abilities. Though she did not say it, Ying obviously considered Fay's death murder. It was a feeling shared by most of the assemblage, though none of the speakers mentioned the shooting. It just hung in the air like a dark cloud. Ying ended, "When you think of what she could have contributed in the future, get angry again."[25]

Mary Dunlap, Fay's colleague from California Women Lawyers and Equal Rights Advocates, read a poem she had written praising Fay's life's work, imagining the enormity of Fay's despair as her myriad friends tried in vain "to lift your pain — to split it up among us into infinitesimal grains."[26] Ruby took a turn at the podium to praise her elder daughter's extraordinary courage. Rabbi Rosen summed up the eulogies, calling Fay a remarkable woman who still lived on through her friends and colleagues. Her message continuing to resonate and to influence the unending stream of those laboring for human justice. Mourners were told that contributions could be made to the Fay Stender Memorial Fund of the San Francisco Bar Foundation. The whole funeral had an eerie quality for what remained unsaid.

During the service, Diana Russell had looked around and spotted only three blacks in the entire crowd, reinforcing her disillusionment. Russell thought that in America, no matter what you do, if you are white, it doesn't matter if you spent your whole life working for blacks. Afterward, she focused her work on race relations exclusively in South Africa. Writer David Horowitz, who was still haunted by the unsolved murder of his friend Betty Van Patter, noticed the same disturbing fact. Fay "had devoted herself to the cause of the black prisoners and their struggle against racism. She had taken their cause into the halls of government, had presented it to the public at large. . . She had defended hundreds of black prisoners. But blacks had not come to her funeral to pay her a last respect." Nor did normally outspoken colleagues address the irony that Fay "had been killed by a black ex-prisoner, who in justifying his awful act, had invoked the memory of George Jackson — the most resonant symbol of Fay's radical life and of her dedication to the cause of the oppressed."[27]

Fay's friend, freelance reporter Karen Wald, was among those circulating among the crowd conducting interviews and taking notes. Most fellow activists agreed with the speakers that Fay played an incomparable role championing prisoners' rights and recruiting teams of lawyers to their defense, but one cautioned, "We should look at Fay as she really was. In many ways, she was domineering. She irritated a lot of people." Wald knew that some people connected with the Soledad case mistakenly thought Fay was "ripping off" the legal defense fund, or that she was getting rich off the profits from George Jackson's book. Wald herself realized that Fay didn't do either, but still the rumors had spread and the erroneous belief persisted. Another colleague noted that Fay was a "catalyst" who gave the Movement direction at a crucial time but was accused by many of being too controlling. Fay faced the constant distrust that outside legal helpers almost always encounter from those inside. Many people resented her "pushiness."[28]

Another colleague defended Fay's lack of humility: "Of course Fay Stender's ego was involved, like any lawyer. She got something out of all her work, a kind of fame, or notoriety. Some people were critical of her for that, but they respected her work. She was strong and tireless and tough. But when she realized she couldn't carry that load any more, she was also quick to pull out. Maybe she was just more honest than the rest of us, who took much longer to admit when we'd had it."[29]

Far fewer people came out to the burial ceremony at Salem Memorial Park in Colma, on a gentle slope just south of San Francisco. Those who did may have noticed its safe location — right behind the Colma police station. It was a short walk up the hillside where they gathered at the roadside grave, not much further into the cemetery than where the remains of Sam Abrahams lay. The rabbi bestowed upon Neal the honor of tossing the first shovelful of dirt onto Fay's coffin. Others lined up behind Neal to add their own symbolic farewell. One of her best friends later told David Horowitz, "You could almost hear her muffled voice — the old Fay, the one we wanted to remember. 'Now wait a minute!' she seemed to be saying. 'Hold on, dammit! There was more to it than that!'"[30]

* * *

Fay's last letters were delivered after her death. When Fay's suitcase came back, it included a three-piece white suit that Fay had brought with her to Hong Kong. Katherine knew it as Fay's prized purchase from an upscale Hollywood boutique, the only time Fay had ever splurged for an outfit like those worn by her Beverly Hills colleagues on the board of

California Women Lawyers. Katherine wore the same size. Fay's family gave the suit to her. She would wear it until it was thread-bare.

* * *

As friends gathered to honor Fay's memory in San Francisco, Huey Newton showed no interest whatsoever in paying tribute to the woman who had been so instrumental in winning his freedom back in 1970. Newton remained at U.C. Santa Cruz where he would be awarded a Ph.D. the next month for the doctoral dissertation, "War Against the Panthers: A Study of Oppression in America."

* * *

Shortly after Fay's funeral, Katherine was among many of Fay's feminist friends invited to attend the June, 1980, swearing-in ceremony for former ACLU board member Marilyn Patel as the first woman on the Northern District federal bench. Katherine decided to wear Fay's white suit. Still grieving for Fay, Katherine was standing in the outer lobby of the courtroom, when Marilyn Patel came out and invited her to sit in a place of honor up front with Patel's judicial colleagues. Katherine had a vivid dream that Fay herself was at the reception wearing her white suit. In the dream, everyone knew Fay was dead, but there she was anyway, standing with a wine glass in her hand, toasting Marilyn's success. As soon as people started saying, "but she's dead," Fay disappeared.

* * *

Marvin and Dru were married on August 3, 1980, at a private ceremony celebrated two days later with a party in Oakland at the home of mutual friends. At the end of September 1980, the California Attorney General's office released an official report of the Bureau of Organized Crime and Intelligence on terrorist activities. It concluded that the attack on Fay on Memorial Day 1979, had been part of "a larger revolutionary effort" to revitalize the Black Guerilla Family. The home

Dru Ramey

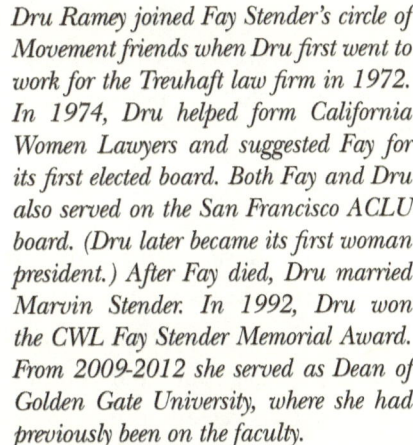

Dru Ramey joined Fay Stender's circle of Movement friends when Dru first went to work for the Treuhaft law firm in 1972. In 1974, Dru helped form California Women Lawyers and suggested Fay for its first elected board. Both Fay and Dru also served on the San Francisco ACLU board. (Dru later became its first woman president.) After Fay died, Dru married Marvin Stender. In 1992, Dru won the CWL Fay Stender Memorial Award. From 2009-2012 she served as Dean of Golden Gate University, where she had previously been on the faculty.

Judith McKelvey

Judith McKelvey was Dean of Golden Gate Law School when she first met Fay Stender. They both served on CWL's first elected board of directors which chose McKelvey as its president. Judy and her husband remained close friends of Fay's for the rest of her life.

Marilyn Hill Patel

Marilyn Hill Patel, first woman Chief Judge, Northern District California, was counsel for the National Organization of Women when she met Fay. They served together on the ACLU board in San Francisco in the mid-1970s, where Fay stood out as a "conscience-pricker." Looking back later on Fay's career, Judge Patel believed that Fay earned a place on a list of great trial lawyers.

invasion was now officially linked both to the twin bank robberies and the unexecuted plan to bomb the electrical plant at Folsom and exchange diplomatic hostages for Hugo Pinell's release.[31]

* * *

Former *Ramparts* magazine editor David Horowitz collaborated with another *Ramparts* alumnus, Peter Collier, to write a biographical piece on Fay. The lengthy article, "Requiem for a Radical," published in *New West* magazine in March of 1981, was even more explosive than Kate Coleman's co-authored exposé of the Panthers three years before. Ten months after Fay's suicide, many Leftists were still recoiling in fear of further violence and reconsidering their own future course. Using Eve Pell as one of their principal sources, Collier and Horowitz painted Fay as a driven and highly effective zealot, with a band of mostly women followers who foolishly romanticized radical prisoners. The article described Fay as "perhaps more deeply typical of the Movement and closer to being the paradigmatic radical" than her more widely known mentor, Charles Garry, or than radical lawyer William Kunstler.[32] Most provocative of all was the authors' conclusion, quoting her friend and colleague Ezra Hendon, that "her death marked an end of an era," a lost cause.[33]

When Fay's mother died, a large gathering of family members met again for Ruby's funeral and burial in the grave next to that of her husband Sam. While the ceremony was being conducted, Marvin separated himself from the group to walk ten rows up and across the service road to revisit Fay's grave alone. Since the day of Fay's burial, an unassuming, foot-high block of dark granite with a Star of David in the upper left-hand corner had replaced the marker at the head of the grave. The epitaph on the polished top could only be read when one stood close. Oriane had chosen its wording:

Fay A. Stender
1932 – 1980
Mother of Neal and Oriane
Wife of Marvin

Marvin wept from the depths of his soul.

Epilogue

Water originally contains no sound.
Touching a stone makes it murmur.[1]
— ZEN PROVERB

Unfortunately, as proud as Ruby had been of her daughter, she did not live to see the ACLU's tribute to Fay. Fay herself would have been amused at her good friend Bernie Bergesen's speech on her behalf at the annual Northern California ACLU Bill of Rights Day Celebration in San Francisco in December 1981. In praising Fay's posthumous receipt of the Earl Warren Civil Liberties Award, Bergesen candidly admitted that Fay was a controversial figure on the ACLU board, often in the minority, stubborn and sometimes divisive. "Though her dedication to civil liberties took many forms - — including her commitment to the rights of prisoners — perhaps her most valuable contribution was as an instigator of change in the way in which the ACLU would proceed."[2] Ying Lee Kelly accepted the award on behalf of Fay's family and friends, explaining as she did so how fitting it seemed. Thirty years earlier, when Ying was a recent immigrant, Fay had taught her much about her own constitutional rights.

* * *

Fay's was a story of lasting resonance. In March of 1983, The *Wall Street Journal* printed "Agonizing Epitaph to a Dilettante of Revolution," by novelist and Beat poet Herbert Gold. If Fay had had the opportunity to craft her own epitaph she might have chosen the same painful words: "She made unbearable errors and, as a consequence, suffered unbearably."[3]

Two weeks later Charles Wesley Coleman, one of the other alleged Wells Fargo bank robbers, confessed that he was the gunman and that Brooks had no involvement in the Stender home invasion. Brooks' new court-appointed attorney filed a motion seeking his client's release from prison based in large part on Coleman's confession. On November 3, 1983, Brooks and Coleman were each transported from their respective prison cells to the Oakland court. Apart from both being of the same race and age group, they did not look much alike. The judge paid close attention as Howard Janssen asserted that both Fay and Neal had been absolutely sure of their trial identification. Coleman had been included in the lineups viewed by all three eyewitnesses and none had picked Coleman out as the gunman.

Reporters could look at the pictures of the two men taken in 1979 and see for themselves how unlikely it was they would be confused. Even when both were made to wear the same blue watch cap, Brooks had a rounder face, with a short, wide nose and a more youthful appearance. Coleman looked all of his thirty years, had heavier eyebrows, thicker lips and a far more sinister look on a narrow face with a prominent chin and angular nose. On December 2, 1983, the judge rejected the confession. Years afterward, Brooks' trial attorney Thomas Broome acknowledged he had been impressed when Fay zeroed in on Brooks' distinctive nervous walk. Broome knew Fay had far too many black clients ever to have confused Coleman for Brooks. Yet Brooks continued to maintain his innocence and pursue the case on appeal. On March 28, 1984, Brooks was stabbed to death in the yard at Folsom Prison. Counting Fay, Brooks' death marked the sixty-ninth known fatality in the chain going back to Soledad prison in 1969.

Later that year, British author and documentarian Jo Durden-Smith returned to San Francisco as a reporter for the British investigative news program "World in Action" to interview Stephen Bingham, who had been a fugitive for thirteen years after the death of George Jackson. Durden-Smith's article focused not only on Bingham — who was Jackson's last visitor before he died — but on the whole history of related violent deaths, including Fay's: "Who is to be blamed for her death, for the long chain of deaths that led up to the events of August 21 and for the long chain of deaths that led away again? The last one home?"[4]

After reviewing the conflicting versions of Jackson's failed escape attempt, Durden-Smith concluded: "There is enough blame here, if you want to find it, for a whole era. It just depends which side you're on."[5] Bingham's trial drew large crowds and media attention back to the fifteen-year-old attempted breakout from San Quentin. On June 27, 1986, after five days of deliberation, Bingham was acquitted on all charges. Bingham broke the chain of violent deaths related back from George Jackson to Soledad and forward through Brooks — at the price of thirteen years of exile.

* * *

Neal planned for himself a life of exile, though he returned to Berkeley to finish his undergraduate education and to attend Stanford Law School to get a degree before establishing himself in Hong Kong with his Chinese wife. Fay would have been immensely proud of Neal's successful legal career specializing in international business. When they came for visits, family and friends in America noticed the features Neal's two biracial daughters shared with their grandmother Fay, who spent her last months on earth in the same city where they were born.

Oriane's adulthood seesawed between New York and San Francisco. Fay would also have been thrilled at Oriane's success as an artist and her belated interest in her late forties in becoming a lawyer herself. Whenever Fay's old friends spotted Oriane at that age in San Francisco, they did a double take. She looked so hauntingly like her mother.

* * *

Marling Mast and Michael Magbie had never lived on Grant Street in Berkeley at the same time. Many years later, they both rented houseboats tied to the Sausalito dock. Somehow in a chance conversation, they both realized they had been Fay Stender's next-door neighbors at different times in the sixties and seventies. They fell into each other's arms and wept.

* * *

In the spring of 1989, Peter Collier and David Horowitz republished "Requiem for a Radical" verbatim as the first chapter in *Destructive Generation: Second Thoughts About the Sixties,* which marked their clear break with their Leftist past and political conversion to neo-conservatism. *The Wall Street Journal* hailed the exposè as "A rare and vivid glimpse into the bowels of hard radicalism." William Buckley of *The National Review* was caustic but also highly laudatory: "If there is such a thing as a must read about the New Left this is it. Collier and Horowitz know the scene from the inside, and they write about it with intelligence, gossipy intimacy, and savage introspection." In contrast, David Burner, the historian who reviewed *Destructive Generation* for *The New York Times,* said the two authors "were deluded in the 1960's [and] have not recovered their senses. . . . Their book is in large part a demolition essay against highly selective and vulnerable targets like the Black Panthers . . . and the Weathermen. . . . They seem to be on the verge of an exploration into tragedy. But in the end what they offer is not tragedy but diatribe."[6]

* * *

On the eighteenth anniversary of George Jackson's death, August 21, 1989, Huey Newton went to a West Oakland housing project to meet a drug dealer named Tyrone Robinson. Shortly after midnight, Robinson, a member of the Black Guerilla Family, shot and killed Newton, then forty-seven years old — the same age Fay had been when shot by BGF wannabe Ed Brooks. When he was caught, Robinson claimed that he acted in self-defense after Newton pulled a gun. But Newton was not carrying any gun. Robinson was convicted of murder and received a 32-year sentence.

EPILOGUE

The New York Times reported that the presumed motive for killing Huey Newton was that Robinson "wanted to be a high-mucky-muck," in the BGF. "He was a foot soldier and he wanted to be a shot caller."[7] Fay would have appreciated the irony that Robinson had participated as a child in one of the Black Panther Breakfast programs Newton had instituted.

* * *

On December 6, 1989, a Canadian in Montreal named Marc Lepine embarked on a shooting spree against "fucking feminists," killing fourteen women engineering students. It resulted in the coining of a new term, "femicide," to describe the growing number of hate killings targeting women. The attack prompted Professor Diana Russell to rethink Fay Stender's death. The question had been gnawing at Russell for ten years why Fay was singled out for execution when there were so many men on the BGF enemies' list that the gang never acted against. In the spring of 1991, Russell published "Fay Stender & The Politics of Murder" for the magazine *On The Issues*. Dr. Russell had concluded that in addition to political motives for targeting Fay, the BGF acted out of sexism. It struck her as not mere happenstance that the highest profile woman attorney in the prison reform movement "was the one to be riddled with bullets." Russell thought Fay was particularly resented because she was a woman who ignored the men who "saw her as their one desperate chance to get out." Russell considered it payback for "daring to finally put her own interests before theirs."[8]

Russell assumed that prisoners initially saw Fay as a "good mother" who "passionately wanted to free them no matter what they had done." As a consequence, "she became the object of her clients' and would-be clients' expectations, hopes, demands and dreams. When she couldn't or wouldn't fulfill their wishes . . . she came to be seen as a betrayer, a 'bad mother.'"[9] Russell's conclusion was that "the misogynistic attitudes and behavior of many men, whether in authority or subject to it, are often unleashed when women don't give them what they want. "Betrayal is what Stender's story is about. Not the betrayal of George Jackson, but the betrayal of Fay Stender — Woman."[10]

* * *

Despite the extensive investigation devoted to Fay's tragic death, no one ever identified the woman who accompanied Brooks to the Stender home on the early morning of Memorial Day, 1979. Nor did anyone ever speculate in print what happened to the confession or who would most have wanted such a document. It would have done Hugo Pinell no good in his isolated prison cell where guards could easily confiscate it and implicate Pinell in a crime he denied any part of. In the summer of 1979, Pinell had called Fay's shooting a tragedy. Cynics might have thought he was just trying to deflect blame. Perhaps he was remorseful only because the attempted execution proved not to be a BGF recruiting tool. Too many fellow inmates and ex-felons found the attack on Fay repugnant. Yet there remained the possibility that Pinell never did in fact order the hit.

The threat to Neal's life in the summer of 1979 obviously stemmed from the fact that he was the key witness against the gunman, upon whose testimony the whole prosecution might have hinged. Oriane was known to have learned something from Fleeta Drumgo. But why did the Black Guerilla Family threaten Ruby Abrahams' life six years after her daughter quit representing prisoners? It smacked more of a personal vendetta against Fay and her family than of political retribution. Another question is raised by the young African-American woman who first pressed the buzzer of the Stender home. If she came along willingly, how did that fit with Dr. Russell's theory of misogyny?

Former colleagues revealed to investigative reporters that Fay made a number of bitter enemies in her career — outside of law enforcement, they were mostly women. Russell had another clue in the offense her lover Donnis took to Fay's question about her "ghetto" upbringing. Though there is no proof, the most likely place the "confession" wound up is in the hands of a sixty-year-old woman for whom the document did hold unique value, a woman whose anger increased exponentially over the years: Hell hath no fury like a reluctant revolutionary mama with two martyred sons.

As an English history buff, there was another lesson Fay could have

EPILOGUE

taken from the twelfth century assassination of the Bishop of Canterbury. Thomas à Becket was attacked in his own sanctuary, where he bled to death, a martyr to his unyielding beliefs. The murder was instigated by King Henry II, obsessing about the stubborn idealist who dared challenge his authority: "Who will rid me of this meddlesome priest?"

The revered matriarch of the Black Guerilla Family had made it clear to anyone and everyone she spoke to in the years following her sons' deaths, how much she loathed Fay Stender's meddling. So Dr. Russell most likely was right to focus on Fay's "mothering" as a motive for killing her, but not because Fay became a "bad" mother for quitting Jackson's defense team. It was because Fay had the hubris to act as his mother at all. Jackson's book editor Greg Armstrong shared Fay's possessiveness of George Jackson: "George's power was our power almost as a fact of ownership. If he had been outside he would never have belonged to us in the same way, but locked away, he was ours. We possessed him and everything he was. We even felt we had the right to live through him."[11]

Georgia Jackson had Fay's address. She had been there with her family and friends mourning her son Jonathan's death in August of 1970, inwardly seething that Fay had the audacity to host the mourners in her spacious Berkeley home. Georgia undoubtedly assumed the Stender home was financed in part with proceeds from the Soledad Brothers Defense Fund. In fact, it was Marvin's injured longshoremen clients who likely footed the bill. Georgia never believed that Fay had barely made a subsistence living from her prison work.

Probably as early as their first joint appearance on George's behalf in February 1970 in Los Angeles, Georgia was uncomfortable with this middle class white woman purporting to speak for her family's pain. Her discomfort grew with time as Fay dared to be both lover and surrogate mother to her son, whom he started listening to more than his own mama. Georgia had found condescending Fay's description of the neighborhood where Georgia and Lester had raised their family as "the ghetto." Yet at first, Georgia held her tongue. Recognizing that Fay had freed Huey Newton, Georgia deferred to Fay and John Thorne's strategy to free George as well. But all that deference later evaporated.

How fitting and simple Georgia could have thought it was to execute Fay in her own sanctuary. But Georgia would not have had to give any orders at all for the Berkeley branch of the BGF to plot such an obvious move. Fay was clearly the person on the 1974 BGF "hit list" whose death would most please the gang founder's mother. Giving the risky task to a wannabe like Edward Brooks gave him a chance to prove himself. Together they would put the BGF back on the map by their audacious bank robberies, kidnapping of diplomatic hostages and bombing of the electrical plant at Folsom to free Hugo Pinell. They would spirit Pinell safely into exile and Georgia Jackson could be handed Fay Stender's confession on a platter.

Many BGF members did believe that Fay betrayed their mission by not helping their founder escape to bring on the revolution. But that was not what motivated Georgia Jackson's anger. Quite the opposite. Her bitterest moment was when she called the Stender home in October of 1970 after reading *Soledad Brother* for the first time and Greg Armstrong answered the telephone in Fay's kitchen. Georgia thought the book sealed her son's fate and blamed both Armstrong and Fay for betraying her son. Georgia assumed that George had been talked into exaggerating his misdeeds. She saw both Fay and Greg Armstrong as exploitative whites ripping off blacks yet again — enriching themselves at her son's expense. The book's proceeds would just make profits for the publisher and fund more lawyers' fees, while George received a death sentence.

Georgia did not realize that Fay had substantially toned down George's rhetoric, not inflamed it. She must have seethed even more over time, bitter that Fay appeared to be revered by her deceased son in perpetuity through worldwide dissemination of his book of letters. Fay would go down in history as George's "small, but mighty mouthpiece." She was admired by some BGF members and by Soledad Brother Fleeta Drumgo and others who had been helped by the Prison Law Project. Georgia may have wanted a confession in Fay's own handwriting to prove otherwise. Then Fay's life would be taken in retribution for the lives of Georgia's two lost sons.

If George Jackson had not been targeted for death behind bars, Jonathan would not have attempted the foolhardy kidnapping at the

Marin County courthouse to try to free his older brother. The grieving mother had long since reached the same conclusion that her younger son had: "A black man doesn't get justice in the courts. If you can't get justice one way, you take it another."[12]

What Georgia utterly failed to realize is that George was the brigand he claimed to be. Without Fay's intervention, he was already headed inexorably for death due to his own outraged response to the killing of his mentor W. L. Nolen. But without Fay, George's death would have made barely a ripple. Fay splashed and thrashed and tried to throw a life preserver to George Jackson. In the process, she facilitated Jackson's wildest dreams, his becoming a revolutionary hero with a worldwide audience. But she could not save him from his own death wish.

Largely through the efforts of Huey Newton, Georgia Jackson and the Black Guerilla Family, Fay's name was practically erased from official Panther history. Yet since 1982, California Women Lawyers has celebrated her life with an annual award given to a woman lawyer with the same demonstrated commitment as Fay Stender "to the representation of women, disadvantaged groups and unpopular causes, and whose courage, zest for life and demonstrated ability to effect change as a single individual make her a role model for women attorneys."[13] In 1992, the award went to Dru Stender Ramey. For Dru, receipt of the award from CWL — where she and Fay had both been founding members — was "particularly meaningful . . . Fay was a real inspiration to me and all the other women who came to San Francisco to raise hell."[14] As she accepted the award, Marvin joined Dru at the podium, where Dru introduced him as "the love of my life."

* * *

Longtime friend of the family, author Peter Dale Scott wrote a trilogy for the new millennium. In the third volume, *Minding the Darkness: A Poem for the Year 2000,* he included a long poem dedicated to Fay Stender. He started his reminiscences by describing a Passover gathering hosted by Marvin and Dru attended by Marvin's son Neal and his two young Chinese-American daughters who had flown in from Hong

Kong. Scott felt Fay's presence at the Seder like that of an unmentioned ghost. After recalling details of her involvement in the prison movement and her violent death, the poem ends with Marvin asking "whether those lawyers who quit because of Fay and the bookkeeper [Betty Van Patter] had in effect betrayed the movement or the movement them." Scott notes:

> My mind's still open on this
> and I in a rare
> moment of certitude affirm
> Good!
> *That's just how we should be.*[15]

* * *

At the urging of Fay's longtime British friend Brian Gluss, who had moved to Berkeley from Chicago, the City of Berkeley declared May 30, 2005, Fay Stender Day, honoring her memory as a Good Samaritan who lived most of her life in Berkeley and "devoted her life to a plethora of good causes," fighting "passionately for disadvantaged groups and people and sought neither fame nor glory nor money, and ultimately sacrificed her life for her good works . . ."[16]

* * *

Fay's most lasting contribution to her service on the San Francisco ACLU board came in her final year on the board when Fay made an impassioned speech urging her colleagues to pick young Dorothy Ehrlich as its new executive director, despite Ehrlich's youth and lack of a law license, which had been required in the past. In the early '70s Ehrlich had demonstrated superior organizational skills, coordinating volunteers for the Coalition to End the Death Penalty, which convinced the board to trust Fay's recommendation. Over the next three decades, Ehrlich exhibited such extraordinary leadership skills that she was elevated to the ACLU's number two position nationally.

EPILOGUE

One of Ehrlich's hirees in the San Francisco ACLU office was Michelle Alexander, whose experience representing ex-felons led her to write the best-seller *The New Jim Crow*. Alexander would then use her national platform as a personal megaphone to awaken millions of Americans to the myriad problems faced by minorities unfairly stigmatized by felony convictions. By 2014, Eric Holder — the nation's first African-American Attorney General, appointed by its first African-American President — was advocating substantial policy changes to reduce the federal prison population, which Loretta Lynch, the first African-American woman Attorney General, carried forward until her own service ended.

Although current Attorney General Jeff Sessions has instead pursued maximum sentences, a growing number of district attorneys, state attorneys general and governors are now seeking to reduce their prison populations. More than a decade ago, Fay's home county of Alameda became the first in the nation to adopt restorative justice as its official policy. Restorative justice is a growing movement to rehabilitate youths headed for expulsion from school and minimize the dropout to prison pipeline. The effort continues.

* * *

Churning inside at injustice and apathy, Fay Abrahams Stender did not merely put her hand in the stream of history, she roiled the status quo and played no small role in changing our society's course.

ABBREVIATIONS USED IN NOTES

BB *The Berkeley Barb*

BPN *The Black Panther Newspaper*

FA Fay Abrahams

FAS Fay Abrahams Stender

FBI-FS FBI file on Fay Stender obtained via Freedom of Information Act request

HPN Dr. Huey P. Newton Foundation, Inc. Collection, 1968 —1994, M864, Green Library Special Collections, Stanford University

I & G *North East Bay Independent & Gazette*

KM Private collection of Katherine Morse [pseudonym]

NYT *The New York Times*

OT *The Oakland Tribune*

KP Private collection of Karma Pippin

RR Private collection of Robert Richter

SFC *The San Francisco Chronicle*

SFE *The San Francisco Examiner*

RMS Private collection of Hon. Richard M. Silver (ret.), Monterey County Superior Court

MES Private collection of Marvin E. Stender

ES Private collection of Elise Stone

EKT Elsa Knight Thompson papers, BANC MSS 2004/101. Courtesy of The Bancroft Library, University of California, Berkeley.

KW Private collection of Karen Wald

Endnotes

AUTHOR'S NOTE

1. Nabeal Twareet, "What Makes A Great Trial Lawyer?" [undated post 2018], Law Crossing, https://www.lawcrossing.com/article/900019978/What-Makes-a-Great-Trial-Lawyer/. The analogy to fighter pilots, surgeons and boxers was attributed to a long-time instructor of federal prosecutors at the Department of Justice's National Advocacy Center.

PROLOGUE

1. The gunman dictated the wording of the "confession" for Fay Stender to write at her desk in her bedroom in the presence of her son and Katherine Morse, all three of whom later testified about the forced confession at his trial. The note itself disappeared with the gunman the night of the shooting and was never found. All of the quotes from the night of the home invasion were from testimony of the victims at the preliminary hearing and the trial in *People of the State of California v. Brooks*, Alameda County Superior Court, Action No. 74625, cited in this book: Act Three, 7. Death Comes Knocking and Act Three, 8. Star Witness for the Prosecution.
2. "Attorney Shot Near Death," *OT Sunrise Edition*, May 29,1979, 1.
3. Dave Cheit, "Political Murder Try?" *I & G*, No. 234, May 31, 1979, 1.

ACT ONE

■ 1 ■
The Battle of Wills

1. Don Jelinek, *Freedom News*, Vol. VI, No. 4 (April 1972), 1, 21.
2. *Ibid.*
3. Elwin LeTendre, "Gold! Gold! Gold!," principal's message, Spring 1949 Olla Podrida (Berkeley High School Yearbook), Berkeley Public Library, www.ollapodridaunse_40.

■ 2 ■
Predestination or Free Will
1. Jelinek, *Freedom News*, Vol. VI, No. 4 (April 1972), 1, 21.
2. FA, August 15, 1951 letter to Robert Richter, *RR*.
3. FA, Aug. 26, 1951 letter to Robert Richter, *RR*.
4. *Ibid.*
5. Jerold S. Auerbach, *Unequal Justice: Lawyers and Social Change in Modern America* (New York: Oxford Univ. Press, 1976), 25.
6. In 1927, Professor Felix Frankfurter of Harvard published an in-depth analysis of the shortcomings of the Sacco and Vanzetti trial in an unsuccessful effort to convince the Massachusetts Supreme Court to order the men a new trial. In response, Harvard received threats from alumni that they would stop contributing to it "unless Frankfurter was silenced." Auerbach, *Unequal Justice*, 47. Harvard's refusal to do so reportedly cost the university over one million dollars in donations. Professor Karl Llewellyn, then at Columbia Law School, also started a futile campaign for complete review of the case, which was supported by the majority of faculty members in half a dozen law schools.
7. "The Army Tells 'How To Spot A Communist," *ACLU News*, June 1955, reprinted in "The March of Civil Liberties Through the Decade" 1950s Fear and Suspicion, ACLU News, Vol. XLV, Aug/Sept. 1980 #6, 11.
8. William Preston, Jr., "The 1940s: The Way We Really Were," *The Civil Liberties Review*, Vol. 2, Winter 1975, 4-38.
9. Vol. II. *FBI-FS*.

■ 3 ■
Intellectual Boot Camp
1. Elaine Partnow (ed.), *The Quotable Woman: The First 5,000 Years* (New York: Checkmark Books, Facts on File, 2001) p. 2635, entry 23, quoting "War and Memory"(1989). "The Woman That I Am," VII, stanza 6, 1.1, D. Soyini Madison (ed.), *The Literature and Culture of Contemporary Women of Color,* (New York: St. Martin's, 1994).
2. Former Ninth Circuit Court of Appeal Chief Judge Mary Schroeder, "Centennial Essays", University of Chicago Law School, http://web-cast-law.uchicago.edu/centennial/history/essays/schroeder.html.
3. Franklin Zimring, "The American Jury Project and the Chicago Law School," *The Maurice and Muriel Fulton Lecture Series* (Chicago: The University of Chicago Law School, 2003), 1–2.
4. Kenneth Dam (1957), "Centennial Essays," University of Chicago Law School, http://webcast-law.uchicago.edu/centennial/history/essays/dam.html.

■ 4 ■
Smitten
1. Sheehy's observation is reprinted in Partnow, *The Quotable Woman*, citing *"Coalescence," The Silent Passage: Menopause* (New York: Random House, 1992) p. 2656, entry 14. The quoted language is prefaced with the

ENDNOTES

words: "The source of continuing aliveness was."
2. In *re Anastaplo* (1961) 366 U.S. 82.
3. *Time Capsule: 1954 — The Year in Review* (New York: Time Inc., 1954, 2004), 13.
4. Joseph Welch, McCarthy-Welch Exchange, "Have You No Sense of Decency," June 9, 1954, excerpted from the Army-McCarthy hearings in Washington, D.C., American Rhetoric Top 100 Speeches, http://www.americanrhetoric.com/speeches/welch-mccarthy.html.

■ 5 ■
Renewed Ardor
1. Forbes Quotes: "Thoughts on the Business of Life," https://www.forbes.com/quotes/672/. The bracketed addition "[and woman]" is that of the author.

■ 6 ■
Starting Out
1. Jane Howard, "Katharine Graham: The Power That Didn't Corrupt," quoting Katharine Graham, *Ms.*, October 1974, Vol. 3, No. 4, 124.
2. See former California Civil Code §§ 69 and 60.
3. Justice Shenk dissenting in *Perez v. Sharp*, 32 Cal. 2d 711 (1948) at 743–44,750.
4. Susan Berman, "Huey Newton's Lawyer," quoting FAS, *MES*, undated clipping, circa November 1970, *SFE & SFC*, California Living, section, 1 C.
5. Allen was disbarred despite pleas for leniency from eminent African-American lawyers in the California Bar — Wilmont Sweeney, Carl Metoyer, Clinton White and Loren Miller. In *re Allen* (1959) 52 Cal. 2d. 762. In 1962, Allen won reinstatement with help from the same lawyers and from the law firm of Garry, Dreyfus & McTernan, where Fay was then employed as an associate. *Allen v. State Bar* (1962) 58 Cal. 2d 912.
6. "Court Decision: Inter-Racial Marriage No Bar to Public Job," *American Civil Liberties Union News*, March, 1958, Vol. XXIII, No. 3, 1.

■ 7 ■
Turbulence
1. The introductory quote by Judith Niemi is from "Bitten by the Jungle," *The Women's Review of Books*, July 1995, Vol. XII, Nos. 10-11, cited in Partnow, *The Quotable Woman*, p. 668 entry no. 13. The full quote refers to another soft-spoken woman named Fay: "Fay raises a plastic cup of siete raices, powerful sugar-cane rum with seven roots that offer endless aphrodisiac and curative properties. It promises long life, it tastes like woody, acrid Mogen David. She surveys the tangled jungle and in her lady-like, 75-year-old voice offers a toast: 'To chaos.'"
2. The ICEA was the brainchild of Los Angeles educator Mary Jean Hungerford, a disciple of childbirth specialist Dr. Fernand La Maze. From its ambitious launching in 1960, the ICEA over the years has grown into a highly developed international organization, offering an extensive variety of services and publications (http://icea.org/about/)

3. FA poem excerpted from letter to Robert Gene Pippin, *KP*, February 2, 1961.
4. FAS testimonial to Barney Dreyfus, "Testimonial Dinner of the National Lawyers Guild San Francisco Bay Area Chapter," June 3, 1979 ("Lawyers Guild Tribute to Barney Dreyfus"), *MES*.
5. Ann Ginger, *The Relevant Lawyers* (New York: Simon and Schuster, 1972) 61, quoting attorney Malcolm Bernstein.
6. FAS, Lawyers Guild Tribute to Barney Dreyfus, note 4.
7. Jelinek,"Conversations with Fay Stender," *Freedom News*, Vol. VI, No. 4, 1, 21.
8. Jessica Mitford, *Daughters and Rebels* [later renamed *Hons and Rebels*] (New York: New York Review Books Classics, 1960, 1989).
9. Charles Garry and Arthur Goldberg, *Streetfighter in The Courtroom: The People's Advocate* (New York: E. P. Dutton, 1977), 48.
10. Warren Hinckle, *If You Have A Lemon, Make Lemonade* (New York, W.W. Norton, 1973), 30.
11. All quotes in the last two paragraphs are from FAS Lawyers Guild tribute to Barney Dreyfus, note 4.

■8■
Joining the Movement

1. Sally Belfrage, *Freedom Summer* (New York: Viking Press, 1965), 13.
2. Paul Harris, "'We are Family': The Not-So-Bloody History of Resolving Internal Conflicts in the National Lawyers Guild," http://www.guerrillalaw.com/guildarticle.html, 3.
3. David R. Davies (ed.) *The Press and Race* (Jackson, Mississippi: University Press of Mississippi, 2001), 88, 91, 100, 102.
4. Davies, *The Press and Race*, 44.
5. *Free Speech Movement Chronology: California Monthly, February 1965: Three Months of Crisis: Chronology of Events*, bancroft.berkeley.edu/FSM/chron.html.
6. For a vivid description of the December 2, 1964 occupation of Sproul Hall and Governor Pat Brown's decision to order the largest mass arrest in California history, see Seth Rosenfeld, *Subversives: The FBI's War on Student Radicals and Reagan's Rise to Power* (New York: Farrar, Straus and Giroux, 2012) 216-22.
7. *The Whole World's Watching: Peace and Social Justice Movements of the 1960s & 1970s* (Berkeley, California: Berkeley Art Center Association, 2001), 37.
8. Brief for Cross-Petitioners, *City of Greenwood, Mississippi v. Peacock et al.* (October Term, 1965) 42–43, *MES*.

■9■
Unfulfilled

1. Rainer Maria Rilke, *Poetry Chaikhana: Sacred Poetry from Around the World*, http://www.poetry-chaikhana.com/Poets/R/RilkeRainerM/Sunset/index.html.
2. Fred Graham, "NAACP Appeal Refused by Court," *NYT*, April 28, 1966, 20.
3. *City of Greenwood v. Peacock* 384 U.S. 808, 854, Douglas dissenting.
4. *Chavez v. Municipal Court of the Visalia District of Tulare County* (1967) 256

Cal. App. 2d 149. A petition for rehearing was denied December 13, 1967, and petition for hearing by the Supreme Court was denied January 17, 1968, with only two of the seven justices voting to grant a hearing.
5. Carmichael later explained that the black power speech he gave after James Meredith was shot by a sniper had been planned by SNCC leadership for some time, waiting for the right occasion to launch that new direction. See interview of Carmichael, https://www.youtube.com/watch?v=4A9SKoMfzek.
6. Susan Berman, quoting *FAS*, undated clipping circa November 1970, *SFE & SFC*, "California Living" section, 1 C, *MES*.

ACT TWO

■ 1 ■
Second Chair at the Latest Trial of the Century
1. "1967: Aaron Mitchell, Ronald Reagan's first and only execution," April 12, 2011, http:www.executed today.com/2011/04/12/1967-aaron-mitchell-ronald-reagan/.
2. Belva Davis interview filmed on August 15, 2013 by director Bob Richter for *American Justice on Trial: People v. Newton*, in San Francisco, California.
3. Belva Davis with Vicki Haddock, *Never in My Wildest Dreams: A Black Woman's Life in Journalism* (San Francisco: Berrett-Koehler Publisher, Kindle Ed., 2011, location 1848.)
4. *HPN* Grand Jury Testimony, Box 11, M864.

■ 2 ■
The Baton Passes to Fay
1. The quote is from the interview of Doron Weinberg by director Bob Richter for *American Justice on Trial: People v. Newton* on February 7, 2014, filmed at Weinberg's law office in San Francisco.
2. "Huey Says He Ordered 'Keep Cool,'" *OT*, Sept. 12, 1968, 7.
3. *Ibid.*
4. *HPN*, Probation Report, Box 11, 4, M864.
5. *Ibid.*
6. *Ibid.*
7. *Ibid.*, 8–9.
8. Gilbert Moore, *Rage*, 36.
9. David Hilliard, *Huey: Spirit of the Panther* (New York: Thunder's Mouth, 2006), 126.
10. Beverly Axelrod, June 27, 1969, to Elsa Knight Thompson and Alex Hoffmann, *EKT*.

■ 3 ■
Freeing Huey
1. Filmed interview of Penny Cooper by director Bob Richter, *American Justice on Trial: People v. Newton*, August 19, 2013, law offices of Cooper & Cooper,

Berkelely, California.
2. FAS letter to Aryay Lenske, January 7, 1969, *HPN* Box 12.
3. FAS letter to Marshall Patner, March 19, 1969, *HPN* Box 12.
4. FAS, handwritten August 1969 note to Charles Garry, *HPN* Box 12,.
5. Matthew Lasar, "Pacifica Radio: The Rise of an Alternative Network," *RALPH Magazine [The Review of Arts, Literature, Philosophy and the Humanities]*, Vol. XVI, No. 2, 1999.
6. Lewis J. Paper, *Brandeis* (Upper Saddle River, NJ: Prentice Hall, Inc. 1983), 268.
7. Philip S. Foner (ed.), *The Black Panthers Speak* (New York: Da Capo Press, 1970) Letter of Bobby Seale from San Francisco County Jail, November 10, 1969, 95.
8. FAS August 19, 1969, letter to Neil M. Herring, Margolis and McTernan, Los Angeles, *HPN* Box 12.
9. Mark Levine, George McNamee, Daniel Greenberg, *The Tales of Hoffman* (New York: Bantam Books, 1970), 55–57, 62, 68–69.
10. Edward J. Epstein, "The Black Panthers and the Police: A Pattern of Genocide?" *The New Yorker*, February 13, 1971.
11. Appellant's Reply Brief, *People of the State of California v. Huey Newton* 1 Criminal 7753, Court of Appeal First Appellate District, January 23, 1970, 107.
12. *Ibid.*, 108.
13. "8 Arrested as Judges Hear Newton Plea," *OT*, February 11, 1970, 1, 4.
14. Roland Young, "Huey's Appeal" *BPN*, Feb. 28, 1970, 2.
15. Charles Garry, letter to Huey Newton, February 16, 1970, HPN Box 12.
16. Young, *ibid.*
17. "Huey: 'BPP Will Go to UN,'" *BB*, June 5–11, 1970, 4.

■ 4 ■
Entering Gladiator School
1. FAS, Introduction, *Maximum Security: Letters from Prison*, Eve Pell (ed.) (New York: E. P. Dutton, 1972), 13.
2. Jo Durden-Smith, *Who Killed George Jackson? Fantasies, Paranoia and the Revolution* (New York: Alfred A. Knopf, 1976), 198.
3. This December 10, 1969, Jackson letter to his father is among official documents produced from his prison file jacket as discovery in *People v. Jackson*, RMS.
4. FAS, Introduction to *Maximum Security*, 11.
5. George Jackson, *Soledad Brother*, 159, letter to FAS, March 23, 1970.

■ 5 ■
My Small but Mighty Mouthpiece
1. Jackson, *Soledad Brother*, 156, 249 "My small but mighty mouthpiece" is a quote from his letter addressed "Dear Fay" dated March 9, 1970. "You're like no one I ever met from across the tracks" is a quote from his letter to FAS dated July 28, 1970.
2. Quoted from March 1970 flyer, *RMS*.
3. FAS, handwritten note to Kathleen and Eldridge Cleaver, Collection of Dr.

Phillip Shapiro, M0928, *HPN* Box 4.
4. Quoted from March 1970 flyer, *RMS*.
5. Eric C. Brazil, "Long Trial Foreseen in Soledad Prison Slaying," *Salinas Californian*, February 25, 1970, 1.
6. Jackson, *Soledad Brother*, 173, letter to FAS, April 1970.
7. The Attorney General later filed a petition to the Supreme Court that included hand-written, sworn statements from inmates Yorke and Worzella describing their interviews by Fay Stender and Richard Silver in Southern California, which the Attorney General's brief relied upon to make accusations that Stender had engaged in witness intimidation. The court could not rely on the inmates' bald accusations against the two defense attorneys.
8. Fred Sorri, "Attorneys Hit Grand Jury Plan," *Monterey Peninsula Herald*, March 17, 1970, 2.
9. Helen Manning, "Judge Enters Pleas For Soledad Inmates," *Salinas Californian*, March 18, 1970, 1.
10. Jackson, *Soledad Brother*, 161, letter addressed to "My Friend", dated March 24, 1970.

■ 6 ■
The Shaping of a Revolutionary Hero
1. Gregory Armstrong, *The Dragon Has Come* (New York: Harper & Row, 1974), Author's Note, x.
2. Jackson, *Soledad Brother*, 152–53, letters to FAS, February 13 and February 26, 1970.
3. *Ibid.*, 152, letter to FAS, February 13, 1970.
4. *Ibid.*, 155, letter to FAS, March 5, 1970.
5. *Ibid.*, 170, letter to FAS, March 30, 1970.
6. *Ibid.*, 169–70.
7. Armstrong, *The Dragon Has Come*, 63.
8. Jackson, *Soledad Brother*, 158–59, letter to FAS, March 23, 1970.
9. *Ibid.*, 159.
10. *Ibid.*, 153, letter to FAS, February 23, 1970.
11. *Angela Davis: An Autobiography*, excerpt reprinted in Clayborne Carson, David Garrow et al., *The Eyes on the Prize Civil Rights Reader* (New York: Penguin Books, 1991), 542.
12. *Ibid.*, 543.
13. *Ibid.*
14. Jackson, *Soledad Brother*, 172, letter to FAS, March 31, 1970.
15. *Ibid.* 164–65, letter to FAS, March 23, 1970.
16. *Ibid.*, 204, letter to FAS, April 17, 1970.

■ 7 ■
On A Roll
1. Transcript of Proceedings, May 14, 1970, pretrial hearing for Soledad Brothers trial, 158, *RMS*.
2. *Ibid.*
3. Ann Fagan Ginger (ed.), *The Relevant Lawyers: Conversations Out of Court on*

Their Clients, Their Practices, Their Politics, Their Life Style (New York: Simon and Schuster, 1972), 282.
4. Jackson, *Soledad Brother*, 242, letter to Joan [Hammer], June 15, 1970.
5. Ginger, *The Relevant Lawyers*, 283.

■ 8 ■
Collision Course
1. Jackson, *Soledad Brother*, 248-49, letter to FAS, July 28, 1970.
2. *Ibid.*, 230–33, letters to Angela Davis, May 29 and June 3, 1970.
3. Paul Liberatore, *The Road to Hell: The True Story of George Jackson, Stephen Bingham, and the San Quentin Massacre* (New York: The Atlantic Press Monthly, 1996), 81.
4. Jackson, *Soledad Brother*, 237–38, letter to Angela Davis, June 4, 1970.
5. Gregory Armstrong, *The Dragon Has Come*, 100.
6. *Ibid.*, Author's Note, x.
7. *Ibid.*, 184.
8. Durden-Smith, *Who Killed George Jackson?* 216.
9. Liberatore, *The Road to Hell*, 83.
10. Armstrong, *The Dragon Has Come*, 130.
11. "Attorney Fay Stender: 'We Are Fighting to Change the Conditions that Destroy Life,'" *BB*, June 19–25, 1970, 12.
12. *Ibid.*
13. *Ibid.*
14. Jackson, *Soledad Brother*, 248–49, letter to FAS, July 28, 1970.
15. Mark Lane, "Exclusive: Mark Lane interviews Huey Newton in jail," *Los Angeles Free Press*, July 24, 1970, 4, 18.
16. Jackson, *Soledad Brother*, 250, letter to Joan [Hammer], August 9, 1970.
17. Armstrong, *The Dragon Has Come*, 134.
18. *Ibid.*, 130.
19. Jackson, *Soledad Brother*, dedication page.

■ 9 ■
Blood in His Eyes
1. Bob Dylan, "George Jackson," http://www.bobdylan.com/us/songs/george-jackson.
2. "Attorney Fay Stender: 'We Are Fighting to Change the Conditions that Destroy Life,'" *BB*, June 19–25, 1970, 12.
3. George Jackson, *Soledad Brother: The Prison Letters of George Jackson* (New York: Bantam Books, 1970), introduction by Jean Genet.
4. *Ibid.*, back cover.
5. Armstrong, *The Dragon Has Come*, 165–166.
6. Soledad Brothers murder prosecution: Defendants' Memorandum of Points and Authorities in Opposition to Change of Venue, filed September 9, 1970, *RMS*.
7. Armstrong, *The Dragon Has Come*, 166.
8. *Ibid.*, 170.
9. *Ibid.*, 171.

10. "Radical Book-In at Quentin Gate," *SFC*, October 16, 1970, 11.
11. Armstrong, *The Dragon Has Come*, 171.
12. All three reviews are quoted in Armstrong, *The Dragon Has Come*, 172–173.
13. Durden-Smith, *Who Killed George Jackson?* Foreword, xv.
14. *Ibid.*, 287.
15. *Ibid.*, 212.
16. Armstrong, *The Dragon Has Come*, 175.
17. *Ibid.*, 176.
18. Jelinek, "Conversations with Fay Stender,"1, 20.
19. Susan Berman, quoting FAS, *MES*, undated clipping, circa November 1970, *SFE & SFC*, "California Living" section, 1 C.
20. Beverly Koch, "Defending Radicals at Risk," *SFC*, November 20, 1970, 24.
21. Jackson, *Soledad Brother*, 215, undated letter to Angela Davis, circa May 8, 1970.
22. Armstrong, *The Dragon Has Come*, 191.
23. Peter Collier and David Horowitz, *Destructive Generation: A Second Look at the Sixties* (New York: 1989) 38, quoting George Jackson's letter to Eve Pell.
24. Jessica Mitford, "A Talk with George Jackson," *Poison Penmanship: The Gentle Art of Muckraking* (New York: Vintage Books, 1980), 184.
25. Durden-Smith, *Who Killed George Jackson*, 269–70.
26. Armstrong, *The Dragon Has Come*, 199.
27. *Ibid.*, 234.
28. *Ibid.*, 97, 99.
29. *Ibid.*, 202.
30. *Ibid.*, 209.
31. Collier and Horowitz, *Destructive Generation*, 44.
32. Armstrong, *The Dragon Has Come*, 202.
33. Libertore, *The Road to Hell*, 115.

■ 10 ■
The Dragon Lady
1. W. E. B. DuBois, *The Souls of Black Folks* (New York: Barnes & Noble Classics, 2003 (first published 1903), 146. The Prison Law Project included the quoted language on a November 1972 Prison Law Project grant application, *ES*.
2. Robert J. Minton, Jr. (ed.), *Inside Prison American Style* (New York: Random House, 1971) 113, poem published under the pseudonym Micha Maguire.
3. Mitford, *Kind & Usual Punishment: The Prison Business*, (New York: Vintage Press, Random House, 1973), 106.
4. *Ibid.*
5. "The First 'Family Day' At Soledad," *SFC*, December 13, 1971, 10.
6. "A Proposal for Prison Reform" *LAT*, April 26, 1971.
7. Libertore, *The Road to Hell*, 98.
8. Armstrong, *The Dragon Has Come*, 211.
9. *Ibid.*, 208–209.
10. Jessica Mitford, unpublished letter to Raymond Benedict, Corona, California, California Rehabilitation Center, July 12, 1971.
11. "Jury Hopelessly Deadlocked in Newton's Trial," *SFC*, August 9, 1971, 1.
12. George Jackson, *Blood in His Eye* (New York: Random House, 1971).

13. Jackson, *Blood in His Eye*, 32.
14. Durden-Smith, *Who Killed George Jackson?* 35-36.
15. Angela Davis tribute to George Jackson, *BPN*, September 4, 1971, 2.
16. *Ibid.*
17. Collier & Horowitz, *Destructive Generation*, 44.
18. Armstrong, *The Dragon Has Come*, 223.
19. *Ibid.*, 223.
20. *FBI-FS*, Volume I.
21. "Berkeley Council Asks U.N. Probe of San Quentin Death," *SFC*, October 27, 1971.
22. "Prison Reform Dilemma: Control v. Rehabilitation," *OT*, Editorial, October 28, 1971, 14.
23. *Ibid.*
24. Tim Findley, "Some Tough Testimony on Reform of Prisons," *SFC*, October 26, 1971, 1.
25. *Ibid.*
26. "Probe of Prison Plots Demanded," *SFE*, Oct. 25, 1971, 1.
27. *Ibid.*

ACT THREE

■ 1 ■
Bitter Fruit

1. Board of Corrections, "Report to Governor Ronald Reagan on Violence in California Prisons" October 7, 1971, Appendix 1, Executive Order No. R-33-71.
2. FAS, "Wardens, Attorneys and Prisoners," *Case & Comment* September-October," 1973/Vol.78, No.5, 13.
3. Board of Corrections, "Report to Governor Ronald Reagan on Violence in California Prisons," 9.
4. Drew McKillips, "Huey Newton Free — Case Dismissed," *SFC*, December 16, 1971, 1.
5. Lloyd Boles and Gaile Russ, "Huey Free as Charge Dismissed," OT, December 15, 1971, 1.
6. *Ibid.*, 24.
7. Douglass C. Rigg, "Letters from 'Inside'—Despair Recorded," *SFE & SFC*, February 20, 1972, 36.
8. Steven V. Roberts, *Maximum Security: Letters from California' Prisons, The New York Times Book Review*, Feb. 6, 1972.

■ 2 ■
Spent!

1. *FBI-FS*, Volume III.
2. Argus (pen name of Don Jelinek), "Conversations with Fay Stender," *Freedom News*, Vol. VI, No. 4, April,1972, 1.

3. *Ibid.*, 19.
4. Greg Armstrong, letter to *Esquire* magazine, circa May 1970, EAS.
5. David Greenberg and Fay Stender, *Buffalo Law Review,* "The Prison as Lawless Agency," 832–833.
6. *Ibid.*, 837–838.
7. FAS letter to Elsa Knight Thompson, June 6, 1972, *EKT*.
8. Peter Sussman, (ed.), *Decca: The Letters of Jessica Mitford* (New York: Knopf, 2006), 441–442, letter to Marge Frantz, circa summer 1972.
9. Judge's Ruling: Quentin Pen Pals Win Right to Visit," *SFC,* July 29, 1972.
10. Bruce Jackson (Professor English & Comparative Literature University of New York at Buffalo) letter, October 28, 1972, EAS.
11. November 1972 Prison Law Project grant application, *EAS*.
12. Mitford, *Kind & Usual Punishment*, 7–8.
13. *Ibid.*, 156–159, 164–165.
14. *Ibid.*, 175–176.
15. *Ibid.*, 267.
16. Tim Findley, "A Grim Finale for Prison Inmates," *SFC,* May 25, 1973, 6.
17. *Ibid.*

■ 3 ■
Cuba
1. Poets.org, "Night on the Great River by Meng Hao-jan [three translations], III: Mooring on Chen Ti River," translated by Gary Snyder, https://www.poets.org/poetsorg/poem/night-great-river-three-translations.
2. Notebook of Emily Jane Goodman, June 1973, private collection of Judge Emily Jane Goodman, June 1973, now in The Collected Papers of Emily Jane Goodman at Brooklyn College Library Archive, City University of New York.

■ 4 ■
The Barb
1. File note, *MES*, Scherr publicity file.
2. FAS letter to *Pacific Sun* reporter Alice Yarish, Jan. 29, 1974, *MES*, Scherr publicity file.
3. FAS note to Marvin Stender, Nov. 1973, *MES*, inside cover of *Grossman v. Striepeke*, Petition for a Writ of Certiorari to the United States Supreme Court, October Term, 1973.
4. Ric Reynolds, unpublished article, "*Berkeley Barb,*" *MES*, Scherr publicity file, p. 7.
5. Susan Berman, quoting FAS, *SFE & SFC,* "California Living" section, clipping, circa November 1970, *MES*.
6. *Hill v. Estate of Westbrook* (1952) 39 Cal. 2d 458.
7. FAS, "Recent marriage case may expand equal rights," *ACLU News,* Mar-Apr. 1974, 10.
8. FAS, letter to Larry D. Hatfield, *SFE*, Dec. 10, 1973, *MES*, Scherr publicity file.
9. FAS, letter to Elizabeth Johnson, KDIA radio station, Jan. 29, 1974, *MES*, Scherr publicity file.

10. This widely repeated quote is from Dr. Stuart Shapiro, Director of Boston's Cambridgeport Problem Center.
11. Alice Yarish, "Max & Jane & Fay & Barb," *The Pacific Sun*, March 14-20, 1974.
12. Beverly Stephen, "Max Scherr's Domestic Triangle," *SFC*, August 20, 1975, 21.
13. FAS, letter to Bergliot Bornholdt [maiden name of Bergie Mackey], March 1974, *ES*.
14. Marvin Stender, note to FAS re CBS News of New York, July 8 [1974], *MES*, Scherr publicity file.
15. Patrick A. Nielson. "*In re Cary:* A Judicial Recognition of Illicit Cohabitation," *Hastings Law Journal* 1226 (April 1974) 25. ("The court has obfuscated California's marital law, distorted the community property system, misunderstood the intentions of the legislature, misapplied the Family Law Act, nullified legislative policy decisions, and raised a myriad of problems for California courts, attorneys and meretricious couples.")
16. Robert Treuhaft, letter to the publisher, *OT*, Feb. 28, 1975, 2.
17. Stephen, *ibid.*
18. *NYT* clipping, *MES*, Scherr publicity file.
19. Diana Russell, "Fay Stender and the Politics of Murder," *On the Issues* (Spring 1991), 30.
20. FAS, letter to Bonn, Sept 1974, *MES* Scherr publicity file.
21. *Marvin v. Marvin* (1976) 18 Cal. 3d. 660 at 680 fn. 18 and 681.
22. Russell, *ibid.*

■ 5 ■
Reflections in the Mirror
1. *FBI-FS*, Vol. I.
2. FAS, "Prisons and the Revolution: Who Killed George Jackson," *SFC*, August 31, 1976.
3. Durden-Smith, *Who Killed George Jackson?* 184–185.
4. David Horowitz, *Radical Son: A Generational Odyssey* (New York: The Free Press, 1997), 311.
5. *Ibid.*
6. Kristina Horton Flaherty, "Witkin award for 'legal giant' Robert Raven," *California Bar Journal*, September 2003, 1.
7. *Ibid.*

■ 6 ■
Temps Perdu
1. Joan Didion, "On Self-Respect: Joan Didion's 1961 Essay from the Pages of *Vogue*," October 22, 2014, http://www.vogue.com/article/joan-didion-self-respect-essay-1961.
2. FAS "Autumn Diary 1978," *KM*.
3. FAS, "Autumn Diary 1978," *KM*, 15.
4. FAS, "Book Reviews: Peggy Dennis, *The Autobiography of an American Communist;* Vivian Gornick, *The Romance of American Communism;* Jessica Mitford, *A Fine Old Conflict,"* *Chrysalis*, Issue 5 (1978), 99.
5. *Ibid.*, 101.
6. *Ibid.*, 99.

■ 7 ■
Death Comes Knocking

1. This is the most quoted line from Jean Racine's 17th century play *Phèdre*, based on the myth of Hippolytus and the 5th century B.C. tragedy *Hippolytus* by Euripides. The French verse translates "daughter of [Cretan King] Minos and Pasiphae [a child of the Sun God Helios]."
2. FAS, "Book Reviews: Peggy Dennis, *The Autobiography of an American Communist;* Vivian Gornick, *The Romance of American Communism;* Jessica Mitford, *A Fine Old Conflict, Chrysalis,* Issue 5 (1978), 101.
3. Peter Dale Scott, *Minding the Darkness: A Poem for the Year 2000,"* Book Three of *Seculum: A Trilogy* (New York: New Directions Books, 2000), 100-01.
4. Transcript of preliminary examination, *People of the State of California v. Brooks,* Alameda County Superior Court, Action No. 74625, August 6, 1979, 34.
5. *Ibid.*, 16.
6. *Ibid.*, 24.
7. *Ibid.*, 34.
8. *Ibid.*
9. *Ibid.*, Don Martinez, "Stender tells her painful story of shooting," *SFE*, January 19, 1980, 3.
10. "Attorney Shot Near Death," *OT*, May 30, 1079, 1.
11. *Ibid.*
12. *Ibid.*
13. *Ibid.*
14. Dave Cheit, "Political Murder Try," *I & G*, No. 234, May 31, 1979, 1.
15. Cheit, "Prison gangs target of Stender probe," *I & G*, No. 234, May 31, 1979, 1, 4.
16. George Williamson, "Radical Lawyer: A Clue in the Shooting of Fay Stender," *SFC*, May 30, 1979, 2.
17. Tim Reiterman and Don Martinez, "Prison-work link in Stender shooting," *SFE*, May 30, 1979, 1, 20.
18. Williamson, *ibid.*
19. Reiterman and Martinez,*ibid.*
20. Cheit, *ibid.*, 1.
21. Reiterman and Martinez, *ibid.*
22. *Ibid.*
23. Peter H. King and Bill Boldenweek, "Jackson letters contain no hint of rift," *SFE*, May 30, 1979, 10.
24. *OT*, May 30, 1979, 1.
25. Bill Wallace, "After the Stender Shooting: I'm No Hero, *BB*, Vol. 29, Issue 21, July 19–Aug.1, 1979, 3.
26. Larry D. Hatfield, "Friends to form fund for Stender recovery," *SFE*, June 12, 1979.
27. Austin Scott, *Los Angeles Times,* June 5, 1979.
28. *Ibid.*
29. Lance Williams, "Stender attack suspect and weapon linked," *OT*, Jan. 18, 1980, Section B,1.
30. Eve Pell, "Life in the U.S. Prison," *MES*, clipping, unknown date, circa July 1979.

31. George Williamson, "Courtroom Brawl in Stender Case," *SFC*, June 19, 1979, 1.
32. Pell, *ibid.*
33. *Ibid.*
34. Don Martinez, "Court security tight on Stender case suspect," *SFE*, June 20, 1979.
35. "Ex-Black Panther Lawyer Threatened," *The Los Angeles Times*, June 23, 1979.
36. Wallace Turner, "Black Convicts Linked to Plot to Kill Lawyer," *NYT*, June 30, 1979, 14.
37. *Ibid.*

■ 8 ■
Star Witness for the Prosecution
1. Undated statement of Hugo A. Pinell, *KW.*
2. Friends of Fay Stender appeal letter, *EAS.*
3. Judy Chicago, "Merger: A Vision of the Future," www.judychicago.com.
4. Robert Kroll, "Stender shooting: new speculations," *I & G*, August 7, 1979, 1.
5. Don Martinez, "Brooks to face trial for Stender shooting" *SFE*, June 30, 1979, 1.
6. Dan Siegel, "Slamming the Cell Door on Prison Reform," *The Los Angeles Times*, July 19, 1979, C7.
7. *Ibid.*
8. Press release, The Intersection, A Center for the Arts and Religion, August 24, 1979, *EAS.*
9. "Stender Wins State Bar Award," *The Recorder*, Sept. 1979, Vol. 107, No. 43, 1; Jim Wood, "Fay Stender found dead in Hong Kong," *SFE*, May 20, 1980, 5.
10. FAS, note to Bergie Mackey, fall 1979, *ES.*
11. FAS, note to Katherine Morse, *KM.*
12. Don Martinez, "Investigators believe Stender the victim of vendetta," *SFE*, Jan. 8, 1980, 4.
13. FAS, letter to Robert Gene Pippin, Nov.7, 1979, *KP.*
14. Martinez, "Crippled Fay Stender identifies defendant in court face-down," *SFE*, January 10, 1980, 10.
15. *Ibid.*
16. Lance Williams, "Dramatic day in court for Stender," *OT*, January 11, 1980, 1.
17. George Williamson, "Shooting Victim Drama in Court — Stender Testifies," *SFC*, January 11, 1980, 5.
18. Williams, *ibid.*, A-12.
19. Williamson, *ibid.*, note 17, 5.
20. Don Martinez, "Stender's son describes shooting," *SFE*, January 17, 1980.
21. *Ibid.*
22. Lance Williams, "Defense fails to shake Stender tale of shooting," *OT*, Jan. 17, 1980, Section B, 1.
23. Don Martinez, "Stender tells her painful story of shooting," *SFE*, Jan. 19, 1980, 3.
24. *Ibid.*

ENDNOTES   463

25. Lance Williams, "Fay Stender tells packed court Brooks was man who shot her," *OT*, Jan. 19, 1980, 1.
26. *Ibid.*
27. Williamson, "Painful Testimony: Stender's Story of the Shooting," *SFC*, Jan. 19, 1980, 2.
28. Martinez, *ibid.*
29. Martinez, "Stender: She was shot for the wrong reason," *SFE*, January 19, 1980, 3.
30. "Odd lineup of Stender witnesses," undated clipping, circa January 22, 1980, *KM*.
31. *Ibid.*
32. *Ibid.*
33. Daniel Borenstein, "Testimony backfires: Defense witness names Stender gunman," *I & G*, January 23, 1980, 2.
34. Williams, "Stender defense questions identification of suspect," *OT*, January 23, 1980, 9.
35. Williams, "Stender friend cites doubt," *OT*, January 22, 1980, B1.
36. *Ibid.*
37. Williams, "Stender defense questions identification of suspect," *OT*, January 23, 1980, 9.
38. Borenstein, *ibid.*
39. Williams, "Lawyers sum up Stender evidence," *OT*, January 24, 1980, Section B, 1.
40. Martinez, "Stender shooting goes to the jury", *SFE* January 24, 1980.
41. Williams, "Stender shooting case goes to jury," *OT*, January 23, 1980, C 1; Williamson, "The Defense Attacks Stender's Testimony," *SFC*, Jan. 24, 1980, 2.
42. *Ibid.*
43. Williams, "Brooks guilty in Stender shooting," *OT*, Jan. 26, 1980, 1.
44. Williamson, "Ex-Convict Found Guilty in Stender Shooting," *SFC*, Jan. 26, 1980, 2.
45. *Ibid.*
46. *Ibid.*
47. *Ibid.*
48. Don Martinez, "Stender defendant found guilty," *SFE*, Jan. 26, 1980, 1.
49. T. Osmani, "Stender Attacker Convicted," *KW*, undated draft article, circa Feb. 1980, 1.

■ 9 ■
Nowhere to Run
1. W. B. Yeats, "The Second Coming," https://www.poets.org/poetsorg/poem/second-coming.
2. FAS, note to her sister, January 1980, *EAS*.
3. Daniel Borenstein, "How the Stender jury reached a guilty verdict," *I & G*, January 27, 1980, 3.
4. *Ibid.*
5. Edward Brooks, statement introduced at his sentencing hearing on

February 23, 1980, *EAS*.
6. Ann Bancroft, "Courtroom violence in Stender case," *SFC*, Feb. 23, 1980, 1 and back page.
7. *Ibid.*
8. *Ibid.*
9. Daryl Johnson, "Fay Stender," Bay Area, *KW*, 2 [undated, circa June 1980].
10. Spring 1980 announcement of Golden Gate University Women's Association, *KM*.
11. T. Osamania, special to *The San Francisco Guardian*, Feb. 27, 1980.
12. Collier and Horowitz, *Destructive Generation*, 64.
13. Wendy Milmore, note to Fay Stender, dated March 29, 1980, *ES*.
14. FAS letter to Katherine Morse, March, 1980, *KM*.
15. FAS, letter to Elsa Knight Thompson, *EKT*.
16. *Ibid.*
17. *Ibid.*
18. FAS, letter to Katherine Morse, April 4, 1980, *KM*.
19. FAS, letter to Bergie Mackey, April 18, 1980, *ES*.
20. Peter Stack, "Folksiness and Feminism, Too" *SFC*, April 15, 1980, 42.
21. FAS, letter to Katherine Morse, May 18, 1979, delivered posthumously, *KM*.
22. FAS, letter to Kay Boyle, May 19, 1980, 4, delivered posthumously. University of Delaware special collection, Kay Boyle correspondence.
23. FAS, note to Sara Levine, May 19, 1980, *ES*.
24. Quotation from colleague of Fay Stender obtained at Fay Stender's funeral, *KW*.
25. *Ibid.*
26. Mary Dunlap, eulogy to Fay Stender, May 28, 1978, *KM*.
27. Horowitz, *Radical Son: A Generational Odyssey*, 311–12.
28. Quotation from colleague of Fay Stender obtained at Fay Stender's funeral, *KW*.
29. *Ibid.*
30. Collier and Horowitz, *Destructive Generation*, 23.
31. "AG Report on Stender shooting," *The Recorder*, Sept. 30, 1980, 1.
32. Collier and Horowitz, "Requiem for a Radical," *New West*, March, 1981, 66; *Destructive Generation*, 22.
33. Collier and Horowitz, *Destructive Generation*, 65–66.

Epilogue
1. Author's private collection, from translation of Zen proverbs collected by Austin Pearlman.
2. *ACLU News*, Jan-Feb 1982, XLVII, No. 1, 3.
3. Herbert Gold, "Agonizing Epitaph to a Dilettante of Revolution," *The Wall Street Journal*, March 9, 1983.
4. Durden-Smith, "The Last One Home: Requiem for a Mass Movement," *California Magazine*, January 1985, 96.
5. *Ibid.*
6. David Burner, "We Were Disinformed," *NYT Book Review*, April 23, 1989, 18 (book review of Collier and Horowitz, *Destructive Generation: Second*

Thoughts About the Sixties). *The Wall Street Journal* and *The National Review* book reviews are quoted on the back cover of *Destructive Generation*.
7. "Arrest in Murder of Huey Newton: Police Identify Suspect as an Oakland Drug Dealer — Self-Defense Claimed," *NYT*, August 26, 1989, 7.
8. Diana Russell, "Fay Stender & the Politics of Murder," *On the Issues*, Spring 1991, 41.
9. *Ibid.*
10. *Ibid.*
11. Armstrong, *The Dragon Has Come*, x.
12. *Ibid.*, 130.
13. California Women Lawyers website, Fay Stender Award, http://www.cwl.org/page/FayStender.
14. Monica Bay, "Fay Stender Award Goes to BASF's Ramey," *The Recorder*, August 3, 1992, 3.
15. Peter Dale Scott, *Minding the Darkness*, 103–104.
16. City of Berkeley Proclamation, May 31, 2005, signed by Mayor Tom Bates at the urging of long-time Stender friend and admirer Brian Gluss, http://www.berkeleydailyplanet.com/issue/2005-05-17/article/21423.

Sources

Individuals:

Among those who graciously gave of their time for interviews and background information for this biography in person, by telephone and via e-mail were Anthony Amsterdam, Ed Bell, Bernhard E. Bergeson, III, Stephen Bingham, Robert Blauner, Kathleen Bouffe, Roberta Brooks, Thomas Broome, Allan Brotsky, Malcolm Burnstein, Kathleen Cleaver, Kate Coleman, Penny Cooper, Steve and Bari Cornet, Belva Davis, Joan DeLasaux, Henry and Evelyn Elson, Peter Franck, JoAnne Garvey, Gordon Gaines, Ann Fagan Ginger, David Lance Goines, Brian Gluss, Emily Jane Goodman, David Greenberg, Lee Halterman, Dag Hamilton, Milton Hare, Hon. Thelton Henderson, Hilde Stern Hein, Ezra Herndon, David Hilliard, Alex Hoffmann, David Horowitz, Howard Janssen, Don Jelinek, Hon. D. Lowell Jensen, Herma Hill Kay, Don Kerson, Ying Lee Kelley, Michael Krinsky, James Larson, David Levinson, Sandra Levinson, Bergliot Bornholdt Mackey, Michael Magbie, Ephraim Margolin, Marling Mast, Michael McCarthy, Jerrie Meadows, Hon. Marilyn Patel, Karma Pippin, Barbara Price, Dru Stender Ramey, Louise Renne, Jae Scharlin, Raquel Scherr, Joanne Schulman, Dan Siegel, Hon. Richard Silver (ret.), Marvin Stender, Don Stone, Elise Stone, Peter Sussman, Hon. John Sutter (ret.), Hon. Jacqueline Taber, Michael Tigar, Karen Lee Wald, Doris Brin Walker, Doron Weinberg, David Wellman, John Wells, Jayne Williams, Alice Wirth, Laura X, and Philip Ziegler.

Special Collections:

Black Panther Collection, archives of the African American Museum and Library, Oakland, California; Department of Justice FBI FOIA Files: The Black Panther Party, Huey Newton, Fay Stender, Student Nonviolent Coordinating Committee; Dr. Huey P. Newton Foundation, Inc. Collection 1968 – 1994, M864. California: Green Library Special Collections, Stanford University; University of California Berkeley Bancroft Library: Meiklejohn Civil Liberties Archives; Elsa Knight Thompson papers.

Private Collections:

Trial notes of Prof. Robert Blauner from *People v. Newton*, 1968; legal files of Hon. Richard Silver (ret.) from his representation of Soledad Brother Fleeta Drumgo; correspondence, documents, and magazine and newspaper clippings of Bergliot Bornholdt Mackey, Katherine Morse, Karma Pippin, Marvin Stender, Elise Stone, and Laura X; Peter Sussman collection of unpublished letters of Jessica Mitford; Karen Wald, newspaper clippings and notes.

Bibliography

Anderson, T., *The Movement and the Sixties: Protest in America from Greensboro to Wounded Knee* (New York: Oxford University Press, 1995).

Armstrong, Gregory, *The Dragon Has Come* (New York: Harper & Row, 1974).

Auerbach, Jerold S., *Unequal Justice: Lawyers and Social Change in Modern America* (New York: Oxford Univ. Press, 1976).

Broussard, A. S., *Black San Francisco: The Struggle for Racial Equality in the West, 1900–1954* (Lawrence, Kansas: University Press of Kansas, 1993).

Brown, Elaine, *A Taste of Power: A Black Woman's Story* (New York: Anchor Books, Doubleday, 1992).

Carr, James, *Bad: The Autobiography of James Carr* (Oakland: Nabat/AK Press, 2000).

Carroll, P. N., and Noble, D. W., *The Free and the Unfree: A Progressive History of the United States* (New York: Penguin Books, 2001, 3d rev. ed.).

Carson, Clayborne, *In Struggle: SNCC and the Black Awakening of the 1960s* (Cambridge, Massachusetts: Harvard Univ. Press, 1981, 1995).

Carson, C., Garrow, D. J., Gill, G., Harding, V., and Hine, D. C., *The Eyes on the Prize Civil Rights Reader* (New York: Penguin Books, 1991).

Churchill, W., and Vanderwall, J., *Agents of Repression: The FBI's Secret Wars Against the Black Panther Party and the American Indian Movement* (Boston: South End Press, 1988, 1990).

_____, *The COINTELPRO Papers: Documents from the FBI's Secret War Against Dissidents* (Boston: South End Press, 1980).

Cleaver, Eldridge, *Target Zero: A Life in Writing* [Kathleen Cleaver (ed.)] (New York: Palgrave Macmillan, 2006).

Clinton, Bill, *My Life* (New York: Alfred A. Knopf, 2004).

Collier, Peter, and Horowitz, David, *Destructive Generation: A Second Look at the Sixties* (New York: Summit Books, 1989).

Darrow, Clarence, *The Story of My Life* (New York: Da Capo, 1996).

Davies, David R. (ed.), *The Press and Race* (Jackson, Mississippi: Univ. Press of Mississippi, 2001).

Davis, Belva, [with Vicki Haddock] *Never in my Wildest Dreams: A Black Woman's Life Life in Journalism* (San Francisco, California: Berrett Koehler, 2001).

Dellums, R. V., and Halterman, H. L., *Lying Down with the Lions* (Boston: Beacon Press, 2000).

Dudziak, M. L., *Cold War Civil Rights* (Princeton, New Jersey: Princeton Univ. Press, 2000).

Durden-Smith, Jo, *Who Killed George Jackson? Fantasies, Paranoia and the Revolution* (New York: Alfred A. Knopf, 1976).

Foner, P. S., *The Black Panthers Speak* (Cambridge, Massachusetts: Da Capo Press, 1970).

Forbes, Flores, *Will You Die with Me? My Life in the Black Panther Party* (New York: Washington Square Press, Simon & Schuster, 2006).

Garry, Charles, and Goldberg, Arthur, *Streetfighter in the Courtroom: The People's Advocate* (New York: E. P. Dutton, 1977).

Ginger, Ann Fagan, *Landmark Cases Left Out of Your Textbooks* (Berkeley, California: Meiklejohn Civil Liberties Institute, 2006).

_____, *Minimizing Racism in Jury Trials* (National Lawyers Guild, 1969).

_____, *The Relevant Lawyers: Conversations Out of Court on Their Clients, Their Practice, Their Politics, Their Life Style* (New York: Simon & Schuster, 1973).

Hilliard, D., *Huey: Spirit of the Panther* (New York: Thunder's Mouth Press, 2006).

Hilliard, D., and Cole, L., *This Side of Glory* (New York: Little, Brown, 1993).

Hinckle, W., *If You Have A Lemon, Make Lemonade* (New York: W.W. Norton, 1973).

Horowitz, David, *hating whitey and other progressive causes* (Dallas: Spence Publishing, 1999).

———, *Left Illusions: An Intellectual Odyssey* (Dallas: Spence Publishing, 2003).

———, *Radical Son: A Generational Odyssey* (New York: Touchstone, 1997).

James, Joy, *The Angela Y. Davis Reader* (Malden, Massachusetts: Blackwell, 1998).

Jackson, George, *Blood in My Eye* (Baltimore: Black Classic Press, 1990).

———, *Soledad Brother: The Prison Letters of George Jackson* (Chicago: Lawrence Hill Books, 1994).

Jones, Charles E. (ed.), *The Black Panther Party [Reconsidered]* (Baltimore: Black Classic Press, 1998).

Keating, Edward M., *Free Huey!* (Palo Alto, California: Ramparts Press, 1971).

Kerr, Clark, *The Gold and the Blue: A Personal Memoir of the University of California 1949–67* (Berkeley, California: Univ. of California Press, 2001).

Knappman, E. W., *Great American Trials* (Detroit: Visible Ink Press, 1994).

Lee, Barbara, *Renegade for Peace and Justice: Barbara Lee Speaks for Me* (Landham, Maryland: Rowman & Littlefield, 2008).

Lerner, Michael, and West, Cornel, *Jews & Blacks: A Dialogue on Race, Religion, and Culture in America* (New York: Penguin Books, 1995, 1996).

Levine, M., McNamee, G., and Greenberg, D., *The Tales of Hoffman* (New York: Bantam Books, 1970).

Liberatore, Paul, *The Road to Hell: The True Story of George Jackson, Stephen Bingham, and the San Quentin Massacre* (New York: The Atlantic Monthly Press, 1996).

Major, Reginald, *Justice in the Round: The Trial of Angela Davis* (New York: Joseph Okpaku, 1973).

Mann, Eric, *Comrade George; An Investigation into the Life, Political Thought, and Assassination of George Jackson* (New York; Harper & Row, 1972, 1974).

McAdam, D., *Freedom Summer* (New York: Oxford Univ. Press, 1988).

Middleton, N., *The I.F. Stone's Weekly Reader* (New York: Vintage Books, 1953).

Minton, Robert, Jr. (ed.), *Inside: Prison American Style* (New York: Random House, 1971).

Mitford, Jessica, *A Fine Old Conflict* (New York: Vintage Books, 1956, 1977)

_____ , *Kind & Usual Punishment: The Prison Business* (New York: Vintage Press, Random House, 1973).

Moore, Gilbert, *Rage* (New York: Carroll & Graf, 1993).

_____ , *A Special Rage* (New York: Harper & Row, 1971).

Newton, Huey, *To Die for the People* (New York: Random House, 1972).

Newton, H., and Blake, J. H., *Revolutionary Suicide* (New York: Harcourt, Brace, Jovanovich, 1973).

Pearson, Hugh, *The Shadow of the Panther* (New York: Perseus Books, 1995).

Pell, Eve (ed.), *Maximum Security: Letters from Prison* (New York: E.P. Dutton, 1972).

_____ , *We Used To Own the Bronx: Memoirs of a Former Debutante* (New York: State University of New York Press, 2009).

Radosh, Ronald, and Milton, Joyce, *The Rosenberg File* (New Haven, Connecticut: Yale Univ. Press, 2003).

Rhodes, Jayne, *Framing The Black Panthers: The Spectacular Rise of a Black Power Icon* (New York: The New Press, 2008).

Rhomberg, Chris, *No There There: Race, Class, and Political Community in Oakland* (Berkeley, California: Univ. of California Press, 2004).

Rosenfeld, Seth, *Subversives: The FBI's War on Student Radicals and Reagan's Rise to Power* (New York: Farrar, Straus and Giroux, 2012).

Scherr, Judith (ed.) *Ying Lee / From Shanghai to Berkeley: The story of an extraordinary woman facing war, waging peace, fighting disillusionment, and inspiring action* (Berkeley, California: Berkeley Historical Society, 2012).

Seale, Bobby, *Seize the Time: The Story of the Black Panther Party and Huey P. Newton* (New York: Random House, Black Classic Press, 1970, 1991).

Scott, Peter Dale, *Minding the Darkness: A Poem for the Year 2000, Book Three of Seculum: A Trilogy* (New York: New Directions Books, 2000).
Sussman, P. Y. (ed.), *Decca: The Letters of Jessica Mitford* (New York: Alfred A. Knopf, 2006).
Time Capsule: 1954—The Year in Review. (New York: Time, Inc., 1954, 2004).
Wellman, David, *Portraits of White Racism* (New York: Cambridge University Press, 1977).
Whitfield, Stephen J., *The Culture of the Cold War* (Baltimore, Maryland: The Johns Hopkins University Press, 1996).
The Whole World's Watching: Peace and Social Justice Movements of the 1960s & 1970s (Berkeley, California: Berkeley Art Center Association, 2001).

Index

A

Abrahams, Elise ("Lisie") Act One, chap. 1, *passim*, 29, 32, 44, 63, 69 (*see also* Elise Stone)
Abrahams, Fay Act One, chaps. 1–4, *passim* (*see also* Fay Stender)
Abrahams, Hank 426
Abrahams, Ruby Act One, chaps. 1–2, Act Three, chaps. 7–9, *passim*, 54, 58, 73, 87, 109, 205, 344
Abrahams, Sam Act One, chaps. 1–2, *passim*, 58, 73, 109, 330, 375, 431
Abramowitsch, Bernhard 13
AFSC (*see* American Friends Service Committee)
Alexander, Michelle 447
Ali, Muhammad xi
American Civil Liberties Union (ACLU) xii, 75–78, 242-43, 247, 322, 349, 437, 446
American Communist Party 86
American Friends Service Committee 32–34
Amsterdam, Anthony 105, 189
Anarchist Cookbook, The 388
Anastaplo, George 56–57
Anna Head School 13–16
Armstrong, Gregory Act Two, chaps. 8–10, *passim*, 181, 264, 274–75
Aryan Brotherhood 185, 203
Attica uprising 253, 320, 358
August 7th Movement 233
Autobiography of Malcolm X 186, 226

Aviron, Harry 10, 79
Axelrod, Beverly and Black Panther Party 118; and Eldridge Cleaver 113, 118, 121-22, 172, 186-87, 384; CORE 111; Council for Justice 101; Free Speech Movement 94, 101-02; and Huey Newton's defense 118-122; self-exile 139-40

B

Baez, Joan 99, 108, 364
Baldwin, James 147
Beatles, The 294
Bell, Ed 256, 266, 270–72
Belli, Melvin 65
Bennett, Fred 233, 237-38
Bergen, Candice 252
Bergesen, Bernie 409, 429, 437
Berkeley Barb, The 205–06, Act Three, chap. 4, *passim*
BGF (*see* Black Guerilla Family)
Bill of Rights 437
Bingham, Stephen 251, 253, 256, 438–439
Bird, Rose 314, 429
Black Friday 82, 83, 99, 287
Black Guerrilla Family (BGF) Act Three, chaps 7, 8, *passim*, 408, 413–414, 432, 440, 444
Black Nationalists 17
Black Panther Party Act Two, Act Three, chaps. 1–2, 5, 7, *passim*, xiv, 3, 22, 287, 337, 413, 441, 445

475

Black Power 5, 110, 186
Blake, Herman 51, 277
Blauner, Robert 127–131
Blood in My Eye 233, 250
Bornholdt, Bergliot *see* Bergie Mackey
Bouffe, Kathleen 52
Boyle, Kay 420, 425–26
Brandeis, Louis 43, 150
Brodsky, Carroll 314
Brooks, Edward Act Three, chaps. 2–9, *passim*, 438–42, 444
Brooks, Roberta 336-37, 416-17
Broome, Tom Act Three, chap. 8, *passim*, 135-136, 411-13, 438
Brotsky, Al 102, 110, 143, 152, 208, 308
Brown, Elaine 223, 277, 316–317, 326
Brownell, Herbert 56–57, 71
Brown, Gov. Edmund G., Sr. ("Pat") 99
Brown v. Board of Education 77
Brown, Willie 189
Brussel, Suzanne 53
Burnstein, Mal 94, 102, 410

C

California Prisoners Union 258
California Rural Legal Assistance 258
California Women Lawyers xii–xiii, 313, 334, 352, 430, 432–33
Camacho, Moe 258-59, 263
Campbell, Gordon Act. Two, chap. 5–7, *passim*
Capital punishment 118 (see also death penalty)
Cappenberg, Julia 278, 370
Carmichael, Stokely 97, 110, 119, 150, 273
Carr, Betsy Hammer 201, 245
Carr, Jimmy 163, 165, 233, 237–38, 245, 252, 275, 318–19
Carter, Alprentice "Bunchy" 210
Carter, Jimmy xii, 110, 210, 339
Castro, Fidel 293–294
Chaney, James 97
Chavez, Cesar 102, 104, 107–09
Chessman, Caryl 113, 349
Chicago, Judy 351, 379
Chicago Seven 19, 154, 205, 207
Chisholm, Shirley 301
Chrysalis 344, 350
CIA 375
Citizen, The 299–300
Civil Rights Act 1964 96, 108

Clark, Ramsey 265
Cleaver, Eldridge 111, 120–23, 137–38, 170, 172, 312
Cleaver, Kathleen Neal 125, 316, 326
Clinton, Bill 4
Clinton, Hillary Rodham 278
Clutchette, John (*see also* Soledad Brothers) Act Two, chaps. 4–10, *passim*
Clutchette v. Procunier 231, 245–46
COINTELPRO 144, 151, 154, 214, 216, 259, 265, 318, 362
Cold War 28, 56, 68, 79, 103
Coleman, Charles Wesley 369, 371–74, 438
Coleman, Kate 321, 363, 434
Collier, Peter xiii, 434, 440
Communist Party 35, 46, 56–57, 86, 186, 343. (*see also* American Communist Party)
Congress of Racial Equality ("CORE") 111
Congressional Black Caucus 277
Constitution ACLU suits 46, 437; Anti-miscegenation law 77; Dreyfus specialty 82, 121; Freedom Summer 97; HUAC victims 46; law class 41, 340; National Lawyers Guild 297, 364; Newton Trial 121, 126, 155; Prisoners' Rights 258; 281; 285; Treuhaft specialty 278; (*see also* Bill of Rights)
Cooper, Penny 126, 143, 147, 352–353, 392
Council for Justice Act One, chap. 8, *passim*, 145, 243, 300
Crime in America 265
Crockett, George 96–98, 104
Cronkite, Walter 273

D

Darrow, Clarence xii, 43, 51, 83
Davis, Angela Act Two, chaps. 6, 8, 9, *passim*, 7, 19, 263–64, 274, 296, 349, 360
Death Penalty Act Two *passim*, xiv, 19, 88, 103, 111, 277, 340, 349, 385, 392, 446
DeLasaux, Joan 7, 19, 23, 58
Dellums, Ron 174, 244, 253, 256, 277, 336
Depression (*see* Great Depression) 9, 17, 22, 322

INDEX

Diamond, Bernard 130
Douglas, William 105, 108
Dreyfus, Barney Act One, chap. 6–8, *passim.*, 111, 121, 148, 152, 364
Drumgo, Fleeta (*See* Soledad Brothers) Act Two chaps. 4–9, 253, 264–65, 270, 360, 369, 374, 377, 388, 442, 444
Dunlap, Mary 430
Durden-Smith, Jo 318–20, 438–39
Dylan, Bob 95, 221
Dymally, Melvin 169

E

Ehrlich, Dorothy 446-47
Eisenhower, Dwight David 71, 77, 90
Equal Rights Amendment 301

F

Fanon, Franz 122, 163
FDR (*see* Roosevelt, Franklin Delano) 59
Federal Bureau of Investigation ("FBI") *passim*, (*see also* COINTELPRO)
Feinstein, Diane 366
Ferlinghetti, Lawrence 415
Fifth Amendment 56, 128
First Amendment 41, 107, 165, 349
Fonda, Jane 3, 205, 264, 360, 367
Foster, Marcus 315
Franck, Peter Council for Justice 101–04, 108, 300; law partnerships 128, 144–45, 152–53, 213, 224, 243, 291, 300, 368; Lawyers Guild 99, 300
Frankenstein, Alfred 13
Frankfurter, Felix 43
Freedom Summer 95-98, 349
Free Huey! 249
Free Speech Movement ("FSM") 46, 103, 111–112, 152, 300
Frey, John Act Two, chap. 1, *passim*, 132, 134
Friedan, Betty 300
Friedman, Monroe Act Two, chap. 12, *passim*; 156–57
Friends of SNCC 95, 110, 123
Fujishige, Amy 355, 385, 401, 409, 418-21, 423

G

Gaines, Gordon 156, 359, 414
Garcia, Inez 339, 349
Garry, Charles xiv, Act One, chap. *passim*, 340, 373, 378, 398–400, 413, 434

Genet, Jean 174, 222, 252
Ginger, Ann xiv, 85, 111, 187, 205, 207–08, 281, 298, 350
Ginsburg, Ruth Bader xi–xii
Girard, Dawn 372–73
Gluss, Brian 69, 446
Goines, David Lance 130, 152
Gold, Herbert 438
Goldschmidt, Neal 109–10
Goldwater, Barry xii
Goodman, Andrew 97
Goodman, Emily Act Three, chap. 3, *passim*
Grier, Henry 128–129, 131, 134, 157
Guevara, Che 122, 168, 265, 289

H

Haley, Harold 265, 275
Halterman, Lee 244, 336–37
Hamilton, Dag 53, 58, 64
Hamilton, Robert ("Bob") 53, 58, 105
Hamilton, Walton 64
Hammer, Joan 202, 232, 318
Hampton, Fred 154, 188
Harper, David 127–128, 131
Hayden, Tom 265, 367
Head-Royce School (*see* Anna Head School) 13–14
Heanes, Herbert 121, 132, 134
Hearst, Patti 315
Hebrew Free Loan Association 10
Heisler, Francis 101, 108, 169
Heller, Joseph 248
Hendon, Ezra 152, 154, 224, 281, 428, 434
Higgens, Marguerite 14–15, 36, 59
Hill, Doug 144
Hilliard, David 120, 125, 129, 211, 249
Hinckle, Warren 88
Hippolytus 4, 410
Hitler, Adolph 86, 163, 342
Hoffman, Abbie 145
Hoffmann, Alex Act One, chap. 8, Act Two, chaps. 1–3, *passim*, 107, 112
Holder, Eric 447
Holocaust, The 149, 336, 375, 429
Horowitz, David xiii, 320–21, 430–31, 434, 440
House Un-American Activities Committee ("HUAC") Act One chaps. 4–7 *passim*
Hove, Harold Act Three chap. 8 *passim*, 211, 411–13

Huggins, Ericka 147, 151, 156, 248
Huggins, John 147
Hughes, Dorthy Pittman 301
Hutton, Bobby 123, 139, 249
Hyde, Lea 15–16

I
International Childbirth Education Association 80–81, 90

J
Jackson, Delora 161, 250
Jackson, George Childhood 50, 161–62; Fay Stender attorney for Act Two chaps. 4–10, *passim*, 3, 5, 19, 293; Forced confession of Stender re 1–2, 356, 360, 441; *Who Killed George Jackson?* 319, 439
Jackson, Georgia Act Two, chaps. 8–10, *passim*, 161, 442-45
Jackson, Jonathan Act Three, chap. 8, *passim*
Jackson, Jonathan, Jr. 250, 266
Jackson, Lester 161–62, 200, 252, 255
Jackson, Penny Act Two, chap. 10, *passim*
Jackson, "Popeye" 317, 319–20, 384
Jackson State Massacre 157
Jamestown Massacre 340
Janssen, Howard Act Three, chap. 8, *passim*, 365, 366, 411–13
Jefferson, Thomas 57
Jelinek, Don 273–74, 358, 384, 417
Jensen, D. Lowell 133, 361, 365, 391
Jet 222
Ji Jaga, Geronimo (*see* Geronimo Pratt) 209, 211
Johnson. Lyndon 96, 459, 464
Jones, Rev. Jim 340
Jonestown 349

K
Kafka, Franz 248
Karenga, Maulana Ron 144
Kay, Herma Hill 314
Keating, Ed 125, 131, 249
Keker, John 361
Kelley, Ying Lee (*see also* Lee, Ying) Act Three, chap. 9, *passim*, 37–46, 63–64, 68, 367, 398, 437
Kennedy, John Fitzgerald 4, 73, 93, 104
Kennedy, Robert 73

Kent State Massacre 157
Kind and Usual Punishment 285
King, Martin Juther, Jr. 95, 100, 110, 123
KPFA 111, 112, 148
KQED 313
Krinsky, Michael Act Three, chap. 3, *passim*
Kroninger, Robert 310–12
Kunstler, William 153, 434

L
Lane, Mark 113, 210, 349
Lee, Betty (*see* Lee, Ying)
Lee, Ying (*see also* Kelly, Ying Lee) 37, 66, 322, 367, 398, 429, 437
Lefkowitz, Louis 9
Legal Realism 47–48
Lenin, Vladimir 82, 163
Levi, Edward 51–53, 65, 68, 70–71
Levine, Sara 385, 417–426
Levinson, David Act Three, chap. 3, *passim*
Levinson, Sandra 287–90
Little Rock crisis 77
Llewellyn, Karl 47, 53, 56–58, 74
Los Angeles Criminal Conspiracy Section (("CCS" or "Red Squad") 215
Lynch, Loretta 447

M
Magbie, Michael 357–59, 363–64, 391, 396, 439–40
Mackey, Bergie (*see* Bergliot Bornholdt) 398, 409, 420
Magers, Mabel "Micki" 232, 250, 266, 271
Mailer, Norman 113
Majors, Reggie 113
Malarkey, Annie Laurie 60
Malcolm X 113, 122, 186, 226
Margolin, Ephraim 429
Margolis, Harry 201, 208, 307, 309
Marin County courthouse shooting 252, 264, 408, 445
Marxism 36, 56
Mast, Marling 129, 424, 440
Maximum Security 248, 270, 282
McCarran–Walter Act 56
McCarthy Era 28, 46, 59, 70, 86–87, 137–139, 161, 165, 174, 188, 240, 242, 268–269, 349
McCarthy, Eugene 87

INDEX

McCarthy, Joseph 28
McCarthy, Michael 137–39, 174, 188–89, 240, 268–69
McClain, James 209
McGee, Willie 98
McKelvey, Judith 313–314, 351, 391, 409, 433
McTernan, Francis 82–83, 152, 208
Meadows, Jerry 171–72
Meisenbach, Robert 82, 83
Mikva, Abner 70, 257
Milk, Harvey 340
Miller, Opie 166, 185, 236
Mills, John 159, 166–168, 174, 177, 189, 193–194, 203, 221, 234, 236, 239, 264
Milmore, Wendy 19–20, 22, 40, 417
Mississippi Summer Project (*see* Freedom Summer) 95
Mitford, Jessica ("Decca") *see also* Treuhaft, Jessica 4, 86–87, 111, 179, 204, 225, 233, 242, 247, 257, 280, 343
Miyashiro, Rand 352
Moonies, The 349, 354
Moon, Rev. Sun Myung 349, 354
Moore, Stanley Act One, chaps. 2, 4–7, *passim*, 14, 74, 100, 231, 274, 343, 418
Morse, Katherine [pseudonym] 2, 322, 326–27, 340, 354–56, 362, 409, 412, 423–24
Moscone, George 340, 366
Muhammad Ali xi
Murrow, Edward R. 59

N

National Association for the Advancement of Colored People ("NAACP") 96, 107, 247, 271
National Lawyers Guild *passim*
National Organization for Women 300-01, 305-06
Neal, Kathleen (*see also* Kathleen Cleaver) 122
Near, Holly 415, 421
Neil, Earl 134
New Deal 82
New Jim Crow, The 447
New Left 231, 336, 440
Newson, Jerry 86
Newsweek 222, 421
Newton, Huey *passim*
Nixon, Richard 243, 266
Nolen, W. L. 166, 236, 317, 445

O

Oakland Seven 118–119, 133, 143, 145
Oakland Tribune, The 15, 118, 123, 308, 359, 360, 363, 422
Obama, Barack 447
O'Connor, Sandra Day xi–xii
Ohara, Margaret 22–23
Our Bodies, Ourselves 309

P

Pacifica Foundation 221, 453
Pan African Conference 149
Park, Jim 251–52
Patel. Marilyn Hall xii, 305–306, 432–33
Peace and Freedom Party 125
Pell, Eve 234, 243, 251, 368, 371–72, 429, 434
People's Park 147, 297, 353, 384
People's Temple 349
Phaedra i, v, 4, 334, 410, 427
Pinell, Hugo 253, 365, 378, 380, 388–389, 392, 414, 434, 442, 444
Pippin, Karma 390, 409–10, 422
Pippin, Robert Gene 40, 73, 351, 389–90
Pratt, Elmer "Geronimo" Ji Jaga 209–10, 214
Price, Barbara 352, 416–17, 420
Prison Law Collective 255, 274, 296, 371, 380
Prison Law Project Act Two, chap. 10, Act Three, chaps. 2-7, *passim*, 235, 268, 270, 287, 295, 304, 318, 322, 327, 380, 444
Prison Lawyers Association 247
Procunier, Raymond 141, 257–59

R

Racine, Jean 4, 347, 410
Rackley, Alex 147, 151
Ramey, Drucilla xiii, 278, 301, 313, 324, 347, 370, 382, 395–96, 433, 445
Ramparts Magazine xiii, 88, 113, 121, 125, 242, 287, 317, 320, 434
Raven, Robert 322, 323–325
Reagan, Ronald xii, 118, 147, 197, 263, 283
Red Squad 215
Red Summer 50
Rehnquist, William xi
Renne, Louise 314
"Requiem for a Radical" xiii, 434, 440

Relevant Lawyers, The 281, 298
Richter, Robert Act One, chap. 2, *passim,* 52, 60, 90–92, 273, 347, 351, 367
Roberts, Patti 240–43, 246, 251, 253, 313
Robinson, Tyrone 440–41
Roe v. Wade xii
Romilly, Dinky 278
Roosevelt, Franklin 64
Rosenberg, Ethel 28
Rosenberg, Julius 28
Ross, Dell 121, 124, 128, 134, 157
Rubin, Jerry 102, 145, 288, 316, 367
Rundle, Frank 241, 429
Russell, Diana 350–51, 354, 306, 430, 441

S

Sacco, Nicola 43, 349, 450
San Francisco Chronicle, The 13, 83, 284, 286, 319
San Francisco Examiner 116, 238, 317, 322, 360, 362–63, 369
San Quentin Six 253, 255, 318, 319, 349
Satcher, Earl 317
Savio, Mario 98–99, 112, 148, 322
Scherr children 297, 307, 309, 370
Scherr, Estela Act Three, chap. 4, *passim*
Scherr, Jane Act Three, chap. 4, *passim,* 370
Scherr, Max Act Three, chap. 4, *passim*
Scherr, Raquel 297, 309
Scharlin, Jae 392–93
Schneider, Bert 223, 252
Schroeder, Mary 51
Schulman, Joanne 304–05, 308, 383
Schwerner, Michael 97
Scott, Austin 367-68
Scott, Peter Dale 445-446
Scott, Rob 27–29, 32
Seale, Bobby Act Two chaps. 1–3, *passim,* 285
Seidner, Stan 39, 92
Sharp, Malcolm 55–58, 64, 71
Siegel, Dan 384, 415
Silliman, Floyd Act Two chaps. 4–9 *passim*
Silver, Richard Act Two chaps. 4–9 *passim,* 249
SLATE 103
Smith Act, Smith Loyalty Act 76, 349
Snyder, Gary 415-16
Sobell, Martin 55, 58
Soledad Brother 225-28, 268, 270, 288, 447

Soledad Brothers Defense Committee Act Two, chap. 5–10, *passim,* 169, 264
Soul on Ice 113, 182
Southern Christian Leadership Conference ("SCLC") 95–96
Spain, Johnny 318
Spock, Dr. Benjamin 174
Stalin, Joseph 35, 46, 343
Steinem, Gloria 301
Stender, Fay (*see also* Fay Abrahams) *passim;* ACLU and 75–77, 348-49, 437; *Berkeley Barb* litigation Act Three, chap. 4; California Women Lawyers 313, 334, 352, 430, 432–33; childhood, Act One chap. 1; college, Act One, chap 2; Council for Justice, Act One, chap. 8; death 424–26; family background 9–10; George Jackson and, Act Two chap. 4–10; law school, Act One chaps. 3–5; Huey Newton and, Act Two, Act Three chap. 1, 5, *passim,* 274, 289, 305, 337, 362, 375, 380, 386, 392, 413, 440-41, 443, 445; shooting 1–2, 356–58; star prosecution witness, Act Three, chap. 8.
Stender, Marvin xiii–xiv, 2–3, Act One chaps. 4–9, Acts Two and Three, *passim*
Stender, Neal 1, 2, Act One chaps. 7–9 *passim,* 323, 333–34, Act Three, chaps. 7–9 *passim,* 435, 438–439
Stender, Oriane 65, Act One chap. 7 *passim;* Act Three chap. 9 passim, 97, 100, 271, 276, 343
Stern, Hilde Act Three, chaps. 6–7 *passim,* 16, 18, 23, 41, 385–86, 390,
Stewart, Lynne 144
Stone, Don 44, 69, 340, 381–82, 416, 426
Stone, Elise (*see also* Elise Abrahams) 277, 350, 351–52, 354, 370–71, 381–83, 393, 407–08, 421–23, 426
Stone, Irving 43
Stop the Draft Week 117–119
Streetfighter in the Courtroom 350
Student Nonviolent Coordinating Committee "(SNCC) Act One chap. 8 *passim,* 121, 123, 256, 271, 273, 374
Students for a Democratic Society ("SDS") 264
Sutter, John 311

INDEX

SWAT Team 315, 382
Symbionese Liberation Army ("SLA") 315, 317, 384

T
Tackwood, Louis 318
Theseus 4, 334, 410
Thomas, Gary 408
Thompson, Elsa Knight 111, 148, 221, 367, 386, 410, 415, 418
Thorne, John Act Two, chaps. 4–10, *passim;* 279, 307, 443
Tigar, Michael 144, 148, 169
Till, Emmett 69
Time 21, 22, 189, 222, 230, 233
Treuhaft, Robert; *see also* Jessica Mitford (Decca Treuhaft) 86–87, 99, 100, 111, 152, 277–278, 280, 296, 308, 312, 433
Tribal Thumb 317, 384
Truman, Harry S. 59, 75
Tse-Tung, Mao 168, 182, 266
Ture, Kwame (*see* Stokely Carmichael) 97, 110, 119, 150, 273

U
United Farm Workers 102, 104, 111
United Nations Commission on Human Rights 49, 256, 334
United Slaves ("Us"); *see also,* Maulana Ron Karenga 144

V
Van Patter, Betty 317, 320–321, 414, 430, 446
Vanzetti, Bartolomeo (Sacco & Vanzetti) 43, 349
Venceremos Brigade 288
Vietnam Day Committee 102, 107
Vietnam War 101, 108, 110, 133, 143, 179, 300, 315, 349, 364

W
Wald, Karen 123, 132, 183, 430–31
Walker, Doris "Dobby" Brin Act Three chap. 4 *passim,* 85, 111, 152, 282
Warren, Earl 43, 70, 88, 105, 437
Watergate 59, 289
Weathermen 182, 209, 252, 440
Weaver shooting stance 356
Weddington, Sarah xii

Weinberg, Doron 133, 295–296, 304, 308, 313, 364–65
Weinglass, Leonard 205
Wellman, David 123, 126, 175, 177
Wells, Bob 88
Wells–Gorshen rule 88
Wells, John xi
White, Dan 366
Who Killed George Jackson? 319. 439
Whyte, Donald 249
Wirth, Alice 52, 59, 67, 71, 91
Women's History Research Center 313

X
X, Laura 313, 350

Y
Yippies 145
Younger, Evelle 279

Z
Zeisel, Hans 70, 128
Ziegler, Phil 151–53, 169, 171, 215, 224

Acknowledgements

I am deeply appreciative of everyone who gave generously of their time and materials as sources for this long-term book project, including by sharing unpublished treasure troves that greatly enhanced my understanding of key events in Fay Stender's life. Their gift was one that kept on giving, providing material I also incorporated in *The Sky's the Limit* and *American Justice on Trial*, which both wound up being published before this biography. I could not have completed any of these books without your input and insights.

I want to single out several people for special acknowledgment. It saddened me greatly when Fay's devoted sister Elise Abrahams Stone died in 2015 before I could share with her this book, the first few chapters and final chapters of which benefitted immensely from anecdotes she told me about their childhood and family relationships. I am grateful as well to Federal Judge Marilyn Hall Patel for inspiring me to write this biography, to Dru Ramey and Marvin Stender for their immediate encouragement of this project, to Fay's lifelong friend Hilde Stern for her unique perspective, to Fay's close friends from college Bob Richter and Ying Lee, to her Newton trial co-counsel Alex Hoffmann and consultant Bob Blauner (both of whom have since died), to co-counsel Richard Silver in the Soledad Brothers pretrial proceedings, to Ann Fagan Ginger, to freelance reporter Karen Wald, to Peter Franck and Fay's other surviving law partners, to Penny Cooper, to photographer Ilka Hartmann, to Fay's dear companion Katherine Morse, for all of their unstinting contributions – and to my oldest daughter, civil rights lawyer Anna Benvenutti Hoffmann, who prodded me last fall to get this biography out now to share Fay's story with the current generation of women activists committed as Fay was to persist in furthering just causes in the face of entrenched opposition.

I want to thank profusely both of my editors: author Sara Houghteling (*Pictures at an Exhibition*), whose deft touch greatly improved every chapter she reviewed; and author Dan White (*The Cactus Eaters* and *Under the Stars*), whose astute comments and suggestions for finishing the book proved just as vital to its birth. I also wish to thank graphic artist Emily Burch for once again working her magic in designing the book cover, and to express my appreciation once more to Mark Weiman of Regent Press and Suzanne Waligore for all their hard work and belief in this project, and to Christopher Bernard for his eagle-eyed proofreading and helpful editing suggestions. Thanks as well to publicist Ellen Whitfield of JKS Communications for her enthusiastic promotion of this book. Special thanks to the Board of Arc of Justice Productions, Inc. for allowing me to use several excerpts from transcripts of its filmed interviews for the documentary project "American Justice on Trial: People v. Newton" [www.americanjusticeontrial.com] and to my late mother, artist Amalia "Mali" Rapaport Pearlman, for her Rabbi sketch. I know my mother would agree I have put it to good use as an illustration in this book. Any opinions expressed in the book are my own; any mistakes in interpreting the results of my research are solely my responsibility.

Thanks again — always — to my wonderful twin daughters Jamie Benvenutti and Amalia "Mali" Benvenutti Glasgow for their research and editing assistance and to Mali for promoting my books through social media; to my sister Leslie Pearlman for her proofreading skills and editing suggestions; and to my stalwart husband Peter Benvenutti — for acting from the get-go as an invaluable sounding board, editor, and chief cheerleader for my completion of this and all my other projects.

www.ingramcontent.com/pod-product-compliance
Lightning Source LLC
Chambersburg PA
CBHW030508080526
44586CB00011B/114